To San —

A lot of
memories !

happy

plus your Dad

Deirdre

12/6/07

# I'm Ready For My Close Up - Anybody!

## By

## Dee Quemby

## Edited by
## John Brindley

Bloomington, IN  Milton Keynes, UK

authorHOUSE®

AuthorHouse™
1663 Liberty Drive, Suite 200
Bloomington, IN 47403
www.authorhouse.com
Phone: 1-800-839-8640

AuthorHouse™ UK Ltd.
500 Avebury Boulevard
Central Milton Keynes, MK9 2BE
www.authorhouse.co.uk
Phone: 08001974150

First published by AuthorHouse 4/19/2007

ISBN: 978-1-4259-7782-5 (sc)
ISBN: 978-1-4259-7783-2 (hc)

Printed in the United States of America
Bloomington, Indiana

This book is printed on acid-free paper.

Logo design Dave Kitto, Clifton Bank Studios

Front cover photo Julie Oswin (www.julieoswin.com)

# INTRODUCTION

THERE are some folk who stand out from the crowd the moment you set eyes on them. Such a woman is Deirdre Quemby.

I remember seeing this petite heavily made-up woman with unusually dark clothing for the first time in the market place of Loughborough more years ago than I now care to recall.

First impressions stay with you, but they are not always accurate. I regarded this vision as out-of-the-ordinary certainly, but not necessarily someone I'd feel comfortable approaching and talking to.

As I continued working on the *Loughborough Echo*, the area's leading weekly newspaper, I got to know a little more about what this woman was all about. She helped to run a local dancing school, was annually organising pantomimes and appearing in charity shows as a female comedian.

I vividly remember going to one of her school's shows at the atmospheric Stanford Hall Theatre and revelling in the sheer fun and mayhem of it all. It made my heart warm.

But it was only when I suggesting interviewing Deirdre several years later that I really met her. She was on the verge of appearing in the top ITV soap *Emmerdale* and it seemed the ideal opportunity to chat.

That was when I began to realise that behind her exotic exterior is a woman whom it is impossible not to like. I felt, at that time, she was on the verge of a big breakthrough.

Like countless of Deirdre's friends, I was glued to that one episode of *Emmerdale* and the appearance of Tallulah Dingle, the psychic arm of that crazy family. I, too, was astonished that wasn't the start of something really big. Never mind... that hasn't been Deirdre's story so far. She has, in many ways, lived on the edge of being well known and may yet make that jump into more nationwide consciousness.

But that is scarcely the point. For in a profession where unless your face fits and you get the right break you remain on the periphery, Deirdre has always found work. And that infectious enthusiasm be it for her stints at working men's clubs or for her travelling panto remains undaunted. She has made countless people look, as I looked that day, and smile.

This is the story of an entertainer with a heart..........................................................

John Brindley

*Getting to know you.................................................................!*

# I'M READY FOR MY CLOSE UP.........ANYBODY!

*Let's go on with the show.......................................!*

**NB:**
Background music tracks at the end of each chapter are suggestions only.  Feel free to play your own choice of music!

# IN MEMORY OF OLIVE AND LEN QUEMBY

A long while ago my Mum gave me a newspaper cutting, it was a picture of a clown with these words underneath:

A clown may be the first in the Kingdom of Heaven, if he has helped lessen the sadness of human life

*Rabbi Baroka*

~~~~~~~~~~~~~~~~~~~~~~~~~~~~~~~~~~~~~~~~~~

Use what talents you possess; the woods would be very silent if no birds sang there except those that sang best

*Anon*

Whatever you can do, or think you can do – begin it.  For boldness has power and magic and genius in it

*Goethe*

Our doubts are traitors, and make us lose the good we oft might win by fearing to attempt

*William Shakespeare, Measure for Measure*

We know what we are, but know not what we may be

*William Shakespeare, Hamlet*

*That's life...........................................................!*

# ACT I

*Another opening, another show..............................!*

# FOREWORD

THIS book is really about a love affair with showbiz!  In the 1960s when I was 14 years old, I went to a working men's club in Leicester for the first time in my life on a Sunday lunchtime, with the Riddles, Audrey and Brian, who lived a couple of doors away.  Brian was the drummer in a very successful 60s group, *Formula Five*, and they were booked to play.

I didn't even know these places existed and I watched in horror as a jaded old comic in a crumpled suit, holding a cigarette between brown stained fingers, reeled off blue jokes, one after another.  In those days you would be booked to do Saturday night, Sunday lunchtime and Sunday night.  Not one person in the packed smoke filled club was listening to him.  You could see the despair in his eyes and he had yet to do the Sunday night performance!

I said to myself "how can anybody want to do that?"

*Deirdre Quemby*

*As Dusty Springfield sang.........................*
*Quiet please, there's a lady on stage!*

For Hannah, Lucy, Lily, Olivia, Amy, Charley, Libby
and Thomas...............the show goes on!

~~~~~~~~~~~~~~~~~~~~~~~~~~~~~~~~~~~~~~~~~~

*I believe that children are our future.....................................!*

# CHAPTER 1

## OVERTURE AND BEGINNERS, PLEASE!

MY first 'public' appearance was on 18 January 1946. I'm well used now to waiting for my turn to appear on a stage late at night but on this occasion, I admit I kept my Mum waiting until 11.15pm before I made my debut into the world at Sommerville Nursing Home in Park Road, Loughborough. There I was Deirdre Doris Edwards Quemby, a daughter for Olive Mary and Len Quemby, a former Warrant Officer with the Royal Engineers.

I soon found out that I was descended from quite an odd mix of people really. My maternal grandmother Flora Doris Edwards (nee Leader) was the granddaughter of Martin Leader, who was a prominent Leicester trades unionist and founder member of the Boot and Shoe Union. Martin's brother was Henry Hardwick, a big shoe manufacturer at Barwell, and many of my Grandmother's relatives were still involved in the shoe trade.

Her other grandfather was Irish and apparently had black hair and a red moustache! At that time, in the large families, older children were expected to move out to make way for the ever arriving new babies, and often came to England looking for work. He was quite bitter about this and never spoke of his home in Ireland, so we never knew where he had originally come from. Coincidentally when I started work at Charnwood Borough Council, I worked with a young Irish girl Caroline who had come to England to meet two elder sisters she had never known!

I always called my grandmother Nan. Nan was very small, 4'11" to be precise, and, later in life, quite portly. Although her name was Flora, she preferred to be called Dolly. She loved having a laugh and had lovely twinkling eyes and she drank a pint of Guinness every day until she died peacefully in her sleep at the age of 90.

My grandfather was Horace Edwards, although to me he was 'Gramp' or 'Grampy'. I also used to call him 'Grampa – tramcar' from the age of four after seeing the tramcars running in Nottingham. Nan and Gramp were publicans – firstly at the Horse and Groom at Kegworth up to 1939, then at the Charnwood Forest Railway Inn at Shepshed, which they ran for 21 years. Landlords at that time carried a lot of respect, they had to be married, have excellent references and they were checked thoroughly.

I'll always remember Nan for her big velvet hats with lots of feathers, fur stoles, fur coats, sparkly jewellery, and lovely cocktail dresses that she had specially made for her job as landlady. All landlords would wear a suit and tie and the landladies would dress up to perfection to stand behind the bar, they really were the Annie Walker's of the day. I used to dress up in her clothes and dance on the beds and around the pub bedrooms.

One skill that wasn't passed down the family line, however, was her ability as a seamstress though I can sew sequins on costumes in all sorts of intricate patterns until the cows come home. She was very adept with a needle and I remember her crocheting numerous lace doilies. Later in life, she crocheted lace cloths for the altar at Rothley Church.

Nan's own mother Lizzie had laid out the dead in Leicester and attended Spiritualist meetings. Nan and her younger brother Ernest had to wait outside and out of boredom used to tap on the windows, much to the annoyance of the people inside. She remembered her mother and the Spiritualist leader coming out to tell them off. But she was staring at something that was of greater significance. She told them that she could see a beautiful light and the impressed Spiritualist told her mother that she had the 'gift!' His judgment was correct, as Nan would often say things that came true and was known to be able to predict things.

Martin Leader, her paternal grandfather, was certainly a trade unionist recognised for the strength of his convictions. It was a time when workers had very few rights and would often be exploited by their employers. He was the secretary of the Riveters and Finishers Union and went as far as to be imprisoned for standing up for the rights of his men. His portrait hung in the well-known and long gone Boot and Shoe Club in Leicester where many club acts started off by appearing in their shop window auditions.

It was thought, however, that Martin's son, Ernest Alfred Leader, had married beneath him and, as a result the family had little to do with them. So instead Elizabeth Anne (known as Lizzie), nee Jeffs, and Ernest ran a grocery shop on Belgrave Gate, Leicester. The problem was that Lizzie liked her drink a little too much and eventually drank away the profits! Fed up with their parents drinking, young Nan and her brother Ernest signed the pledge and marched in a procession through Leicester holding 'Ban the Demon Drink' banners. This didn't go down well with Lizzie however as when she saw them she promptly dragged them away and gave them a good hiding!

When Lizzie died my Nan was married and my Mum was a small child. Nan took her young brother in at 3 Barfoot Road in Leicester and my Mum and Ernest grew up more like brother and sister.

Strange as it seems, Nan later in life ran public houses while Ernest went in entirely the opposite direction and joined the Salvation Army in London. Later in life he became a lay preacher and came back to Leicester several times to preach.

Gramp came from a family that had roots in Buckinghamshire and London. His parents were Thomas and Mary Edwards (née Williams).  Gramp lived in Chilton in Buckinghamshire with his many brothers and sisters and his mother came from a Romany gypsy family who were Welsh horse traders.  My Mum told me that her grandmother was known in the village as 'Gypsy Mary'.

Gramp's grandfather lived in a cottage, he was a very handsome man with long black ringlets and he made many pots and pans. He had horses and ponies tethered nearby on common land and he had trained one of them to go to the cottage door and rattle the knocker early in the morning to wake him up.

Grampy remembered walking across many fields with his mother at the age of three years as the church bells were tolling for the death of Queen Victoria in 1901. They went to the burning of a gypsy caravan of a deceased Romany relative, attended by Romanies from all over the country.

Gramp's grandfather however had a prison record!  The local Lord and Lady had driven out of their gateway of Chilton House and killed my great-great-grandfather's horse that was pulling his cart.  My 90-year-old Great-Grandfather did no more than get out of the cart, roll his sleeves up and engage in a punch-up with the chauffeur, ending up a 'guest' of the local police station for the night!  The rift was apparently healed as Her Ladyship later on did attend Great-Grandad's funeral.

Great-Granny was a tough 'no nonsense' woman.  Gramp at the age of three years had thick black hair - the thick hair he kept up to his death at the age of 85 years, a lovely tanned skin, big brown eyes and wore a gold earring.  He had been playing outside his front door, this was not thought of as unsafe then, and when Great-Granny went to call him in, he was no longer there.  Earlier in the day gypsy caravans had gone through the village.  Great-Granny ran after them and there was Gramp sitting up front, with a man, holding the horse's reins.  Great-Granny climbed up and snatched him back.  The gypsies had obviously recognised one of their own kind!

Gramp loved animals and as a child had a cat.  This cat was quite happy to be carried around all the time by Gramp over his arm, and had a permanent dent in its stomach!

Gramp's elder brothers enlisted to fight in the First World War and he was so keen to go with them that he lied about his age. He was only 15 years old at the time.  They were all in different regiments and all fought in the battle of The Somme where thousands of soldiers met their deaths.

Gramp told me that the young soldiers were ordered to jump over the trenches as the Germans fired at them.  The soldier in front of him was petrified and wouldn't jump.   Gramp jumped in his place, the soldier then followed in Gramp's place and was immediately shot dead.  Amazingly, at roll call the next day, all three brothers had survived to tell the tale.

After the war, however, there was little for the men to come back for.  There were no benefits in those days and you had to work to earn money to live.  So Gramp and one of his brothers stayed in France for two years rebuilding the roads.  It was here that he learnt to speak French and it was to prove useful even in his 80s.  For when our next-door neighbour's daughter's young French pen friend came to stay, he was able to converse happily with her as he spoke the same dialect as she did.  When he did come back to England, there still was no work around so Gramp and his brother came to work at Bardon Quarry. It was in nearby Leicester that Gramp met my Nan and they were married on Christmas Eve 1923 at St Saviours Church, Leicester.

Gramp used to take any work that he could, cycling from Leicester to Nottingham every day to be able to feed his family. This took such a heavy toll on him that he needed an operation. A sister had moved to Nottingham so he now could stay with her in the week and come home at weekends as a lot of men used to do in those days. He even went as far as Ireland to work in order to support his family.

I remember my Gramp as being a quiet, kind, very handsome and distinguished man, more than six feet tall and with thick white hair. He never ever lost that lovely soft Buckinghamshire accent! He was always immaculately dressed in a suit, and proudly wore a gold Hunter watch and chain, a diamond tiepin and a diamond ring.

Gramp went into hospital at the age of 85 for a minor routine operation. The day before the operation he suffered a massive stroke and died.

My parents were married at Holy Trinity Church, Loughborough on 11 January 1945 almost exactly a year before I was born. My Mum was 20 years old and I always thought her wedding dress was made from the material that parachutes were made out of, as were many brides' dresses during the war. But staff at the museum service where I have donated many well kept items from the World War II years and my grandparents' pub, have since told me it was actually pure silk that would have been virtually impossible to get at that time. Nan and Gramp had many business friends through the pub, so it was probably thanks to one of them.

My Mother told me that with rationing, couples didn't normally have a cake for their wedding day, as it was too difficult to get the ingredients. Instead a box would be iced over and put on a table for show. But my grandparents had friends who ran a restaurant on Frog Island, Leicester, called the Browns. They saved up the ingredients and my Mum did get to have a real wedding cake, after all. My Mum was given a contraband dinner service as a wedding present. This had been taken off an enemy ship sunk during the war and every piece is still intact to this day.

My Mum was a very well read, well educated and a deeply religious woman. Even at the advanced age of 80 she hated the idea of being in the dark about anything interesting and I would be sent off to buy books on many different subjects. I had to buy one on tennis so she could watch Wimbledon on TV and understand the scoring. She read all the Harry Potter and the Lord of the Rings books – and I took her to see all the films. She kept a Thesaurus and a dictionary on a tray, as she couldn't use her fingers due to rheumatoid arthritis. She would 'thumb' through them both using the bottom of her hands. She said it infuriated her to come across a word she didn't know the meaning of. Proof that they were well used was that I had to buy her new ones every year. She read at least eight books a week. She loved history and we had many books, especially on the Tudors. She also loved a good old fashioned 'who dunnit' and every day did the crossword in the *Daily Mail* even though she was blind in one eye and the sight in her other eye was fading fast.

My Mum had many friends and relatives both here and in America and Australia and wrote at least two letters a day, usually many pages long. She also

4

sent many picture postcards, mostly from our London and Stratford-upon-Avon day trips. Cinema and theatre were two more of her loves and as a child she had a big crush on the American movie star Robert Taylor. She also badly wanted to learn how to dance. Back then in the 1920s it would have been far too expensive for her parents who were just making enough money to survive, but as soon as I could walk she made sure I went!

When my Mum was a child living at 3 Barfoot Road in Leicester, she regularly went with Nan and Gramp to Saffron Lane working men's club, as it was their local club. Nan told me she had an Uncle who used to sing in the clubs.

My Mum was a beautiful-looking child and had inherited the thick jet-black hair and lovely slightly tanned skin from Gramp's Romany side and the big brown eyes. Mum loved to sing around the house although she never knew the right words. It didn't bother her though she just used to make them up! She sang at one time in the St Peter's church choir, as she wasn't a brilliant singer I think they must have been short of members at the time! She adored Judy Garland, Deanna Durbin, Shirley Temple and, of course, Robert Taylor.

My Mum was a wonderful storyteller and she really didn't know how funny she could be. When she recalled her days in the Land Army we would have tears running down our faces. During the Second World War, everybody had to contribute to the war effort. Young girls either worked in munitions factories or on the land in the newly formed Land Army. They wore military style coats and hats with badges.

My Mum joined the Land Army and worked at Shepshed. She and another girl delivered the milk in churns with a pony and cart. Being two very pretty girls, people would save them a treat everywhere they went – be it an apple or a biscuit and would give the pony a carrot or an apple core. Naturally this meant it took them longer to finish the round and, in Mum's own words, made her the plumpest she had ever been! Eventually an inspector was sent to see why they were getting back to the depot so late and went with them on the next round. Mum and her friend took the milk into the cottages and houses, politely refusing any treats. They explained why they were in a hurry but, unfortunately, when they got back to the cart and the inspector there was one big problem – the pony was having none of it! He stayed firmly put until he was given his carrot or apple core and the Inspector cottoned on to the reason why they were always late! Needless to say this earned Mum and her friend a telling off.

The pony was an old hunt pony and one day they were going down a lane when the pony's ears pricked up. He had heard a hunting horn as there was a hunt going on, on Freddie Mee's land. Old habits die-hard! The pony snorted, threw back his head and started to gallop down the lane with Mum and her friend holding on for dear life as the milk churns flew off the cart in all directions. They just prayed the pony would stop before they came to a hedge or a fence and the pony tried to jump it! My Mum loved the Land Army and spoke about it all her life.

My Mum's great passion was ironing which she did every day. It was very unusual to go in the house and not see the ironing board out. Anything she could iron she would; she read that Jackie Kennedy, America's First Lady at the time, had her tights ironed and so did we after that!

My Mum's favourite colour was green. I grew up in houses painted green with green curtains, carpets, pots, towels, sheets, bathroom and kitchen. If she could have had a green cat she would have! No need to say that her favourite shop was Harrods with the commissionaires in their green uniforms. We never bought much, usually a couple of green Harrods' pens which I had to queue up and pay for separately so she could have two green Harrods' bags to put raffle prizes in for the Mothers Union meetings. The majority of her clothes were green and she said that you had to have some Irish in you to be able to wear green. I couldn't stand the colour but since my mother died I find that I am very much drawn to it. Funny that, considering green is supposedly an unlucky colour to wear on stage!

My Mum was an only child but, with her books and interests, said she didn't mind being on her own. She said she was never at a loss for something to do. As an only child I, too, was quite happy on my own, I could always make up stories, dances, play act and my imagination would run riot.

My mother spoke beautifully without any regional accent, known in acting circles as RP (received pronunciation). This is how people who took elocution lessons would speak, as a lot of children did in the 1950s and 1960s. To be an actor you have to be able to do RP and if I ever audition for a part that requires this I just think of my Mum's voice.

My Mum was not really that interested in clothes and fashion but she always bought lovely outfits. Even in her 80s she would wear a nice tailored suit or dress, a pearl necklace and a pair of earrings. With that lovely white hair swept up in a chignon she always looked so chic. All the doctors, nurses and specialists at the hospital on our many visits would always compliment her on her appearance.

In the 1950s, I especially remember her wearing a wool full skirted purple dress that had black felt ballerinas on it; another full skirted dress was in yellow chiffon adorned with small flowers, the skirt was in three-tiers and every edge of the dress had a small seam of brown velvet. I remember vividly as a child going with her to Pearl's ladies dress shop at the bottom of Church Gate in Loughborough. She bought a lovely black sleeveless shift dress that had little white velvet lilies on it, and a matching bolero jacket. She had wonderful 1940s style jackets and suits that are still fashionable today. She would always have a camel hair swagger-coat every winter.

My Mum's other passions included pots and soap. Everywhere we went her eyes would light up on seeing a pot shop and would often come home laden down with cups and saucers, plates, and bowls that she didn't need. They would be put away in a cupboard somewhere and never seen again. On our trips to London we would have to go to the pot floors in Harrods and Selfridges and she was thrilled when we found a sale pot shop just up the road from Harrods. Soap was the best present you could buy my Mum. She went into raptures over boxes of soap and put a bar in every drawer that contained jumpers, underwear and scarves.

In later life, although disabled and in a wheelchair, my Mum would look forward to the many trips we made together to her beloved London and said as soon as she as we got there it felt like home to her. We would catch the 9.45am train from Loughborough. We would wander round London with me pushing Mum in her wheelchair reading all the historical wall plaques found everywhere and then we would go to see a matinée performance of a show. After the show it would be off to Garfunkels' restaurant in Leicester Square, where they always looked after us, and still do me, for a meal (they have a wonderful salad bar) and then we would catch the train home.

We had booked in January 2005 to go to the *Old Vic* to see that wonderful actor Sir Ian McKellan in *Aladdin*.  We had never been to the *Old Vic* before and my Mum was really looking forward to it when she was admitted to hospital for two weeks treatment.  She had been in for several days but the hospital allowed her out for the day so I could take her to London.  We loved the panto at the *Old Vic* and Sir Ian McKellan made a fabulous 'naughty' dame.   We went round to the stage door at the end.  Christopher Biggins came out and said hello to us, he had been visiting backstage.  Then Maureen Lipman who was playing Wishee Washee came out to see us, much to my Mum's delight.  We walked down from Leicester Square to the famous theatre, looking at all the landmarks.  On the way back it was dark and Mum was enthralled to see these famous sights so beautifully lit up.   Sadly it was to be our last London trip together.

My Mum died two weeks before her 81st birthday in May 2005.  Many people said that my Mum was a real 'lady' which was a comfort to me. I liked the fact that people thought of her like that because, for her, everything had to be done right.  Second best would never do.   Manners and behaviour were everything.  My friend Janet Holmes, a popular local amateur and very good actress, seeing my Mum for the very first time was so taken with my Mum's beautiful white hair piled high into a bun said:  "Deirdre, your mother looks like Russian royalty!" I was so proud.   Nurses in the hospital would love doing her thick waist-long hair and each time I went it would be in a different style.  She wasn't always very impressed, however, and would wait patiently for me to go and put it back into her normal bun.

My mother was buried in the family grave at Rothley alongside my Dad and Nan and Gramp.  The service was held at St Peter's Church and as my Mum loved singing I asked for a choir but was told they didn't have one anymore.  I contacted friends who sang in St Botolph's choir at Shepshed.   News quickly spread and many people from other choirs contacted me asking if they could come and sing including a lady at Quorn well into her 90s who had known my Mum.  My Mum had her choir and the church was packed.  My Mother's good friend Christine read out her memories of my Mum and it was a fitting tribute to a wonderful lady.   In all honesty I have never known anyone so kind and generous as my Mum, she always saw the best in everyone even if nobody else could!

My Father Leonard Quemby came from a poor family in Shepshed.  He was naturally brilliant at maths and in the 1920s he won a scholarship to a school where he was always known as, and called, the 'poor boy'.  He went on to gain a degree in mathematics.

My Father joined the army in 1933 and rose to Warrant Officer Class 1 in the Royal Engineers.  He was for many years in the Middle East, where he quickly learnt to speak fluent French and German. My Father loved opera and in the Middle East before the War saw all the great opera stars that would perform in the many theatres and luxurious casinos.  He was also a very good ballroom dancer and, as a young man, danced in competitions in Blackpool before the War. He loved Morocco and said if there was one place he could choose to live it would be there.   During the Second World War he turned down all further promotions, as he wanted to stay with the men under his command.

My Father fought at the Battle of Crete and was left for dead, but an Australian battleship docked and rescued survivors and he was taken to Jerusalem.  He had to have an emergency operation In a makeshift army hospital that left him slightly deaf afterwards, meaning he was no longer fit for active service.   Because he could speak fluent French and German he was sent to secret offices in London

7

*Dee Quemby*

Road, Leicester, for the duration of the War to train as Officer-in-Charge of the army of occupation in Germany. He was sent to Germany in this post when the war ended and hated it. He said he couldn't bear to see women, children and old people rummaging through ruins struggling to survive, but all soldiers were ordered not to help 'the enemy'.

My Father would not watch the Remembrance Service on television. He said it brought back painful memories of the young men under his command who had not survived, and for whom he would wear his Remembrance poppy on his commissionaire's uniform with great pride. One Sunday me, and my Mum were watching the Remembrance Service on TV when my Dad rushed into the house looking like Al Jolson, covered from head to toe in black soot but without the smile! He had been cleaning a convector heater outside in the yard and it had exploded. We had thought that the explosion was the firing of a cannon on the TV! He was quite narked that we hadn't rushed out to help him.

As I was born the year after the war ended my Father came out of the army. He first worked as an Assurance Agent, and then worked at Herbert Morris Ltd in the Time and Motion section. When he retired he joined the Corps of Commissionaires and was well known as Loughborough Town Hall's commissionaire. With his ear for languages he quickly picked up many of the new languages being spoken in the town so he could help people.

My Father was a quiet and very disciplined man. Even in his 70s, he would get his bike out and fetch pensions and shopping for elderly people who couldn't get out. The grass would never be allowed to grow over ½" thick and everything was done by the clock. If I said I was going out at 7pm my Father would make sure I was! I remember going out one night and a man who worked with my Father jokingly said; "Has your Dad clocked you out?"

Every Friday night after I had finished at the dancing school, I would go home for my dinner, this I continued to do after I left home. My Father always finished eating first and he would sit there waiting impatiently for us to finish. You daren't put your knife or fork down because as soon as you did your plate would be whipped away from you. If we had guests we had to warn them to keep hold of their cutlery! When the table was cleared my Dad would spread the newspaper over the dining table and out would come the boot polish, Brasso, cloths and brushes. He spent a long time lovingly polishing boots, belts, badges and medals with great pride and military precision ready for catching the bus the following morning to go on duty at the Town Hall.

My Father would always go to bed dead on the dot at 9.30pm, and rise early a throw back to his soldier days. He also took part in the Civic Events at the Town Hall and received many letters from a succession of Mayors commenting on his smart appearance. He was on duty when Prince Charles and Princess Diana visited Loughborough

I was told by ladies who worked at the Town Hall after my Father died that if they ever went to pick anything up or move anything my Father wouldn't let them do it, he would do it. When he died, they were amazed to find out that he was 77 years old. They thought he was much younger. They wouldn't have let him lift and carry things if they had known! Sorry girls, I can see my father putting up with that! All of the Town Hall staff attended his funeral.

Another lady stopped me in Loughborough and told me that he was the only person in the town who let her inside and found a room for her to feed her baby, no where else would let her do this.   No baby change rooms in those days.  When my Father died we received so many cards from people we didn't know but who had met my Dad by going in the Town Hall.

My Dad was a regular every Saturday and many weekdays and evenings when other functions were being held at the Town Hall.  At his funeral we had pall bearers from the Corps of Commissionaires and a young soldier sounded the last post. My Father was buried in his uniform in the family grave at Rothley.

All have now gone; it only seems like yesterday that we were all together.

*Unforgettable, that's what you are!*............................................!

Ernest Alfred and Elizabeth Anne Leader

Thomas and Mary Edwards

Great Granny Edwards and a young Gramp on the right

Gramp in the First World War at the age of 16

Nan and Gramp

Nan and my Mum

Gramp in the Police Force in Leicester

My Mum as a teenager during the Second World War

Mum and friend at the Charnwood Forest Railway Inn,
Shepshed during the Second World War

My Mum

Mum doing her bit in the Land Army

Granny Quemby with a young Dad on the right

My Dad in the Royal Engineers

My Mum and Dad's Wedding Day at the Holy Trinity
Church, Loughborough on 11 January 1945

The Wedding Group

Me and my Mum and Dad

A 1946 post war baby

18 months old

Dad's retirement from Herbert Morris (Albert Mear second in on right)

Dad on duty at Loughborough Town Hall

A proud Dad on duty for Prince Charles and
Princess Diana's visit to Loughborough

Mum and Muffin in Mountsorrel

Mum and Muffin

# CHAPTER 2

## GROWING UP IN SHEPSHED

My first memories of Shepshed are of living 'over the bridge' – this was how the block of terraced houses including ours, number 266 on Charnwood Road was known in the village. Our little terraced house had the added modern luxuries of a bathroom and inside toilet. It wasn't my very first home as when I was born we had lived in a Victorian villa house on what is now the site of the East Midlands Hotel in nearby Loughborough before my parents and I made the short trip – and for a short while – to 193 Derby Road in Loughborough.

Number 266 had the old original, but by this time unused, outside toilet at the bottom of the garden. For those who don't know these were 'earth toilets'. Inside these toilet huts was a wooden bench with three holes in, two big ones and one small one. This was so that father, mother and one child could all go together! A metal container would be underneath the bench to collect the waste material. Men were still employed to come and empty these toilets as they were in use in some areas up until 1953. At that time a lot of houses were not connected to water and electricity, fortunately we had both!

The 'panman', as he was known, would come from the council with a horse and cart. He would go down to the bottom of the garden with a trolley, lift up the wooden seat and remove the metal container that contained all the waste material. He would then wheel the trolley up to the cart and the waste would be put into a tank on the cart and the now empty container would be taken back to the wooden hut.

Some of these wooden huts would have a partition at the back that slid across so the panman could remove the metal container. It was not unusual for a family to be sitting there during their performance as it was being removed.

A friend, John Hall, as a child living in Rothley, remembers the panman from Barrow Council coming to fetch the waste from the outside toilet. He was wheeling the trolley up to the cart when his false teeth dropped out into the full metal container. He did no more than go into the kitchen, rinse his teeth under the tap and put them back in!

Another friend in Mountsorrel, Noel Wakeling, remembers two 'panmen' bending down to pick up a full container. One of the men's jackets fell into the full tank, and he pulled it out! The other panman said to him: "you're not going to put that on now, are you?" "Oh no" replied the other; "my lunch is still inside the pocket!"

We stayed 'over the bridge' for a short while. We moved to the public house the Charnwood Forest Railway Inn, number 186 on Charnwood Road, where we now lived with my grandparents due to my Mum not being well. Our pub was better known in the village as the 'Top Railway' and the Railway Inn, which was just the road at Ring Fence, was known as the 'Bottom Railway'.

I really can't remember too much about seeing my first-ever show. It came when I was just 18 months old and my Mum had suffered a nervous breakdown after having a stillborn baby boy, and we were living in Loughborough. One night when my Dad was working she said she felt so upset that she picked me up out of my cot, dressed me and went to the *Theatre Royal* Market Street. She thought I would fall asleep in the seat but I sat there to the end of the show taking it all in. My eyes apparently never left the stage and my laughter made her feel so much better. That must have been where my love of theatre came from.

My Mum was determined I was going to dance and at the age of 18 months I was taken to the Molyneux Academy in Loughborough. When we moved to Shepshed we had to catch the bus into town and back. As no mothers were allowed in to the dancing school, my Mum had to walk round Loughborough for an hour or more in all kinds of weather. These were the days when there weren't endless cafés to pass the time away in and the few that were there would shut at 5pm.

All little girls went to dance classes at that time – the late 40s and early 50s, dreaming of becoming a ballerina. Nowadays they all want to be pop stars or just 'famous'! Our playtime didn't then include such things as ice-skating and ten-pin bowling and we didn't have gyms and leisure centres to go to. Boys tended to play football and 'Cowboys and Indians'. Though all children would 'play act' the latest film they had been to see with their parents in the many cinemas in the area at the time. It was a time when you had to use your imagination and we did. You never heard children then saying they were bored and had nothing to do like today.

I had a framed picture of Moira Shearer, the ballerina in *The Red Shoes* film on a wall in my bedroom. She was very different with her red hair. All ballerinas at that time would have jet-black hair and dodgy sounding Russian names. Alice Marks for example was better known as the world-famous prima ballerina, Alicia Markova. Many years later, I would meet her sister, Doris Barry, an ex-Windmill girl who would be one of the members of the panel of judges at an audition for *Opportunity Knocks*.

When one dancing school closed you moved on to another. As a child I went to lessons at the Molyneux Dancing School, the Kathleen Freeman Dancing School that became the Poole Academy all in Loughborough, and then at Molly Dodd's in Shepshed for a short while. All ballroom dancing schools at that time would run a Saturday morning children's tap and ballet class.

All the many dancing schools in those days produced shows either at the Town Hall or the *Theatre Royal,* the latter down Market Street being very special with its large, sparkling crystal chandeliers and doormen looking so smart in long coats and military style caps. We had many big names at the *Theatre Royal,* Shirley Bassey appeared there in the early days of her career.

My stage debut was at the age of two, in the Molyneux School of Dancing's production of *Dick Whittington* in the Corn Exchange. This was what Loughborough Town Hall's auditorium was called then, a throw back to the town's market days when local farmers really did exchange corn in this big room. The entrance door had a brass plaque above it proudly bearing this name.

I was in the Sunbeam troupe and there were seven of us 'tinies'. Other troupes were the Footlight Girls and the Molyneux Starlets. I've learnt from my own experience as a dancing teacher that there's always one child who stays on the stage lost in the magic of the moment after all the other children have skipped off, the star of the show no doubt to the appreciative audience and at the age of two years I was that child! On one photo in panto at Loughborough Town Hall, the rest of the 'Sunbeams' have left the stage and I am proudly pointing my foot, my head down looking in admiration at my new pink leather ballet-shoes that I still have to this day! I just loved being on the stage and that has always remained with me, come what may.

All dancing troupes had 'special' names back then. At the age of four, I attended lessons at the Kathleen Freeman School of Dancing. In the school's production of *Jack and the Beanstalk* at Loughborough Town Hall, I was now a Freeman's Sunbeam! The other troupes taking part were the Freeman Panto Babes, the Freeman Lovelies, the Freeman Juveniles and the Freeman Starlets. I don't ever remember making the Freeman Lovelies troupe! I love these names, it's such a shame this tradition hasn't carried on.

In the Kathleen Freeman School of Dancing pantos we had a wonderful traditional 'dame', Roy Johnson. He also constructed and painted all the scenery. Roy in recent years, though in his 80s, has been a big part of many shows at the *Little Theatre* in Leicester and for many years played dame in the pantos at Coalville in Leicestershire. Roy wrote and appeared as Dame Durden in *Jack and The Beanstalk* in 1950 at Loughborough Town Hall. I was a four-year old Freeman Sunbeam and a certain teenager, Joan Jarram, played Princess Gloria.

In 1952 the Poole Academy based in Leicester, bought out the Kathleen Freeman School in Loughborough and retained the teachers, among them the young student teacher Joan Jarram who would have a big influence in my life later on! We 'Sunbeams' now became the 'Poole Academy Juveniles and Tiny Tots'!

That same year, for her first show, Margaret Poole produced *The Pied Piper* panto at the Theatre Royal, Loughborough. I was six years old and appeared as a rat, a villager and a herald. There was only one man in the cast and he was playing 'Mrs Winkler' the Dame. He came from Nuneaton and was very young, and tall and thin. His stage name was Billy Breen. He went on to become the so loved and much missed Larry Grayson. At that time he was working as a semi-pro comic; in the first half of his act he appeared in drag and the second half as himself. A lot of club audiences never realised it was the same person and many working men's club entertainment secretaries thought they had got two 'turns' for the price of one, and that the first act really was a woman!

My Mum, throughout her life, filled many albums and scrapbooks with pictures and programmes of everything I appeared in. All proud parents took numerous photos of all the children in those days; in these sad times this practice has to be carefully monitored or even stopped!

My Mum made up a wonderful album of my early dancing days. One of my first dancing teachers was Margot Turner, today better known in local amateur operatic circles as Margot Elliott. There is a newspaper cutting in the album of Margot, with Pauline Farren as the principal boy in *The Pied Piper*. Larry Grayson is standing alongside them dressed in a very ordinary 40s style cotton frock.

Margaret Poole, the principal of the Poole Academy, was a friend of Larry's and had asked him as a favour to her to play the 'dame', as she wanted to make a good impression in the town with her first show. He absolutely refused to wear the traditional dame outfits. Instead he wore the fashionable women's clothes of the day. Margot said: "Like all drag queens he had fabulous legs and he looked great in high heels." He would not wear wigs either; he grew his own dark hair into a bob and combed a long fringe over his forehead. Looking at the photos now, he looks just like E*astEnders'* Dot Cotton!

Margot recently told me Larry Grayson was a very kind and charming, extremely camp, and private young man. He would sit in his dressing room on his own. When he was backstage however, he loved talking to the mums, and the children appearing in the show. I do wish I could say I was one of them but it's so long ago I can't remember!

Years later I met him when he was appearing in the De Montfort Hall panto in Leicester. I told him I was trying to become a comic and he said: "Where are you going to work, all the theatres are closing down?" I showed him the photo of himself as dame with Margot. He autographed the programme for me and sighed wistfully on seeing the photo: "I loved that print frock!"

Larry Grayson also told me that he had appeared in the chorus of many musicals all over the country during the Second World War, as there was, unlike today, plenty of theatres and work around. He particularly recalled being in the chorus of *The White Horse Inn,* one of my all time favourite operettas, in London. I had tears rolling down my face as he recalled: "They shouted bring on the legionnaires. Of course all the real men were in the army and out we all 'swished' to: *Give Me Some Men Who Are Stout Hearted Men*!"

Larry Grayson appeared as dame in two of the Poole Academy shows, the other being *Cinderella*. As Margot recalled, he was indeed a very private man. At a British Comedy Society event in 2006 a plaque to Larry was unveiled at the *Empire Theatre*, Shepherds Bush in London, the home of his hit TV show *The Generation Game*. His friend and manager Paul Vaughan told us that, at the height of his fame wherever he was appearing, he would always stop his chauffeur-driven car and go into a nearby church for a quite moment to himself before a show.

Our pub had wooden floors that were great to tap dance on and I would often go in the bar and dance for the regulars, how they must have looked forward to that! We had a cupboard in the living room that ran from floor to ceiling and also ran the length of the wall and it was always full of jams and pickles and cake tins. One day my Nan was cleaning this cupboard out and there was some chocolate on the table that I took into the bar, I did my tap dance and then handed out the chocolate to the men in the bar. Little did I know that it was a chocolate laxative, one man going to work that night had to stop the bus and run down someone's entry!

There were many regulations in running a pub and you were not allowed to keep many things on the premises. We could only have 2-lbs of sugar at a time in case we were brewing and selling our own beer instead of the brewery's beer.

I went to St Botolph's Church of England Infant and Junior School in Shepshed from the age of four. I was already quite advanced for my age in reading and writing, thanks to my Mum. Those were the days when you said what each letter was and then attempted to say the word. Most children would be proficient readers and writers at an early age. I find it quite odd today when a child looks at a word and grunts and still can't pronounce the word. What kind of progress is that? Children in those days read a lot of books both at school and at home. There were very few comics then for children though I do remember having one called *The Girl*. I was always warned about the germs in newspapers and comics and told never to read anybody else's comic papers as you never knew what you might catch!

We had spelling tests every day at school, yet nowadays spelling correctly seems to have been abandoned all together. It's amazing today how not only children, but also a lot of adults, have no idea how to spell even the simplest of words. The amount of official documents I receive today with blatant spelling mistakes is unbelievable. If they can't be bothered, neither can I, straight in the bin!

Safety was not an issue then, as every family in the village knew each other and children really were safe out and about on their own in the village. A lot of children would walk down to the school and back every day with a friend or even on their own. Mums and dads didn't have cars to take their children to and from school. Mind you only the bravest of children would walk to school by way of the cemetery. There was a tree in the cemetery with a very knarled face and we all knew a really nasty witch who captured children lived in it!

Discipline was very different back then too. You stood up when a teacher entered a room and when they left. All teachers were 'Sir' or 'Miss' and you would never talk during a lesson unless told to by a teacher. You would do what you were told, and not only did you not use the teacher's first name like today, you wouldn't even know what it was. Even adults would not use another adult's first name unless they were told they could! Every child would say 'please' and 'thank you' without having to be prompted.

Bad manners were not an issue, as they were not tolerated. Any child who misbehaved would soon be brought into line. Parents would be appalled to receive a letter from a teacher about their child's bad behaviour as it reflected on them and they would punish their child accordingly for showing them up.

Children were taught to be quiet and only speak when spoken to. Any child who was rude would be said to come from 'a rough family' who wouldn't know better. Of course children would get noisy in the playground. We would play with skipping ropes that would be a piece of your mother's rope washing line – no plastic ones then - soft balls, wooden tops and whips, snobs, diabolos and yo-yos. Both boys and girls would play the still popular 'Hopscotch'. But children would never be noisy out in the street or on public transport. That would be totally unacceptable. You had to speak properly and schools even gave marks in end of term reports for speech. Slang words would not be allowed, not that we knew many of these anyway until the American shows started appearing on TV.

It really was a time of great respect and good manners. All men would offer their seat on a bus to a woman or an older person and children would not occupy a seat if adults were standing. People would open doors for everybody else and say 'after you'. All adults and children would say 'excuse me', 'please' and 'thank you'. People would queue (stand in line) and wait for their turn quietly and patiently. No one would ever push in front of anyone else. All men wore hats and when passing a lady they would raise their hats and nod their heads. When I started working at the Herbert Morris crane company in Loughborough in the 1960s we even had a manager who, if a director rang him, would put his hat on and stand up to attention for the entirety of the call! If a funeral procession went by in the street everybody would stop and stand still. Men would remove their caps and hats and bow their heads. When someone died in your street every house would have closed curtains in the front windows as a mark of respect.

It was very hard to buy clothes after the War as rationing carried on for a few more years. Clothes had to last and were only bought new when you had outgrown your old ones. Clothes were expensive and not that easily available. Even children had to have a clothing ration book. After my Mother died I found three ration books with our individual names on with a few of the unused ration slips still inside.

Most children wore clothes their mums had made and knitted. Boys and girls had knitted woollen gloves sewn onto a long piece of elastic that would be threaded up one coat sleeve and then down the other so they didn't lose them. Girls had knitted 'pixie' hoods that buttoned underneath with a point on top of the hood and pom-pom hats and boys wore balaclavas and cloth caps. In the winter, to keep warm, girls wore a liberty bodice; this was a tight fitting thick fleecy vest with rubber buttons.

All mums, grannies and girls had hand knitted 'twin sets'. A twin set was a short-sleeved jumper with a matching long-sleeved cardigan or 'cardi' as we called them. Mums and grannies would buy endless knitting patterns for these and other garments from the wool shops in Loughborough. All women's magazines would contain knitting patterns for every garment imaginable.

Boys wore short trousers, usually grey flannel, with braces even in winter. It would be unthinkable then for boys to wear long trousers, as it was for girls and women, long trousers were for men only! Boys had sleeveless V-neck pullovers usually striped in all colours, as these would be knitted by their mums from the wool they had left over, to wear over their white cotton shirts and they all wore ties and wool knee length socks. These pullovers would come back into fashion for adults in the 1970s as 'tank tops'!

All mums and grannies would darn the holes, called 'potatoes' in children's, and men's socks over and over again. Coat and dress hems and sleeves would be let down time and time again for growing children. In those days most children grew upwards not outwards like today. Clothes would then be passed on to smaller members of the family after you had outgrown them for good. Younger brothers and sisters all grew up in 'hand-me-downs'. If people couldn't afford to go to the cobblers to have the soles of their shoes mended they would line the shoes with cardboard!

## Dee Quemby

There was no Lycra in those days and on day trips to Skegness, Chapel St Leonard's, Cleethorpes and Mablethorpe (usually on a bus provided by the firm or business your father worked at) children had knitted bathos with matching boleros. Unfortunately as wool retains water you would wade out into the sea and struggle back with your 'cosi' pouring out water from either side of the gusset. You certainly felt that you weighed a lot more than when you went into the sea! I still have a pink and blue one that my Mum knitted for me. All women's magazines of the day would contain knitting patterns for these 'cosis'.

There had been a bad polio epidemic in the late 1940s and you could see a lot of children at school wearing leg irons. Many also had National Health glasses with a plaster stuck over one lens. A mouth full of black teeth was also a common sight, as people didn't go to dentists regularly like today. It was far too expensive then.

Most people seemed to lose their teeth about the age of 21 and had to have false teeth. It was something you just expected to happen. It was almost like a 21st birthday present! When, as a child, visiting friends' or relatives' houses, on going into the bathroom there would nearly always be someone's false teeth in a glass on the wash hand basin shelf.

Luckily, my Mum took me to the dentist as soon as I was old enough in Granby Street, Loughborough. My Mum had asked for something to sedate me as she herself was terrified of going and didn't want me to be frightened. This was promptly done but, as soon as the dentist came near me, I shot out of the chair and 'legged it'. The dentist and my Mum had to run after me, through Queen's Park! I still hate going to this day, but am grateful that she took me, and I have my own teeth. A lot of my friends at that time were not so fortunate.

This was also a time when you had to pay to see a doctor, so all mothers and grandmas would brew up the old tried and trusted traditional medicines. Mum and Nan regularly went to see Nurse Christian in Loughborough. We used to get lots of little cardboard pots from her with thick yellow ointment in. Whatever it was, it seemed to cure just about everything. Children were not pumped full of antibiotics and other drugs from an early age as they are now. We all had the usual colds, coughs and children's ailments, but there didn't seem to be the illnesses and viruses there are today. Most people seemed to die of old age, with a lot reaching their 80s and 90s, even though most smoked and ate many things now considered bad for our health. Mind you, there weren't the pesticides about then and animals weren't given drugs. As rules and regulations changed Nurse Christian was forced to stop making her famous ointments and had to close down, as she was not a 'recognised' practitioner.

All grannies and mums would treat abscesses, boils and other infections themselves with a hot poultice. Bread would be mixed with boiling-hot water or milk, spread thickly onto a linen bandage and then left on all night on whatever needed to open up for the poison to come out. I can remember these 'hot poultices' being red hot and steaming. A more simple tried and trusted way to treat chilblains at that time was to dip the inflamed toes in a recently used chamber pot - in other words while it was still warm! In wintertime people would go outside and put their inflamed toes in the snow. As a child, if I had a headache, a spot of 4711 eau de cologne or lavender water would be put on my forehead, children would not be given drugs as they are today.

Most grannies and mums brewed up all sorts of remedies and beauty aids, as there were very few to buy in a village and not much money to buy them with. Most women at that time, with all the scrubbing, cleaning and washing that they had to do, had very rough hands. Not my Nan, she would mix glycerine and lemon juice together. She kept this mixture in a small bottle at the side of the open fire. She would always be massaging this liquid into her hands and, right up to her death at the age of 90 years her hands were still soft and supple. One of Mary Queen of Scots many escape attempts failed due to her not having 'washer-women's hands', as they were called when I was little. Disguised as a washerwoman she left the fortress she was imprisoned in with the other women on their way to be rowed back to the mainland. As soon as she held out her hand to the boatman the game was up and back she went!

We children would pick flowers from the garden and put them in jam jars full of water to make our own 'scent'. Lavender would be grown in the garden, dried out and then put in little bags made out of the material from old cotton dresses. These 'lavender bags' would be put in wardrobes and drawers to keep the moths away and make the clothes smell nice. Nan would also make her own little white linen 'dolly bags' to put the blue block of powder in for the 'white' wash. I was always fascinated by the 'bachelor buttons' Nan had in her button tin. These were for unmarried men as men didn't sew or mend in those days, apart from tailors and men working with leather, it was a mother's or a wife's job. These 'bachelor buttons' were white bone buttons with a metal hook at the back that you could push through fabric. A small metal loop like a hairgrip (bobby pin) went through the hook to keep the button in place.

People had to make use of what they had and nobody would ever throw away newspapers. We had our own recycling system in those days! Newspapers would be used to light fires and gas rings and even to wrap up presents. Our 'gift wrap' then was to buy sheets of shiny brown paper and tie a parcel up with string (though we did have decorative paper at Christmas time). I was always fascinated watching my Nan seal the string around a package with hot red wax if it was going to be sent through the post. Men working outdoors would put sheets of paper inside their shirts and jackets to keep warm. Newspapers would also be cut into handy size squares and have a hole punched in one corner so you could tie a loop of string through them. They would then be hung up on a nail on the inside of the outside toilet's door for use as 'toilet paper'. If you hadn't read the newspaper before it was cut up and the piece you were about to use contained an interesting story you would frantically search through the other hanging pieces to find the rest of it. Some dads, according to my friends, would even search through the sheets of newspaper to find a picture of a politician, they didn't like, to use first. These days they'd be spoilt for choice! Toilet rolls were a luxury at that time for most people and the ones that you could buy then were made from stiff white, shiny and very odd smelling paper. Today's luxury toilet bathroom tissue in pastel colours was a long way off and who could have ever imagined then a bath, toilet and wash hand basin in any other colour than white!

We also had visits at school from a nurse. You would stand there in your vest and knickers and she would examine you, checking your height and weight and then looking through your hair for head lice. We never knew her name but we children called her 'Nitty Nora, the hair explorer'.

One day at school we had a lecture on rabbits. A local man brought two to the class. These were 'Dutch' rabbits that were half black and half white. One rabbit had a 'broken saddle' where the line is not straight between the two colours. As he couldn't exhibit this one they both needed a good home otherwise something unfortunate would happen to them. Nobody spoke up, so guess who took the rabbits home!

29

Nearly all children grew up having pets in the 1950s and 60s. We always had a cat at the pub, as did most business premises. The cat would earn its keep by monitoring the mice population. As we lived in the country, mice quite happily took up residence in everybody's house. People did not flea or worm pets or take them for annual inoculations or have them neutered; these things weren't done then and you never heard of anyone being allergic to a cat or a dog. Come to think of it we'd never heard of allergies! I can remember my Mum being very indignant when our American friends 'The Emricks' who were living here in the 1950s, asked why our cat wasn't wearing something called a 'flea collar' as all cats did in the States. My Mum was adamant our cat was very clean and didn't have fleas! There was no vast array of pet food products stacked on numerous shelves either as in supermarkets today. Pets would be fed the remains from the family meals. Poor cats would be put out at night to hunt for their supper whatever the weather even if they were curled up asleep in front of the fire. I can remember my Dad often carrying an indignant half-asleep cat over his arm to the back door at night.

The Emricks also mentioned something called 'babysitters'. We had never heard of such people then. When you had a family you stayed at home together and if you went out you all went out together. My Mum thought it was awful, as no doubt all mothers would in those days, that parents would leave children with strangers and pay them for it. It was a mother's job then to stay at home with her children. Dads might nip out to the pub but it would be a long while before their wives would go with them. Women did not go out together at night; it would have been considered indecent not to be accompanied by a man. Mums would however sometimes meet up in someone's home for tea in the afternoon while the children were at school. A lot of mums would be members of the Mother's Union at that time and other church groups.

If you had told anybody then, that some time in the future, they would have to take home their dog's 'business' they would have thought you were 'off your rocker' as we say in Leicestershire. It was completely acceptable to walk the dog and leave its 'business' wherever. I do concede that this is one of the few improvements in life today, along with paper 'hankies'! I can remember walking to school every day in complete amazement at how many different colours of doggy 'poo' there were along the way! But then being in the country there would be horse-dung and cow pats everywhere and we were well used to horse-dung on rhubarb and other things that were growing in the garden, outside earth toilets and chamber pots. Chamber pots were always called 'guzzunders', because as we say in Leicestershire they 'guzzunder' under the bed. It all was perfectly normal and acceptable; nobody was squeamish about these things then! Life was life and we just got on with it.

Shepshed was, at that time, renowned as the biggest village in England. It certainly had more pubs than most of the towns. We had long hot summers and freezing cold winters. Often the snow would be very deep and last for days, even weeks, but life went on without the assistance of snowploughs and gritters. In the mornings the streets would be full of dads digging their way out of their front doors and making paths for elderly neighbours.

These days even mild winter conditions shut down many schools and offices, yet then very few people had cars and though most people worked in the village some had to walk or bike to Loughborough and Hathern to get to work and still did even in severe weather conditions. The bus would not make it to the village; we would be completely cut off. The children would put on their wellies and trudge through the snow to school. The free milk would still get delivered even though it was frozen solid and you had to wait for it to thaw out in the cold schoolroom. People got to work regardless. If you didn't you would not get paid and today's many benefits and sick pay were unheard of. You either worked to feed and clothe your family or you went without, it was as simple as that. It was a big disgrace to be out of a job if you were able, and people were too proud to accept any help that they called 'charity'.

Most people had coal fires, not the central heating we have all come to expect these days. If you couldn't afford coal you just put on extra clothes and went to bed earlier with a hot water bottle to keep warm. Nan had several big old-fashioned stone beer bottles that she would warm up and fill with hot water. She used to wrap a towel around one of these bottles and put it in my bed every night in the winter. People flocked to buy electric blankets when they became available. We had a massive walk-in airing cupboard. When it was a freezing cold morning my Mum or my Nan would take me in there in the warmth and change me in the dark and the sparks would fly off my nightdress as it was pulled over my head. Gramp would keep his bottle of horse oil lineament at the side of the fire. If I woke up in the night with 'growing pains' as they were called, this would be rubbed all over my legs. The smell was very strong, but it certainly worked.

I remember living in the pub as being something special. People would look at me quite differently, or so I thought, on first meeting me to be told 'she's the landlady's granddaughter'. It always made me feel a bit remote in some way. There was nothing plastic in pubs in those days. We had proper drinking glasses, solid glass ashtrays, big heavy mirrors, solid oak stools and tables with heavy wrought iron legs like the Singer sewing machines, they were so heavy you could hardly pick them up. We had many pot Bambi and Guinness ostrich ornaments. In my bedroom I remember I had a fireguard with a very pretty girl wearing a pilot's helmet advertising some brand of cigarettes, we also had a fireguard advertising Black Cat cigarettes.

We had a 'phone in the lounge and I used to sit on my own at night watching the nine-inch screen television while all the family worked in the bar. I loved the old films with stars such as Bette Davies, Jean Arthur, Errol Flynn, James Cagney, Humphrey Bogart, Jean Harlow, Joan Crawford, Robert Mitchum and the many Brian Rix *Whitehall Farces.* There would often be a knock at the door and a customer would poke his head round the door and say: "It's all right your grandma said I could use the phone." As very few people had phones in their houses this would happen often during the evening. I wouldn't even notice them. I would be lost in the magic of the film I was watching.

There were no colour televisions then (or coloured photographs) and I loved the old 1940s black and white films that were on the TV. It was Orson Wells who said: "Everybody acts better in black and white" and I quite agree with him. There's nothing as creepy as a thriller in good old black and white. My favourite film was *The Big Heat* made in 1953 starring Lee Marvin, Glenn Ford and Gloria Grahame. Lee Marvin is the 'bad guy' and he throws scalding hot coffee in Gloria Graham's face, and she has to wear a veil over the badly scarred side of her face for the rest of the film; needless to say he gets sorted out good and proper by Glenn Ford at the end! To me Gloria Grahame was the most beautiful woman, apart from my Mum I had ever seen. At the age of seven years I said to myself: "That's it, I'm going to be a film star and call myself Deirdre Grahame!"

Our pub would get packed at night. Many men would also nip out of their homes in their slippers, carrying jugs and bottles (or even a glass vase on odd occasions, needs must!) to buy beer at our pub's 'off-sales', to take back home to drink. Most people smoked and many would roll their own cigarettes. Looking back at old black and white photos two things always strike me, everyone, when out in the open, has a hat on and all men are holding a lit cigarette! I can also remember a coin 'cigarette' machine fixed on a wall in Shepshed where you could put your money in and two cigarettes and a book of matches would drop down into a tray at the bottom of the machine.

Life in those days was very safe, children played out and we all went to play at the farms our friends lived in, walking over many fields on our own to get there. You never heard people rowing or swearing. It may have been done behind closed doors, but never in front of other people and certainly not children. We didn't have any trouble or fights in our pub. I'm sure if anyone tried to start something my Grandad, being over 6'0" and well built, would have thrown them out by the scruff of their neck. People did not put up with anyone's bad behaviour in those days. We never heard of any murders, rapes or assaults. If you did it was usually in London or some other big city far away and probably only happened about twice a year. You would never expect it to happen where you lived. People would be horrified then, nowadays it's something we have come to expect to happen almost daily!

People left their doors open and never got robbed. Villagers all knew each other, helped each other and trust was the natural thing. These days you're lucky if you know the neighbours next door. There weren't the same problems with noisy neighbours then. Most people only had a radio and everybody listened to *The Archers*. The vicar visited his parishioners at night and told my Mum he would put his ear to the door and if they had *The Archers* on would move on to the next house as he knew they wouldn't want to talk to him until the programme had finished. So influential was this programme that when in one episode a member of the cast died in a fire in the stables, the BBC in London was inundated with wreaths! The only thing I can remember personally about *The Archers* was that there was a character called Walter Gabriel who used to say "oh ar oh ar me old beauty" a lot. At the 1953 Shepshed Wakes, Mrs Fairbrother of *The Archers*, actress Joy Davies, was the guest of honour and I was a proud attendant on the Carnival Queen's float.

I loved the radio on a Sunday afternoon, particularly programmes like *The Clitheroe Kid, Life With The Lyons, The Huggetts* and *Two-Way Family Favourites*. We would have our dinner. There was no such thing then as 'lunch'. Then I could go to the sideboard and have a bar of chocolate as a treat. Children did not eat sweets all the while like they do today.

Meals were not available in pubs as they are today, but there would be snacks for sale in the bar, plain crisps with a little blue bag of salt inside (no different flavours then), cheese and onion cobs and cheese and biscuits in packets. A big jar lay on its flat side with a big screw off lid that contained Crawfords cream biscuits; why people would want to eat sweet biscuits with beer was beyond me? There was also a card hanging on the wall with little bags of nuts and raisins attached. On the bar was a big glass jar containing little packets of snuff.

I used to love Old Poll, as she was known, one of the pub regulars. She was a little overweight lady in her late 70s. She always wore a long black dress and a big hat with lots of feathers. She would come into the bar, have a couple of drinks then buy a packet of snuff. She would put some of the snuff on the back of her hand, sniff it up and go back home on her own, no worrying about walking alone in the dark then.

My Grandmother cooked every day for the family.   I loved her steam puddings, 'spotted Dick', 'plum duff', treacle tart and treacle pudding, all served with a big bowl of custard.     All children would sit patiently waiting whilst their mother or grandmother whipped up the ingredients for a cake so they could lick the bowl out at the end.   That was a big treat in those days.

One day every year would be set aside for making jam, pickling onions and red cabbage.  All the glass jars would be labelled carefully with Nan's very flowery writing with big fancy capitals at the start of each word and put inside the big cupboard. This would last us the year, ready for the next jam making and pickling session.  This would be a ritual that was performed in every house yearly.    We drank full cream milk, Nan's fruit cake would be cut into slices and then buttered one side with thick 'proper' butter before eating, a piece of bread would be smeared with thick dripping and then heavily salted.    No food health fads in those days and oh my, did everything taste good!

Most people sat down to a 'dinner' at midday of at least, two veg and meat every day followed by 'pudding' apart from washday on Saturdays.  Food was scarce, there wasn't much to go round so most families kept chickens and rabbits in their back gardens and it was not at all unusual for children to see these animals and birds being skinned and plucked.  I remember only once seeing Gramp pluck a turkey in the garage.   There were feathers everywhere and I hated seeing the poor dead bird strung up.

People ate an enormous amount of rabbit meat in those days. My Nan recalled how she and her brothers and sisters had sat and sobbed when they were served their first rabbit meal.  Their dad was shouting at them because they wouldn't eat it. All they could think of looking at the meal on their plates was the rabbit they had spent weeks playing with!  We never ever ate rabbit meat thanks to Nan's childhood experience.

We didn't have microwaves, fridges and freezers then, so all food had to be bought, prepared and cooked every day.  Vegetables and fruit were bought loose and straight from wherever they had been growing locally.  Potatoes were always covered in dirt and they all had to be scrubbed thoroughly and the potato 'eyes' cut out.  I hated having to shell peas and peel the rind off runner beans, as it always made my fingers so sore – yes even young children helped prepare the family meal then!  It wasn't until the 1970s when I first went to California that I saw vegetables and fruit in bags ready prepared and washed.  It always amazes me that tomatoes are fruit and not vegetables.  The Victorians called them 'love apples'.

All the family would have a hearty 'fry-up' breakfast followed during the day by dinner, tea and supper before going to bed.  My Gramp would often cut a thick wedge of cheese, spread lots of butter down one side and eat it like a piece of cake.   As a child a lot of people would put condensed milk in their cups of tea instead of milk.  I went to a friend's house and was nearly sick on being given this to drink.  The family that eats together stays together was the saying then and it certainly seemed so.

Nan had come from a wealthy family, but as said before her parents had wasted away all their money.  As a young wife and mother and having a younger brother to look after money was scarce and there were very few benefits.  You had to have money to live.  She and her sisters and friends would go down to the factory gates and wait outside to see if there was any work for the day and she was always chosen because her sewing was so good, she said she felt so sorry for the other women begging to be given work to feed their families.

During their early-married life, Gramp was working with a 'gang' of diggers in Leicester. It was Christmas Eve their wedding anniversary and he had no money to get Nan anything. As he was digging he saw something gleam, he looked down and saw the 'old Queen's head'. It was a gold Queen Victoria sovereign. He quickly put it in his pocket, took it home and gave it to my Nan. This meant more to her than any other present she ever got from Gramp. Nan kept it safe for years only to have it stolen, amongst other things from her house in her last years, and I sincerely hope that whoever stole it had their hands drop off!

Nan had a best friend Aunty Hilda who had married Ralph Ward, a budding businessman. He was buying up terraced houses cheap, doing them up and renting them out. At one time they ran a pub and I presume this is how my grandparents got started in the business. Aunty Hilda and Uncle Ralph even had an ice cream parlour in The Rushes for a while. Ralph Ward was a very good businessman and bought a lot of property in Loughborough, at one time he even had a string of racehorses. He became a self-made millionaire in the 1930s when most people were struggling to make a living. Aunty Hilda and Uncle Ralph had no children of their own. They thought the world of my Mum and even asked Nan and Gramp if they could adopt her. As if!

Even when my grandparents had made money, my Nan still kept little habits from their hardship days. She would never write on an envelope to immediate family. You would be given your birthday or Christmas card but when you took it out of the envelope, she would take the envelope off you and put it in the bureau to use again. On Christmas Day she would open her presents carefully then lay the wrapping paper flat on the table, pick up a desert-spoon, smooth out the creases, fold the paper up and put it away safely to use for someone else the next year. Old habits die hard, and I admit that I never write on envelopes for my husband's cards to this day and, like Nan, save the envelopes. I also when cracking an egg smash the shells so 'the witches can't sail away in them', that probably came from my Nan as she was very superstitious and very afraid of the unknown, probably due to her mother's involvement with mediums.

My grandparents' first pub was the Horse and Groom at Kegworth that is now no longer there. Pubs always had a cat to keep the vermin down and the Horse and Groom was no exception. Next door was a baker's and cockroaches would find their way into the pub cellar. However this particular cat didn't have the killer instinct! He would lick the cockroaches and some had become transparent according to my Mum. My grandparents moved in 1939 to take over the Charnwood Forest Railway Inn, an old coaching inn, in Shepshed with Gramp as Landlord.

People used to go round houses and pubs selling books that my Nan would buy. We had lots of books with vivid pictures of people burning in Hell that I used to play with. We even had a hardback copy of *Mein Kampf* by Adolf Hitler! My Nan had written inside in her flowery writing 'To Horace with best wishes from Dolly Xmas 1942'. What a Christmas present during the War!

At that time you were either one of three things 'Church, Chapel or Catholic'. Oh those infamous threes! Mum and Nan always told me that there were three things you never talked about which were religion, money and politics as they always caused rows, especially in a pub! We used to attend St Botolph's Church in Shepshed and every Sunday we would all dress in our best clothes to go. I always had a pretty silk dress with matching ribbons for my ringlets, a rabbit wool bolero, white lace gloves, straw hat, white ankle socks, white bag and my 'Alice in Wonderland' shoes as I called them.   I had an Alice in Wonderland doll with black shiny shoes that had ankle-straps and I loved them.   I still like black patent shoes with a strap to this day and still think of them by this name. Even the very poor people would save a 'best' outfit for Sundays.

My long hair was put in six 'ringlet' rags every night.   The rags would be made from an old white cotton bed-sheet; we didn't have coloured bed linen in those days.  I would sit there holding tight on to the end of my hair-rag with my eyes getting wider and wider as my Mum wound the other end around my hair. She would then take my end of the rag, wind that round as well, knot both ends together tightly and then start all over again on the next 'ringlet'.   The rags had to be pulled tight to hold the hair and I think it's due to this that I have big eyes! It was always a bit uncomfortable at first trying to sleep with the knots in the rags.   Little girls in those days either had long hair or a short 'pudding bowl' cut and we all wore hair ribbons.  I remember other mothers bringing their daughters to my Mum to learn how to do ringlets and all the little girls sitting on a bench in our sitting room, where we lived over the bridge at Shepshed, as their mums twisted the rags in their hair under my Mum's supervision.

Food was still scarce as it took a long while after the War for things to return to normal.  So you had to grow what you ate.  Most people had an allotment to grow vegetables on.  Bananas came back into Britain after the War.  Children had no idea what these strange things were and had to be shown how to peel them.

Whilst my Mother was pregnant with me, an American serviceman used to visit her.  His wife was having a baby at the same time and he was very homesick. He used to take my Mum things that were very scarce that he, being an American serviceman, could get.  One day he took her an orange, she ate it and it made her sick.  I could not eat oranges or drink the free orange juice that was given to post-war children as it always gave me a sore throat.  Unfortunately his baby died and my Mum never saw him or heard from him again.

If children were orphaned, relatives and friends would take them in and bring them up with their own.  There is a 1987 John Boorman film *Land Of Hope And Glory* that is based on his childhood memories of growing up during the Blitz. One scene shows a little girl standing shell shocked in a big pile of rubble that used to be her house, another little girl tells her mum; "She's lost her house and her mam and dad." The mother holds out her hand and the shell-shocked girl takes hold of it and walks off with them.  You just know she is going to be well looked after and loved by this family.  To me this says it all about this generation of wonderful people.  They had nothing but gave everything.

My Mum baked the best chocolate cake ever.  Friends used to say: "Instead of a present, can I have one of your Mum's chocolate cakes?"   People used to ask for the recipe but they could never ever bake a cake as good as my Mum's! Joan Neal, my dancing teacher in the 1960s, had a chocolate birthday cake from my Mum for many years until rheumatoid arthritis stopped my Mum from doing so many things.

Mum and I used to listen to Radio Luxembourg at night.  I remember *Dan Dare* and the film star Margaret Lockwood in a programme as a nurse.  I was an Ovaltiny and still have my Ovaltine mug with a cover that looks like a nightcap. Hi-Fi systems, DVDs and video recorders hadn't been invented.  We were one of the few families with a television.  TV programmes finished early and the National

Anthem was played before closing down. People even stood to attention in their own homes as they watched the young Queen on her horse at the trooping of the colour.

Our pub had been a coaching inn and was massive with four bedrooms and a bathroom as big as the living room. The pub door still contained shrapnel from the Second World War. A 'stray' German bomber on the way back from the devastating bombings in Coventry had let fire at the street hitting the pub door. Fortunately nobody had been in the street at the time. I would sit on the front doorstep waiting for the man with the 'camels' to walk by - at the age of three I didn't know they were greyhounds!

Our pub was very popular during the Second World War with the American GIs stationed in Woodhouse. Gramp said there would often be a knock at the pub door late at night and it would be the American Military Police looking for the GIs who hadn't made it back to the barracks.

At one point my Mum had been engaged to an American GI and then she met my Dad, and that was that! My Mum told me Nan and Gramp would often run a raffle in the pub during the war and the prize would be for one onion or such like. As food was rationed, many tickets would be sold with all the pub regulars hoping to be the winner!

One of my Mum's cousins Margaret came from Leicester to work in a nearby munitions factory and lived at the pub for the duration of the War. Another cousin Norah was in the WAF doing 'her bit' for wartime. Norah met and married a very handsome American airman, Alan Swindler, my Mum being one of the bridesmaids. She was one of the many GI Brides who went to live in America after the War. Norah and Alan first lived in New Orleans, but she has now moved to Florida. 'Aunty' Norah is now in her late 80s and we often phone each other.

Mum had a friend called Narina, whom I loved. She was a pretty young Italian girl who, when her village had been liberated by the British troops, had met and got engaged to a British 'Tommy'. She had come back with him to Shepshed to get married. Narina always made a fuss of me and bought me lovely presents for my birthday and Christmas. I sometimes see Narina at the Thursday market in Loughborough and she still has the lovely Italian accent she had back then. She recently told me that she had spent her honeymoon night at the pub as they had nowhere to go and my grandparents invited them to stop there. She also said she used to alter my many dancing costumes as I grew.

Shepshed was a very pretty and clean village. You would never throw any rubbish down in the street. If you had sweets you put the wrappers in your pocket and put them in the dustbin when you got home. Cleanliness is next to Godliness, we were told. Very few people had a bathroom complete with all fittings. Most people had to manage with outside toilets and tin baths. Luckily, living in a pub, we had a massive bathroom with a bath, wash hand basin and toilet. It was quite usual in many families on 'bath-night' (Fridays) for a tin bath to be filled with hot water in front of the fire. The whole family would use the same bath water. Father bathed first, then mother would get in followed by the children from the eldest down. Mothers would often bathe small children in the kitchen sink. A lot of people would go to Loughborough to the swimming baths in Granby Street (now the Charnwood Museum) to the slipper-baths. They would take their own towel and soap to have a proper all over bath once a week.

Saturday would be washday and with the old fashioned wash tubs and ringers it meant your mum or grandma would be hard at work all day, and you had a 'catch what you can' meal of what was in the pantry usually tomatoes on toast. There were no fridges, readymade meals, automatic washing machines and tumble dryers in those days! It really did take all day and the whole house would smell of soap!

Being an only child growing up in a pub meant I was often on my own and one of my favourite things to do, apart from watching the old black and white films on our television, was to walk through the 'jitty' (small lane) near our pub. At the end was a shed-cum-garage where the coffin maker worked. He had coffins stood up against the wall and hedge and I used to sit and watch him sand them down for hours.

One Christmas I had a wonderful gift my Nan had had made for me. It was my own shop! It was wooden about 18" high and 6" wide and painted green. I opened the sides and inside was a counter that you fixed to the two sides. On one side of the box was a glass shop window with QUEMBY'S STORES painted at the top in black capitals. The other side was full of shelves and there were many boxes and tin miniature replicas of items you could buy at that time. There was a switch near the door and the light actually worked! It must have cost a fortune at that time to have it made for a child. I am proud to say that my little shop is on display at Snibston Discovery Park in Coalville, Leicestershire.

As children had very few toys in the 1950s we would find our own things to play with. I remember my Nan had a very ornate tin full of different buttons. I would often fetch it out and quite happily play for ages with the buttons.

When I was six years old, I had a turquoise metal pedal scooter with small red wheels, a real luxury then for a child. I loved going up and down the road on it on my own or zooming round our massive sloping pub car park. Children really were safe out on their own then. One day there was thunder and lightening and I was terrified it would strike the metal scooter. I dropped it and ran all the way back to the pub. Gramp had to search the streets looking for it in the pouring rain and he eventually found it. Opposite the pub were many fields with big rocks and most children would go and play there. My Mum didn't think it was safe, so I never played there.

As my parents worked during the day, Nan and Gramp took me out a lot in the car when the pub was closed in the afternoons, usually to see Nan's relatives in Leicester. Gramp used to keep a bucket and spade in the boot of the car, as living in the country with lots of horses and ponies you would often find something large and steaming in the middle of the road to shovel up and take home for the garden. Often the bucket would be full to the brim long before we got home and I would have to sit in the back of the car holding my nose for the rest of the journey!

Looking back I think most of my relatives were quite bizarre and eccentric but I loved going to see them. There was an aunt and uncle who had bought some farmland and were building a house. They had bought an old double-decker bus, sunk it into the ground and taken all the seats out. They had made it into a house and it was massive inside. I loved playing in that.

We would go to Bardon to see Gramp's brother Uncle Walt (Walter) and his wife Aunty Poll (Polly). Gramp and Uncle Walt both worked at Bardon quarry after the First World War. Aunty Poll was enormous and clasped every relative to her very ample bosom that looked like a bolster, nearly suffocating you! The powder from her heavily made-up face, and her overwhelming strong 'scent' would go up our noses. We would all sit there for the entirety of the visit with big 'red lips' on our cheeks. On the journey home, we would frantically try to rub Aunty Poll's dark red lipstick off our cheeks with Nan's lace hanky; no such thing as paper ones then. My Dad and Gramp would keep well out of Aunty Poll's way when she came to visit us!

Another aunt, on my Nan's side of the family, had two terraced houses in Leicester with an adjoining door from one landing to the other. You went up the very steep stairs in one house opened the door and down the stairs into the other. That was great fun.

My Grandad would often take me up to Mount St Bernard's Abbey at Oaks in Charnwood. Not all the monks had taken a vow of silence and Gramp was friendly with some of them. One time he bought a pair of candlesticks from the abbey, they stood for many years on our mantelpiece in the pub. Many years later my mother donated these candlesticks to St Peter's Church, Mountsorrel after it had been burgled.

My Nan would walk me round numerous graveyards and read all the inscriptions on the gravestones out loud to me. If it were an inscription for a child she would cry. To this day I have to read all the gravestones when in a cemetery.

I used to love the Licensed Victuallers' 'do's. Nan and Gramp would really dress up to go. The men wore their best suits. Gramp would put on his gold watch and chain, diamond ring and tie pin, and the women would have beautiful cocktail dresses, tailored suits, furs, jewellery, big hats with feathers and veils. They all talked very 'posh' and only the best would do, they would even dress like this when working behind the bar! Never underestimate the landladies of those days; they looked like ladies but they were as tough as old boots and worked very hard every night behind the bar, then scrubbing and cleaning the living accommodation and the pub every morning. Most publicans didn't employ other people to work in the pub, as they couldn't afford to, though I do remember we had a barman called Charlie who always wore a white jacket behind the bar.

Nan had clothes made for working behind the bar. She had a beautiful green satin shift dress with a black lace dress that went over it. I would dress up in her clothes. There was a mustard crepe blouse with sparkly bits on it and a beautiful big black velvet hat with lots of feathers. I would dance on the bed looking at myself in the dressing table mirror pretending I was dancing on the stage.

Grandmas in the 1950s all seemed to look alike, not very tall, stout, with no waists and would always wear a floral wrap-over pinny, and they all proudly sported the tight white 'granny perm'! No self-respecting grandma would have dyed her hair in those days, they were very proud when it turned white. It was almost a badge of office. They would go to the hairdressers, have it cut very short and then tightly permed 'so it lasts' and then come home and say: "It'll be alright when it drops". Of course when it did they went straight back to the hairdressers for another tight perm! At home in the day they would cover their hair with a fine hair net to keep the curls in and put a thicker one on at night to sleep in. It would be a decade later when grandmas would have the blue, pink and purple rinses on their white hair, long before the punk era. Trendsetters those grannies!

Most little girls accompanied their grandma to see the corset lady. This would be an annual outing as grannies always had new corsets which they wore every day. You would go to a terraced house and the lady who lived there would be an agent for the Spirella Corset Company of Great Britain, like Tupperware, Avon and Ann Summers today! Nan would stand there in the front room in her slip as she was carefully measured. These measurements would be sent off to the Spirella Company who would make the corsets at their factory. A few weeks later we would go back to the house to pick up the new corsets. Nan would stand in the living room in her slip again and the lady would open a large white cardboard box and hold up triumphantly a pink 'concertina' with suspenders attached, full of whalebones, eyelets and dangling laces, tabs and buckles, in all a frightening sight!

The corset-lady would then place the corsets around my Nan and start the long task of fastening all these things up. Nan would get a bit red faced and breathe in a bit sharply, they would be taken off, Nan would dress and we would go home with the 'concertina' in the box. If you ever touched your granny's tummy it was like touching a block of concrete! How they ever bent down or walked around in those things I'll never know. I recently found an old diary of my Nan's and there is an entry in her flowery writing: Joan Kilgallon, Patterson Place, Shepshed, new corsets two pairs August 1974. Joan must have been the corset agent at that time.

All women wore girdles and as you became middle aged, you moved on to a corset that would be worn daily. If one of the suspenders broke, Nan would get a sixpence to use to fasten her stocking to the suspender. During the daily housework they would undo their stockings and they would be rolled down around their ankles so they didn't ladder them. When stockings disappeared during the 1960s and tights were in fashion, my Nan would cut tights in two to use with her corsets.

I remember in the pub when my Nan would say at any time during the year "should we have a Christmas?" We would snuggle up under a tartan car rug on the leather settee with orange velvet cushions, in front of the roaring fire. She would put a couple of tangerines in front of the fire to warm up and crack a few Brazil nuts open. We would also have a few wedges of Chocolate Orange. We would sit there as various Gracie Fields and *Birds In A Monastery Garden* records played in the background.

Nan always vetted friends, I couldn't play too much with any one friend as she said people would think the family were getting free drinks and the other regulars would complain.

I had a friend, Pearl Miller, who lived in one of the terraced houses that were built up to the pub. I loved Pearl that much that I would say to my Mum: "Why didn't you call me Pearl?" over and over again! Another friend Jackie is on a lot of photographs with me and Gramp and his car. Very few people had cars so a ride out would have been a great treat. Another friend was June Riley who had a younger brother David but I didn't like him because he would eat worms! June kindly came to sing in the choir at my mother's funeral. I often see another friend, Carol Freeman from my childhood days 'over the bridge' as she now lives in Mountsorrel.

Looking back at photos of Pearl recently, I suddenly realised after all these years that her and her family's skin was a lot darker than other people in the village and they had black tightly curled hair. Her grandfather had originated from St Helena but it had never occurred to any of us then that we were in any way different and it really would have been different back then.

Each bed in our pub had a satin top sheet and a matching satin eiderdown, in green, mustard gold, dark rose pink and pale pink each one elaborately embroidered with the same colour thread. Pearl and I were always chosen to be part of the tableau on Mothering Sunday as 'children of all nations'. Pearl would be dressed as the Hawaiian girl and I always had to represent India because I had long dark hair. At that time, we had never even seen children or adults from that part of the world or most anywhere else come to that! I would be wrapped in the dark rose pink satin sheet off the bed as a sari and my Mum would put a dot of her red lipstick on my head. As Romanies originate from Asia perhaps I was the best choice after all.

On my birthdays at the pub because we had big rooms nearly all of my classmates would come to my parties as well as Jackie, Carol, Pearl, June and another friend Kathleen White. As my birthday is in the panto season, Nan would also let me take a friend to see the big professional pantomimes in the theatres in Leicester that have now long gone. This was probably where my love of pantomimes came from. After the panto we would go for tea in a posh restaurant.

It was quite usual in the 1950s for a child to be given a spoonful of liquid paraffin before they went off to bed as constipation was looked upon as a sin. If a child were constipated, mothers and grannies would first try California syrup of figs or liquid paraffin. If either of those were not successful, they would then brew up senna pods in the teapot and you would have to drink this foul smelling liquid that almost made you sick. You prayed this last resort would work because if not the nurse would be sent for. She would come armed with a black bag and proceed to give you a soapy water enema. I remember this vividly. I had to sit on a pot in the living room in front of the nurse, Nan and Mum as they sat chatting on the settee and drinking tea waiting for me to perform!

My Grandad used to mop the wooden floors and would sit me on one of the tables and sing all the old music hall songs to me. I loved *Me And Jane In A Plane, Oh Mr Porter, Daisy Daisy, Can't Get Away To Marry You Today, My Wife Won't Let Me* and *The Spaniard Who Blighted My Life* and I would sing along with him. The highlight of the pub week was the barrels of beer being delivered. The cellar doors were in the ground and they would be lifted and the barrels would then be rolled down into the cellar. I used to sit and watch every time they came.

I went past an old boarded up shop the other day called 'The Glory Hole' and it struck me that I had not heard this name for many years. When I was a child every house had a glory hole, it was usually a cupboard under the stairs with lots of shelves where everything would be put out of sight. If you couldn't find anything in the pub you would always be told; "I bet it's in the glory hole" and it always was.

People rarely left the village, there were no cars and there was only one bus into Loughborough. Sometimes this didn't turn up, so you just went back home with your parents and waited for the bus another day.

Shops had strict rules during the 1950s and 60s. As shops were open on a Saturday they would have to have one half day closing during the week and it would be on a different day all over the country. In Leicestershire it was a Wednesday and the shops would shut dead on the dot at 1pm. If you needed food for a baby or any other necessary item no matter how urgent, even medicine, you would have to wait until the shops opened the next day. On half day closing there would often be a knock on your door and a neighbour asking if they could borrow half a cup of sugar or an egg and you would always oblige. No big supermarkets open all hours then. Even today a lot of village shops retain the one half day closing tradition. Half day closing in London at that time was on a Saturday, if you went on a bus trip by the time you got there all the shops would be shut.

Going to church was a big part of people's lives then and Sunday was Sabbath Day. No one would go into a church, even children, without wearing a hat. When women first started wearing trousers it was considered indecent to wear them on a Sunday even in your own house! Nowhere would be open at all on a Sunday and any form of sport or recreation was banned. Sunday was the day you rested. Children would go to Sunday school and all families would attend a church service. When regulations were relaxed and football was played on a Sunday afternoon it was illegal to charge admission on the Lord's Day. There's always a way round anything! People would be sold a programme and admission to the game would only be by having a pre-sold programme. Years later when we had a Sunday performance of a dancing school pantomime we also had to sell 'admission' programmes in advance otherwise the performance could not have gone ahead. How different it is today. Now there are some musicals and plays in the West End that have Sunday matinees and are 'dark' (closed) one night of the week.

Loughborough was also a big part of my childhood. I was taken every Saturday afternoon on the bus with my Mum and Dad to the *Empire Cinema* that over the years became *The Essoldo* and then the *Curzon Cinema*, to see the latest film. The *Curzon Cinema* has recently been very nicely and tastefully refurbished, complete with a beautiful art deco style 'chandelier' in keeping with the original building and now has another name, *Reel Cinema*.

The *Essoldo Cinema* was a very classy place to go in those days. It was a lovely art deco building with its own ballroom above the cinema. In the daytime people would go to the Palm Court at the cinema for tea and cakes and there would be three musicians dressed in black playing classical music in the background in front of a waterfall. I particularly remember a very large lady in a long black dress looking very serious as she played the violin, balancing pince-nez on the end of her nose. Rumour has it that live musicians and the waterfall may be making a comeback soon!

In those days there would be one main film on for the week, accompanied by a really dreadful 'B' movie. If the main film proved popular it would be held over for another week. There was no such thing as multi-screen cinemas then so if you had already seen the film a week before you just didn't go until they changed the film, or you would go to one of the other two cinemas in the town. At that time the cinemas would have 'stills' in glass-cases of the main film they were showing. I used to love looking at these richly coloured photos of the stars. If you knew anyone working at the cinema you might be lucky enough to be given one of these 'stills' after the film had been taken off.

The National Anthem was always played in the cinemas at the end of the last showing. A few rude people would get up quickly as the film credits were rolling, grab their coats and caps and rush out to avoid having to stand to attention. Not me, and my parents! We all three proudly stood there, as did most people.

After the film we would go to Ruby Hall's fish and chip shop in Wood Gate. This was near to the magistrates' court buildings and has recently been demolished. You went through the chip shop to the restaurant at the back where the tables would have white lace trimmed cotton table clothes and it was a proper sit down meal.   I remember having a piece of bread and butter cut in two diagonally on a separate plate with the fish and chips and a glass of Vimto – a real treat for children in the 1950s.

The other two cinemas in Loughborough that we went to were the *Victory Cinema* on Biggin Street and *The Odeon* on Baxter Gate.   Herbert Morris, the town's well-known crane manufacturing company where my father worked and I later worked at myself, used to hire the *Victory Cinema* at Christmas on a Saturday morning for their employees' children to have a free cinema show and a present from Santa.   Presents for the girls would be wrapped in pink crepe paper and blue for the boys.   On the way out from the *Victory Cinema* you would be given some sweets and an orange.

After going to the cinema, on the way back home to catch the bus from the bus stop at the side of Queens Park, we always looked in Clemersons' toyshop across the road from the Town Hall.   They would have the latest doll in the window that, at that time, was probably be once a year.   Even if the doll was there in May you were always told you'd have to see if Santa would bring it to you for Christmas. And wait you did!   Most children had toys that their parents had made and I was no exception.  My favourite doll was a lovely black pot doll, which my Mum would knit clothes for.   Nan's brother in Leicester, Great Uncle Frank, made doll's furniture, so I had a doll's house and the lovely doll's furniture he had made.

Loughborough was a really nice little market town at that time.   There were permanent cattle pens in the Market Place that hosted the weekly cattle market.   Simpkins and James shop was on the corner of Market Street and was Loughborough's equivalent to Harrods. All the 'posh' folk bought their groceries there  - their cakes and 'dainties' were a big treat.  I also recall clearly a big draper's shop at the bottom of the market, currently home to Boots the chemists and a men's-outfitters shop.   The entrance was a long glass corridor with a mirror in the ceiling.   Inside the large shop were many counters displaying gloves, scarves, stockings, socks, hankies and jumpers. When you paid for your purchases, the money and invoice were put in a metal container that would run up the wall, along the ceiling and upstairs to an office.   Your change and receipt would be put inside and it would be sent along the same route back to the assistant to give to you.   All the assistants would be smartly dressed. I immediately think of this shop when watching the re-runs of *Are You Being Served?* In those days a shop job was an important one and you would have to have impeccable references and background to work there.

I would go with my Mum and Grandma to the little hat shop in Swan Street in Loughborough (in recent times *The Echo* newspaper office).   It had a big bay window with many elaborate and colourful hats on stands.   In those days no one would leave the house not wearing a hat.  You could stand in front of the window and watch the ladies sitting down in front of the mirrors trying these hats on with a smartly dressed assistant holding another one for them to try.  When the assistant came to take one out of the window she would see you there and motion to you to move away.   But if you went to C & A's big department store in Leicester, the hats were all out on display for anyone to try and all the children did.   We used to look forward to trying all the different sorts of hats on and looking in the many mirrors.

One of my favourite shops in Loughborough was the ribbon shop down Market Street. Most little girls wore hair-ribbons in their plaits and ringlets in the 1950s. This was a tiny shop with lots of shelves and a glass cabinet, full of rolls of different coloured plain and patterned ribbons. My Mum would always match the ribbons to my dresses as, apparently, I wouldn't wear them if they didn't. A diva at that age!

There was also a dolls' 'hospital' in Loughborough. This was where you took your 'poorly' doll, for her arm or leg, or even her head to be put back on! She would be in for at least a week and then you would fetch her back. Most little girls at that time would only have the one doll so she had to be looked after.

The large dry cleaners shop was on the other side of the Market Place. There was a pretty young woman machinist sitting in the window mending stockings. They were very expensive so if you laddered them you took them to her to mend. There would often be a crowd of people watching her as she carried on oblivious to the interest she was creating. There were very few cafés or restaurants, but there was one at the top of Market Street where we used to have a cup of tea on shopping day.

A big event to look forward to was the annual fair in Loughborough in November. The centre of the town and a lot of side streets closed, with traffic being diverted for three days. The town would be filled with rides, food-stalls and stalls with hats and toys for sale. My parents would take me every year and they would always buy me a fairy doll with a big sparkly skirt off one of the stalls.

Looking back I realize how lucky I was in having four people to bring me up, four to love and look after me, as well as four to discipline and educate me. I never remember being rude or cheeky to any of them, always respecting them. I was very lucky that, with rationing carrying on in the 1950s after the war, with my grandparents in business and both my parents working they were able to get me things most children at that time would not get a lot of. I always had nice clothes, dresses with matching ribbons for my ringlets, fluffy angora boleros, a pair of white gloves, a straw hat for Sunday school, and a new coat at Easter. But I would always wait for things and Santa would usually bring them at Christmas.

My Mum always got me many film books for Christmas mainly *Picturegoer*, *Film Review* and *Moviegoer* which I would read avidly over and over again, I still have most of them to this day. Most little girls would get film books as Christmas presents as going to the cinema was a big part of children's lives in the 1950s.

Walking round Loughborough these days it now looks like any other town complete with mounds of rubbish. It has lost all of its character and I do so miss the lovely little town of my childhood days.

The town centre houses the most horrendous 'statue'. People were asked to go to the Town Hall to look at all the suggestions for a town centre statue and voice their approval. The design that got the town's population approval was of a large bell with two children standing on top, very appropriate as Loughborough is famous the world over for its bell foundry. However the Council decided against the majority vote and commissioned 'The Sock Man!' Well, we did have a very thriving hosiery trade at one time in the town but it wasn't thriving when this was happening, in fact it had long gone resulting in a loss of many jobs! To add insult

*Dee Quemby*

to injury we have a very capable art department at Loughborough University and this 'chosen' design was commissioned from miles away!

When the green nude Sock Man was unveiled, I was asked, by the Town Centre Manager what I thought of it and I replied: "If I want to look at a fat man in the nude putting a sock on, I can stop at home."

I used to have to pass this statue early in the morning as I was on my way to work, before the streets had been cleaned, and it had always been defaced with chips, hamburgers and the like in the night. The best however was one morning when I was walking by; someone had put a chocolate Mars bar up his 'bottom' and it was melting. Well that says it all for me!

*Walk on by...............................!*

The 'over the bridge' gang at Shepshed

Me and my Nan on my 4th birthday

St Botolph's Infant and Junior School photo (third row back, third in on the right)

School photo aged 4 years

School photo aged 7 years (and still got the ringlets!)

1953 Shepshed Wakes with Carnival Queen Lorna
Lee (I'm the one with the ringlets!)

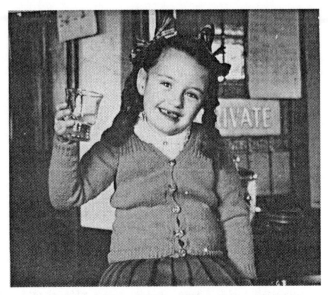

Cheers!  Sat on the pub bar singing along with Gramp

Children of All Nations at Shepshed (me in Nan's rose
satin bedsheet and Pearl as Hawaiian girl)

2 years old and ready to dance in panto

Molyneux School of Dancing's *Dick Whittington* at Loughborough Town Hall
(2 years old, the only 'Sunbeam' left on the stage in the Corn Exchange!)

Yvonne Haywood, Jennifer Mee, me, Ann Walker and Beverly
Collins in acrobatic pose *Dick Whittington* 1948

A rat in *The Pied Piper* at the Theatre Royal, Loughborough in 1952

Kathleen Freeman School of Dance *Babes in the Wood* at
Loughborough Town Hall in 1951 (third from the left)

Kathleen Freeman School of Dance fairies in *Babes in the Wood* 1951 (with
Kathleen Denley, Pamela Fowkes, Yvonne Govus and Jacqueline Parry)

*Does Santa Claus sleep with his whiskers over or under the sheet?* Song and dance routine from *The Pied Piper* 1952 (back row second in on left)

A villager in *The Pied Piper* 1952

A fairy in *The Pied Piper* 1952

Margaret Turner, principal girl in the pantomime "The Pied Piper," which pupils of a Loughborough dancing school are giving, is here seen with two of the young dancers, Iris Bettison and Elizabeth Smith, and the principal boy (Pauline Farren) and dame (Billy Breen).

Margot Turner and Billy Breen

Billy Breen in the panto finalé

Larry Grayson (Billy Breen)

On holiday with Mum and Dad at Butlin's

Children's beauty competition at Butlin's – Come on in number 145!

Eileen Taylor and Joan Jarram as Jack Durden and Princess Gloria
in *Jack and the Beanstalk* 1950 at Loughborough Town Hall

Joan Jarram as Sleeping Beauty

Roy Johnson (the dame par èxcellence!)

Nan and Gramp behind the bar at the Charnwood Forest Railway Inn

Gramp, Jackie and me out for a car ride

Nan and Gramp, Mum and me (always ready to tap dance!) in the pub

1953 Coronation Tea Party on our pub lawn

Me, my Mum, Nan and Gramp, Granny Quemby and Narina (2nd in on right)
Shepshed trip to the Festival of Britain, Pleasure Gardens, London 10 July 1951

The Charnwood Forest Railway Inn (top Railway)
today (courtesy of Brian Buhler)

There's always been a cat!

Pull 'em up dear!

Another school photo for my Mum

Me and my Mum (no ringlets!)

# CHAPTER 3

## THE BIG SCHOOL

YOU sat the 11+ in your last year at junior school. Those passing would gain admission to an academic school. Some would be 'borderline' and have an interview. Those failing would go to a secondary modern school. I was 'borderline' and so I went for an interview. The headmaster, Mr Westoby, knew I was interested in history and I was asked if I knew any of the Kings and Queens of Great Britain. He later told my mother he couldn't believe a child of that age could name every British King and Queen and in the right order. Because of this I was recommended for an academic school.

Most children had a new bike bought for them if they passed the 11+. When my Mum asked me what I would like I asked if I could have Charles and Mary Lamb's *History of Great Britain – The Tudors and the Stuarts*! Apparently Capricorn children are very solitary and serious.

Unfortunately I was not very popular with the history teacher at Rawlins, as she would often get things wrong about the Tudor period and, Adrian Mole like, I felt obliged to inform her. My mother said: "If she's wrong she should be told!" I always remember a friend at Limehurst High School for girls in Loughborough telling me the foreign history teacher there had told the class that one of Henry 8th's wives was Jane Eyre. I was totally horrified! I'm surprised I didn't write to him. Looking back it wasn't arrogance on my part. I was a very quiet and serious child with an unusual love of history. I, very innocently, thought these teachers would be pleased to know the correct facts! I was always amazed how all Limehurst's pupils had to write everything in Italics, for some reason. They spent the first year there learning how to do this. They could only ever write that way even as adults

Leaving the pub at Shepshed and going to live in Mountsorrel came about because my mother had got a job at Rolls Royce and we waited to move there until I was ready for the 'Big School' which was going to be Rawlins Grammar School for girls at Quorn. My mother's job at Rolls Royce, in Mountsorrel, was a very good one but she had to travel from and to Shepshed every day on two buses.  My grandparents were nearing retirement and they decided to buy some land in Mountsorrel near the Old Vicarage guesthouse on Loughborough Road, Mountsorrel.  A builder from Shepshed built two adjoining bungalows for us.  We had a third of a field as a garden with horses at the bottom and my Dad used to grow many vegetables for us.

Next door to us there was a big house that belonged to a local farmer Tom Pepper and his mother.  I used to go round to see Mrs Pepper who always sat in a big high-winged chair.  She always wore a long black dress and had her hair in ringlets.  I felt a real affinity with her.  She always reminded me of Miss Haversham in *Great Expectations.*  I used to play with the many cats and dogs they had.

We moved first and my grandparents' bungalow was fully furnished waiting for them to retire.  It made a fabulous playhouse for me.  Nan and Gramp never lived in this bungalow as after a few years they sold them and bought two of the new houses that were being built on the corner of Castle Road and Cross Lane, Rothley by Jelson Homes.  Later on due to boundary changes this became Cross Lane, Mountsorrel.

I remember my first day at Rawlins very well, as I didn't know a soul.  Every other girl there had moved up with friends, it was a very lonely beginning.  Rawlins was a very foreboding place in those days, the very serious and ladylike Headmistress, Miss Sawdon, looked like a big black vulture standing on the stage every morning at assembly.  She wore her black gown all the while, her hair was scraped back and she always wore bright red lipstick and could have been a teacher from any of Charles Dickens' novels.  She could never say my name right.  She always pronounced it Daredry Quemby.  Perhaps she didn't like Irish names.

At Rawlins dress code was very strict; long black coats, gymslips, blouses with ties and a cardigan during the winter, blue or yellow cotton check dresses and blue blazers in the summer and berets always had to be worn.  We had black 'gym knickers' horrible baggy things with a pocket on the front to put your hanky in although nobody ever did.

When I first started long hair had to be plaited or cut short, absolutely no fancy underwear.  If you were found to be wearing an under-slip with lace on it you had to take it off and wear it over your dress or gymslip for the rest of the day as a punishment.

Nevertheless there was the greatest respect for all the teachers.  We listened and we learnt.  You were also taught that when you were outside the school in uniform you had to behave as it reflected on the school.  How very different to behaviour today.  Miss Sawdon must be turning at a rate of knots in her grave!

The secondary modern schools taught their pupils a lot of practical things, boys would be taught carpentry and how to build a wall amongst other things, as they would more than likely go into the building trade or on leaving school serve an apprenticeship at one of the factories in the area.  Girls would be taught all the requirements for their future roles as wives and mothers such as cooking, sewing, cleaning and some schools even taught baby care.  They would also be taught how to type and how to do Pitman's shorthand.  A lot of girls would go into office jobs.  Most of my friends from secondary modern schools went into factories or became hairdressers.  These jobs paid a lot more money than the admin jobs at the time.

Academic schools expected their pupils to go to university but even so girls would be taught 'domestic science'.  This was a fancy name for cooking, cleaning, mending and dressmaking!  We were also taught to embroider, darn socks and how to knit various items of clothing.   Some schools even had their own little house on the school premises.  Girls would have to clean and look after this house for a few days and cook meals for the teachers to eat.

We had to make our own domestic science overalls in the first year.  My skill with a needle, knitting pin and sewing machine, unlike my Nan's, was more than limited to say the least.  I was yet to discover that my creativity lay in a completely different direction! My Mum sympathised with me as she couldn't sew either, which was very unusual in those days.  After a year of both of us struggling, she paid someone to finish it for me.  The other girls had been wearing theirs for months.  My Mum did however manage to embroider my initials on it for me.  Now if they had wanted it decorating with sequins, I would have been in my element!

I didn't like any of the practical lessons especially cookery.   I would fling everything into the bowl, stick it in the oven on the highest setting while the other girls carefully weighed every ingredient and checked the oven settings; mine would always come out perfect, there's wouldn't.  The cookery teacher hated giving me good marks for my cavalier attitude.  A lot of the girls' cookery efforts would be thrown into the stream on the way back home.  My culinary efforts would always be taken home and eaten with great pride by my parents.

The worst was Christmas when you had to mix the Christmas cake ingredients with your bare hands, no spoons allowed.  It made my stomach turn over.  This was supposed to be the traditional and best way to make a Christmas cake, try telling that to an Environmental Health Officer today!

I hated biology!  We had a very short woman teacher with an American accent who had to stand on a stool to reach the blackboard.  She had a bad temper and would often throw chalk at pupils.  It wasn't long before you would be expected to cut up dead animals but I never did.  The first time I was expected to do this I looked at the poor dead mouse on a dish in front of me, walked out the classroom and went straight home!  My Mum totally sympathised with me and some agreement with the school must have been reached because I was never asked to do this again.

We also had to do Latin for a year as we were told all European languages came from Latin, and it would be a great help when learning French and German.  Well it certainly wasn't to me!

At Rawlins I joined the Guides and after two weeks of crawling round on the grass on my stomach and getting dirty learning how to track animals, I decided this wasn't for me and somebody else could track them!   I've never been one for roughing it!   How many animals were we going to find on a school playing field anyway?

All children had to exercise.  There would be many gym lessons, cross country runs, hockey and rounders for the girls and football and cricket for the boys.  Overweight children were a rarity and according to the odd ones, it would always be due to their 'glands.' We also had to do country dancing, I really hated that class it was so boring, and no sequins on the outfits!

Drama was not really encouraged at school apart from reading Shakespeare and very boring dramatic plays. A career as an actress would have been frowned upon then. Though I did hold a certain secret ambition to be a Shakespearean actress at one time! In fact at that time all actresses were considered to be loose and immoral women. It is interesting to see that a drama college in London has started running acting courses for mature students up to 70-years of age, as they, quite correctly, say a lot of creative and talented people were discouraged from pursuing acting careers in the 1950s and 1960s.

A rather strange woman, Dr Barbara Moore from London could be seen walking the length and breadth of Britain in 1960 and this started off a craze that got everyone mega fit. Six of us schoolgirls from Rawlins walked from Loughborough to Leicester and had our picture in the *Leicester Mercury* as a result. Barbara Moore said with all this walking that she would live to well past 100. Unfortunately whilst walking coast to coast in the USA she was hit by a car and killed, she was in her 50s! This craze brought to the fore a local 'celebrity'. A very tall heavily made-up strange woman (on reflection it could have been a man!) with wild eyes wearing bright flowing frocks used to walk the main road from Leicester to Loughborough and back all day long and became known as 'Lay-by Lil'. Everybody would look out for her and report back sightings!

School trips out would always be day trips on a coach. We went to London, Stratford-upon-Avon, Newstead Abbey and Twycross Zoo. It would be many years before children would be taken on trips abroad by their schools. Family holidays would be to British seaside resorts, we never heard of anyone going to another country for a holiday.

At school at that time children were still children even up to 16 years of age. We lived in a very protective society. Girls' comics would be full of adventure stories, with no problem pages or romantic stories. Films and programmes on television contained no swearing, nudity or even mild sex scenes, nobody even mentioned sex and most teenagers probably didn't know what the word meant. In films all married couples slept in twin beds, if a woman were in bed and a man, usually dressed in a suit, sat on the bed British Censorship dictated that the man would have to have one foot on the floor for the whole of the scene or it would be cut from the film before release in the cinemas. If in a film or TV programme a couple kissed it would be very short and on closed mouths. Censorship even dictated the time a couple could do this, which was believe it or not a maximum of 3 seconds! Not at all like the big open mouth sloppy kisses in films and TV programmes today where even the audience gets wet! It certainly looked more romantic in the censorship days.

Sex education at school, at that time, was virtually non-existent. If a girl did get pregnant she would be sent away 'to stay with an 'aunt' or ' grandma'. Having had her baby, she would come back a few months later; the baby would have been put up for adoption. This was a big social sin; an unmarried mother who kept her child would be virtually shunned.

In the 1960s D H Lawrence's book *Lady Chatterley's Lover* was taken off the censorship list and published. Girls would fill the school toilets wide eyed and open mouthed listening to whoever had managed to get a copy of the book reading aloud passages during break time. Going back to classes you could hear girls in total disbelief saying: "My mother wouldn't do that!" and "I bet the Queen doesn't do that!" My Mum was thoroughly horrified to learn that she had been taught at school in Leicester by one of the author's mistresses.

The film *A Taste Of Honey* came out in 1961, it starred Dora Bryan, Robert Stephens, Rita Tushingham and Murray Melvin. I was 15 years old and went to see it with my school friends. It was a black and white 'kitchen sink' film set in the 1950s, nothing like the films we had seen before. We were shocked at how bad a mother Dora Bryan was, that Murray Melvin was playing a homosexual, and that Rita Tushingham was not married and pregnant by a black sailor. Very shocking stuff at the time, it wouldn't even raise an eyebrow today.

I was very unhappy at Rawlins and hated being at an all girl school. My father saw Miss Sawdon and I was allowed to leave at the age of 15 provided that I went to Loughborough College of Further Education for a year.

As I left early, I never sat for any GCEs at school but later in my life in my 40s when taking a French language night course at Rawlins Community College I was told by the tutor, I ought to take the present day equivalent of English and French GCEs as I would easily pass them. They were not at all as hard as they were in my day. So I wouldn't even have to study much. Once again how is that progress?

I was at a disadvantage at Loughborough College as most of the girls on this course were from Secondary Modern Schools and were quite good at shorthand. One girl, Olive, had actually been working for three years! Fortunately my mother had sent me, as a schoolgirl, with two women from the Rolls Royce for typing lessons. I used to meet them at the bus stop in my gymslip and go on a bus to Loughborough, then another one to Shepshed to a Miss Angrave for lessons at her house. I learnt how to type on an old heavy black Imperial typewriter with blank keys.

My Mum was a shorthand typist and must have been disappointed that I couldn't get to grips with it; the College compromised, they were just starting a new course, dicta-phone typing and I could start it early, I was one of the first to go on this course. Shorthand was beginning to lose its appeal as with the introduction of dicta-phones your boss could be dictating a letter while you were typing up previously dictated letters, therefore saving time, so all in all it had been a good change of course. I'm proud to say I was the first person to gain a certificate in dicta-phone typing at Loughborough College of Further Education.

Typing classes at college were great fun. We had an erratic middle-aged male tutor, who threw our rubber erasers out of the window and said we shouldn't be making mistakes, and we typed in time to music. He didn't have records, he had the very antiquated black cylinders and a player, the music was always very lively and I loved it. We had one boy in the class and that was very unusual. Men did not type, it was considered a woman's job. He was learning how to do shorthand and typing, as he wanted to be a reporter. It was a very brave and groundbreaking for him to be in the class and I hope he did eventually become a reporter. There was also a girl, Aileen, who could only use one hand and she was being taught to type. She became very fast and accurate at it.

On Friday afternoon we had to pick a leisure activity and the choices for girls were either painting or cooking. We listened in horror how two of the girls had gone to the painting class to be confronted by a male nude model! The swinging sixties had only just started and it would take a long time before you could apply this term to Loughborough, though it might have been earlier if we had all gone to the painting class!

I decided to opt for the cookery lessons, judging by my world beating time of baking a cake at school, I would be finished before the others and be able to catch the bus to go home early. I didn't enjoy the classes and once again slung everything in and got perfect results! One afternoon I was the only person in the large class to completely finish the chocolate éclairs. I went home with perfect éclairs complete with cream and chocolate whilst the other girls were still waiting for the basic cakes to come out of the oven. I eventually got so bored making things I could go and buy anyway, that I joined the men's rifle class instead!

We were encouraged to do a bit in the college show by another very eccentric male tutor. Olive, the very large girl who had been at work for three years, was going to do a tap dance. Wasn't there anything this girl couldn't do? Others were playing instruments or singing. The Charlie Drake record *My Boomerang Won't Come Back* was a big hit in the charts believe it or not, it really was a very different time then! I worked out a routine with me in my grandma's fur coat, wellies and a straw boater miming to Charlie Drake with other girls being aborigines and various other characters. A couple of days before the show I didn't think it was very good and decided we wouldn't do it  This tutor got to know of it and demanded to see what I had come up with. He sat there as we went through our paces and at the end he said; "This is great it's in the show" and it certainly did go down well on the night particularly as everything else on the bill was very serious. Years later my Mother told me he had rung her up after the show and said: "Your daughter should be at drama school."

Talking of drama, whilst I was at Rawlins a very big 'drama' unfurled at Mountsorrel at the Rolls Royce factory.................................................................................

After the Second World War, Rolls Royce had purchased a factory from an aircraft propeller manufacturer in Mountsorrel. By the 1960s this factory was huge and employed over a thousand people from the village and surrounding area. Then disaster struck on Wednesday 13 May 1959, during a heat wave! Molten metal that had been poured into a mould exploded, the hot metal hit and set fire to the high ceiling. Fire extinguishers could not reach the ceiling and for some reason the water hose didn't work. There were two sections in the roof and the flames took hold in the supposedly flameproof ceiling and ran another 50 yards then blew a hole through the roof.

My future husband, John, was a young apprentice at Rolls Royce then. When the fire alarm went off, he was actually sat on the toilet. The toilet block was at the end of the building with 17 cubicles that were always full. He went back to his workbench in the factory that was now beginning to fill with smoke. A new expensive metal, titanium was being used in aero engine manufacturing and the foreman in desperation tried to save as much as he could with not much success. John, now realising how bad this fire was ran back to the toilet block banging on the cubicle doors shouting: "There's a fire in the factory!" He was met with a chorus of: "Sod off and find your own toilet." Followed by John shouting back: "I'm not joking get your f*****g  a***s off the toilets, they're evacuating the factory!"   John, in desperation, had to find the Union official to get the men out.

Brian Riddle of *Formula Five* fame was also an apprentice at Rolls Royce. He was in a booth welding when someone banged on the door shouting: "Get out the factory's on fire!" Brian was on piecework trying to earn as much money as he could, as he was getting engaged that weekend. He thought one of the apprentices was playing a pre-engagement joke on him! His reply was: "f\*\*k off!" until he looked up and saw the flames in the ceiling. He was also ordered to save as much titanium as he could. The apprentices frantically rolled this metal out into the yard with flames lapping at their feet.

People were gathering outside in the yard. From an open window a manager was throwing out the old very heavy Imperial 66 typewriters one after another shouting: "Catch!" One apprentice did just that, as he was instructed to, and very nearly broke both of his arms! The rest of the typewriters then proceeded to smash to pieces as they hit the floor, watched by all the other apprentices!

Another manager was throwing paperwork and contracts out of the windows of the front office block. Apprentices were instructed to put these documents in neat piles in the yard near the bike sheds. The fire engines took a while to get there; but when they did, they ploughed straight through the yard scattering these papers here, there and everywhere, never to be found again!

The factory was burnt to the ground. All the glass was hanging and girders were actually twisted. The only parts of the Rolls that escaped the fire were ironically the front offices and the toilet block! Perhaps the men would have been better off staying put reading their papers! Miraculously, nobody was injured, apart from the 'typewriter catching' apprentice!

Later that night John went back to the workstation and on the metal workbenches were the workmen's tools all intact, the wooden toolboxes that they had been in had been burnt to cinders.

That night Audrey, Brian's fiancée, rang him to ask if they were still getting engaged the following weekend, as he was now out-of-work? They did get engaged, but at a much later date.

I remember getting home from Rawlins that day. Everywhere was grey and there was a horrible smell all over the village that lasted for days. The whole village was sad and in mourning.

All employees were given three weeks paid leave. John reported on the starting back day and said he couldn't believe his eyes when he got there, coaches were lined up from the Hilltop Garage (at the top of the hill) all the way down the Leicester Road. They must have commissioned every spare bus in the county. Workers were then shipped out every working day to other factories in Ilkeston, Hucknall and Sinfin in Derby whilst the factory was being re-built and this took nearly two years.

The rumour in the village was that when this factory had been built during the Second World War, the men putting in the flameproof insulation had actually been taking it home to use as firelighters!

Gradually things got back to normal, but the Rolls Royce decided to lay off the married women. At that time a husband was expected to provide for his wife. A few married women worked for extra money, which at that time would not have been very much, to provide a few luxuries and this was known as 'pin money'.

My Mother's boss came to see her and said her job was safe but she found out that a young girl in another office was getting married in a few months' time

Dee Quemby

and they had decided to let her go so my Mum could stay. My Mother wasn't having this. Our neighbour's family had a button and zip factory, Thomas Firth in Mill Lane, Leicester and she was offered an office job there which she took.

Looking back, it's amazing how much the 'Riddles' have been in and out of my life. As a teenager, I went with them when the *Formula Five* played in Leicester in the working men's clubs. After leaving school, I worked with Audrey in the offices at Herbert Morris Ltd. At the Neal Academy of Dancing, Audrey was to play Prince Charming to my Cinderella, but on finding out she was pregnant, she had to pull out as she was advised to rest. Her son, Anthony, for many years appeared in my touring panto and, Brian and Audrey helped look after my Mum during her last years.

My Mum loved working at 'the Rolls'. Every morning she would walk down the road to go to work with Jackie Gould a young girl who was a few years older than me. My Mum was sorry to leave the Rolls and Jackie remained a loyal friend to my mother right up to the day my Mother died.

Many years-later workers were transferred to other Rolls Royce plants. The factory at Mountsorrel was demolished. The land was sold for a housing estate to be built on it in 1993. An end of an era!

*Burn baby burn, disco inferno...........................................!*

Formula Five

Brian Riddle on drums

Mum out with the girls from The Rolls on a Christmas 'do'

Firemen inside The Rolls on 13 May 1959 (courtesy of Noel Wakeling)

The 'flameproof' roof at The Rolls (courtesy Noel Wakeling)

# CHAPTER 4

## GROWING PAINS IN THE SWINGING SIXTIES!

THIS is not an accurate, historical or chronological chapter of fashion, music, radio, film and television. It is how I remember it happening in the Midlands.  So please no boring letters telling me I got this and that wrong……………………………………………**write your own book!**

THE women of the 40s and 50s were the most glamorous ever.  They dressed plainly but were very tailored and chic.  They wore hats and gloves, high heels and stockings, tailored suits and dresses and they would always wear red lipstick and rouge and their hair was beautifully dressed.  In the 1950s the designer Norman Hartnell's dresses were high fashion; they were full skirted with a belt to emphasise women's slim waists.  Women flocked to buy these new full skirt dresses as with rationing during wartime it meant material was scarce and dresses and skirts had to be straight and short.  At that time there were not the cosmetics and treatments that we have now but for the all the beauty aids and clothes about today, no one has ever had the style, class, glamour and sexiness that the women of these two decades had.

In the 1950s you would hardly have any choice of shampoo and conditioners were unheard of.  You would wash your hair once a week in a bowl in the sink using jugs of water.  If you had fair hair you would add lemon juice to your final rinse and vinegar for dark hair.  To keep your hair dark you would dip the blue bag, used on washing day for making sheets and pillowcases white, in your final rinse.

People would stand in front of the sink or wash hand basin for an all over wash in the mornings.  If you had a bath in your house it would only be used once a week.  This was because not many houses had hot water and it had to be boiled up.  If you had an immersion heater or coal boiler it would take a long while for the water to get hot and would be used up in one go and that's why it was not uncommon for a family to all use the same bath water one after each other.

These days there seems to be very little dress code and class which is a great pity. Hopefully it will all change round again.  When I was a teenager the first jeans appeared but I was not allowed to wear them on a Sunday and you only wore them to play or do manual work in.   My Grandfather hated seeing people going out in them as he had worked in France where the material originated from, a place called Nimes, 'de Nimes' gradually changing to 'denim'. This coarse thick material had been specially woven for the workmen's overalls, not for clothing.

When I started work, men had to wear a suit and tie and could not remove their jackets.  During a very hot summer in the 1970s permission was given for the men to remove their jackets and ties before they passed out with the heat! How unlike today when you see people in offices casually dressed, even jeans and, worst of all, shorts in the summer!

Women had to wear stockings all the time absolutely no bare legs and no trousers.  Arms were usually covered and you would never have gone to work in the low cut tops you see today, never mind T-shirts or trousers.  You would definitely never wear a chain around your ankle, as then it would mean that you were a prostitute!  As for showing your stomach, bosom or underwear, as is the trend nowadays, people would have been horrified and you would have probably been charged with indecent exposure!

Standards were very different; women would not go in a pub without a man or anywhere else, as they would be classed as loose and immoral.  Most people smoked, but a woman would never be seen smoking in the street or anywhere else out in the open, as she would be called common.   Women could not buy a house on their own or enter into hire purchase agreements and for women in those days the trend was engaged at 19, married at 20 with a first baby at 21 (usually followed by a trip to the dentists to have all your teeth out as mentioned before!).  It was very unusual to find an unmarried woman and if you did she was usually older and had probably lost the love of her life in the war.

Most newly married couples had to live with parents or rent one room.  There were no new houses with all the mod cons then; if you did manage to save enough to buy a house, the house was all you had, relatives and friends rallied round and gave you old furniture and bits of old carpets, fitted carpets and central heating were unheard of.  I remember going to a young married couple's house as a child and we had to sit on orange boxes, as they couldn't afford any furniture.

Holidays were usually a day trip to the seaside once a year.  We were lucky enough to be able to have a week's holiday in a B & B in Skegness every year, a great luxury then.  It was unheard of to have a holiday in a foreign country or to see many, if any, foreigners in your town or village but then again your father had probably fought all over Europe during the war and was perfectly happy to stay in his own country anyway.

People had nothing, but they all seemed happy with their lot; the more you have the more you want. Today we have everything, the house and everything to go with it, the foreign holidays, the cars, TVs, DVDs, computers, music centres. People can go out every night of the week if they want to.  In those days a couple had to work hard and save to get even the most basic item.  You really appreciated what you got and knew how hard your parents had worked to be able to get you things.  You really respected and loved them for what they did for you – you didn't expect anything so when you were given something it was a real treat. You would never see a child screaming for sweets or some toy they wanted like you do today. There wouldn't have been any point as nobody had any money.

Teenagers of the 50s did not really need a lot of money like today. There were only sweets and comics for them to buy. Most children would leave school at the ages of 15 and 16 years. They would go straight into a full time job to earn much needed money to help their parents; especially if they had younger brothers and sisters who needed feeding and clothing. A lot of children took on a paper round to get some extra money. My mother would never let me do this as she thought it was dangerous especially as I somehow never managed to properly ride a two-wheeled bicycle. Somehow my feet never seemed to reach the pedals. I lost all sense of balance. Each of my friends had a bicycle, as this would be their only mode of transport, as it was for many adults.

When I was at school, the 60s opened up a new world for teenagers; suddenly we needed money for the clothes, records, boots, hats, bags and jewellery. During one summer holiday we went to work full time at a crisp factory down Wharncliffe Road in Loughborough and it was the dirtiest place I have ever seen in my life and put me off crisps for many years. However the pay was very good. I then got a Saturday job in the children's section in the very large clothes shop, C & A, in Leicester. C & A were the initials of the two Dutch founders of the company, but everybody said it really stood for 'coats and 'ats'! I then moved to a Saturday job in the very much missed Woolworth's in Loughborough town centre where my Dad's sister Emma was the supervisor. I would finish work, run to catch the bus home at Packe Street, then later on at the side of the *Odeon Cinema* (now a Bingo Hall), get changed, catch the bus back into town to go the Town Hall dances and then catch the bus home afterwards. The bus stop later moved to the High Street near the Cross Keys pub outside a very smelly public toilet that thankfully has gone and is now the outside drinking area of the pub.

When the 60s started I was 14 years old. If you went out you usually went with an adult. I remember vividly going with my Mum to see the Walt Disney film *Old Yeller* starring Dorothy Maguire. The first and last time I have watched a film or TV programme about animals! I sat and sobbed all the way through it, it upset me for months and I absolutely hate the song *Old Shep*.

Cinema was the place to go in the 1950s and 60s and nearly every village would have their own small cinema. There was a cinema in Shepshed but I don't remember much about it as my parents took me every Saturday afternoon to the big cinemas in Loughborough.

I was 11 years old when we moved to Mountsorrel. Mountsorrel had its own little cinema. This was the *Rock Cinema*; probably so named because Mountsorrel had, and still has, the largest granite quarry in Europe. However this cinema was better known as 'Bert's Bug House' to the village children! Bert Baum owned it as well as another small cinema, *The Futurist*, in Sileby, a nearby village. Bert was a tall thin man and always wore a suit. He would charge round the cinema looking harassed and shouting and spluttering just like Basil Fawlty in *Fawlty Towers*! I can remember that he would stop the film if the kids got too rowdy, and this happened quite a lot. Bert's wife was American, and their very large son, known to the kids as 'Hairy Ken', also worked there, as did Bert's brother. In those days a film would run for three days and then change over with the film being shown at the cinema in Sileby.

Sometimes one film would be screened in both cinemas on the same night, but at different starting times! When the first reel of the film had been shown in the Mountsorrel cinema, it would be given to a cinema employee. He would ride his bike frantically to the other cinema in Sileby and give it to the projectionist there, for him to show the first reel in that cinema. This poor employee would then bike back to Mountsorrel to pick up the next reel, and so on and so forth. Some films would have as many as seven reels! I bet he loved them. And I bet he was pretty fit by the end of the week!

When he was 15, my husband to be, John worked at the cinema as an usher, ticket collector and ice cream seller. He would stand with Bert behind the iron fence that would concertina up to let the screaming kids through ready for the 'Tuppenny rush' which was a film show for young children without adults. Bert would get very annoyed if the kids hadn't got 'tuppence' and needed change. The balcony nicknamed 'the chicken run' was made up of three rows, with approximately six seats per row. To sit in the balcony you had to climb up a wooden ladder! What would Health and Safety make of that today?

We would sit and watch Laurel and Hardy, Abbott and Costello, black and white cowboy films especially *Hopalong Cassidy* and singing cowboy Roy Rogers and Trigger. This horse could do 52 tricks on command and Roy had him stuffed when he died, there's gratitude! Apparently, the actors needed more retakes than the horse! There were many episodes from the 1930s film serial *Flash Gordon* starring an actor by the wonderful name of Buster Crabbe, and the many Norman Wisdom films. My favourites were the St Trinians' films with a very young George Cole, the many 'Road to.........' films with Bob Hope, Bing Crosby and Dorothy Lamour, Dean Martin and Jerry Lewis comedy films, anything with Margaret Rutherford and Peggy Mount in, the series of 'Doctor' films starring Dirk Bogarde and Kenneth More and the films with Ma and Pa Kettle. The Ealing comedies were another big favourite of mine especially *The Ladykillers*, along with other films like *The Card, Passport To Pimlico, Kind Hearts And Coronets* and *The Lavender Hill Mob* and these films seem to get more enjoyable with the passage of time.

John eventually graduated to spooler. This consisted of giving the next reel to the projectionist and then rewinding, by hand, the used reel. Reels would also have to be mended and spliced.

John would sometimes sit in the projection room keeping an eye on the carbon rods that shone through the film as they would burn down and would have to be replaced just at the right time. There was also a seat in the auditorium for the usher with a light above it. If the projectionist were ready for the next reel he would flash the light as a signal for the usher to fetch it. John recalls often being engrossed in a film and on looking up seeing the light being flashed madly by a desperate projectionist!

Brian Buhler, who helps out at the dancing school and the shows with his wife Connie, whom he met at Bert's Bug House, worked at the cinema at the age of 18 years. He was an apprentice at Rolls Royce but wanted to earn extra money. Brian also graduated to being a spooler and recalls many times standing on the outside balcony whistling at the girls walking by in the street and being shouted at by Bert to find the next reel quick as the kids were stamping their feet as the screen had gone black! Even today both Brian and John when going to the cinema still look out for a little black dot in the top and bottom right hand corners of the screen that signifies a reel change is coming up! A lot of these village cinemas were little palaces and very Victorian in their décor. All the cinema staff would wear smart military type uniforms and some of the cinemas would have exotic names like *The Bijoux* and *The Ritz*, though round here they were the less exotic the *Lawn Cinema* and the *Rock Cinema* probably due to living in the country. Unfortunately most of these village cinemas are now long gone, but the memories live on.

At the cinemas we went to as children and teenagers everybody would rush out as the credits started rolling. Not me I love reading 'who dunnit?' and still do! John will sometimes get quite annoyed if I am still sitting there when everybody else has left the cinema. It's amazing how many people are involved in making a film nowadays. One recent film had about forty carpenters in it, with each one named in the end credits! In case you didn't know, mega movie star Harrison Ford was a carpenter at the Goldwyn film studios where he was 'spotted' mending the front porch and given a screen test!

I would look at the end of the American films to see if the 'gowns were by Irene', Adrian or eight times Oscar winning costume designer Edith Head. Edith Head was actually nominated an incredible 34 times for an academy award for costume design. Then I would wait to see if William Tuttle or one of the many Westmore brothers, Perc, Frank, Ern, Monte, Bud or Wally had been responsible for the make up. Their father, George Westmore was born on the Isle of Wight, where he ran a barber's shop. George emigrated and went to Canada and then moved to America. On the film sets he saw that actors had to do their own make up and that they weren't very good at it, so he founded the first movie make up department in 1917 in Hollywood.

George Westmore also made wigs and he had to make fake curls for Mary Pickford as many of her fans would get too close and out would come the scissors for a souvenir to take home! Little did 'America's sweetheart' know that the curls she paid $50 each for were made from hair that George obtained from the 'ladies' at *Big Suzie's French Whorehouse*! My Nan loved Mary Pickford and I have two much cherished autographed sepia photographs that she got when Mary Pickford visited England.

Not only were the Westmores in charge of movie stars' looks but they also had to be responsible for making up numerous amounts of different animals, at one time even having to black out a chimpanzee's private parts as well as making up 'A' list stars such as Bette Davis. Let's hope they didn't use the same make up brush!

So successful were 'The Westmores of Hollywood' that Cecil B De Mille wouldn't make a film without one of the Westmore brothers being in charge of the make up department. 'The King', as Clark Gable was known then, would only let a Westmore see him without his false teeth.

At that time Clark Gable was the undisputed King of Hollywood and won an Oscar for *It Happened One Night* in 1934, even though he wasn't first choice for the lead, which had been Robert Montgomery. Clark Gable didn't want to do it but was made to by the MGM studio for turning down a role opposite Joan Crawford in another movie that was probably due to Clark Gable having an intense relationship with her at the time.

The film director Stephen Spielberg recently bought at an auction, Clarke Gable's Oscar for the film *It Happened One Night,* and also the two Bette Davis' Oscars for the 1938 film *Jezebel* and the 1935 film *Dangerous.* He has presented them back to the Academy.

Oscars are actually Academy Awards. Bette Davis is said to have named hers after her then husband bandleader Harmon Oscar Nelson, although the Academy's Executive Secretary, Margaret Herrick, was overheard saying that the gold knight standing on a reel of film looked like her Uncle Oscar. Both ladies are credited with the Academy Award's much better known name.

The female lead in *It Happened One Night* had only two costume changes in the entire film. Because of this, most 'A' list female movie stars such as Bette Davis, Myrna Loy and Carol Lombard turned it down. Those gals liked their clothes in those days! Eventually Claudette Colbert agreed to do it. She asked for double the salary and also insisted her part was shot in 5 weeks as she was going on a skiing holiday! She won an Academy Award for best actress even though, during filming, she said it was the worst film she had ever made.

In one famous scene Clark Gable took off his shirt and revealed a, never before seen on screen, bare chest. Sales of undershirts dropped dramatically on the film's release! *It Happened One Night* is one of the rare occasions when a comedy has won an Academy Award for best picture, in fact this Frank Capra film had five nominations and won them all.

So popular now were the brothers, that at one time every major film studio in Hollywood had a Westmore in charge of their make up department and most 'A' list movie stars would only let a Westmore do their make up. Some stars were made up very early in the morning at their homes before even setting foot on a film set.

As we got older we went on the bus to the larger cinemas in Loughborough, mainly the *Essoldo Cinema*, now the *Reel Cinema*. It was the time of the Hammer Horror films with either, or sometimes together, Peter Cushing and future Bond baddie, Christopher Lee, taking the lead as Dracula or some other blood thirsty well dressed baddy surrounded by busty, long haired, over made up women often in see through nighties. Oliver Reed and Ingrid Pitt would often make an appearance in these films. We had gone from the 50s films where if someone got shot there wouldn't be any blood to gallons of blood everywhere and these films frightened me to death. I went later with friends to see *Psycho* and spent most of the time looking at the floor, even though the film was in black and white it was very scary. Watching re-runs of these films on TV it is hard to see what was so frightening but then again we are used to it today and it doesn't have the same impact.

The older teenagers in the village would go to Mountsorrel's working men's club on a Thursday night as this was rock and roll night, dancing to records from 7pm to 10pm, the admission price being 9d. I went to see the Everly Brothers at the De Montfort Hall, Leicester in 1960 when I was 14. I was allowed to wear my jeans even though it was a Sunday. I had pleaded with my Mum to let me wear them as all my friends would be wearing theirs. We all wore our very fashionable short swagger style duffle coats. Mine was white with red toggle buttons. When I got home my Mum said it had been on the news that an American rock star had died in a car crash but she couldn't remember who it was. The next morning I found out it was the great Eddie Cochran and we all flocked to buy his memorial double LP.

When I was 15, I was allowed to go out on Saturday nights with friends. We caught the bus into Loughborough and went to the Saturday night dances in the room above the *Essoldo Cinema* that was usually full of students and we found it very boring but there was nowhere else to go. The Town Hall started putting on live rock and roll bands on a Saturday and we were allowed to go with older brothers and sisters.

The girls would dance together until the pubs closed. After closing time it would get packed. In would come the boys in their 'teddy boy' suits. The long fitted jackets (drapes) had the cuffs and lapels trimmed with velvet. The trousers were straight and tight and known as 'drain pipes'. These suits were styled on the very elegant Edwardian gentlemen's suits. Black 'brothel creeper' suede shoes with thick crepe soles, a pair of pink florescent socks, a white frilly shirt, a 'boot lace' tie and one gold earring would complete the look. An essential item was a comb to constantly slick back their thickly coated Brillcreme DA (duck's arse!) hairstyles. When walking down a street they would always stop to look at their reflection in a shop window and out would come the comb.

We learnt to dance with the older boys who had been rock and rolling in the 1950s. You can always tell a rock n roller from that time as they are so good, not at all like ballroom rock n roll which is too 'stagey' and done with floppy arms and none of the throwing through the legs and over the shoulders which is really jitter bugging. There were some brilliant dancers and only the best danced together regularly, some of the boys would dance with two girls at the same time twirling them using both hands. A new dance craze from America, The Twist, came out and everybody was standing on the spot twisting their knees and feet seeing how low they could go, even parents and grannies, but it didn't take over from rock 'n' roll, in Loughborough anyway. At the Town Hall Saturday night dances there would probably only be a couple of Twist numbers in between the serious dancing.

Every pub, club and dance hall would have live music. Most places certainly the working men's clubs, would be packed at 7pm and if you wanted a seat you had to get there even earlier. We saw some great rock and roll bands at the Town Hall like Johnny Kid and the Pirates. I'll never forget seeing the 'infamous' Screaming Lord Sutch and his band at the Town Hall. He walked out on stage in a leopard-skin outfit with a toilet seat round his neck and blew his nose on the curtain, shocking stuff at the time! I never imagined then that many years later my grandparents' pub would become his official headquarters when he tried to stand as a Member of Parliament for the Monster Raving Loony Party!

One Saturday night we went to the dance at the YMCA on Wharncliffe Road in Loughborough, known as the 'Y Dub' for some reason; it was just a man on stage with a record player that we thought was terrible. Where was the live band? Now everywhere you go its on disc or taped, completely unthinkable then, we wanted live artists. In that day and age most children learnt to play a musical instrument and that's when the great bands of the 60s were being formed, I can't today think of a band as just singers. It all seems so untalented and they don't seem worthy of having that title.

The new small 45rpm unbreakable records came out and we had nothing to play them on as our parents had the old sideboard style gramophone record players. These players had a big heavy arm that you had to place on the record and would only play the big and very breakable 78 rpm records with an 'His Master's Voice' label showing a bewildered dog looking into a big horn of an old gramophone. These old players would be in your lounge or living room as part of the furniture and only operated by your parents though my grandparents always let me use the one in the pub. The idea of children having their own record players in their rooms would be completely unthinkable!

Pat Boone was an American singer second only to Elvis Presley in the early 1950s and a real heart throb in Britain. His hit record was *April Love.* A friend gave me this record for my 11th birthday in 1957, even though I had nothing to play it on! I put the record on my 'tall boy' and would just look at it! I had to wait for a year to play this when my Mum bought me one of the new turntables in a red and cream box with a spindle that would take one record only. Pat Boone made all the newspapers when he was making his first film, *April Love,* as he refused to kiss the actress he was appearing with, as he was a married man. Haven't times changed!

We went to Woolworths to buy records and later to Eugene Cooper's record shop up Church Gate always looking in on the way up in Johnny Mars second hand jewellery shop for a good deal on gold gypsy earrings. The records we bought then were 45rpm priced at 6s 8d (a third of a pound) which would be a small fortune and you would have to save up your pocket money. These 45s were usually cover versions of the American chart hits sung by British pop singers of the day, we had no big international pop stars of our own. I went to see my first Elvis film the very dramatic *King Creole*, with a friend and her older sister, and when Elvis sang *If You're Looking For Trouble* I was almost in shock! I had never seen anything like it before! If you were lucky enough to buy the original American 45s you had to go to Eugene Coopers to buy the plastic inserts that clipped into the centre of the discs as the holes in the middle of the American records were much bigger than the British ones. We were now getting the soggy sentimental teenage films from America with stars like Troy Donahue and Sandra Dee.

As the large 78rpm records were fast going out of fashion, children would lay them in the sun and, when they were warm shape them into vases and bowls!

The television children's shows were beginning to change, the powers that be realised that teenagers wanted music not the normal children's shows and the educational programmes that we got. In one of the educational TV shows I remember Mick Jagger's father lecturing on rock climbing with a very young Mick Jagger, who would turn to a different sort of rock later, demonstrating!

Kent Walton's 15-minutes TV show, *Cool For Cats* aired in 1956. Me, and my Mum would watch this show late at night. *Cool For Cats* featured live dancers, which of course I loved. Then in 1957 came *Six-Five Special*, this was followed by Jack Good's all live music TV show *Oh Boy* in 1958 and we began to see Marty Wilde, Billy Fury, Adam Faith, Cliff Richard, Lord Rockingham's XI, The Shadows who were originally called 'The Drifters' but had to change their name because there was already an American group by the same name, The Tornadoes, Joe Brown, Leicester's Dallas Boys and the Vernon Girls who sang and danced and always wore shorts, blouses and stilettos. One in particular, Margaret Stredder, became very well known as she always wore her glasses something you didn't do on TV then. *Six-Five Special* had a lot of top guest stars, I remember seeing Brenda Lee, Gene Vincent, Shirley Bassey and Leicester born singer Engelbert Humperdinck on the shows.

One of the most remembered shows started on the BBC in 1959 *Juke Box Jury* hosted by David Jacobs. A panel would sit and listen to a record that had just been released and then vote it a 'hit' or a 'miss' by giving it points. This programme made a star of a young Birmingham girl, Janice Nicholls, who nearly always said; "I'll give it five" In a very strong Brummie accent. She even had a big hit record with this catch phrase. Janice Nicholls auditioned for *Crossroads* but was turned because of her genuine Brummie accent; it was thought that no one would understand what she was saying! *Juke Box Jury* was such a hit that it attracted star names as panellists including Thora Hird, Roy Orbison, Spike Milligan and even the Beatles.  ITV hit back with a pop show *Thank Your Lucky Stars* in competition.

We would listen to David Jacobs' show on the radio *Pick Of the Pops* but radio still did not play much 'pop' music though you could listen to more if you tuned into Radio Luxemburg.  Then came the pirate radio ships.  They were moored in the North Sea and played pop music for 24 hours!  Government officials tried in desperation to have them shut down.  The DJs had to use pseudonyms; if they had used their real names they would have been arrested when they set foot on British soil!

The popular Loughborough based SAGA Radio (now 'Smooth' Radio) presenter and panto fan Steve Merrick was one of these.  His real name is Mike Willis, but he still uses his 'pirate' radio name for professional reasons.  Steve started his pirate radio career broadcasting from the ship *Comet* moored in the Firth of Forth and was known by the nickname 'Marjorie' on air! He then moved to Radio Caroline and broadcast from the *Mi Amigo*. He eventually became 'legit' in the 1970s and worked as a broadcaster on Radio 1.  I was a guest on his show many times when he worked at the radio station GEM AM based in Nottingham; he then moved to OAK FM based in Loughborough.  He has been to see many of my pantos accompanied by his wife Julia a former dancing pupil of the Neal Academy.  These pirate DJs became household names with the new generation of teenagers.  DJs Tony Blackburn, Dave Lee Travers and Simon Dee were probably the biggest stars to emerge from these illegal broadcasts.  Simon Dee went on to have one of the most popular shows on TV and even made a few film appearances before it all went pear shaped for him.

Attitudes were beginning to change and then the real explosion happened.  A group of four mop-haired young men from Liverpool; formerly known as the Quarry Men, Johnny and the Moondogs and the Silver Beetles, with a slight spelling change to the Silver Beatles, that had become shortened to the 'Beatles', appeared on the scene!

At last British teenagers had their own identity.  The Beatles' haircut had never been seen before on men, well perhaps on the popular Benny Hill in one of his sketches in his hit TV show.  Their clothes were so different, gone were the lapels on the suit jackets; they had high round necks and they wore pointed suede slip on shoes.  They wore black roll neck tops under their jackets and we searched the shops desperately for these tops.  I was working in Leicester at the time at William Davis Manufacturing and a little shop round the corner was selling them for 5 shillings.  I used to have to fetch them for all my friends.

Women's clothes were the most dramatic change of all.  Mary Quant brought out the mini skirt.  I had a desk at Herbert Morris where I had gone back to work that I measured my skirt against.  If my skirt hem didn't line up with the top of the desk I would shorten it went I got home.  You couldn't wear stockings and suspenders with mini skirts and so tights suddenly appeared which was liberation day! No more having to wear those horrible girdles.  At last we girls could breathe properly again!  Stilettos looked very odd with a short skirt and the 1940s thick heel shoes came back into fashion again.  We all had our hair cut in a Mary Quant bob.  We used black eyeliner and the pale pink lipstick that was now in fashion.  False eyelashes were a must and we all used lots of black mascara, that came in a square flat plastic ('plaggy') box with a little brush, and a bit of 'spit'.

Jean Shrimpton became the top model both here and in America and a very thin Cockney model, Twiggy, became a national icon with a boyish haircut. All girls copied her eye make with the must-have grey 'socket' line and painted on lower eyelashes. Blusher appeared in little pots that was almost like Vaseline and we used to go out with shiny sticky cheekbones. Black nail varnish was all the rage.

Mary Quant produced a mini skirt in PVC. This had previously been used for kitchen tablecloths! Suddenly all clothing began to appear in PVC and everything went black and white. I had a black and white PVC coat and hat to go with my white boots and white lace pattern tights. In the 60s plastic jewellery appeared. We had black and white hoop earrings and big chunky rings and bangles. PVC 'Baker boy' caps were all the rage. Mary Quant's daisy logo could be seen everywhere. Accessories became must have fashion in the 1960s. We all bought the fitted black or brown leather gloves with a hole in the middle which older people called 'kissing gloves' from the days when men used to kiss a woman's hand. The leather was very thin and it moulded to the shape of your hands and the gloves had a snap fastener at the wrist. The doctors' bags from the Victorian area known as Gladstone bags were immensely popular. They were very large and square, with lots of metal fasteners and were made in black or brown leather.

Before the Beatles we had swooned over British singers Cliff Richard, Billy Fury, Eden Cane, ex-milkman Craig Douglas, Anthony Newley, Jess Conrad, Shane Fenton and the Fentones (Shane would reinvent himself later as Alvin Stardust) Marty Wilde and Adam Faith who would also appear in a hugely successful TV drama series *Budgie*. But now live groups were emerging every day and storming up and dominating the charts with names like Freddie and the Dreamers, The Small Faces, Gerry and the Pacemakers (I used to love how the drummer of this group finished each number with a pose), Credance Clearwater, Cream, the very handsome Dave Clark Five, Wayne Fontana and The Mindbenders, The Mersey Beats, The Move, Procul Harem, The Archies, Amen Corner, Vanity Fair, Edison Lighthouse, The Honeycombs with a girl drummer which had never been seen before in a pop group, Herman's Hermits, The Fortunes, The Ivy League, The Troggs, The Bee Gees, The Kinks, The Foundations, Manfred Mann, The Animals, Marmalade, The New Seekers, The Rockin Berries, Swinging Blue Jeans, The Moody Blues, The Merseys, The Who, The Tremeloes, Lulu and the Luvvers, The Hollies, The Rolling Stones, Georgie Fame and the Bluenotes, Dozy Beaky Mick and Tich, The Applejacks, The Yardbirds, The New Vaudeville Band, The Pretty Things, The Searchers, Billy J Kramer and the Dakotas, and many more and the great comedy pop group The Barron Knights. Billy J Kramer was the most handsome well dressed man, but he had an unfortunate habit of continually licking his lips when singing which was a bit off putting.

So many British solo singers hit the charts - Cilla Black, Helen Shapiro, Gary Puckett, Cat Stevens, Rod Stewart, Dusty Springfield, David Essex, Petula Clark, Donovan, Peter Sarstedt, Gilbert O'Sullivan, Jonathan King, Paul Jones, Long John Baldry, P J Proby, Chris Farlowe (oh how I loved his hit single *Out of Time* and still do!), Dave Berry, Sandie Shaw who never wore shoes when singing, Alan Price, Marianne Faithful, Leo Sayer and of course Tony Christie who has just seen his career reborn with *Amarillo* thanks to Peter Kay. Peter Sarne had a hit record with *Come Outside* that featured Wendy Richard, who would become Pauline Fowler in *EastEnders*, answering him back and we had some of the best British singers ever in the charts Shirley Bassey, Engelbert Humperdinck and Tom Jones. All these would be regularly appearing, almost nightly, on the many popular variety shows throughout the week on TV. When do you see a singer in a show on the TV nowadays? Come to think of it when do you ever see a show!

We had an Israeli husband and wife, Esther and Abi Ofarim, top the charts with *Cinderella Rockerfella* which they performed on *Sunday Night at the London Palladium*. British duos in the charts were Scaffold with Paul McCartney's brother and Peter and Gordon, Peter being the brother of Paul McCartney's then girlfriend Jane Asher who now makes cakes. However it wouldn't be until 1974 when ABBA, one of the best and most remembered groups of all time would win the *Eurovision Song Contest* with *Waterloo*.

In 1968 a young very good looking busker, Don Partridge, appeared on *Opportunity Knocks* with his one man band and he was an instant success which led to him having a number one hit record with *Rosie* and then he seemed to disappear out of sight. A few years back I met him in Mountsorrel. He was living on a houseboat and came into a local pub. He told me he couldn't cope with being organised and managed and even though he had become a successful recording star he had gone back to busking. He wanted to do his own thing, a true free spirit. He also told me how surprised he was when appearing on tour with the great comic Les Dawson. He had expected him to be cracking jokes all the time but said how serious he was. He would often find Les Dawson sitting in the dressing room reading very serious books like *Homers Iliad*.

America hit back and the best they came up with was husband and wife duo, Sonny and Cher and The Monkees with their wacky TV series that was very much like the 1970s British TV series *The Goodies*. There was much speculation in the press at the time as it was rumoured that The Monkees couldn't actually play any of the instruments and they had been put together purely on their looks to rival the Beatles. The Monkees had one English member Davy Jones, who had appeared in *Coronation Street* as Ena Sharples' grandson. Violet Carson who played Ena Sharples, one of the greatest characters *Coronation Street* has ever had, had in fact been the pianist on the Wilfred Pickles' radio show *Have A Go* that I listened to as a child.

With the 1960s we went from hardly any music, to music everywhere, in shops and at work. You had to make the biggest decision of your life in the 1960s and that was whether to be a 'mod' or a 'rocker'. Mums and dads changed too, and horror of horrors mums started to wear mini skirts! How dare they?

With all the records we were now buying, a new turntable came out in a box with a spindle that actually held eight discs at once, dropped them down and played them one at a time. It was called a 'Dansette' and it was a revelation, though it didn't do the records any good.

*Oh Boy* gave way to *Ready Steady Go* in 1963 with Cathy McGowan as host. She set a new fashion trend for white tights and 'A' line dresses with a white Peter Pan collar. It seemed that hundreds of groups and singers were emerging from Liverpool every week. Cilla Black set a trend for mini length 'Empire' style dresses that she always wore on TV. That's dresses where there is no waist but a seam under the bust like the women wear in *Sharpe* with Sean Bean. They had baggy sleeves that had elastic at the wrists that had a frill that flopped down over your hand. They often had another big frill around the neck and yes I had one too. I remember buying a pink one in a boutique in Bournemouth on holiday with my friend Janice Lauder and her parents.

*Top Of The Pops* came out on TV in 1964 and brought us the sexy dancers Pan's People, who then became Ruby Flipper, then Legs and Co which I think is a great name for a group of dancers. Arlene Phillip's even more raunchy Hot Gossip appeared later which resulted in a lot of complaints from Mary Whitehouse, the 'clean-up' TV campaigner, and a few outraged parents, though all these girl dancers were very popular with everybody's dad!

A rough rugged Welsh singer, Tom Jones, had a number one hit in the charts with *It's Not Unusual* and me and my Mum never missed his TV show on a Sunday night. We'd never seen anyone move like he did, we looked forward to it all week.

I can remember watching the Beatles on the 1963 *Royal Variety Show* at the *Prince of Wales Theatre* and my favourite Beatle, John Lennon, saying to a very posh audience: "Those in the cheaper seats clap, the rest of you rattle your jewellery!" The Royal Variety shows, unlike today, always had very restrained upper crust audiences at the show so it came as a bit of a shock to them.

A French singer, Francoise Hardy, hit the British charts. She had long straight hair and a fringe down to her nose that set off another hair change. We had no electrical hair 'straighteners' in those days, so you would set up your mum's ironing board, lie with your face near to the board, put brown paper over your hair and iron it straight! Straight hair was now so popular that a lot of hairdressers had to close. During the 50s and early 60s you would visit a hairdressers at least once a week for a shampoo and set, a perm or to have your hair dyed. The hairdressers' shops then were usually packed and a lot of my friends went to work as hairdressers and they got a really good wage certainly better than mine working in an office. Most women would sleep every night with rows of big pink plastic rollers in their hair covered by a net in between trips to the hairdressers for a shampoo and set and very uncomfortable it was too.

In the 1950s and early 60s, all women had their hair dyed. There was no such thing as brown hair! You had to have black, blonde or red hair, once again the infamous all things in threes. Backcombing had been very popular with the rock n roll set, the higher you could get your 'beehive' the more fashionable you were. We used to buy bottles of 'Madam Pompadour' hair lacquer from Woolworths which looking back I think was really glue! It set your hair rock solid and you couldn't comb it out, you had to buy green liquid soap to wash your hair from the chemists where McDonalds now is in Loughborough. If you used a regular shampoo you would have white bits all over your hair when it dried. You slept with your hair backcombed and then pushed it back into shape in the morning and put on more lacquer. You could always tell the girls who weren't very good at backcombing, as they would have a great big hole in the back of the beehive. There was a real art to smoothing it over! I have seen girls at that time with a beehive probably ten inches high and stood and looked at them in awe!

The Beatnik era also dawned. Women would wear black tights or black tight trousers to the knee which were called 'pedal pushers' and 'sloppy Joe' jumpers which were very baggy, black ballet pumps, long straight black hair and pale make up, very much Audrey Hepburn; men would wear all black too, but this didn't catch on in Loughborough.

Another explosion was in film where all the big movie stars were American; British films and stars were considered a bit 'naff' by the teenage set……………. but then came *Dr No* and our first introduction to James Bond starring a then unknown Sean Connery. We had never seen anything like it and neither had the

85

rest of the world.  Sean Connery took the world by storm.  Previous British male film stars had treated women with kid gloves but here was a man who, if the women turned out to be 'baddies' slapped them around and even shot them after making love to them and we couldn't get enough of it!  More British stars became international movie stars - Michael Caine, Julie Christie, Terence Stamp, Albert Finney, David Hemmings, Tom Courtenay, Roger Moore, Lynn Redgrave, Glenda Jackson and many many more.  It was so 'cool' and 'fab' to be British.  Yes, we had our own language now too.

During the 50s and 60s the American musical dominated the world especially on screen as in *Seven Brides for Seven Brothers, Singin' In The Rain, An American In Paris, Kismet, High Society, The King And I, Easter Parade, Paint Your Wagon, On The Town, Calamity Jane, Kiss Me Kate, Anchors Aweigh, Gigi, Pyjama Game, Damn Yankees, Call Me Madam, Carousel, Showboat* and *Oklahoma* to name but a few.  We had had a few British musical stars gain success in America such as Noel Coward and Jack Buchanan but these were not familiar names to British teenagers.

As everything British became popular, Michael Crawford went to Hollywood to appear with Barbra Streisand and Walter Matteau in *Hello Dolly* directed by Gene Kelly.  Julie Andrews starred on Broadway in *My Fair Lady* but lost out in the film version to Audrey Hepburn, even though her singing voice had to be dubbed, as the film moguls wanted a star name in the title role.

Julie Andrews took the title role in *Mary Poppins* and with this became an overnight 'A' list star.  The first choice for the title role of the English nanny was Bette Davis until Walt Disney went to see a Broadway show *Camelot* starring Julie Andrews and the rest is film history!  Revenge is sweet however, as Julie Andrews picked up an Oscar for *Mary Poppins.*

We could have had a British star in the American musicals long before.  After the break up of the dazzling dancing partnership of Fred Astaire and Ginger Rogers in 1939 as Ginger wanted to pursue an acting career, Fred had taken a shine to our own Jessie Matthews who was the most wonderful dancer and starred in many British films and stage musicals in the 1930s and later on in life would be Mrs Dale in the popular radio show *Mrs Dale's Diary*.  Fred Astaire wanted her to be his dance partner but due to their individual work commitments this never materialised.  Somehow 'Fred and Jessie' doesn't sound quite so magical and unforgettable as Fred and Ginger so perhaps it was for the best!

Kung Fu films hit the cinemas with Bruce Lee in *Enter The Dragon* and we all flocked to learn Kung Fu, me included I went with Eric Smith who was in my men's dancing troupe and also appeared in the dancing pantos, to a Dojo at Melton Mowbray.  I was the only girl there in class of at least 40 men and this was in a time before strict controls of fighting came so there were plenty of mishaps and I was the one who had to bandage them all up. However I prided myself on being told I had got 'killer' elbows.

The much loved 'Carry On' films became a national institution and are still watched today in affection by the older generation and an eye opener to the younger generation.  Nothing has ever been funnier and more popular, just look at all the box sets of these films that are being sold today

The 1960s produced probably the most popular and well known Western film ever, *The Magnificent Seven* that was based on the 1954 Japanese film *The Seven Samurai*.  This film starred Yul Brynner, James Coburn, Steve McQueen,

Eli Wallach, Robert Vaughan, Charles Branson, Horst Buchholz and Brad Dexter with a stirring music track by Elmer Bernstein. All the actors became household names with this film and Yul Brynner and James Coburn won Academy Awards for best actor and best actor in a supporting role respectively.  I do also want to mention the many years later Steve Martin film *The Three Amigos* which although a spoof on *The Magnificent Seven* is actually a very good tribute as well.  Elmer Bernstein also did the music score for this picture

The Union Jack started to appear on T-shirts, bags, mugs and even underwear much to older people's disapproval.   Second hand military uniforms were being worn, the more decorative the better and could be bought from Portobello Road by the hundreds.

A new car, the Mini, was brought out and sold all over the world and three of these cars starred with Michael Caine, Noel Coward, Irene Handl and Benny Hill in the cult and never bettered 1969 film *The Italian Job*.

Television began to lose its snobbery.  You had to have a cut glass accent if you were on the 'box' in the 1950s and early 60s, one of the women presenters on the BBC at the time looked and sounded exactly like the Queen.  This type of presenter was portrayed by, that great actress, Maureen Lipman in a *Dr Who* episode.  Dramas were usually boring and most of the other programmes were educational.  Regional accents were coming to the fore.  You didn't have to be ashamed any more because you didn't speak 'proper' and elocution lessons went out of the window.

Grittier TV dramas were now being produced as were the 'kitchen sink' films such as *Saturday Night And Sunday Morning* with a new young actor Albert Finney and *A Kind of Loving* with Midlands born actor Alan Bates.  *Look Back In Anger*, probably the forerunner of these films, had just missed the 60s as it came out in 1959.  More realistic working class films aimed at young people were in the cinemas *Up The Junction, Blow Up, Georgy Girl, Whistle Down The Wind, To Sir With Love, Poor Cow*.  Michael Caine was swept to stardom with *Zulu* and then had us on edge playing a British, glasses wearing, cook and secret agent Harry Palmer.  We now had an International 'A' list star with a very strong Cockney accent.  Who would have believed it?

Whoever would have thought that a new TV show from up north about working class people first shown in December 1960 with a planned six-week run would still be on the box today.  Yes you guessed it *Coronation Street*.  This was originally going to be called Florizel Street and, if it had, would probably have only run for six weeks!   *Emmerdale Farm* began its run in 1972 and we would have to wait until 1985 for *EastEnders*.

Betty Driver who plays Betty 'Hotpot' Turpin in *Coronation Street* was born in Leicester and worked for many years as a band singer and sang on many of the 1950s radio shows.  She also worked alongside George Formby in one of his films, but George's jealous wife, Beryl, had Betty's bit cut from the film!

*Coronation Street* has probably had over the years the most members in their cast with a variety background and that probably accounts why it is always tops on the comedy side.  These include the great all rounder Roy Hudd, comics Bradley Walsh, Paul Shane (Ted Bovis in *Hi-De-Hi*), Bobby Knutt (Albert Dingle in *Emmerdale*), Johnny Leeze (Ned Glover in *Emmerdale*) and Peter Kay.  Debra 'Frankie' Stevenson started out as a child singer/impressionist, Jayne 'Yana' Tunnicliffe was a comic banjo player, Amanda 'Alma' Barrie was a dancer.  Michael

87

*Dee Quemby*

Ball was a singer as was Barbara 'Rita Sullivan' Knox and Liz Dawn and Bill Tarmey 'Vera and Jack' and Kym 'Michelle the barmaid' Marsh sang on the club circuit before her break in the TV manufactured short lasting pop group *Hearsay*. Lynn Perrie 'Ivy Tyldesley' sister of comic Duggie Brown started out as a vocalist in the working men's clubs. Noddy Holder of *Slade* fame also appeared on the show briefly. I do think he's a wonderful actor, why don't we see more of him? Violet Carson (Ena Sharples) was a pianist and started her career by playing the piano in cinemas accompanying the silent movies.

Years ago, I did a comedy spot for the Miss Echo personality contest with Lynne Perrie at Loughborough Town Hall. What a nice down-to-earth lady she was. She walked in to the dressing room and said: "Hello love" and then turned to her husband and said: "Get the little girl a drink", and he did.

Two of the greatest names in British entertainment also appeared in *Coronation Street,* Max Wall and Sir Norman Wisdom. I was thrilled to sit next to and have lunch with Sir Norman Wisdom recently at a British Comedy Society event. I said to him: "thanks for making me laugh as a child", his eyes filled with tears and he squeezed my arm tightly. He then jumped up, performed his trademark funny walk and did the raffle draw - and he's well in his 90s! Old troupers go on forever!

You never know how a popular actor or actress started or what he or she can do. I remember seeing Clark Gable in the 1939 MGM musical *Idiot's Delight* and he was tap dancing and very good he was too! I hasten to add that I did not actually see it in 1939! Oscar winning actor, and supreme 'baddie', Christopher Walken was a dancer (in showbiz terms a 'gypsy' or a 'pony') in many stage shows. Sean Connery was 'spotted' building up his muscles in a gym and ended up on a London stage in the chorus line of *South Pacific,* alongside a certain other young man Larry Hagman, pre their 'James Bond' and 'JR' days! Kevin Costner started off in marketing. Rock Hudson was a postman who delivered mail to a showbiz agent. John Wayne was a studio props man and was 'spotted' loading furniture into a van. Actor, director, musician and composer Clint Eastwood was 'spotted' delivering parcels to a film studio. Shirley MacLaine was a dancer on Broadway. She was covering the star of the show Carol Haney (in showbiz terms an 'understudy' or a 'swing'). Carol Haney was unable to appear one fateful night and so, out into the spotlight went Shirley MacLaine. Unbeknown to anyone, in the audience that night was a Hollywood producer, and the rest is history. In the end, it's all down to luck!

An actress, musical star, principal boy in panto and big friend of Larry Grayson, Noelle Gordon, hosted a lively lunchtime TV show from 1956 called *Lunch Box*. There was music and chat and this show was the forerunner of all the morning shows in this vein. Noelle always had a lovely 50s dress on with a skirt so full it completely covered the chair she was sitting on. Noelle Gordon went on to appear in 1972 as Meg Richardson in the cult soap *Crossroads* famous for its awful dialogue and moving (when it shouldn't be) scenery. We would always watch it as it was on just when you got home from school or college. *Crossroads* was one of the most popular shows in TV history and had wonderful characters like Amy Turtle and Benny! Unfortunately a recent vamped up version of *Crossroads* was a big failure. The public loved things going wrong and unbelievable characters and most of us were hoping the 'revival' would have the same characters but it just didn't work 'glammed up' and it had really had its day.

We went to Loughborough Town Hall one night and there was a couple dressed in 'mod' clothes dancing apart! This was the new Mod dancing and we all quickly learnt how to do it. The part of the town near The Rushes was the 'cool' part to go now. We had a coffee bar 'El Chico' (previously occupied by students and now a restaurant) serving frothy expresso coffee in Pyrex cups and saucers and there was a small silver jukebox on one wall. On the other side of the road the Lion Café became a Wimpy bar, and a nightclub with a gambling room at the back further down the road became a disco 'Il Ronde'. Live groups were still popular but now the DJs were beginning to appear. Trendy boutiques started to open up in the town as well.

The Beatles appeared at the De Montfort Hall in Leicester. I wasn't allowed to go as we had heard of all the incidents on the tour, screaming girls being crushed, people passing out and other things to make my Mum say 'No'! A rumour quickly went round Mountsorrel that the Beatles were staying the night at Rothley Court, a very expensive hotel at the back of where we lived. My Grandad took me up there in his turquoise Austin car. We parked on the road outside for ages, me clutching my autograph book, but eventually gave it up as a bad job and went home.

So now it was the 'swinging sixties'. The world looked to England; Liverpool for music and London for fashion. Instead of the 1950s' British teenagers wanting to go and live in the States, the American teenagers now wanted to live here, especially in Liverpool.

The Beatles' success was phenomenal and we were invaded with tourists from all over the world. Everybody wanted to be part of the British 60s scene. The Beatles brought so much money from overseas into the country that in 1965 they were each awarded an MBE and didn't that cause some trouble when their names were announced in the forthcoming Honours List! There was a lot of opposition to this and several MBE holders threatened to send their awards back.

Colour television had arrived but there were problems in the early days with filming in colour. I went to the Teddington Studios to film *Opportunity Knocks* with Hughie Green. The make up girl was frantically powdering the blond hair of the drummer in a group that was also appearing. Apparently peroxide hair came up green. She told me a lot of stars had to have a drink before filming but they couldn't any more as their noses came up red on screen and nothing would hide it. She also told me that anything white came up fuzzy and that the nurses' and doctors' uniforms in the very popular medical drama *Emergency Ward 10* were actually yellow but appeared white on screen.

British music, fashion, films and every day life was rapidly changing and it had a knock on effect worldwide.

The 60s brought about the most notorious political, exciting and glamorous scandal ever 'starring' Tory Minister for War, John Profumo and two high-class callgirls, Christine Keeler and Mandy Rice-Davies. It was talked about on the bus, at work, in shops and even at school. This was an age when politicians were scandal free, respected, looked up to and were seen to be church going 'pillars of the community' family men.

John Profumo was married to the beautiful elegant British actress, Valerie Hobson, and the papers were crammed full of stories of prostitutes, Lords, an osteopath, Russian spies, MPs and sex parties at a time when we didn't even know what Tupperware parties were! These days we don't bat an eyelid at exposures like these that seem to happen on a regular basis but at least, the women they were involved with in the 60s were glamorous............come to think about it so were the men! The famous black and white photo of Christine Keeler sitting on a chair in the nude is still an ageless classic today.

The 'Great Train Robbery' was also a much talked about, and to us very exciting, event. This sort of big scale crime didn't happen here! The newspapers and TV were full of it and the whole country couldn't get enough. We followed every little detail as it all happened in Buckinghamshire where Gramp came from. Everybody knew each of the train robbers by name they were the 'reality' stars of the day.

The pill became available to married women only. A lot of employers would sack women when they first became pregnant. This was the reason why you weren't given a lot of responsibility, as you weren't expected to stay long in a job (remember first baby at 21). Building societies would not even give mortgages to single women, or put the names of married women on the mortgage, as they would all be considered a risk financially. When a young woman became pregnant with her first baby the battle of all battles would begin. Mother and mother-in-law would slug it out to be the one to buy the Silver Cross pram, the most prestigious, and expensive, gift you could buy for your first grandchild. This was also a time when you would be kept in hospital for a lengthy stay after having had a baby. When you got home the whole family would rally round so you could take it easy. Mums would stay at home to raise their child and only take short walks out in the village with baby in the pram. There were no easy access buses then, as no one would expect you to go on a bus ride with a new baby in a pram. My Mum used to push me in my Silver Cross pram and walk from Shepshed to Loughborough and back. Mums didn't have jobs, apart from those who had been widowed during the war, as with no husband to provide for the family they needed money to live. The benefits then were pitiful especially for war widows. A woman with a husband and children having a career, unthinkable in those days!

As the pill slowly became available to all women, you now could get a mortgage and live on your own even though it was not socially acceptable. You did not have to go down the traditional route of engaged at 19 and so on, as mentioned before, if you didn't want to.

National Service stopped in the 1960s. With National Service, when boys reached 18 they would have to serve two years in the forces usually abroad. This gave them discipline, a career and a sense of purpose. My husband John just missed out on this but all his friends who did National Service have great memories and, all in all, really enjoyed it especially those sent to Hong Kong.

There were no shops for teenage girls like today. Clothes were a mini version of what your mother wore and she bought them for you. In the 1950s and early 60s most girls made their own clothes, not me I could sew sequins on anything but actually make a garment - never!

C & A in Leicester started to carry the mod trends in clothing and I bought my first trouser suit from there. Trouser suits were a major change for women and the first ones were double breasted in grey flannel with turn-ups (called 'cuffs' in America) on the trousers. I used to buy mod dresses from C & A for £1.50 that was very expensive then as a woman's average weekly-wage would have been £5.50.

Second hand fur coats became fashionable and there was a woman who sold them on Leicester market. They were piled high usually smelling of mothballs and looking a bit 'manky' and moth-eaten - but what the heck, it was fashionable. You couldn't be anything else in the 60s!

In the 1960s with the mini skirts, women's knees got bigger! Nature compensates, as when cold air hits a part of the body not exposed to the elements before, the fat piles on, just as today with the 'fashionable' hipster trousers that have been fashionable before anyway. I had hipster trousers in the 70s. Even the slimmest girls today have a roll of fat hanging down around their trousers hip line. You can't fight nature!

At that time all the boutiques were in London and to get the really trendy clothes you had to go there. I walked into the newly opened Biba store in Kensington High Street in my mini skirt and had a shock; the girls there were wearing them four inches shorter than mine was! I wasn't as fashionable as I thought I was, time to get the needle and cotton out again! Biba clothes were fabulous and unobtainable anywhere else and so the famous Biba mail order shopping catalogue came into being. You could go into Biba's and see celebrities like Sonny & Cher, Twiggy, Julie Christie, Brigitte Bardot, Yoko Ono and Barbra Streisand trying clothes on with everybody else.

Kensington High Street and Carnaby Street were full of boutiques and trendy shops. Petticoat Lane market in Middlesex Street and Portobello Road were also the places to go. Big old houses in these streets were open, you could walk in and there would be stalls everywhere selling the latest fashion trends, shoes and jewellery. I bought my first pair of white platform boots in such a house for £25 (a fortune then!) and still wear them to this day when playing Dame in my touring panto – what a bargain!

Out came a trendy fashion magazine *Honey* aimed at young women, unheard of before, and was published monthly. Biba produced their own make up and perfume, girls started to use the new men's fragrance 'Hi Karate' instead of perfume for some reason and yes I was one of them. We used to pour 'Aquamanda' into our baths (Friday night was usually bath night) it smelt so strong you nearly passed out. It must have been a Friday night when we heard President Kennedy of the USA had been assassinated because my Mum rushed up stairs to tell me as I lay there soaking .......Yes I'm one of the many people who remembers where they were when Kennedy was shot.

*The Avengers* was a massive TV hit and was broadcast live. We all wanted to be Cathy Gale. In Loughborough, I actually bought a suede skirt suit that had been made for Diana Rigg (Mrs Peel). She always had two copies of every outfit she wore in *The Avengers* and this one had never been used and had ended up in a boutique that had just opened in Loughborough in the High Street opposite the Cross Keys pub. When Joanna Lumley became Purdy in *The Avengers* we all went to the hairdressers to have a 'Purdy' haircut.

The first boutique opened in Leicester, called 'Viva Caran'. It was an upstairs shop on the right hand side of the road going up towards the train station. Two very trendy girls worked in the shop and it's just occurred to me that the name of the boutique could have been Carol and Ann amalgamated. The shop was full of the latest trends, feather boas, long sequin earrings, tops and dresses with psychedelic prints and the shop was always full of customers

## Dee Quemby

What a change from the 50s and early 60s when we wore a V neck sweater with a plastic rose brooch pinned to it that had a centre that you put cotton wool in and put perfume (called 'scent' in those days) on usually a cheap one like 'California Poppy' and 'Paris by Night', we had never heard of Designer perfumes then.    We had full rock 'n' roll skirts, wasp belts, and those awful can-can underskirts in red, green, yellow, orange or pink florescent net so rough and sharp that they shredded your stockings as you rock 'n' rolled and left red marks on your legs.    When the can-can underskirt went limp you put it in the bath with a solution of hot water and sugar to stiffen it up again, if you got really hot the sugar solution would start to melt and make your legs sticky.    Some girls wore suspender belts and seamed stockings but most girls wore a girdle with suspenders attached. We rushed to buy the new 'pearlised' winkle picker stilettos from Marriott's shoe shop, in which you had to run to catch the last bus home, which I think was about 11pm.    It was compulsory to have sleepers in pierced ears, then later on the big gypsy hoops that are now fashionable again.    Only the not very brave women would wear clip on earrings!

At work screams could be heard coming from girls in the ladies' toilets at break times as their friends kindly pierced their ears for them armed with a needle and a cork and they would all be queuing up to have it done and then go back to their desks, white faced, with blood dripping from their earlobes. My Mum was having none of that.    I was sent to Peabody's jewellers in Shepshed on the bus to have it properly done, the woman in the shop marked my ear with a pencil she had licked (had she never heard of health and hygiene?) and then produced a needle and a cork! My Mum had omitted to tell me that when she had had her ears pierced she had felt so sick after the first one that she had to be taken home and then go back later on to have the other one done.

To me the 60s clothes were the smartest fashion for young people and then the 70s came and everybody turned into hippies................quel dommage!  People changed overnight from smart and trendy into scruffy and shapeless.    Flares came into being, as did tank tops, and suede waistcoats that tied at the waist and then the suede was fringed down to your knees.  You wore your hair long and lank and tied a scarf around your forehead.  You bought a caftan and an Indian frock coat and you had to have a bell on a chain round your neck!  I bought my bell from the Portobello market in London.

Alongside this we had glam rock and fashion was exciting in a new way. You wore your platform boots with soles that were so thick that in the winter you never had cold feet.  It took a while to get used to them and even seasoned wearers could sometimes be seen losing their balance and falling over.  The disco scene appeared with clubs opening up everywhere; you had to dress in bright florescent colours, silver PVC, feather boas, and have the new Afro hairstyle and put on lots of make up.  Bouncers wouldn't let you into discos and nightclubs unless you were dressed in colourful over-the-top outfits.  Hairdressers were now back in business with the Afro perms, even men had them as well as blond highlights and 'mullets' that were also known as 'lion' cuts.

The disco scene will never be repeated.  Never again will you get people wearing the over the top outfits like hot pants, flares, tank tops, dresses made out of thick lace curtains and tablecloths, outrageous make up and hairstyles but it was a real fun time and everybody really did look fab.

John Travolta wowed us in *Saturday Night Fever* and men in white suits, open to the waist black shirts and gold medallions could be seen everywhere.  People were out for a good fun time, of course as in the 50s and 60s there was the odd punch up, more so in the 60s with the mods and rockers, but it wasn't like today with stabbings, rapes and murders nearly every week. Nowadays, a lot of young girls I know never go clubbing anymore, as it can be frightening and downright dangerous. As one young woman said to me recently "You're lucky, you've got so much to look back on, we've got nothing" which really is very sad. Later on in the 1980s the dances on a Saturday night in the canteen at Rolls-Royce factory canteen became very popular. I remember at that time it was fashionable to buy the long brushed nylon nighties from Dorothy Perkins to wear as dance dresses. I can remember having a long black one with frilly sleeves. Women were starting to go bra-less at this time but you couldn't dancing in a brushed nylon nightie then, it was too painful on the 'raspberry ripples'!

Television closed down during the war but it didn't worry anyone as no one had a set. It must have been the luxury of millionaires then. Radio was the big star maker during the war and afterwards. We listened to *Workers' Playtime*. This radio show had started during the war to boost the morale of the nation but carried on a few years more after as it was so popular. The show went to a factory's canteen 'somewhere in Britain' and was put on live during the lunch break hence the title. *Workers' Playtime* featured a lot of the top variety acts at the time and these included Peter Sellars, Frankie Howerd, Cyril Fletcher, Julie Andrews, Morecambe and Wise, Bob Monkhouse, Elsie & Doris Waters, Ken Dodd and many more.

I loved *Have A Go* hosted by Wilfred Pickles and his wife Mabel that would be broadcast from various church halls up and down Britain and had an incredible audience of 20 million listeners. Me, and my Mum being two of them! Wilfred would get people up on stage with him and encourage them to tell stories about their working class lives, sometimes sad but more than often heart warming and would nearly always ask them: "Are you courting?" He would then ask them some simple questions so they could win a prize off the table. He would say: "What's on the table, Mabel?" and Mabel would tell him. The prizes never got more exciting that a tin of peas or a postal order for five bob (shillings) or seven and six but we never missed listening to it. At that time five bob (25p today) was known as 'a dollar' and 2/6d (12.5p) as 'half a dollar', (also as half a crown) that tells you a lot about the exchange rate then! Wilfred had a pianist on the show, and in the audience and at home we would all sing along "Have a go Jo, come and have a go" as she played.

Many years later when I was filming *Opportunity Knocks* at the Teddington Studios with Hughie Green, Wilfred Pickles was filming a sitcom with Irene Handl *For the Love of Ada*. I was thrilled that he opened a door for me and said 'hello'. I loved to watch Irene Handl on TV when she played the dotty granny in *Metal Mickey*.

Tony Hancock's radio show was not to be missed, nor was *The Goon Show*, *The Navy Lark*, *Life With The Lyons*, *Meet The Huggetts*, *Ray's A Laugh*, *The Clitheroe Kid*, *Two Way Family Favourites* and *Round The Horne* which has recently been produced on stage in the West End, and many more. Young children sat engrossed at *Listen with Mother* and mums and grannies never missed *Women's Hour*.

We would listen to all the comedy greats such as Ted Ray, Richard 'Stinker' Murdoch with Arthur Askey, Tommy Trinder who would in the future be one of the *Sunday Night At The London Palladium* comperes, Frankie Howerd, Tommy Handley and his *ITMA* (It's That Man Again) radio show that toured military bases 'somewhere in England' during the war. Due to its popularity it continued on the radio in peacetime. *ITMA* also featured Hattie Jacques and Derek Guyler. I loved Mrs Mopp; you would hear the door being flung open and a woman shouting: "Can I do you now Sir?" Then there was Mona Lott who always said "It's being so cheerful that keeps me happy" in a very monotone voice and Ali Oop who always wanted to sell his postcards.

So popular was this show that in 1947 the ITMA broadcast from Broadcasting House had in the audience their Majesties King George VI and Queen Elizabeth along with Princess Margaret. There was a corgi called Patsy in the show and a lot of 'Down Patsy' just like years later we would all be saying 'Down Shep' when *Blue Peter* came on TV. There really is nothing new under the sun!

Other comics we would listen to were Cyril Fletcher, Harry Secombe, Jimmy Edwards, Two-Ton Tessie O'Shea, Jimmy Wheeler, Al Read, Rob Wilton, Vic Oliver, Beryl Reid, Joyce Grenfell, Sandy Powell, Hattie Jacques, Avril Angers, Jimmy James, Stanley Holloway and many more. Who could ever forget the Glum family, Pa, Ron and Eth in *Take It From Here*? The whole nation wanted to laugh having gone through the second World War and there were plenty of great comics who could make the whole family do that many having served their apprenticeship during the war in E.N.S.A, apart from Frankie Howerd who failed his audition!

ENSA stood for Entertainments National Service Association. Though the ordinary soldier, sailor and airman affectionately re-named it: 'Every Night Something Awful!' ENSA was a branch of the military and its members wore uniforms. ENSA went where the troops were fighting all over Europe during World War II and put on shows to keep the force's morale high and give them a laugh. It is impossible to get the original ENSA stripes for costumes today as it was a very small unit and like most service people after the war they were glad to get rid of their uniforms. But a military friend of my Dad managed to get me a pair made in India of all places for my 40s show uniform exactly as they would have been during the war, white capitals on a black background.

The *Carroll Levis Discovery Show* was a very popular radio talent show. Carroll Levis was a very large and tall man, Canadian by birth. This show switched to BBC television in the 1950s and I can remember watching a young Scottish boy in a kilt playing a piano accordion on roller skates competing.

The whole family would sit down to listen to *The Archers* that started in 1951. *The Archers* came about because of a Lincolnshire farmer who said the radio ought to do a farming radio show similar to the very popular *Dick Barton* show, another of our favourites, and the BBC did at the latter's expense as *Dick Barton* was taken off to make room for *The Archers*! *The Archers* original format was 50% educational and 50% fiction and is still running today.

Ken Dodd's radio show was another of our favourites, as was *Educating Achie* starring Archie Andrews who was, believe it or not, a ventriloquist's dummy with Peter Brough as the ventriloquist………. on the radio! Well we certainly never saw his lips move! The show also starred a young actress Beryl Reid performing her naughty schoolgirl routine. She also did this on *Sunday Night At The London Palladium*. When I first started doing comedy in charity shows I too dressed up as a schoolgirl. *Educating Archie* at one time had 16 million listeners and launched the careers of Benny Hill, Harry Secombe, Eric Sykes, Tony Hancock, Julie Andrews, Bruce Forsyth, Max Bygraves and Beryl Reid.

Princess Elizabeth became Queen in 1952 and her Coronation was in 1953. It was announced that the Coronation would be shown on television, but very few people had television sets. Television sets would be rented from a TV Rental shop, we had ours from Radio Rentals. You would have to go every week to the shop to pay your money and have your rental card stamped. If you didn't pay they would come in a van and take the TV set back to the shop often as the family sat there watching! Though I hasten to add this never happened to us.

As we were one of the fortunate families to have a television set, we crammed as many people into our lounge as possible, as did other families, to watch the whole Coronation ceremony in black and white. It would be years before we could see this in colour on the television. We all flocked to the cinema to sit through the Coronation again in glorious 'technicolor'.

Children used to save the cellophane wrappers from sweets that were coloured but you could see through. They would hold them over their eyes when watching television to make the picture appear coloured. At that time we only had one channel and that was the BBC. A few years later we would have our first commercial channel.

When the commercial channel started in Britain it was expensive to have the new sets and so not many could afford to do this. Envious children would wait for invites to go for tea from school friends who had the new channel so they could watch the American shows and the adverts! This would happen all over again when colour TV came into being.

Quiz shows were all the rage in the 1950s with one of the most popular being *What's My Line?* After an announcement: 'Will the next contestant sign in please', a contestant would write his/her name on a board, perform their mime of their everyday job, and then the panel would have to guess what it was in ten questions. The host of this show was ex-boxer, Eamonn Andrews. Years later he would carry a red book and say to astonished celebrities: "This is your Life!" The *What's My Line?* panel was made up of Gilbert Harding, Barbara Kelly, David Nixon and Leicestershire's own ex-doctor turned celebrity, Lady Isobel Barnett. The quiz shows *Double your Money* hosted by Hughie Green, *Take Your Pick* and *Spot The Tune* with the popular singer Marion Ryan we never missed. Everybody loved the 'Yes/No' game where you would be asked questions and have to answer without saying 'yes' or 'no', it sounds easy but just you try it. I used to do this sometimes if there were older children at parties when I was a children's entertainer and they would all want to keep doing it. So simple and so much fun as was 'open the box'.

All the radio comics went on to have successful TV shows and I will always remember seeing Jimmy James, Eli Woods, 'Our Eli', and a very young Roy Castle and the 'animals in the box' routine time and time again and it still made us laugh as did the endless supply of the Old Mother Riley films being shown on TV.

Many of the quiz shows and variety shows featured Sabrina who really didn't do anything, she just seemed to stand there but she always wore glamorous long tight low cut evening dresses with fishtails and had long blonde hair and was very well endowed! A very popular radio singer, Val Doonican, had his own TV show and he always seemed to be sat in a rocking chair, this obviously went down well as his show ran for 24 years.

*Quatermass* was a hugely popular radio sci-fi show for adults, it was made into a TV programme, in 1955 and children were not allowed to watch it. I remember my Mum having to go to bed after seeing it as it made her feel so ill and apparently this had happened to other people up and down the country!

95

## Dee Quemby

A popular programme and probably the first British 'soap' was the BBC series *The Grove Family* that ran from 1954. A quarter of the population tuned in including the late Queen Mum who apparently was also a big fan. I can only remember 'dad' who always seemed to be sat in an armchair in his suit smoking his pipe and a rather 'dotty' grandma.

*The Good Old Days* televised from a theatre in Leeds was a very popular show. There would be many variety acts on stage, a master of ceremonies dressed immaculately in a tail suit, continually banging his gavel on top of his table taking ages to announce the acts with words we'd never heard of as in the old music hall days and the audience dressed in Victorian costumes. I particularly remember one Christmas 'special'. Outside the theatre it was snowing heavily and the Chairman announced to the audience they were expecting an important guest that turned out to be an actress as Queen Victoria arriving in a black horse drawn coach and then sitting in a box and watching the show. This show ran for many years and there is nothing that comes close to it today.

Nowadays the commercial break is when we put the kettle on, let the cat out or nip to the loo. This was definitely not the case when commercial television first hit our screens in the 1950s. The first commercial shown in this country was for Gibbs toothpaste in September 1955 and I was nine years old. Those lucky enough to have commercial television were transfixed with the adverts, many were better than the programmes and so many of the musical themes to the commercials became so well known that you could hear people singing them everywhere. Remember singing: "The Esso sign means happy motoring", "Coates comes up from Somerset" "You'll wonder where the yellow went", "All the dust, all the grit", " "Murray mints Murray mints", "Hot chocolate drinking chocolate". I bet a lot of you can still finish these jingles off and we loved them all. Katie the 'OXO' mum became a big star, everybody put a tiger in the car petrol tank, children pleaded; "Don't forget the fruit gums mum", one little squirt did all the washing up, we were never alone with a Strand and we all knew the answer to "what's got a hazelnut in every bite?" The whole family would all sit and laugh at the antics of the Brooke Bond monkeys. We would sit there eagerly waiting for the ends of parts one, two and three to see if our favourite commercial would be shown. These days I can't understand most of the ads! If I sit there perplexed as to what the commercial is trying to sell I know for sure it is going to be an ad for a car!

Rented television sets and television aerials were suddenly sprouting up everywhere and the TV set was affectionately known as the 'goggle box'. Children's shows I remember watching were *Heidi, The Adventures Of Sir Lancelot, William Tell, Andy Pandy* (all little girls had a Looby Loo doll knitted by their mum or grandma), *Bill And Ben, Blue Peter, Mr Pastry, Whacko, Billy Bunter, The Sooty Show, The Clangers, Pinky & Perky, The Buccaneers, Ivanhoe* with a very young Roger Moore who could be seen in women's magazines modelling knitwear, *Robin Hood, Muffin The Mule* with Annette Mills (actor John Mill's sister) playing the piano. Charlie Drake went from one show to another for many years but he was always Charlie Drake so they all seemed like the same programme. I also watched a children's show that I can't remember the name of it but I do remember this rhyme: "Billy Breen built a machine to see what it could do, he built it out of sticks and stones and lots of pots of glue!" Larry Grayson used the stage name 'Billy Breen', when he started out as a semi-pro drag queen and comic in working men's cubs. Perhaps this is the show that he got it from?

It is hard to believe today that up until 1957 television would close down from 6pm to 7pm, this was known as the 'toddlers' truce' and this would be for mums to put young children to bed.

Television was full of cowboy shows - *Hopalong Cassidy, Davy Crockett, The Lone Ranger, The Cisco Kid, Champion the Wonder Horse* with a fabulous title song sung by Frankie Laine and the more adult one's *Gun Law, Maverick* (a young Roger Moore crossed the 'pond' to appear in this), *Sugarfoot, High Chapparel, Bonanza, Bronco Layne,* the name of which children used to think was hilarious due to the horrible tiny hard sheets of cheap Bronco toilet paper at school, *Cheyenne, Lawman, Wyatt Earp, Laramie* and many more.......the most popular being *Wagon Train* starring Ward Bond and Robert Horton that was based on John Ford's 1950 film *Wagonmaster. Wagon Train* attracted big name guest stars such as James Coburn, Clint Eastwood, Henry Fonda, Bette Davis, Mickey Rooney, Barbara Stanwyck, Shelley Winters and a future USA president, Ronald Reagan. John Wayne made his only dramatic TV appearance in this show as General Sherman. We watched all of them. My Dad loved his cowboy films and books. He would watch the films over and over again. When we had our first colour TV set a John Wayne film came on and I said: "You're not watching this film again you've seen it times" and my Dad said indignantly: "But not in colour!"

My Dad also loved the wrestling on TV. He would get so excited and thump his armchair. My Mum would say: "We'll have no furniture left!" Wrestling was a big part of people's lives in the 60s. Most men would watch it on TV and a lot of women would too. The wrestling stars became big names and one, Jackie 'Mr TV' Pallo even appeared in *The Avengers.* He was knocked out cold for real, by Honor Blackman as Cathy Gale in an episode that was shown live at the time. Loughborough Town Hall staged live wrestling bouts once a week in the Corn Exchange, as it was then known. So popular were these nights that the queue would stretch all the way down the road, waiting for the doors to open.

Clint Eastwood became a massive star as 'Rowdy Yates' in the enormously popular *Rawhide.* How many times have I heard the theme tune of this cowboy show still being sung in clubs today!

Clint Eastwood moved into films with the 'spaghetti' westerns, so called because they were shot in Italy, *The Good, The Bad And The Ugly, A Fistful Of Dollars* and *For A Few Dollars More* these made him an A' list star and ponchos and blanket coats the height of fashion! He even starred alongside Lee Marvin, he of *The Big Heat* fame, in a musical western *Paint Your Wagon* in 1969. Lee Marvin had a surprise hit record in the charts with *Wand'rin' Star,* one of the songs from the film. Brilliant actor that he was, a singer he wasn't!

One of my favourite TV programmes as a child was *The Army Game* that started in the late 1950s when National Service was still compulsory. William Hartnell, who would become the first *Dr Who* from 1963 to 1966, Michael Medwin, Alfie Bass, Charles Hawtry, Norman Rossington and Bernard Bresslaw starred in the first series. So popular was this show that the theme tune sung by some of the actors reached number five in the charts in 1958 and yes I bought a copy but by then I had a record player to play it on! William Hartnell appeared as the Sergeant Major. When William Hartnell left the show, the popular actor Bill Fraser stepped into the Sergeant Major's boots! Bill Fraser and Alfie Bass later appeared in another massively popular TV show *Bootsie And Snudge,* that was a spin off from *The Army Game.*

## Dee Quemby

We had, as children, all watched Jack Warner (brother of Elsie and Doris Waters the popular variety act) in *Dixon Of Dock Green* on TV that ran for 21 years as he upheld the law in his very British way. The film *Alfie* starring Michael Caine is said to be the first time an actor spoke directly to camera but PC George Dixon did this at the end of every episode of *Dixon Of Dock Green* years before! PC George Dixon was originally a policeman in the very successful 1955 film *The Blue Lamp* although he was bumped off at the start of the film by the character played by Dirk Bogarde - the writer Ted Willis resurrected him for the TV series!

Police dramas such as *Z-Cars* and *No Hiding Place* followed and then came the American cop and private detective dramas which were much faster paced and became 'must see TV', particularly first of all the black and white shows *Dragnet, G-Men* followed by *77 Sunset Strip.* Ed Byrnes was the young man 'Kookie' who parked the cars and occasionally helped the two 'star' detectives solve crimes. His trademark was taking out his comb, combing his blond quiff and using the hip talk of the day. He had a No 1 hit record and I can still hear myself singing: "Kookie, Kookie lend me your comb!" *Hawaiian Eye* was another one of my favourites. Drama series such as *Dr Finlay's Casebook* and *The Forsyte Saga* drew in audiences in their millions, as would *Upstairs Downstairs* later on. *Upstairs Downstairs* was an international hit and received an amazing 26 International awards and seven American Emmys.

Our medical knowledge improved from 1957 with *Emergency Ward 10* in which Richard Thorpe who plays Alan Turner in *Emmerdale,* appeared as Doctor Rennie and it had viewing figures of over 16 million. We all swooned over Richard Chamberlain in *Dr Kildaire* and then again in his Australian hit drama *The Thornbirds*. Michael Parkinson presented a film review show that me and my Mum never missed and it was great to find a male fan of Gene Kelly, at that time most men would never admit they liked a male dancer! We also never used to miss the new satirical show *That Was The Week That Was* hosted by David Frost with Millicent Martin singing the theme tune every week, followed later by *The Frost Report* in which we were first introduced to John Cleese, Ronnie Corbett and Ronnie Barker in their famous 'he looks up at me, I look down at him' sketch.

We also loved the new exciting British TV spy/thriller series that seemed to run for ages called *Top Secret.* *Armchair Theatre* was a one off drama televised once a week. I remember me, and my Mum watching Diana Dors being murdered on a bed and the murderer on the floor putting money into a suitcase when her hand flopped down on to his head. You heard her croak off camera "Give me the money", it frightened us both to death as it was late at night, and yes it was in black and white. I had to keep my bedroom light on all night! Even now I can see her hand coming down from the top of the TV screen and the hairs on the back of my neck stand up. What an actress!

We never missed *On The Braden Beat* with Bernard Braden. Canadians Bernard Braden and his wife Barbara Kelly were big stars in Britain and Barbara Kelly was one of the panellists on *What's My Line?* This was a real mix of a show with news, cabaret and investigations into all sorts of odd things viewers wanted putting right. There was a woman who had been going to a tap class for many years and wanted to complain about how much she had been taught which wasn't a lot. They had her troupe on the show and it seemed all they could do was a few hops, triples and the odd Suzie Qs. She had a very strong point, as this is very basic stuff that four year olds can do! The dog from *Opportunity Knocks* that growled 'sausages' made an appearance on this show as did a very young female researcher Esther Rantzen who eventually took over the show that became *That's Life.*

98

Then came the thrillers and private detectives. We always watched *Danger Man* with Patrick McGoohan. Later on we watched him as Number 6 in the cult show *The Prisoner* starring alongside a big bouncing balloon which we really didn't understand but thought was great. We all went round saying "I am not a number!" So popular was Patrick McGoohan in the 60s that he was actually offered the part of James Bond which he and Cary Grant both turned down and a young unknown hot headed Scottish actor by the name of Sean Connery, who on being asked to audition for the part thumped the table and stormed off which led the producers to believe he was the ideal 'James Bond' and he was! Then came *Callan* that started in 1967 and starred Edward Woodward and had a hugely popular character, 'Lonely', who was very 'quiffy. *The Professionals* with Martin Shaw and Patrick Mower, *The Saint* with Roger Moore, *Baretta, Man In A Suitcase, Jason King, Perry Mason, The Persuaders* and many more and then the cult TV shows *Kung Fu, The Fugitive* and *Man From Uncle* and our own top cop show *The Sweeney.*

More glossy detective shows followed with unconventional heroes *Starsky And Hutch, Kojak, The Streets Of San Franciso* with Karl Malden and a young Michael Douglas always in a light coloured raincoat as was *Columbo* but his was scruffier, *Charley's Angels* and *Miami Vice* starring Dan Johnson who always had his designer jacket sleeves rolled up and never wore socks. So another fashion was born, even girls rolled up their jacket sleeves. *Dr Who* complete with 'Daleks' and 'K9' still had children hiding behind settees. New children's shows like *Basil Brush, Thunderbirds, Stingray, Joe 90, Fireball XL5, Captain Scarlet* and *Torchy the Battery Boy* started to appear.

One of my favourite children's shows was Australian, starring a kangaroo! If anyone had an accident or needed help they would tell the very talented animal star of *Skippy The Kangaroo* as he would understand every word they said to him! He would hop off and find someone who would come to help them, as they would also understand every word he said as well! You really need to watch an episode to understand this, believe me!

Sci-fi TV programmes from America appeared on British TV with *Lost in Space, Buck Rogers* and *The Invaders* being the most popular alongside our own *U.F.O.*

Long before we knew what drag queens were we had the wonderful *Stanley Baxter Show* where he would appear as many famous people, usually glamorous women stars, in all types of routines, Hollywood musicals and famous films, he even did a take off of the Queen in one show. Stanley Baxter had been on television from the 1950s. His BAFTA award winning shows must have cost a fortune to put on. They were well worth the money as they were fabulous! Paul O'Grady as 'Lily Savage' in his show late at night a few years back did a wonderful take off as 'Shanghai Lil' from the Ruby Keeler and James Cagney number in the 1933 film *Footlight Parade* and this is the closest TV has come to this much missed show in years.

From America came the comedy programmes that the whole family would watch at teatime, the Emmy winning *Phil Silvers Show* starring a former vaudeville burlesque performer and small part movie actor Phil Silvers, *Beverly Hillbillies* with Buddy Ebsen the great song and dance man playing Jed Clampett, *The Munsters* with glamorous movie star Yvonne de Carlo as Lily Munster. *I Dream Of Jeannie* starred Larry Hagman the future 'JR' of *Dallas,* son of American musical comedy star Mary Martin.

I really liked *Green Acres* with Zsa Zsa Gabor and Eddie Albert. I don't think I ever missed an episode. Another one of my 'never miss' shows was *Hey Jeannie*. This was about a young Scottish girl who goes to live in New York and befriends a taxi driver who always used to shout out of his cab window, yes you guessed it "Hey Jeannie!"

*Candid Camera* was a very different show to what we were used to. One of the 'hosts' of the show was Bob Monkhouse. This show was revolutionary in using actual members of the public in set-ups. Groundbreaking TV at the time! I remember Bob Monkhouse wandering around London as a foreigner with limited English asking where 'Keapsidi' was. Of course no one knew. After a lengthy conversation and being secretly being filmed on a hidden TV camera, he showed them what was written on the paper, which was actually Cheapside! I like millions of others always remember the car in the garage with no engine and the man running in and out of the dry cleaners eating fishes out of an open tank which were actually slices of carrots. I used to do this at children's parties and of course the kids loved it.

The magician David Nixon had his own TV show. Leicester's Bill Maynard with Terry Scott appeared in a comedy show *Great Scott, It's Maynard*. We even had TV cooks then with their own shows one being Philip Harben who looked like Phil Mitchell but spoke very posh and dressed like a French waiter. Then there was the immortal Fanny and Johnny Craddock. She was very aristocratic and dressed up to the nines in cocktail dresses and diamanté jewellery and always snapped at Johnny. Poor old Johnny always seemed to be in the background holding an opened nearly empty wine bottle and of course Benny Hill did a wonderful parody of this on his TV show, he as Fanny and Bob Todd as Johnny.

Fanny and Johnny were, unintentionally, as funny as the comedy stars and made astonishing gaffes on live TV. It is alleged that on the programme when Fanny made dumplings, Johnny said at the end "and make sure your dumplings turn out like Fanny's!" The next week he made a similar remark about smelly fish! A lot of people maintain he said this about her donuts too.

'Fanny Craddock' is actually Cockney rhyming slang for haddock that probably came into use after the unfortunate 'fish' show! At this time the very naïve rather pompous heads of the BBC would have no idea what people were laughing at but certainly would have noticed how the ratings shot up. This was also the case with the top radio show *Beyond Our Ken* that changed into *Round The Horne* with listener figures of over 15 million. One of the stars of this show was the wonderfully witty Kenneth Williams. He had originally been part of *Tony Hancock's Half Hour*. Tony Hancock hadn't liked his style of comedy and so Kenneth Williams left.

In *Round The Horne* starring Kenneth Horne, Kenneth Williams and Hugh Paddick played a very camp pair called Julian and Sandy and every week they would be in a different job as interior decorators, gents' tailors, photographers, antiques dealers or such like. They even ran a boutique one week called 'Bona Drag'. They would talk to Kenneth Horne in 'Polari' or 'Polare'. 'Polari' is a slang that originated from Romany gypsies. They would speak this language amongst themselves, like Cockney rhyming slang, so nobody else would understand what they were talking about. It was picked up by the acting profession and then by gay men, but has not been used for several years now.

Kenneth Williams would say, amongst other things to Kenneth Horne and God knows how he managed not to burst out laughing each week: "How bona to varda your dolly old eek" (how nice to see your handsome face again). As landscape gardeners he offered to shove a couple of creepers up Kenneth Horne's trellis and how about 'varda the naff hommie with nante pots in the cupboard' (look at him with his bad teeth). We still use 'naff' today, as Princess Anne quite often does, when we mean awful, though it can also mean heterosexual.

Kenneth Williams would also do a spot as a folk singer, Rambling Syd Rumpo, you wouldn't understand a word of it and in reality it was utter rubbish but you would have tears streaming down your face putting your own interpretation to it as he sang "as he traggles his nagger" and other weird and wonderful phrases like 'dangling your lallies', 'cordwranglers' and 'grunting your futtocks'! One song had the introduction of "This is a taddle gropers dance, sung by the villagers of Musgrove Parva and it heralds the coming of the oak apple fairy, or sanitary inspector as he is called." Wonderful stuff!

Some of the names of characters in the show were Dame Celia Molestrangler, played by husky voiced Betty Marsden, J Peasemold Gruntfuttock and Daphne Whitethigh amongst others. Not only was this radio show very camp and hilarious it was also extremely clever and very witty. This is something we seem in short supply of today. If the top powers at the BBC at that time had realised what Jules and Sandy were really talking about the show would have been cancelled immediately.

This was a time when homosexuality was illegal and such private lives would be kept very secret, as homosexual men would face a prison sentence. Many of them did go to prison. Now there's a novel way to punish homosexuals, lock them up for months, or even years, with a lot of other men, that'll teach 'em!

Lesbianism was not, and never has been, illegal. When a Bill to prosecute lesbians was put before Queen Victoria she absolutely refused to sign it, as she would not believe such a thing could happen between women and would not allow it ever to be mentioned to her again. Mary Whitehouse, the clean up TV campaigner, who obviously was a bit more worldly-wise than the BBC (and Queen Victoria) at that time, complained about the content of *Round The Horne* with little success. There was no way the BBC was going to stop its top show.

In Polari 'camp' actually means original, outrageous, amusing, unusual, 'bona' is fabulous and wonderful like kids use 'wicked' nowadays. 'Cod' means rubbish and amateur and is used in showbiz terms to describe an act today. You can buy the Kenneth Williams and Hugh Paddick sketches from *Round The Horne* on several CDs and if you want to really have a laugh go get 'em. Just because they're old doesn't mean they're not funny! A recent BBC TV drama title *Tipping The Velvet* starring Diana Rigg's daughter, Rachael Stirling, is also Polari slang and if you watched it you would know what that means as does 'cleaning the cage out' but I think the BBC went with the right title!

My ex-dancing pupil Stephen Mear told me that when he got his first professional job as a dancer over 20 years ago in the West End in the chorus of *Evita* all the male dancers were at least 10 years older than he was and they spoke Polari in the dressing rooms. He used to sit there looking totally bewildered and they had to explain all the phrases and words to him.

One of the most popular TV shows was the variety show the *Black And White Minstrel Show* with one of the minstrels actually coming from Shepshed. *I Love Lucy* seemed to be on all the time, as did the *Dick Van Dyke Show*. The *Arthur Haynes Show* was not to be missed and *Sunday Night At The London Palladium* made massive stars of whoever compered it, such as Tommy Trinder, Bruce Forsyth, Jimmy Tarbuck and Norman Vaughan with his catch phrases 'Roses Grow on You' from his Cadbury's chocolate commercial and 'Swinging' holding up his thumb.

In 1961 the papers were full of a horrific murder, a couple had been shot in a car. The man had died but the woman had survived though she would be paralysed for the rest of her life.    This is sadly something that doesn't shock us these days, but in the 1960s murder was practically unheard of.    We still had the death penalty, and everybody was talking about it.    James Hanratty was arrested, found guilty and sentenced to hang.  The Sunday after he was executed I, at the age of 15, remember vividly Norman Vaughan walking out on stage to compere *Sunday Night At The London Palladium.*  His opening line to the audience and the many millions watching being "James Hanratty swinging" and holding his thumb up!

There were so many comedy and variety TV shows featuring variety stars such as Mike and Bernie Winters, Ken Dodd, Spike Milligan, Max Bygraves, Des O'Conner and a brilliant young impressionist Mike Yarwood.  Now pop stars were getting their own TV shows, like Cilla Black, Dusty Springfield and Tom Jones. Guest stars were the well-known comics of the day and each show always had a team of dancers.  All the top British chart stars were appearing on *Sunday Night at the London Palladium* and even great artists from America like Frank Sinatra, Bob Hope, Dean Martin, Jerry Lewis, Danny Kaye and many more previously unseen live on British TV.    *Sunday Night at the London Palladium* actually got members of the audience, usually newly weds, to take part in 'Beat the Clock', which consisted of party games for big prizes and whoever was the star compere for the show had to rush them through in time for the commercial break as this was a live show. Variety shows were a big draw both on television, and in theatres and seaside resorts; variety acts were needed and TV talent scouts toured the working men's clubs to find them.

I used to love the variety show *Seaside Special* on a Saturday night from various seaside resorts.  It had all the top stars of the day headlining and a wonderful group of dancers, Dougie Squires' Young Generation that later became known as the Second Generation.  These dancers were so different, gone were the feathers and sequins and high heels, they were young and danced in the fashions of the day and were full of energy.  Oh how I miss shows like this.

*Opportunity Knocks* had started as a radio talent show hosted by Hughie Green and now moved to television.  My friend, Karen West's Mum, Judy Reeves, a singer in the working men's clubs in Leicester, was a winner on *Opportunity Knocks* on the radio.  *Opportunity Knocks*, and later *New Faces*, made overnight stars of acts that had worked for years on the club circuit with limited success. Some of these were Freddie Star, Les Dawson, Cannon and Ball, Little and Large who, with all their experience took to this new genre like ducks to water.  They could work to children, teenagers and adults and pensioners alike and all the family loved them.  *Opportunity Knocks* was probably one of the most successful TV shows ever and along with real talent they also had the more 'unusual acts'. I remember a man playing a tune on leaves and these had to be specially flown in from Ireland on the day of the recording, a dog that said 'sausages' and Tony Holland 'The Muscle Man' who was a body builder and moved his muscles as the band played a cha-cha medley.  The TV quiz shows changed  - gone were the cheap prizes we had been used to, now you could win as much as £100 or even a washing machine, I saw a woman burst into uncontrollable sobbing when she won a tumble dryer!

*Adam Adamant* aired in 1966 and me, and my Mum would never miss this unlikely series about a Victorian gentleman being frozen alive and thawing out in the 1960s to solve crimes. Ten years later we would never miss the hugely popular *Duchess Of Duke Street* drama series based on a true story and *A Family at War* with a young John Nettles who would later on be better known as *Bergerac,* and later still from *Midsomer Murders* fame.

Morecambe and Wise came later. Their first TV series *Running Wild* being a huge flop! Eric Morecambe carried one critic's write up in his wallet to his dying day which said "The TV set, the box in which they buried Morecambe and Wise." How wrong can you be! They were TV's biggest stars ever and rightly so, I never missed their shows and neither did the rest of the country. Famous stars were pleading to appear on their shows and they did. Pubs and clubs were empty while their shows were televised. Even the Royal Family re-organised their Christmas meals so they could watch the Morecambe and Wise legendary Christmas show that, at one time, had an audience of 28 million viewers! These days the TV people rave if a show gets six million viewers and sometimes the top shows pull in eight million, that seems to be about the maximum they do get now.

*The Andy Williams Show* was very popular and was watched by all the family. This show always had top guest stars, such as Judy Garland, Sammy Davis Jnr, Tony Bennett, Ella Fitzgerald and Jerry Lewis and many others. These shows often featured a very popular group of very cute and very polite little boys called 'The Osmonds' all dressed in matching suits and bow ties, I wondered what happened to them! At that time whole families would sit down together to watch TV. No remote controls then, so there was no 'surfing' of channels. There were very few of them anyway.

Probably the most successful comedy show of all time was the *Benny Hill Show* that started in 1953. Benny Hill was on British TV for an incredible 36 years before the political correctness lot very kindly forced him off! Benny Hill was the first comic to achieve TV stardom and was now shunned by British TV but was fêted as a massive star in America and France. I saw him on French TV receiving an award and was astounded that he could speak fluent French. He died on the same day as another of our great and much missed comics, Frankie Howerd. When the legendary Greta Garbo was found dead in her New York apartment, on the floor were Benny Hill videos that apparently she watched all the while even though she 'wanted to be alone'.

*The Dick Emery* show was another national favourite TV show full of eccentric over the top characters, vicars, skin heads, and in particular, his long haired dumb blonde 'Mandy' character who would push or smack some man really hard and say very breathy like Marilyn Monroe "Oh you are awful, but I like you" and quickly walk off in her high heels! I still hear people saying this today. It is a great tribute to a great comic actor.

It was the start of the golden age of the British sitcom and comedy shows that over the next two decades gave us *On The Buses, It Aint Half Hot Mum, Are You Being Served?* (this sitcom was actually based on an idea by Joanna Lumley), *Father Dear Father, Steptoe And Son, Thicker Than Water, Rising Damp, Hancock's Half Hour, Love Thy Neighbour, Mind Your Language, The Lovers, The Rag Trade, George And The Dragon, Just Good Friends, 'Til Death Us Do Part, Sykes and A...., The Likely Lads, Bless This House, The Liver Birds, Meet The Wife, Up Pompeii, In Loving Memory, Hugh And I, Harry Worth, George And The Dragon, The Good Life, A Sharp Intake Of Breath* starring a young unknown actor by the name of David Jason, *Porridge, Open All Hours, Up Pompeii, To The Manor Born, Last Of*

103

## Dee Quemby

*The Summer Wine, Hugh And I, Please Sir, The Gaffer, Doctor In The House, All Gas And Gaiters, Terry And June, Oh No – It's Selwyn Froggitt, Monty Python's Flying Circus, Some Mothers Do 'Ave 'Em!, Butterflies, Allo Allo, Fawlty Towers, Hi-de-Hi, Man About The House, George And Mildred , Yes Minister, I Didn't Know You Cared* and *Robin's Nest*......... to name but a few!

How many sitcoms over the last few years can you list today that appealed to such a wide age group, apart from *Only Fools and Horses* with the now Sir David Jason as the legendary 'Del Boy'. Oscar winning actor Jim Broadbent was the original choice for Del Boy. However he did make a few appearances in *Only Fools and Horses* as Roy Slater, an East End gangster.

My three favourite sitcoms, though it is hard to pick favourites as they were all so good, are the wonderful *Dad's Army*, Diana Dors in *Queenie's Castle* and Hylda Baker and Jimmy Jewel as Nellie and Eli Pledge in *Nearest And Dearest* set in Pledge's Purer Pickles factory. I can remember Jimmy Jewel, the hen pecked brother, secretly smoking in the living room and using his father's urn on the mantelpiece as an ash tray and Hylda Baker dusting, picking up the urn and saying "father's putting on weight!" *The Two Ronnies* and *Minder* made an appearance and both shows went on for years. From America came the over the top soaps *Dallas* and *Dynasty* which were watched by millions worldwide with *Dynasty* giving our own fabulous glamorous everlasting Joan Collins another burst of stardom.

*The Comedians* showcased unknown comics from the working men's club circuit drawn from all over Britain. Johnny Hamp, the producer and whose idea it was, wanted as many different regional accents as he could get. A band *Shep's Banjo Boys* played the odd number during the show. *The Comedians* was revolutionary TV and had such an impact at the time. All these comics became stars 'overnight' after many long years on the working men's club circuit, holiday camps and the summer season circuit. These included Mike Reid, George Roper, Tom O'Connor, Duggie Brown brother of Lynn Perrie, Bernard Manning, Frank Carson, Colin Crompton, Charley Williams, Ken Goodwin and Stan Boardman to name but a few and I am proud to say I have been the support act to two of them. At that time I could never have imagined that one day I would appear on Granada TV's *The Comedians,* the second woman to ever appear on the show, the first being Pauline Daniels.

One of the 'spin-off' TV shows from *The Comedians* was *The Wheeltappers And Shunters Social Club* with Colin Crompton as chairman. A young Liz Dawn, later on to be 'Vera Duckworth' in *Coronation Street* appeared weekly as a barmaid. Another one of these shows was the *Star and Garter*, a fictional pub in London. Both shows featured working men's club acts. I remember seeing a male singer on stage in *The Wheeltappers And Shunters Social Club* TV show being heckled by a man in the audience who did no more than get up on the stage with him. We all held our breath but it turned out to be a double act Little and Large who went on to have one of the most successful shows ever on Saturday night television. Apparently this is how this duo got together in the first place! Other successful acts from the TV talent shows were getting their own Saturday night shows like Cannon and Ball and Les Dawson and were watched by millions.

The Beatles' ever growing popularity saw them make their first film. Twiggy sang and danced in the film musical *The Boyfriend* and Cockney ex-sailor Tommy Steele crossed the Atlantic to star in two American block buster musicals *The Happiest Millionaire* with Fred MacMurray, Greer Garson and Gladys Cooper and *Finian's Rainbow*, with Fred Astaire and our own Petula Clark. Tommy Steele had made a few musical films beforehand in England with great success especially *Tommy The Toredor* accompanied by a chart hit single *Little White Bull*.

More quiz shows were coming on TV, in particular *The Golden Shot* with Bernie the Bolt.  Critics at the time said the third word of *The Golden Shot* had the wrong vowel in it!  Bob Monkhouse took over from the male Canadian compere Jackie Rae.  Bob had a giggly blonde, Anne Aston, as his assistant who couldn't add up.  But the viewing figures did!  With Bob at the helm they went from two million to 16 million viewers and the show ran for many years.  Bob Monkhouse hosted so many successful quiz shows among them my favourite *Celebrity Squares* that he became known as the Quiz Master King of TV.  Larry Grayson took over the *Generation Game* from Bruce Forsyth and had Isla Blair as his 'sidekick'.   So successful was he that he had over 18 million viewers.  Whenever I see excerpts of Larry Grayson in this show the tears roll down my face.  Why oh why do we have no one like him today?  A true genius!

One of the worst quiz shows for me was Ted Rogers in *3-2-1* asking cryptic questions that nobody understood and this made a star of the rubbishy 'dusty bin'.  The trouble being we still watched it!  Rumour has it that this show might be coming back on TV -  **Ahhhhhhhhhhhhh**!

In the 1960s with the ever growing popularity of the pirate radio ships, the BBC decided to fight back and BBC Radio Leicester opened, the first regional radio station in this country.  The presenters became big names.  They opened shops, were guests of honour at galas and other events, judged local talent shows and even appeared in local professional pantos.  Once again listening to these first broadcasts little did I know that in January 2004 I would have my own BBC Radio Leicester three hour live 'phone-in show and a weekly 'soap watch' with the popular radio presenter John Florance.

One of the 1960s comperes of *Sunday Night At The London Palladium* was the 'fifth Beatle', as he was known, Jimmy Tarbuck, a cheeky, young Liverpudlian comic who through this show became a massive star.  Every top showbiz name from here and America appeared on this show and on the famous revolving stage at the end.  This has recently been removed from the theatre.  Jimmy Tarbuck had actually been support act to the Beatles on their early tours and with his hairstyle being the same, this had resulted in him being called the 'fifth Beatle'.

I will never forget the night Jimmy Tarbuck was compering a television show in 1984 in which Tommy Cooper was appearing.  Tommy Cooper was wearing his trademark red fez and a massive kaftan.  The curtains were drawn behind him and he was producing all sorts of things from his kaftan; a stagehand behind the curtain was so obviously sliding them through, when suddenly he sank gracefully down on the floor; all you could see was his fez.  People in the audience were laughing hysterically, the front curtains came down, and Jimmy Tarbuck came out looking very flustered.  We went straight into a commercial break.  I said to my Mum; "Something's wrong, I think Tommy Cooper has just died" and he had.

What a way for a performer to go!  Ironically the show was called *Live From Her Majesty's*.  *Her Majesty's Theatre* in London is one of the few theatres that changes its' name from time to time.  If we have a King on the throne it will become His Majesty's Theatre.  The whole country went into mourning for Tommy Cooper as they would later on for Eric Morecambe and Les Dawson.   No such comics have ever been loved by the public like these were and never wIll be again. An end of an era!

Most of my best times and memories were probably during the 1960s. There never has and probably never will be a more exciting, fun filled and life changing decade like the swinging sixties ever again!

*England swings...........................................................!*

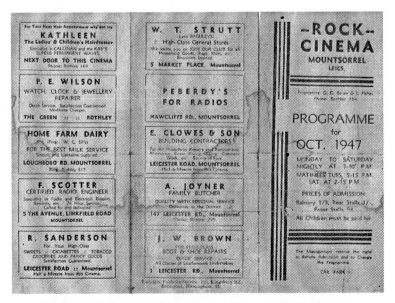

1947 Rock Cinema programme (courtesy of Noel Wakeling)

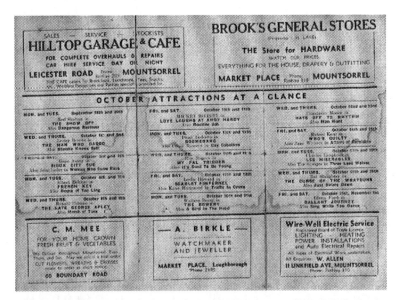

Films showing at the Rock Cinema 1947 (courtesy of Noel Wakeling)

Demolishing the Rock Cinema (courtesy Brian Johnson)

The Rock Cinema as engineering works in 1991 (courtesy of Brian Johnson)

# CHAPTER 5

## STEPPING OUT!

WHEN I went into full-time employment at the age of 16 for the princely sum of £3.8s.0d a week on 25 April 1962, little did I realise how it would change my life! It was as a trainee Dictaphone typist at Herbert Morris, a well-known Loughborough crane company where my father had worked for many years in the Time and Motion Department.

I took to Joan Neal who was in charge of the typing pool at once, as she looked so much like my childhood 'idol' the ballerina Moira Shearer. She was fabulous looking, very tall and slim and so elegant with long dancer's legs. Joan always wore tight dresses with a belt, high heels, red lipstick and red nail varnish, with her red hair piled up in a bun. A lace hanky would always be tucked into her belt. She also loved her big chunky plastic earrings and had boxes of them at home. But she was often one short at work! When she answered one of the many phones in the typing pool, she would take off an earring as otherwise she couldn't get the phone to her ear! She could never remember to put it back on again after the call ended; so we girls used to spend a lot of time trying to find the missing earring for her! Born Joan Jarram, she had been a student teacher at the Kathleen Freeman School of Dancing from the time when I was two years old. She was also principal girl in some of the early pantomimes I was involved in.

By the time I met Joan again at Herbert Morris, she was married to Derek Neal and was 30 years old. She immediately recognised my name from my 'Sunbeam' days at the Kathleen Freeman School of Dancing and the Poole Academy. Joan had just opened her own dancing school in a factory unit down Meadow Lane in Loughborough and was moving her few pupils to new premises in Bedford Square. I wanted to finish off my dancing exams and Joan helped me to not only pass these, but my teaching exams too. We also took our Fellowship exam together and from the age of 17 I started teaching at the Neal Academy of Dancing.

Joan certainly looked the part of a ballerina and, as a teenager, had gone with her mum as chaperone to audition for Margaret Kelly (Miss Bluebell) for the famous Bluebell dancing troupe in Paris. Margaret Kelly later in life worked with the dancers at Bally's Casino in Las Vegas and the male dancers there are still known as *The Kelly Boys*. Joan actually passed the audition, but perhaps it was just as well that she never took it up for Joan was absolutely terrified of birds and feathers and the Bluebell girls wore these all the time. Many years later when the dancing school put on *Mother Goose* because of Joan's fear of feathers we had the goose costume made out of lace and it looked pretty good on stage I must say; but even so Joan kept well away from the 'goose'.

Joan and I would finish work at 5pm. We would call in to see Joan's parents, Doll and Harry, for a quick cup of tea, then walk past the Bell Foundry up to the bus station, where The Rushes Retail Centre is now, and through to the dancing school. I would walk through first shooing off all the pigeons, so Joan could pass quickly through. We then moved to The Volunteers where we had a room above the pub. I would catch the bus into Loughborough on a Saturday morning, go to The Volunteers and pick up Joan's shopping list. Then I'd fetch cakes from Simpkins and James and go up Church Gate where Kath and Arthur (Beane and Hull) had their ballroom dancing studio. Joan and Derek went there for ballroom classes and I went too on Saturdays to pay Kath Joan's club book money, then I would finish off the rest of the grocery shopping.

I would get back in time for the beginners class to help Joan with the new pupils. One Christmas I got to The Volunteers and Joan was standing outside looking very pale and distressed. She hysterically said: "I can't go in - go and look!" Inside there was a massive plucked turkey slung over the banister. It was unwrapped with its head and feet clearly visible. I went into the bar and asked the landlord if he could move it. He told me that it was first prize in the pub's Christmas raffle and, as it had not been won by one of his regulars, it must belong to one of the mothers from the dancing school. He moved the turkey and we all went upstairs and all the mums looked at their raffle tickets. Guess who had won it? That's right it was Joan! I had to sling the very heavy turkey over my shoulder, walk through the town and take it down to Joan's parents, Doll and Harry who laughed like 'drains' as we say in Leicestershire, as I staggered into their front room! Hopefully that was the first and last time I get the bird!

Exams were held in Derby at the AAD, Association of American Dancing Headquarters in Friar Gate. We would hire a bus for all the pupils. The mums would wait in Friar Gate until all the exams were over, then we'd ride back to Loughborough with a stop at the Navigation pub that was in one of the neighbouring villages All the children and the mums used to look forward to this day out.

Very few dancing schools had their own premises in those days, not many people were happy hiring out rooms where young children were concerned and so when you had worn out your welcome you had to do the rounds to find another place to teach in which we often had to do. When I first started dancing with Joan, she had a room above a printer's office in a lovely old oak beamed building on the corner of Victoria Street and Bedford Square. Now sadly demolished, a concrete block of flats has been built on the site. We then had rooms in a succession of pubs among them The Volunteers, now 'Showboat' and 'The Golden Fleece', where a ladies clothes shop QS now stands.

In desperation, in between premises, we even taught in the tiny front room of a terraced house that belonged to a relative of a pupil's mother for quite a while! With each new premise we would also have to find a piano. There would be many people wanting to get rid of them as in the 40s and 50s every front room would have one for a family get together sing song and this was fast dying out in the 1960s.

We then had our own premises in South Street that is now part of a furniture shop. We used to hire the NALGO building at the Council just up the road every Saturday morning as we now couldn't fit all our ever growing amount of pupils in this one up and one down small roomed building with an outside toilet. Pupils of all ages would run from one building to the other in leotards and often wearing tap shoes watched by bemused Saturday morning shoppers.

The best would be when the November Fair was held as our little street would be home to the donkey rides for three days and nights, and would not be cleaned until the fair had left. When opening the door children would often be followed in by a donkey. Have you ever tried to push a donkey backwards out of a door? And needless to say most pupils and mums had managed to tread in something 'nasty' that they walked in and out all day!

We then moved to the large classrooms at the back of the United Reformed Church in Loughborough where we still are to this day and we also have schools in Mountsorrel and Shepshed where we hold general lessons and United Teachers of Dance examination classes.

In 1963 Herbert Morris Apprentice Association asked Joan if she would produce a panto for them. She held auditions for the parts in *Cinderella*. I went to audition for the title role and, as nobody else turned up to audition, I got it! Another girl from Herbert Morris Jennifer Geary, also a dancing pupil, was Dandini. Dancing school pupil Angela Basford was the Fairy Godmother and, as with all amateur productions, being short of men to take part, her mother, Mrs Basford, played Baron Hardup! Audrey Riddle, who also worked at Herbert Morris, was to play Prince Charming but had to drop out, as she was pregnant and had been advised to rest and was replaced by a fellow dance pupil Diane Tuer. Two apprentices Mick Winterton, many years later to become a popular local policeman in Loughborough, and David Wooley played Snatch and Grab, the brokers' men. Danny Shaw, another Herbert Morris apprentice, and Eric Giles played the ugly sisters. A lady living in Mountsorrel, Joan Adams made my *Cinderella* 'rags', fabulous ball-gown and finale wedding-gown. At that time we only had three troupes of dancing pupils - Neal Babes, Neal Juniors and Neal Seniors, totalling about 26 pupils in all. Our accompanist for the show was Mrs Irene Harrie-Cornish.

In January 1964 Joan's production of *Cinderella* ran for three performances at Loughborough Town Hall. Joe Pepper from Herbert Morris was the stage manager and Harry Gosling was in charge of the lighting. Cinderella's coach was hired from Emile Littler, the impresario from Birmingham, and a local man provided two Shetland ponies that often 'ad-libbed' on stage! Luckily I had a big fan that I would wave frantically as the curtains closed for the interval. The ponies' owner would rush onto the stage with a spade and bucket and shovel it up to take home for his rhubarb. Needs must, in those days! Apparently the ponies loved chocolate, but it didn't like them. He would give them a little bit to keep them happy, but rumour had it that one of the apprentices would give them a bar each just before their appearance!

The man, who was to play Buttons, dropped out just before the panto was to open. His wife, Bettine, Audrey's sister, knew the part as she had helped him learn his lines. She stepped in as no one else had the time to learn this big part at such short notice.  I realised then that I would rather have done that part than *Cinderella*, but it really was a man's part.

My parents did not have a car and so, I caught the bus into Loughborough to appear in the shows at the Town Hall.  On the last night somebody kindly took my costumes home for me. I caught the last bus home clutching what I could carry, plus two massive bouquets!  In those days, all the men in the show would get a 'bouquet' as well.  These would be specially made at the florists and would contain carrots, Brussel sprouts, parsnips and other vegetables, and were a real work of art.

The following year, however, we were going to do *Aladdin* and I auditioned for and got the part of Wishee Washee.   It was to be a turning point in my life, although I wasn't to know it at the time.    Something technical went wrong at one of the performances and there was a big pause.  I instinctively walked forward to the audience and told a joke - the laughter that came back was one of my greatest moments and it was there and then that I realised I had to do comedy.

Joan's friend June Davidson, who also worked in the typing pool and made a lot of her dresses, took on making panto costumes and we are still in touch today. We went on to produce *Dick Whittington* the following year for the Apprentice Association with other apprentices such as Geoff Sewell, later to become a popular local football referee, taking part.

At one of the shows the lights failed and I went down in the auditorium to the front of the audience with another girl, Maureen Adams, who held a huge torch on me to pick my face out in the dark.  I entertained the waiting audience with a few jokes while the Town Hall electrician sorted the lights out, a job that took him a good fifteen minutes or so.   Well you do what you have to, as every performer knows the show must go on!

In 1967 Joan produced *Cinderella* at Loughborough Town Hall again for Herbert Morris' Apprentice Association, but this time I was playing Buttons. We had two young brothers Martyn and David Wilson playing the broker's men, 'Snatch and Grab'.   David would be 17 years old at the time and is better known today as Loughborough-born actor David Neilson who plays 'Roy Cropper' in *Coronation Street*.  David's brother Martyn produced the programme and I did a comic tango with Martyn in the panto.  For this show, we had the Ray Allen Band led by Ken Wright.  I performed a song and dance number at the end, *Second Hand Rose,* with all the men behind me, including David, resplendent with top hats and canes.   I was black and blue at the end of the week from being poked with the canes during this number!

The school was getting many pupils now and, as with all dancing school shows, the more pupils you have the more tickets you sell.  Every pupil's mum will round up relatives and friends to come, willing or not, to see her 'little star' perform, even if he or she is only making the shortest of appearances. Professional pantos in the 1950s and 60s would always visit local dancing schools to pick juveniles to dance in their show as they knew that this would guarantee 'more bums on seats' from tickets sales by proud mums and the panto company did not have to 'paper the house'. This is a show business term that means to hand out free tickets to try to compensate for poor sales.

We entered troupes for the new series of *Hughie Green's Says Opportunity Knocks.* The Neal Seniors passed and appeared doing a dance routine as cowboys to *There's A Coach Coming In.* Later on the junior tap troupe, the 'Little Ten', also appeared dancing a routine to: *When The Saints Go Marching In.* I appeared later on the same show as a comedian, which I'll let you know about later.

My junior Tuesday night troupe was asked to appear on Yorkshire TV's very popular show *Junior Showtime*, as we had been recommended by the *Opportunity Knocks* production team. We travelled to Leeds on a coach, staying overnight in a bed and breakfast and then filmed in the studios the next day. This show regularly featured a young girl dancer with a squeaky voice and long ringlets, Bonny Langford. Every dance routine she did on that show would finish with the splits, I wonder what happened to her?

Joan now decided to produce her own pantos and we were now putting on our annual panto at Stanford Hall for two weeks with many shows sold out. We had no taped music in those days, so it all had to be live. Mrs Cornish had been our pianist and now we had a new pianist, Mrs Childs or 'Aunty Lil', as we all called her. When she played the piano her top set of false teeth would keep dropping down without her knowing, but we never dared to laugh. At an exam rehearsal, in between pianos, she brought a plastic toy trumpet and played every child's exam music on it. She always wore a belted rainmac and hat and I often think of her when I see Dot Cotton in *EastEnders,* as there was a big similarity in looks.

Auntie Lil hated shows running over time even by a few minutes as she was always in a hurry to get home. We would always know if the show was running late, as Aunty Lil would play all the music a lot quicker. Pupils dreaded dancing in the last troupe of the show, as the music would be so fast you could almost see sparks coming off their tap shoes! Then at the finale, as we all stood to attention on stage, we would see her in the orchestra pit standing up playing the National Anthem on the piano with one hand while putting her other arm in her coat ready to go home. Her false teeth would be clattering away and she never ever took off her hat and scarf throughout any of the performances. At that time the National Anthem was always played at the end of all films and shows in theatres.

Stan Boneham was our next pianist. When we moved to Stanford Hall to put on the shows he would play the organ there. This would rise mechanically and majestically out of the orchestra pit. I often sat with him at the organ as it did this! I loved it! Uncle Stan, as we called him, would hold up my cue cards in the orchestra pit for my 15 minute spot at the end of the shows, but he often got them in the wrong order! Later on, he and Aunty Lil would play piano and organ together for the dancing school shows at Stanford Hall. He recalls me saying from the stage: "Aunty Lil and Uncle Stan, they're not married, they're just good friends" and Aunty Lil being miffed; apparently this was quite suggestive then. Haven't times changed!

As the school was getting so big, the professional scripts we were using for the pantos didn't have many opportunities to put in the many dance troupes we now had. Joan asked me to write the script for *Cinderella* for the dancing school to put on. This I did and it was one of my proudest moments to see my script produced on stage and giving me credit for writing it in the programme. I went on to write many more for the dancing school and then later on for my own professional touring panto and I have given permission for many of these scripts to be used by other societies.

Joan now decided to do an annual *September Show* just for the dancing pupils. She said they didn't get a chance to do a lot in the pantos and this would be their show. She was also going to let examination pupils perform their medal winning solos and duets.    The first was put on at Loughborough Town Hall. Joan and I did a solo tap number each for the finale, the difference being that I wore tap shoes and Joan had tap plates put on to her stilettos! I was now also doing a 15-minute comedy spot in each *September Show* and appearing in local charity events. The pantos were gaining in popularity and Joan now started to take part herself as principal boy and what a wonderful principal boy she made with those long legs.

I now had a men's tap troupe, this was made up of dads and friends and men who took part in the pantos and really started as a bit of fun.   Keith Hassall, one of the dads had a TA meeting on a Monday night before the tap lesson and he used to rush in and dance in his uniform and army boots!

I always dressed them as 'ladies'. They did the Can-Can, a dance as French 'tarts' in black split straight skirts, stockings and suspenders, striped tops, blonde wigs and berets and who will ever forget the 'Brownies' and many more such 'numbers'.   These routines proved very popular in the local charity galas, the men's troupe always being the highlight of the September shows.  The men got really good at tap but the hardest thing I found was teaching men how to skip, they just found that so difficult!    The men even took a couple of tap exams with all of them passing.   At the exams the examiner asked them about their lessons and they said they spent an hour at the bar beforehand.  She was very impressed; she thought they meant a ballet barre!

There were so many families taking part with mums and dads dancing and playing panto roles, or helping backstage and front of house.  Some of the many family names I remember are Shand, Pierrepoint (yes they were related to Britain's last hangman), Varney, Adams, Green, Ballard, Bond, Bull, Mear, Manners, Parker, Smith, Tolley, Alldread, Mullis, Edwards, Buhler, Bettoney, Salmon, Sharpe, Davis, Taylor, Farrer, Baddeley, Davie, Thornton, Brown, Rose, Stephenson, Pawlyn, Gent, Gartshore, Evans, Orton, Alldread, Makin, Hawksworth, Newton and Hassall.   Some are still with us today bringing their grandchildren. If I have missed anyone out I do apologise but there were so many.

We still have one of the original mums from the early days of the Neal Academy of Dancing still helping at the shows, along with her friend Nadine!  I remember going to Joan's dancing school for the first time and seeing this very pregnant well spoken elegant lady dressed in a fur coat and diamante earrings. Her name was Joan Shand and her young daughter, Vicky, was a pupil.  Due to a shortage of adults for parts, Vicky at the age of 12 played a very mature and elegant Dandini in our 1967 production of *Cinderella*.  Later on Joan's other daughter Karen and the new baby Tracey, would all become dancing pupils and so would Karen's son, Sean many years later.  Joan is in her 80s and loves coming to help with the refreshments at the interval of the dancing school shows that are now held at Loughborough University.   Vicky now lives and works in Florida and we are still in touch.

One of the dads, Mick Green, said to me that since joining the dancing school, when he and his wife went into town on a Saturday morning to do their shopping they couldn't believe how many people said "hello" to them.

Joan died in the Leicester Royal Hospital at the age of 68 years.  It all happened so suddenly; we were so close to our September Show.  Paula Wood, another teacher, and myself decided that we would carry on as the Neal Academy of Dancing with Paula as principal and myself as secretary.  Most parents thought that we would have to cancel the show but that wouldn't have been what Joan would have wanted. Just before she died I said to Joan "Don't worry I won't let you down" and she said "You never have", that was the last thing she said to me, and the best that she ever could have.

We all pulled together and the show went on. At Joan's funeral it was so comforting to see so many past and present pupils and parents at the service, the church being packed. As Joan had no family, Paula had the heartbreaking task of arranging the funeral and I was asked to say a Eulogy. There was so much to say and I could see the Vicar keep looking at his watch but it all went so well and it was a 'finale' Joan would have been proud of. I placed in her coffin a pair of pink satin ballet shoes.

Even after Joan's sad death, the Neal Academy of Dance has remained a very important part of my life – and still is today. Time goes by so quickly, it's almost unbelievable to think that I have now been involved as pupil and teacher for 45 years! At its height I was teaching there four nights a week, rushing straight from work, and Saturdays. Whilst today it is an integral part of my routine on a Tuesday night and Saturday mornings. In addition I take classes at the Memorial Hall in Mountsorrel on Fridays. Paula Wood the Principal is also involved on Tuesday and Saturday as well as taking classes at Vine House in Shepshed on a Monday evening. Helen Farrer, our other teacher, takes classes at our Loughborough headquarters. We have just had a teacher 'retire'. Katie has just had her third child and has also taken over the running of the Waterside Inn and restaurant in Mountsorrel, and unfortunately won't have time to teach as well! Her mum, ex-dancer and at one time half a cow in a panto, Sonia, has also 'retired' from being involved with the sound system for the shows. Paula, Katie and Helen, as children, were all pupils in my classes many years ago. Oh yer razzer (as we say in Leicester), that makes me feel even older!

Joan's rule for her school was that each and every pupil regardless of ability, shape or size would appear in the shows, and this tradition we keep to this day. In the past I have had girls from some other dancing schools that have never set foot on a stage having been a pupil there for years. They were told they weren't good enough and only the best dancers could perform in shows, even though they were capable enough dancers for an amateur show. I have been at a dancing school where diet sheets were handed out to larger girls with strict instructions to follow, otherwise they wouldn't be appearing in future shows.

Joan also started a dance troupe for older ladies and mums, and even a few grandmas, who wanted to learn to dance and this troupe still appears in our annual shows and is affectionately known as 'the big girls troupe'. One of the dancers from this troupe, Sandra Hall, also sang in St Botolph's church choir and kindly gave her time to come and sing at my Mum's funeral.

Nobody is expecting a West End performance at an amateur show. For a start, West End shows cost millions of pounds to put on and employ the best professional artistes and technicians available worldwide. So long as everybody taking part in an amateur production gives it their best shot, along with 100% enthusiasm, a show can be as enjoyable, and on the odd occasion sometimes more so, than a top professional show.

We have been based at the United Reformed Church in Frederick Street for the last decade or so and, yes, we still perform the annual *September Show*, just as Joan would have liked. As soon as the panto has ended in January we get on with the show that has, for the last few years, taken place at the Sir Robert Martin Hall Theatre at Loughborough University, having previously been at the very atmospheric, but slightly off-the-beaten-track Stanford Hall. In other words it's way out in the country!

Joan's idea as previously mentioned was that, as the opportunities for children in the panto were limited, the *September Show* was the show for all the pupils to showcase their talents and all the dancing school pupils would take part. We usually have a theme such as 'Around the World' for the first half; with a selection of numbers from the many West End and Broadway shows and film musicals for the second half.

Even after being involved for such a lengthy time, there's a great atmosphere and excitement about the shows. The children perform Thursday and Friday and then twice more on the Saturday with the younger children swopping over every other show.  It's impossible not to get excited for them. They love the make up and costumes and stand transfixed at their reflection in front of the mirror in the changing room, completely oblivious to anything else going on around them.  Of course standing at the side of the stage to make their entrance, not being used to wearing make up, there is a lot of rubbing of eyes and mouths and many end up coming out looking like 'Coco' the clown!

Everybody wants to see the 'little ones' strut their stuff on stage.  Nobody wants to see them come out on stage and perform perfectly, and these juveniles never let you down!  In one 'tinies' ballet dance, a little girl of three years wouldn't go out on stage.  Her dad and grandparents were seated proudly in the audience! I pushed her out and she stood for the whole of the dance motionless with her head down and sucking her thumb at the back of the stage.  The audience were laughing throughout the whole routine.  As the others skipped off she walked off after them, head down and thumb still in her mouth.  Another three-year old one year decided to walk to the front of the stage and stand there for the entirety of the routine picking her nose as the other fairies danced behind her! Children always fidget at the side of the stage and one little girl had taken off her 'pillbox' hat that had a piece of material hanging down at the back of the hat. She rammed it back on as she was skipping out and danced with the hat on the wrong way round unable to see, completely nonplussed.  I remember years ago a three year old whilst dancing, stopping, turning round and looking curiously at the backcloth.  After a few seconds, she did no more than walk upstage, pick the backcloth scenery up and peep underneath to see what was there while the other children were still dancing.  We have even had a punch up between two tiny 'fairies!  Pure magic and well worth all the hard work!

Naturally, we couldn't do anything without the volunteer helpers; there's Paula's husband, Paul selling tickets, many mums and dads helping with the shows. Joan Shand, with Nadine, serving the refreshments.  Alan and Robert looking after the music and sound equipment, Steve and Irene Farrer, Barbara Thompson and the Buhlers, Connie and Brian with their daughters Helen and Claire, who help around the kitchen at the dancing school in raising much-needed money for the huge costs involved in running the school, essential equipment and the ever increasing costs of putting on shows.

The Buhlers have a long history with us as Connie and daughters used to dance, with Brian taking an acting part in the pantos and then moving on to stage manager.  Their son Robert is now our panto 'dame', and Claire and Helen also take parts.  In addition their grandson, Helen's son, Elliott Wysall got down to the last four boys in a bid to become Billy Elliot in the London musical of the same name and he, like his Uncle Robert, also plays leading parts in local amateur operatic societies of which there are several in Loughborough.

115

Robert was a sensation locally as Melvin P Thorpe in *The Best Little Whorehouse* and as the Major General in a wonderful production of *The Pirates of Penzance,* as was nephew Elliott as the Artful Dodger in *Oliver,* all at Loughborough Town Hall.  Where oh where were those film and TV talent scouts that used to look for talented performers in such shows many years ago.  Both of them would have been put under contract immediately back then, as indeed would some of the other excellent players in the casts.  Now if they went on a TV reality show................!

Dancing classes are still very popular, particularly since *Pop Idol*, the popular TV talent show, emphasised that to be successful you need to be able to move as well as sing and of course the wonderful *Strictly Come Dancing* that many TV critics predicted would be a huge flop!  Even so we have never got over the taboo of it being something for boys to do. There are literally only two or three boys in the school today.  What a shame and what a misunderstanding to think somehow that dancing isn't for them.  A lot of football clubs nowadays use ballet as an excellent way of strengthening leg muscles.

John and I recently went to see the musical *Footloose* in London that was full of young men who danced brilliantly and very energetically for nearly the whole of the show.  John is a huge sports fan and has played cricket and football all his life.  As we came out of the show he said: "If this show had been a football match, all the players would have wanted to be substituted at half-time.  They wouldn't have had the stamina to complete the second half!"  Get dancing lads!  Women love a man who can dance - believe me.

We hold classes for tap, ballet, modern, cabaret, song and dance, lyrical and gymnastics to exam level, but we do our absolute best to incorporate modern methods of dance and music into our classes. We haven't quite managed a break dancing class yet, but who knows what might be around the corner.  I can assure you it won't be me taking that class!

Political correctness, of course, rears its head everywhere nowadays and the dancing school has had to adapt to all of this.  For example, adults taking photographs of the children have to get the permission of every pupil's parents in the picture beforehand and sadly we have had to stop videoing the shows for the parents to buy copies as a keepsake for their children.  Looking through all the photos and many mementos my Mum had saved for me before the PC days, I have some wonderful memories that today's children will never have to look back at.

We now have endless forms to fill in to get permission for our school-age pupils so they can dance for a few minutes on an amateur stage to raise money for local charities.   There are so many in fact, that it is putting a lot of amateur theatrical societies off from using school-age children in their productions.  Once again the good kids are losing out.  You don't have to fill in forms for permission to be a hooligan or a vandal!

It is such a shame these days that most children aren't really 'allowed' a childhood with modern life today.  Their world is crammed full of computer games, DVDs, mobile phones and I-pods.  As a teacher I find that, in a lot of cases, this has led to a loss of confidence in their own human-abilities, and they have very little or even no imagination at all, how sad!

Having said that, I am proud to say that I have had quite a few pupils go on from the dancing school and develop what they have learnt.  Former pupils

Jeanette Davis, now Patrick, and Carl Edwards are well-known choreographers in local amateur operatic societies. And of course many ex-pupils are to be seen strutting their stuff in the chorus lines of these shows. It's always great to see them again and to have a natter with them afterwards.

Over the years hundreds of pupils and mums have come and gone and many times a woman will come up to me in the street and say I taught her dancing when she was little and how much she enjoyed it. It is always nice to hear this and I am always surprised that they can still recognise me!

I do hope Joan looks down on us, and similes. Hopefully she is happy how her school is carrying on with the traditions and standards that she left us with. Joan's life was dancing and dancing was her life.

*Dance ballerina dance.................................................!*

As *Cinderella* in 1964 at Loughborough Town Hall

In finalė ball gown for Cinderella

David Wooley and Mick Winterton as 'Snatch' and 'Grab' in *Cinderella* 1964

Danny Shaw as ugly sister 'Gloria' in *Cinderella* 1964

*Dee Quemby*

With Angela Basford, Howard and Paul Ferrier and those dear little ponies!

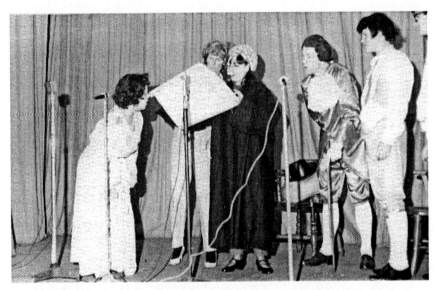

As Buttons in *Cinderella* 1967 (David (Neilson) Wilson on the right)

Finalė of *Cinderella*, Joan Neal and Lesley Pierrepoint centre, Vicky Shand on right, David (Wilson) Neilson third back on right and me on front left

Neal Academy panto cast for *Mother Goose* at Stanford Hall

Neal Academy cast of *Jack & The Beanstalk* at Stanford Hall 1977

With the ugly sisters in *Cinderella*

Oh no it isn't!

The Neal Academy on Parade at De Montfort Hall, Leicester

Joan Neal as Prince Charming 1967

Two of the Can Can ' girls'

Those French 'tarts'!

Neal Academy panto cast for another version of *Cinderella*

At Stanford Hall in Dick Whittington Tommy the cat, me and Paula Wood

# CHAPTER 6

## FROM BROADWAY TO BROADWAY!

SOMETIMES you get a pupil who has that extra special something and, in my case, it was a young boy called Stephen Mear. I first came across Stephen when he was three years old. He was running about in our small and very old building in South Street, Loughborough, the then home of the dancing school. He wasn't even there to dance. He had come with his mother Fay, who helped out with the beginners' class on a Saturday morning and who also danced in one of the adult troupes in the shows. His older cousin Fay Simmons was already a pupil and his two sisters Diane and Joyce came for lessons later on.

Fay, Stephen's mum (or 'big Fay' as we called her because of Stephen's cousin) had a brother, Phil who sang on the Leicester club circuit. She used to keep going on and on at me to do a shop window in Leicester as a comic as she had great faith in my abilities, but I never had the confidence to give it a go professionally at that time.

I was so pleased when Stephen asked if he could dance as we rarely had any boys in the classes. In the early 1960s in the Midlands there was a lot of opposition to a boy wanting to take dance classes but Stephen had the full support of Fay and Albert, his mum and dad. The general feeling at that time was that it wasn't a 'manly' thing to do exactly like in the film and hugely successful West End show *Billy Elliot – The Musical*. Stephen's dad, Albert, worked with my father at Herbert Morris for many years long before I ever got to know Stephen and the rest of his family.

The girls wore blue leotards at lessons and Stephen was quite put out, as he wanted a dancing school uniform too. Fay had a cat suit with flared trousers made in blue that Stephen used to wear with a white shirt and bow tie, quite a little dapper at three years of age. He always stood so upright and proud in class. He recently told me that he was that wrapped up in his dancing that he insisted on going to junior school wearing his cat suit and bow tie. Of course he came in for quite a lot of stick from the other children at school but he didn't care because his outfit meant that he was a dancer!  The fact that Stephen was the only boy in the class never bothered him and it's that kind of attitude and determination you need to succeed. Too many people are afraid to give things a go because of what other people think.

Goodness knows how Stephen even came to be such a good dancer considering the dancing premises we had at the time.  18 South Street consisted of a very old dilapidated tiny building, one room down and one room up and an outside toilet.  The floor downstairs was an uneven concrete one with very old lino over it that was breaking up. As Stephen danced I would pick up the larger pieces of lino and place them in front of where he would be dancing next.  We still laugh about it today and, yes, he also helped me push the donkeys out of the downstairs room every November.

When Stephen was young we did a duet together. I would be in my 20s. We had black tail suits made, bow ties, top hats and canes and tap danced to *Stepping Out* which we performed at charity shows, always making his mother Fay cry. The first time I saw her do this I thought we must have been terrible, but she reassured me that she always sobbed when she was happy!

During the many power strikes in the 1970s, we taught by candlelight; the strikes weren't going to keep us from dancing classes that's how keen we were. It was a good job, however, that we had white tap shoes as all you could see in the dark was the flame of the candle and the tap shoes.  Health and Safety would be horrified today!

Stephen passed all his exams with flying colours and at the age of 15 he received the second highest mark for his disco style modern dance sequence in the whole of the American Association throughout the country and this resulted in us both winning trophies.   The same year he also took first prize in the Carnival talent show at Shepshed.

Any chance Stephen could get to dance he would take. He would often do cabaret numbers at the Mediaeval Banquet Hall down Meadow Lane where best selling 'Adrian Mole' Leicester authoress Sue Townsend was often a diner.  She took a great interest in Stephen.   Stephen left school and went to work first of all at the Spa shop at Shelthorpe and then at Mansfield Hosiery Mills offices in Loughborough.  On a Tuesday night he would cycle up to the offices where I worked in the Town Hall passage, pick up the dancing school key and go and open up ready for me to take my classes.

Stephen never missed any of his examination classes with me even if he was really poorly and he passed all his dance exams with top results.  Not only did he want to dance he had the passion for it and he was now dancing in several troupes taken by myself, and Joan Neal, appearing in our annual shows.

Stephen was at the Neal Academy of Dancing until he was 16 years old. He grew up amazingly in a house on a street just named 'Broadway' on the Shelthorpe Council estate in Loughborough.  I could never have imagined then, however talented he appeared, that he would ever be lucky enough to make it all the way to the more famous American Broadway or The Great White Way as it is better known!  It's almost like the plot of one of those old Mickey Rooney, Judy Garland films – pure Hollywood fantasy!

At the dancing school I loved having a lot of children tap dancing all over the stage in big show numbers and loved doing 'quirky' numbers.  At that time children at dancing schools performed on stage in tutus and pretty dresses. I choreographed numbers like the 'Frog Ballet'. I danced with the children and we had green tights, green long sleeve 'all-in-ones', green net tutus, I had a hood with those metal eyes on springs sewn on and flippers, long before the Olivier award winning musical *Honk!*

For another number, we had old ripped raincoats with paint thrown all over them, fishnet tights over faces, bright coloured wigs and old boots! I also did a number with dresses made out of black bin liners, red and green net underskirts and wigs streaked with red paint, needless to say the children loved dressing up in these outfits far more than the pretty ones! These would be quite controversial outfits in their day.

As a young teacher I found the then modern dancing boring; it was performed to show numbers and was more like cabaret, whereas we now had *Top of the Pops* on television with *Pans People* and *Hot Gossip* and I wanted to do this new style of dancing. So I started a modern/disco troupe, that grew so big, I had to split the pupils into three different classes. I mentioned these classes to the examiner at the next exam session, and she said put them in for a medal and I'll mark it. This I did and so the disco medals began in earnest and the children loved dancing to the chart music.

Stephen also has a love of big numbers and tap dancing. At the London studio, as he was so good at tap and they didn't have many teachers who taught this, he started to take tap classes for them. To this day Stephen still teaches whenever his busy schedule allows and regularly puts together workshops for the students at Millennium Dance.

Whilst training at the London Studio, Stephen danced in clubs around London with a couple of girls for experience and extra money. He also danced in cabaret with Wayne Sleep. Stephen's first professional booking on leaving the Studio was dancing in the chorus of *Aladdin* in Gravesend with the then Dr Who Peter Davison. Also appearing was his then wife Sandra Dickinson. We had a coach party from the dancing school travel to see Stephen and he was soon appearing in shows with Grace Kennedy, Janet Brown, David Essex and Lionel Blair.

The London Studio sent Stephen to many auditions where Robert Stigwood spotted him and wanted him for *Evita* in which he made his West End debut on 5 March 1984. I went to see the show at the Prince Edward Theatre and Stephen looked so young compared with the other male dancers. He said that, as he was the newcomer, during the balcony scene where they throw clothes at the poor people, they all threw them at him as part of an initiation ceremony! They also had put sausages round the 'corpse' in the opening scene where 'Evita' is lying in a coffin that Stephen had to dance round.

Stephen went on to dance in many big productions including *Cats, 42nd Street* and *On Your Toes* where he injured himself badly dancing on a shack with a corrugated tin roof. His ever growing CV went on to add *Anything Goes, Follies, Grease* and *Some Like It Hot*, where he understudied Tommy Steele in the lead part at the age of 28 years, the role played by Tony Curtis in the film version.

When Tommy Steele was injured at a performance I had a phone call from Stephen to say he had got me a ticket as he was playing the lead for two weeks at the Prince Edward Theatre in London. I sat next to a Canadian girl who thought Stephen was incredible; it made her day when I took her backstage to meet him.

When Stephen appeared in *42nd Street* at Drury Lane he danced alongside a young girl Catherine Zeta- Jones, I wonder what became of her? He was also part of the company chosen to dance for the 1985 Royal Variety performance.

However it wasn't all plain sailing for Stephen in the early days of his career. He auditioned and re-auditioned time and time again as although being a brilliant dancer his height was always against him. The minimum height for a girl dancer is 5'6" and when costumed on stage, wearing heels and a wig their male partner has to be at least 6'0" tall. Stephen never gave up and just kept going back time and time again. He took endless dance classes to keep himself in 'tip-top' shape ready for when the next audition came along. A lot of people do not appreciate how hard it is in the harsh world of showbiz. A driving ambition is always the best motivation for an aspiring performer but so is the realisation that you have to start at the bottom and work and take a lot of knocks along the way. It is a lifetime of hard work, pain and rejection and only the very few, like Stephen, ever make it to the top!

Stephen's first brush with choreography was for the Youth Theatre's amateur production of *Oliver* for which he received a Charnwood Arts award. Today he is a successful and famous choreographer both here, in America, Europe, Australia and even Japan and frequently works alongside the great theatre impresarios Sir Cameron Mackintosh and Sir Trevor Nunn. Stephen has choreographed *Anything Goes, How To Succeed In Business, Cabaret, Just So, Soul Train, Acorn Antiques, Singin' In The Rain, Sinatra At The London Palladium, On The Town, Tonight's The Night* and many more and has also choreographed pop videos for top groups such as *Oasis*. Stephen won the Laurence Olivier Award in 2005 for best choreographer, jointly with Matthew Bourne, for *Mary Poppins*.

The night of the 2005 Olivier awards (which were not being televised) Stephen rang me and said he was just off to the awards ceremony and, even though it was his third nomination, he had no chance of winning. I said to him: "third time lucky" and a few hours later he rang me absolutely over the moon that he and Matthew Bourne had won for *Mary Poppins*. Those threes again!

Stephen has *Mary Poppins* running on Broadway and will have the honour of being the first non-American choreographer for the Disney Corporation when he choreographs *The Little Mermaid* on Broadway in 2007.

Stephen's idol is Ann Miller, one time girl friend of the great Hollywood film mogul Louis B Mayer. Ann Miller was probably the best female dancer at the time of the great Hollywood film musicals. She could manage 500 beats a minute in her tap shoes and did just that in film musical greats *Easter Parade, On The Town* and *Kiss Me Kate*. Ann Miller was discovered dancing in a theatre by Lucille Ball, the star of *I Love Lucy* and the first woman ever to head her own TV studio. Lucille Ball was in the audience with a talent scout from RKO. Texan born Ann Miller stood tall on the stage at 5'6"; her hair was dyed jet-black. She wore blood red lipstick and nail varnish. She was dressed in high heels and white fur stoles. Because of her amazing talent as a dancer, she was immediately snapped up and signed to RKO by the talent scout. Incredibly, and unbeknown to them, she was only 13 years old. She had lied about her age and was wearing false boobs! She always carried two birth certificates, one real and one fake!

Ann Miller was taken to ballet classes as a child because she had rickets. This was a children's disease, softening of the bones, that many children suffered from then and, fortunately we don't hear much of these days. Her mother hoped these lessons would strengthen her legs. They did – and how!

One of my favourite Ann Miller dance routines is to *I've Got To Hear That Beat* in the 1953 film *Small Town Girl* where she tap-dances on a floor with holes in it. Musicians were under the floor and only their arms and the various musical instruments they are playing can be seen as she dances around them. This number was directed by, that master of film dance sequences, Busby Berkeley.

Ann Miller starred alongside Fred Astaire and Judy Garland in the 1948 film musical *Easter Parade.* Cyd Charisse was originally cast in the part but due to an accident was unable to dance. Ann Miller was 'borrowed' from Columbia Pictures by MGM to cover the role. She was then put under contract to MGM for a further 10 years. It really was a case of 'break your leg' in both senses for Cyd Charisse and Ann Miller!

*On the Town* was one of the most successful movie musicals. It was also very ground breaking in actually being shot on location, not in a studio. Ann Miller was, at the time, Louis B Mayer's girlfriend and she pleaded with him to film part of the musical in New York, as she had never been there! And so the rest is history as they say!

Stephen always tries to pay homage to his idol Ann Miller in his shows with the angular arms and hand shimmy shakes which he used to great effect in the dance numbers for Julie Walters in *Acorn Antiques – The Musical*. Stephen loved working with Victoria Wood and Julie Walters. He said they were two of the nicest and down-to-earth women he has ever met in the business!

When Stephen was appearing in *Follies* in the chorus in 1988, Eartha Kitt, who was playing a starring role in the Sondheim musical, invited Stephen to join her for tea at *The Savoy*. When Stephen got there another lady joined them, it was Ann Miller his idol! She was appearing at *The Savoy Theatre* with Mickey Rooney in the hit vaudeville show *Sugar Babies*. Eartha Kitt was a big friend of Ann Miller and knew how much Stephen admired her and she had arranged the surprise tea party meeting! Stephen said he was so dumbstruck he just sat there and could have kicked himself later as there was so much he would have loved to ask her about.

Recently the legendary Shirley MacLaine went to see *Sinatra At The London Palladium* and Stephen asked if there was any chance she would kindly go backstage at the end of the show and just say a few words to the cast as it would be much appreciated, expecting to get his head bitten off. She immediately said yes and was very charming. A few days later Stephen had a message from Shirley MacLaine's agent inviting him to go and have lunch with her at the famous showbiz restaurant, The Ivy. Not bad going for a boy from Shelthorpe council estate, Loughborough!

The *Supercalifragilisticexpialidocious* number in *Mary Poppins* is actually contrived from sign language that Stephen knows how to do as his partner, Mark, is deaf. Stephen stamps his own brand of brilliance and creativity on this well-known number, and it is also his tribute to Mark.

I go to see all of Stephen's shows and visit him backstage and his, more than often, dance captain, Nikki Woollaston, and often stay with him. If I am down for an audition he will always rush to see me in his break time even if he really hasn't the time to spare. He has never forgotten where he started, even if it did involve pieces of lino and a donkey!

There is, as yet, one unfinished piece in my story with Stephen. He talks enthusiastically about a vivid dream he had in which we are dancing together. Who knows, it could yet still happen? At my age it will probably have to be in something like 'Miss Marple - The Musical'! If so, can I please have sequins and diamantés on the tweed suits, stiletto heels on the 'sensible' lace-up shoes and perhaps a few feathers? On second thoughts scrap the feathers; don't want to be too over the top? I wonder, did Miss Marple ever wear leopard-skin.................?

*Gotta Dance.....................................................................!*

A 4-year-old Stephen Mear in Neal Academy panto (front row on the left)

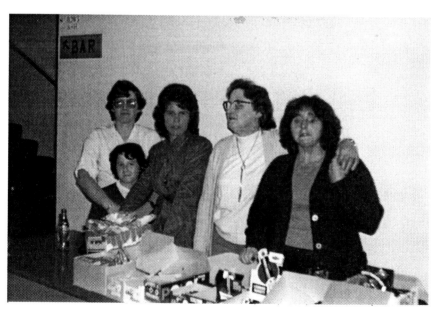

Sweet stall for dancing school panto at Stanford Hall. Fay
Mear (second on left) and a young Joyce Mear

A young Stephen Mear strutting his stuff!

A 15 year old Stephen and me with our teacher and pupil awards

Stephen's first West End Show *Evita* at the Prince Edward Theatre, London 1984

Stephen in dressing room at Prince Edward Theatre 1984

Stephen at *Theatre Royal, Drury Lane* in 42nd Street

Stephen and me in 2006 outside Prince Edward
Theatre, London the home of *Mary Poppins*

# CHAPTER 7

## NEVER WORK WITH CHILDREN!

I AM quite 'chuffed' that I have been the subject of two University studies; one was by a former pupil, Sally Boon, of Boon's Boatyard and the B & B in Mountsorrel. Sally was at Uni on some sort of comedy/drama course and had a boyfriend who was working on the alternative comedy circuit. She said the whole class was as well! She wanted to ask me about what it was like on the working men's' circuit and also being a female stand-up comic at a time in the early 1980s when there really wasn't many in what was then a male dominated side of show business. We had a great laugh it's always nice to see someone who danced with me as a child and hear what they have gone on to do. A woman on the train a few weeks ago stopped me and said: "You taught my son to dance when he was little" and when I asked her what he was doing now she said: "He's modelling for Dior!" The other Uni study was by a young man living in Mountsorrel, who was working on a project on Punch and Judy. He came to my house and we set up the booth and showed him how it all worked with the puppets and he took loads of photos.

Unlike W C Fields and the children's entertainer in *Hi-de-Hi*, I really like children. Years ago I was asked to do a 'turn' in a charity show to be held in a working men's club in Leicester. A fairly well known woman singer on the club circuit was compering. Her introduction to the packed audience of what was to come included: "We have some lovely little children from a local dancing school. We all love to see them. It brings tears to our eyes, bless 'em." She then walked off and said loudly backstage: "Keep them f*****g kids away from me, I hate 'em!"

In all honesty, I would say that becoming a children's performer and working with drag queens were the two best experiences I ever had in shaping me as a performer. Another person's world opens up your own.

How did I get into children's entertaining? Well I had performed a panto at a working men's club in Leicester and the ent sec asked me if I could do an Easter show for the kids in the day. I didn't even know they did shows for kids at Easter in the clubs. I said I would do it as the prospect held no fear for me being a dancing teacher for so many years in contact with all ages of children from 18 months up. I had clown outfits from the dancing school shows, I worked out routines with all sorts of props, sent for some very easy magic tricks, pinched a few ideas from programmes I had seen on the television, like the Yes/No answer game and another quiz idea taken from the very popular children's show *Crackerjack* where you had to hold all sorts of things if you got the wrong answers and taped a few of the panto participation songs.

I also decided to do a few games as these use the time up well and kids can get very restless having to sit all the while and it was going to be at least a two hour show. This is how the custard pie game came into being. All the kids stood in a circle, we passed round a custard pie on a paper plate and when the music stopped the child with the plate could pick either of the two kids either side of him or her and gently push the pie in their face with myself supervising and standing by with a towel to wipe it off their face and they were all instructed to avoid the eyes. Well we could have done this for hours the kids absolutely loved it.

A couple of years later doing this same game at a party in Loughborough there was a girl from the dancing school and her younger brother about six years old stood in a circle. Well he didn't wait for the music to stop as soon as he got the plate he smacked it straight into his sister's face. He had the biggest smile on his face as his sister wept loudly and his mother was screaming at him!

I can still see his smiling chubby face even today. The look on it was priceless and I have just seen that same look again. *Marilyn Among Friends*, the book about Marilyn Monroe by Sam Shaw and Norman Rosten has just come into my possession. There are many photos of Marilyn in that famous white dress from the 1955 film *The Seven Year Itch*. There is also a photo of the man operating the wind-blowing machine under the grating for Marilyn's billowing skirt scene. He has the same look on his face as that little boy!

I was asked by many parents if I would do house birthday parties and now needed to come up with some 'kiddy entertainer' name for my new career in show biz and eventually decided on 'Dippy Dee' the clown. I placed an ad in the *Leicester Mercury* and was amazed how many people rang me in desperation and at their wits end for entertainment for their children.

I now needed more things to do and so sent for some modelling balloons. I had the book and spent hours trying to shape these weird and wonderful creations described step by step in the manual but could only ever do a dog. At one party I had a rather sullen plump boy stood next to me insisting he didn't want a dog, he wanted a car! I made a dog and told him it was a 'rover' and off he went quite happy! Children always amaze me how you can tell them something they accept quite happily. At a dancing school show a little girl wanting to go home said to me: "Deirdre, when's the finale?" I said: "At the end" and off she went quite happy too. It's very surreal.

I had my own magic words, for a simple trick it would be 'fish fingers' and for a really hard one it would be 'five fried fish fingers on a Friday' as well as 'Dippy Dee Dippy Dee make this magic work for me'. Of course the best magic word for a trick was 'knickers' children love to hear an adult say this as well as 'bum' even in these enlightened days.

I was getting so many bookings, I would go to someone's house and it would be the same kids that I had already performed to before as one mum passes your phone number on to another. "They can't want to see me again," I wailed as I walked into a room full of the same kids for about the eighth time. "Oh yes they do" said a mum: "You have a real affinity with children, they really like you." I carried on setting up my stuff with tears in my eyes!

Over many years I performed for children in working men's clubs, bingo halls, houses, galas, schools, village halls and even at Althorp, the childhood home and final resting place of Princess Diana. This came about from doing a party in Leicester and someone's relative lived in a beautiful house in the Althorp grounds. There was a huge courtyard with a dovecote and entering through the massive door a huge foyer greeted me with a staircase either side, straight out of a fairy tale.

I was asked to do a children's Christmas party in Nottingham in a working men's club, it was very run down as the area itself was. The children were wonderful and very polite and obviously came from poor families. I had a magic picture book trick in which you show the children that it has blank pages. Then you 'magic' drawings in and ask the children to shout out colours and throw them at the book and the pictures become coloured. One little boy about six years old in a gaudy tank top and patched up trousers just stared at me "Wow that's real magic" he said wide eyed. "Please can I buy it, I've got some money?" He pulled the few coppers he had got out of the pocket of his patched up trousers, and held them up to me. Another truly humbling moment that still brings a lump to my throat today!

I took this magic book trick to work and one of the men I worked with, David, was so fascinated by it I had to get him a copy of the book so he could do this trick for his two daughters.

I was asked to do a Bank Holiday show at the Lonsdale Pub in Loughborough near the train station in an upstairs room. How we performers love upstairs rooms having to lug all that equipment up the stairs and then back down again at the end of the show! I was now 'Professor' Dippy Dee as I had added Punch and Judy to my children's parties and whatever anyone says it is still very popular today even with adults. I would model dogs and then ask the children who could laugh the loudest, cry the loudest, had the best smile and who could pull the most horrible face. Each winner would get a balloon dog. This is great if out in the open air as the noise attracts more children before you start the actual Punch and Judy show. Once inside the booth you are literally tied in and there is very little room.

It is imperative that you have a 'bottler', your sidekick who stands at the side of the booth, for certain children will sneak round and try to get in and it is a real 'no, no' to show anyone your puppets they must be packed in the case out of sight when finished. I used to come out at the end with a Teddy bear puppet 'Fred Bear' that I had bought from a stall in Covent Garden. Fred Bear sat on my other arm as I moved his arms and all the children really believed he was real and I would be surrounded as they all wanted to touch him.

However back to the Lonsdale, I was in the middle of Punch and Judy when John whispered: "I'm going downstairs for a pint".........big mistake! As soon as he left a shower of fish paste sandwiches and fairy cakes hit me on the head, being thrown through the booth opening by the kids!

139

We did many summer group sessions and there would always be a few older glum looking boys who could have been trouble so we used to ask them if they would mind being in charge of the music that was on separate tapes and also play the pop music for the countless games. It always worked because now they had a job of importance. They even told the younger kids off if they started to misbehave.

At one gala in Mountsorrel where John was on the committee I saw two of the dancing school children's mums in clown suits for the adult fancy dress competition. I asked if they would stand either side of the booth while I did the show as John was otherwise occupied. The bottler also has to pick up the baby that Mr Punch throws out and not let the kids get their hands on it. I was inside the booth saying over and over "pick the baby up!" with no success. I hadn't reckoned on the mums being a bit the worse for wear due to their earlier appearance in the beer tent. They were stood either side with big grins on their faces, swaying from side to side, wigs akimbo. I had to shout at the kids to tell the 'deaf' clowns to pick the baby up! Not only didn't they make the fancy dress competition nobody ever saw them again all afternoon!

How did I get into being a Punch and Judy Professor? Well I was considering becoming a Punch and Judy performer on seeing an advert in *The Stage* for a course down south and you could buy the puppets as well, all in all it was pretty expensive. A friend of one of the mothers from the dancing school had worked as a barker on the fairs and told John about a friend he had in Nottingham who also made these puppets and off we went to see Ted Corbin, in St Anne's in Nottingham. Ted's house was wonderful to behold; he had a Punch head door knocker and lying in the garden were carousel horses and the pots and pans you see on water barges, all these he was painting in vivid colours. The whole house was a tribute to Punch and Judy, with ornaments and paintings everywhere. What a nice man he was. He showed me a video of himself performing and gave me many tips on how to get started. He carved and dressed all the puppets for me and made my concertina booth. He gave John the measurements for the booth covering and off John went to the rope makers to order the traditional red and white striped covering. Ted had a choice of backcloths he could paint for the shows as well.

My ever-realistic (as he likes to call himself, though I and others think pessimistic is better!) husband thought I would be too clumsy to handle the puppets. I decided to do a try-out show and invited friends at work to bring their children to my house on a Sunday afternoon. I also handed out leaflets to local children and dancing pupils. The show was free but there would be a tin for donations to an animal charity as I had just got my first two poor little rescued kittens.

We have a massive garage. We actually bought the house as having a garage for four cars! What the previous owner had done was build up the brick garage from the bottom of the long garden to the front of the house and yes you could get four cars in one behind the other if you wanted. John put down cardboard on the concrete floor and we put in seats and benches and set up the booth and puppets. We had a full house and everything went so well, even John was amazed.

I added Margaret Thatcher to my puppets. It was the time when she was Prime Minister and in pet shops you could buy dog toys 'pets you hate' with plastic heads of politicians. I rang Ted who said he could make the body for the head and he did. Maggie came back with a blue frock and even a string of pearls.

I never used the gallows and the coffin as in traditional Punch and Judy shows, I'd got enough on my 'hands' with the puppets, but I did have a prison, which was hinged and swung to the front so Punch was seen behind bars.  There was a lot of talk at that time of prisons closing down and Maggie appeared to check the prison out in my show.  In Leicester when Maggie appeared everybody would cheer but she got a lot of boos in the Nottingham area.    I also added a ghost and a dog that weed.

Oh how the kids loved my Toby the dog.  He was plastic and on a stick.  I had a superb Batman water pistol that I squirted at the audience in between Toby's legs.  He really was the star of the show!  In the old Punch and Judy shows they would have a real dog, usually a Jack Russell or a Terrier, who would wear a clown frill around his neck and a pointed clown hat complete with pompom.  He didn't actually perform in the show; he would sit at the side of the booth.  This probably wouldn't be allowed today................another performer out of work!

I loved the Mountsorrel Galas.  These Galas would always attract a huge crowd of people from all over and raise a lot of money for local charities.  Every year we would enter a float with many of the dancing pupils fighting for places on it.  Being at a dancing school, we had so many costumes we could come up with endless ideas for our entry.  One year we had performed a panto in which the men's troup had been dressed as Norman knights and the ladies in long straight dresses and pointed hats as they danced to *Greensleeves,* composed by Henry 8th himself no less!   The children had jesters' outfits and also long dresses and so we did a mediaeval themed float.  We had cardboard horses that Stephen's mum, Fay, had made for the panto that the men wore over their costumes and the men's own legs were the horses and false legs were either side of the horse and they also carried jousting poles.  These are still intact in my attic today – the horses that is not the men!

For a display two free fall parachutists were going to jump and land, one on The Green in the centre in Mountsorrel and the other in the field where the games for the Gala where being held.   John that year was playing cricket and quite a strong wind got up and the cricketers saw an off course parachutist land in very deep floods in a field next to the cricket game.  An announcement came over the tannoy-system that he was in trouble and sinking fast.  In a split second four of my gallant 'knights' pulled a canoe off another float's tableau, which I think was the Towns Women's Guild, 'Boating Down The River' theme and they quickly ran to help.  The cricket team stood there gaping as four Norman knights carrying a canoe charged down the field and yes they did rescue the poor unfortunate, very wet and also very bewildered parachutist who probably thought he had gone time travelling just like Dr Who!

Becoming a children's entertainer helped me get my Equity Union membership card.  I was so in demand that on a Saturday I would be at dance classes in the morning, a children's show in the afternoon and then off to a working men's club at night to do a comedy act.  Most of these would be in different parts of the country.

You can't fool kids, if I had a Gala appearance after dance classes, I would go to the dance classes with my own original clown make up and my wig on as I wouldn't have time afterwards to get ready, all the kids would come into the lessons and not think anything was unusual.  One Mountsorrel Gala I was dressed as Jemimah Puddleduck, I waddled down the road in the costume, flippers and bonnet to the field the Gala was being held in, the huge beak covered my face. A child shouted across the road; "Hello Deirdre", I asked: "how did you know it was me?" to which she answered matter of factly; "nobody else would dress up like that!"

A woman recently stopped me in Leicester and said I had done all her children's birthday parties for many years and said: "All my children grew up with you." What a lovely thing to say! Later on a young woman would say the same to me about the touring panto.

For many years walking round my village where I performed in the village gala, sadly now no longer held as is the case in most of the villages, due to lack of support in helpers, I would hear children say: "That's the puppet lady."

Ted gave me the address to join the Punch and Judy Society as an Associate Member. I couldn't become a full member as I was unable to use the swazzle to make Punch's voice, but I could do this without anyway. David at work had my swazzle and could use it brilliantly; he didn't want it for a show however, he used it unbeknown to anyone, in his local pub when it was full and he would then sit bemused looking at the many startled people looking round to see whom it was with the peculiar voice!

I would say at that time all the children were well behaved and polite apart from the odd one, In the early days parents would want to be part of the party, too. They would sit with the children and join in and take photos and video the show with my consent. How unlike today as already mentioned, that you have to have all the parents' consent to take a photo and if one says 'no' that's the end of that. What memories will children of today have to look back at?

However over the years there has also been a big change in attitudes. We would get to a village hall or wherever and a mother would inform me: "Here's the kids, any problems we don't want to know, we've got some bottles in, we'll be in another room, see you at the end!" We were now doing many parties with no adults present at all.

One show I will always remember was in Quorn many years ago. Now Quorn is a very nice village and so are the people and you wouldn't expect bad behaviour from children there in those days. We got to the hall and about 15 boys, ranging from five to eight years in age, were running wildly round the room, screaming, throwing themselves on top of each other, biting and kicking and punching. A very well spoken mother came up to me and said: "They're a bit boisterous." Extremely badly behaved, I'd have said!

Off she went and disappeared somewhere. Her boy whose birthday it was came up to me as I was carrying a box in and started to thump and kick me, I 'unfortunately' dropped the box on his foot and this obnoxious child now hopping on one foot said: "You've got to do what I say, my mother has already paid you." I bent down to him and said in my best authoritative voice: "Listen sunshine, your mum can have the money back. I'll go home and you can entertain your friends for the next two hours and then they'll all be saying what a crap party yours was!" Whereupon he sat down sulking and never bothered me again for the duration of what turned out to be a very good show with the other kids.

For many years a man called Larry Peace in Wigston, Leicester got me to do his massive annual charity fund raising show in Wigston and then hit on the idea of one year breaking the *Guinness Book of Records* number of clowns together in one go. Larry always seemed to think I could do the impossible and I reluctantly agreed to help him do this as well as the entertaining. I rounded up friends and dancing school pupils and mums and I think that we did actually break the record that year. I was too worn out at the end of the day to find out if we had!

At one of Larry's shows it was boiling hot. I had gone into the booth to do my Punch and Judy show and pouring with sweat in an enclosed space had to strip off my clown outfit and performed the show in bra and knickers. I had just finished my show when over the tannoy-system at the other end of the field Larry's voice could be heard loud and clear. "Can Dippy Dee come and present the prizes now, the Lord Mayor of Leicester is waiting?" Have you ever tried to get dressed quickly in a clown suit with a hula-hoop round the waist of the trousers in big clown pants (costume tip: much better than whale bone!) encased in a small booth? I nearly knocked the whole thing over but managed to do it and run from one end of the field to the other.

All in all entertaining children was a great experience and very touching too when you see how little some children have but it was now time to move on for me. Even today with all the gadgets and computer games children have they still like the more simple 'old fashioned' entertainment even if many 'grown ups' don't think they do.

I have many wonderful memories of being a children's entertainer. It is one of the most unappreciated jobs by other people in the world of showbiz; for in those two hours or more that you are performing it is probably the hardest and most responsible, but very rewarding performance, you will ever do.

*The party's over.................................................................!*

A happy Professor Dippy Dee at the start of the show

A not-so-happy Professor Dippy Dee at the end of the show with toilet rolls!

My Punch and Judy booth at Wigston, Leicestershire

Watching Punch and Judy at Wigston

'Eviction technicians' for Punch and Judy

Those 'deaf' clowns

The gallant Norman knights

As Jemimah Puddleduck (note the webbed feet me duck!)

# CHAPTER 8

## OPPORTUNITIES KNOCK?

THESE days you hardly ever see one and yet they used to be everywhere.........
and that is the talent show, one of the best ways in which amateur performers
such as myself could enter to get going on the professional circuit. When I
was starting out they would be held in every club and pub going as well as on
television. For with the local talent shows came the agents and sometimes even
the TV talent scouts. In those days they were always on the look out for new
acts.

I got through to the semi finals at Ann Oliver's Talent Show in Leicester. I
didn't make the final and so I went along to see the friends I had made compete.
The 'star' judge for the finals was Bill Maynard, the locally based entertainer and
actor who became the much-loved Greengrass in *Heartbeat*. The acts had all
done their 'turns' when Bill stood up and said: "I feel very sorry for the winner of
the show!" We all waited holding our breath wondering what was coming next!
He went on to say that he had appeared in lots of talent shows when he started
out as a comic on the club circuit and had never won one. All the winners he
had known had never been heard of again! It could be the kiss of death for
some entertainers!

Years later I was appearing in Christmas cabaret at The White House, Scraptoft.
This was a very posh audience, mostly consisting of wealthy businessmen in their
designer black suits and their wives and partners in expensive outfits (why do all
women wear black dresses?). Bill, the nation's favourite as 'Greengrass' and his
then wife Toni Berne came down to see the Leicester entertainer Bruce Bateson,
who was also appearing, about a business deal. The landlord invited Bill to stay
and watch the cabaret and set another table up quickly. In walked Bill dressed in
his gillet and wellingtons, with his wife. At the end they invited me into the bar
with them and Bill said to me: "Very good and very professional." I went home
walking on air that night.

In this industry you have to be prepared to put yourself in the all-too-likely firing line for rejection, if you hope to get anywhere. Watch *The X Factor* auditions on TV and you regularly see would-be 'stars' arguing back with the 'experts' about their opinions of their 'talent' and chances of getting on in the business. But that really isn't the way to do it. Believe me, this is a very intimate, close-knit industry and saying the wrong word out of line to someone with top contacts will definitely be remembered. You have to take the rejection and criticism and carry on and that's what I've done, probably more times than I care to remember.

Many of the talent shows I entered I found advertised in *The Stage,* the theatrical newspaper that is published weekly. In those days there was always news of many auditions, castings and talent shows. Nowadays there are more adverts for boy bands and lap dancers, a sign of the times! In recent years, I actually saw an advert for a saxophonist for a boy band that read: No experience necessary, image is everything. That says it all today!

I probably started at the end. The biggest talent show I ever entered, or am likely to enter in my whole life, was the very first and they didn't get any bigger than *Opportunity Knocks*. Filmed at Teddington Lock in London, it was compulsive viewing for Monday night audiences of an amazing 20 million on ITV during its hey-day from 1968 to 1978. Imagine taking part in such a top TV show as a comic of all things when I'd never even been on a professional stage before.

Before appearing on *Opportunity Knocks*, my 'career' as a comic had been the round of dancing school shows, charity events, residential homes and village halls. Don't misunderstand, I loved such events and I still do. But it remains a lot easier to make relatives and friends laugh than it does to crack the frown of hardened professionals and an audience made up of people who do not know you at all. However bad you are, with family and friends, you will always get a friendly smile and hear them saying: "You're better than anything on the TV." Well you are to them!

Over the years *Opportunity Knocks* brought fame to such stars as comedian Freddie Starr, Scottish singer Lena Zavaroni, Mary Hopkin (she won for 10 consecutive weeks and was fortunate enough to be 'spotted' on the show by Twiggy who brought her to Paul McCartney's attention and with his help had a No 1 chart hit with *Those Were The Days),* pianist Bobby Crush, Bonnie Langford, Les Dawson, Pam Ayres, Little and Large, Tom O'Connor and Frank "It's the way I tell 'em" Carson!

The 'star' of the show was Hughie Green, a film star in his youth, and the host of many popular TV quiz shows, before he took on this TV talent show that would run for years. Many people still remember Hughie Green's catchphrase which he said on every show "And I mean that most sincerely, folks" even if he didn't!

My audition took place in Nottingham at a time when I was playing Billy Crusoe in *Robinson Crusoe* in the dancing school panto at Loughborough Town Hall. When I got there I found out that a lot of acts were given exactly the same audition time to appear. I was one of many who had got 3pm on their card! The programme's producers did this as they knew that a good half of the would-be acts were likely to bottle out. This meant that you could be sat there hours waiting for your name to be called to perform. The room was jam-packed full with musicians and singers when I turned up. This was a time when all pubs and clubs would have live groups playing several times a week and live resident backing for singers. Musical equipment was set up everywhere and there was scarcely any room for anything else. Most of the acts waiting to audition were 'professional turns' hardened and sharpened by the working men's club and pub circuit, but I couldn't claim any similar experience. Can you imagine how nervous and worried I was as I had never even been on a professional stage before?

Judges included Len Marten, a comedian who appeared in John Cleese's wonderful *Fawlty Towers* and Doris Barry, a former Windmill Theatre showgirl and sister of the prima ballerina Alicia Markova. Some of the acts were so bad that a couple of the judges were laughing quite openly at them. The few male club comics auditioning got on stage, said a few words only to hear someone bellowing loudly: "Next!" Not the most encouraging of signs for a nervous young amateur comic hoping and praying to make them laugh. My heart was sinking fast and I was beginning to wish I were somewhere else. I honestly didn't think I could do it. But something made me stop.

When they eventually called my name, I made what seemed like the longest walk of my life up to the stage dressed in my safari panto costume in front of hundreds of people. I knew I'd be something of a change for the judges as there was a real shortage of female comics at the time. In fact there wasn't any that actually stood on a stage and told jokes! I did about ten minutes of my panto routine, throwing in tap dancing and singing to *Happy Feet*! To my surprise, they laughed and asked me to go down and talk to them. Thrilled though I was, I could really have done without them asking me to have a short rest and then do the whole routine again. The reason was that they wanted to commit my voice and act to reel-to-reel tape. They did not have mobile film equipment at auditions in those days. I was even more terrified now. I'd made these important TV talent judges and audience laugh once, surely they wouldn't laugh at the same routine again? When you've heard a joke – you've heard it!

As I walked back to the end of the hall to prepare myself again I was met by the unfriendly glare of people waiting to audition and I heard a woman singer say loudly: "It's amazing what you can get away with when you're young." Well, I never saw her appear on any of the shows! I did the whole routine again and the judges once again laughed but not the now highly envious audience made up of people waiting to audition! Though I felt the judges' laughter was a bit forced second time around, I also felt they were doing it to encourage me and it did.

I was told by some of the production crew the format behind the casting of the show. It wasn't a case of picking the best performers as we all thought. The producers were looking for an area balance – a singer from Wales, a comedian from the Midlands and a dancer from the south, for example and they actually kept a book with entertainers they liked listed under where they came from not by their names or type of act   This would give the show a widespread regional appeal as is evident by the voting for acts in the *Eurovision Song Contest* and *The X Factor* shows even today.

Doris Barry, Len Marten and Royston Mayoh the director were very nice to me and very encouraging and said there had only been one female comic on the show in the past. I felt so sorry for some of the other acts auditioning even though a lot were really dreadful and probably had only ever sung into a wet soapy scrubbing brush in the bath! Mums were going off in a huff, arms around sobbing daughters saying loudly; "you're better than anything on the TV, that lot know nothing." Where have we heard that before?

After *Opportunity Knocks* finished Doris Barry went on to be an audition adviser at the London Studio for dance and drama where my former pupil, Stephen Mear, attended many years later. He mentioned to her that I had taught him dancing and she said; "Oh yes I remember Deirdre." I was very touched and surprised after all these years.

After your successful audition, you would get a letter to say you had passed and then you would have the agonising wait for the phone to ring to say that you had been selected for a show. If the present series ended with no phone call you would be sent for to audition for the next series. Doris Barry told me that a lot of good singers on their next audition had, over the year, ruined their voices in the cigarette smoke-filled working men's clubs and never ever made the show. My second audition was at another venue in Nottingham and I thought I needed to give the judges something different. I did my new policewoman routine and when I had finished they said: "Why didn't you do the safari act, we liked that!"

The news that my opportunity had arrived this time came through the post a couple of months later. My big moment was in 1970 when I was 24 years old. I was asked to send my script up to the producers and Len Marten himself vetted it. It was then returned to me with bits altered and added in red ink for me to learn.

On the weekend of the recording, I went to Teddington Lock TV studios and was greeted by, of all people, Wilfred Pickles, who opened the door for me. Benny Hill was there too. I couldn't believe that for a funny and cheeky comedian, he was such a painfully shy human being. He could barely face the autograph hunters. Irene Handl who was filming *For The Love Of Ada* with Wilfred Pickles walked into the canteen. She had a two little Chiwowa dogs with her and walked over to my Mum and said: "Hold these for me dear" and went and queued up at the counter. She came back with her meal and sat with my mother and talked to her like she had known her for years. She obviously had recognised another animal lover.

We were taken up to the band room that was situated above the studio where the acts would be filmed. Hughie Green used to joke with 'Uncle Bob' as he called the conductor of the band during the show. He seemed to be such a jovial man to TV viewers, but I was to find out otherwise. I sat there with Len Marten and a stern looking Uncle Bob said: "We'll play her intro." They blasted out this great 'jungle safari' tune and I couldn't help but laugh. Uncle Bob shouted: "What's she laughing at?" very indignantly and glared at me. Len Marten smoothed things over by saying: "She's not heard it before, it's come as a surprise." Nevertheless I was glad to get out of the band room and relieved never to see Uncle Bob again. This was my first experience of the 'nice' people you see on TV not being so 'nice' in real life!

Hughe Green was a massive star at that time. At the incredible age of 14 he was given his own BBC Radio Show and, by 15, was the highest paid child star in Great Britain. During the 1940s he appeared in many British films, particularly the very successful and hilariously funny Will Hay films. He went on to host the popular TV shows *Double Your Money* and *The Sky's the Limit*. His last and most controversial 'appearance' came after his death in 1997 when it was revealed that he was the real father of TV presenter Paula Yates.

Hughie Green didn't speak to any of the acts and seemed very serious, even a bit grumpy. He had an assistant with him and was very much in control of everything happening on the studio floor. I was amazed when I rehearsed my comedy act that Hughie Green took the time to stop and listen. He also made the studio workmen stop hammering the set together and stand still! I was that embarrassed I could have crawled under a stone!

As we 'turns' waited to go on and the band was playing the opening music, Hughie Green came and sat down beside me and asked me how old I was, he was surprised when I replied that I was 24. He had thought I was more like 16! He then gave me some sound advice encouraging me to continue performing by saying: "Keep on going, you can do it. Don't ever give up, we need people who can make us laugh."

The format of the programme was that each act took along a friend who acted as their 'sponsor'. Mine was Peter Bull, later known as the managing director of the *Loughborough Echo* and in the local sporting world as Mr Shepshed Dynamo FC! I knew him very well as his daughter Diane was a pupil of mine and she performed in the dancing school shows. He and his wife Joan used to help out at all the dancing school shows. I'll always remember Peter with a big brush sweeping up in the dressing rooms after all the children and mums had gone home moaning about how much rubbish they had left. A lot of them still do at the end of a show today; some things never change!

Each act's 'sponsor' sat and spoke with Hughie Green to introduce the act they knew. The show itself was recorded over a weekend and shown on TV on a Monday. My 'turn' was actually shown on an August Bank Holiday Monday. I did my *Robinson Crusoe* act, complete with safari hat, but not the song and tap dance. My performance was probably only a few minutes long, but you can imagine when you're out there how long it seems. How did I cope with the idea of performing in front of 20 million people? Well, the answer is very simple – I didn't! There was a very small audience in the studio itself and all acts could have tickets for three friends and that's whom you are realistically playing to. It is totally impossible to imagine 100,000 folk, let alone 20 million, and it's probably easier on the nerves not to.

Huge stars such as Freddie Starr and Jim Davidson have revealed that they get so nervous at the prospect of facing an audience that they sometimes throw up before a performance. Jim Davidson said he feared for his long-term health and the diva herself Shirley Bassey threatened to quit altogether if she ever got so worked up again after a particularly bad bout of nerves. As for me, I seem to be at my best in front of an audience and love making contact with them. A lot of performers don't like to actually see the audience they are playing to, but I'm just the opposite. I insist on having the house lights on, so I can see their faces. I like to see the enemy!

After my 'turn' came a nail biting wait to see what the studio audience made of my performance. The 'clapometer' was a source of much intrigue for viewers. At the end of the show the applause for each act, was measured by a wavy line appearing across the bottom of the nation's TV screens. But far from being a piece of hi-tech equipment, it actually consisted of nothing more than two stage hands in long brown coats and caps looking just like Morecambe and Wise in a certain well known TV sketch holding a piece of hardboard working the sliding scale with their hands. There was then the postal vote to be taken into account. Only the winner would be informed of the outcome and watching the next show it was once again the girl who played the guitar and sang. Never mind I was in pretty good company by not winning. Nottingham's Sue Pollard, of *Hi-De-Hi* fame, once appeared on *Opportunity Knocks* only to be beaten by a singing dog. She was to get her big break later and what a break that would be!

I was also intrigued to see that the set, that had taken a full day to set up, was made up of bits of scenery with *Callan* written on the back on every piece. This was obviously part of the set for the very successful *Callan* TV series at the time starring Edward Woodward.

However it was not to every act's advantage to appear on the show. The great Max Boyce, that hilarious, large-leek bearing Welsh entertainer, said that after appearing on *Opportunity Knocks* he actually had some bookings cancelled. Victoria Wood, undoubtedly one of the best comics ever, reported that she scarcely worked for two years after winning *New Faces*.

In reality there's two sides to a national TV appearance. Not only could it interest agents and ent secs in you and provide you with work, it could also change the minds of some people who had already booked you in for their venue.

I remember seeing a very well known club comic on *New Faces* that was being shown live. He was doing the Tommy Cooper 'different hat' routine when he completely lost his bottle and walked off the stage. He said it was the worst thing he had done going on the show. He had many bookings in the clubs for at least a year and they were all cancelled after his disastrous appearance.

As for me, however, appearing on *Opportunity Knocks* certainly didn't do me any harm. But, on the other hand, it fell short of making showbiz my career as, to be quite honest, merely taking part in such a big TV show as this wasn't enough to impress club land agents to give a female comic a chance but it certainly inspired me to give it a go in a much bigger way.

*New Faces* was the British television talent show on ITV that in many ways followed *Opportunity Knocks*. It was popular in the 1970s and 1980s and, unlike its predecessor, was known for its hard-as-nails judges. The host was Derek Hobson, previously of *ATV Today*, but the people it will more readily be more readily be remembered for were panellists Tony Hatch, one half of a very talented musical partnership with wife Jackie Trent, producer Mickey Most, a big name in the music industry, and Nina Mishkov, who was a TV critic with *The Sun* whose biting comments often reduced acts to tears.

*New Faces*, like *Opportunity Knocks*, catapulted some very talented 'unknowns' to national fame. The long list included Marti Caine (who later went on to be its presenter), Lenny Henry, Michael Barrymore, Roy Walker, The Chuckle Brothers, Victoria Wood, Les Dennis, Leicester's Showaddywaddy, Jim Davidson and Gary Wilmot.

Some auditions for the new series of *New Faces* were being held at a nightclub in Birmingham during the day. The place was packed and we sat in a corridor going through our various routines. As usual on such tense and frustrating occasions, there was plenty of moaning and groaning, as people waited none too patiently for their long overdue turn. I inadvertently made things even worse after I finally got my call later that afternoon. I can't recall all the names of the three judges but one was Richard Holloway, a very prominent TV producer, his recent TV shows being *Pop Idol*, *The X Factor* and *The Sharon Osbourne Show*. I did my 'turn' and they kept me behind for quite a while after I had performed as they wanted to talk to me and that now meant all the other acts were kept waiting even longer to audition. I was chuffed the judges thought I had been at it for a while and not the rank amateur that I really was.

The judges were great with me and had laughed at my whole routine but even so I was still surprised when I received a letter afterwards to confirm that I'd been successful. Even that, however, didn't mean I was actually in the next series and, as Saturday nights came and went without any further communication, I began to take it as though I wouldn't be. There would always be next year, I told myself, unaware at that time that this would be the very last series.

Yet in the end I so nearly made it (the story of my life!) I got a phone call totally out of the blue, saying that someone had dropped out of the show at the last moment and inviting me to audition for one last spot. When I got there I was told that it was between me, and a comedian called Billy Pearce. Billy Pearce was already a professional comic and tap dancer, as his mother ran a dance studio up North. He obviously performed better than me at the audition as he got the place on the show and he went on to have such a very well deserved successful career. What has been nice is that I've met Billy Pearce on several occasions and he has always been very apologetic about the fact that he got the spot. A very nice and talented man is Billy. How I would have gone down in front of those stern TV judges I will now never know, which is perhaps just as well!

At this time, I was doing my best to get down to any talent show I could and making some very good contacts along the way. This was always going to be far more important than the £50 prize that was usually on offer. The problem was that female comedians were never really in vogue. Even in the hey-day of the clubs, now long passed, the call was for singers, comedy vocalists and impressionists and alternative comedy was now beginning to dominate the TV screen.

One show that did me a great deal of good, was the one I referred to earlier run by Ann Oliver. She is a businesswoman forever associated with her dancing school from which many girls went on to dance professionally. She decided to host a cabaret evening on a Thursday evening where her girls would dance and any act could get up on stage and give it a go. I used to perform quite regularly on a Thursday and this got me in *Showcall*, a variety journal that every producer has a copy of that you simply had to be in if you wanted to get anywhere. This led to me making an appearance on the *Showcall* showcase held at Anne's venue even though I hadn't really got going professionally.

I was very nervous once again being on such an important showcase, with reviews of acts in *The Stage*. As I stood on the stage waiting for the curtain to open a professional comic, Andy Feet, who had recently had a very successful appearance on a TV show, crept up to me, held my hand and said: "Take a deep breath and go for it, you can do it!" Bless him! I did and got a really good review of my act in *The Stage*.

But even so how was I going to get working as a professional comic? Well help was at hand when I met a very important person in my life through doing another talent show at Hemington Court, near Castle Donington. It didn't appear to be the most promising of evenings. Here I was in a room with large rotund columns making it hard for the audience to see who was performing – a comic's nightmare. I was also once again on the bill with many singers.

I got talking to a man who was sat at the same table and through him to his wife Joy, the compere for the show. Joy was a professional singer who worked as 'Joie Hearts'. Joy and Mike, her husband, were impressed that I did comedy and asked me to go to venues in Nottingham with her where she was working in charity do's and do some short spots there.

My first show with Joy produced unexpected results. We were sitting in a certain club until 11pm waiting for my short spot and John, not surprisingly, was thinking it might be better to call it quits and go home. "Nobody is going to want to listen to comedy this late at night" he said, and I must admit I thought he had a point. I was thinking much the same myself. But, anyway, I did get on, had a fabulous time and was offered more work there and then by the agents who had gone along with their acts who were also appearing in the charity show.

I used to go along and do a 10 or 15 minute act at Joy's bookings and she was only too happy to help me further my career. Comics and singers were paid separate rates in the clubs and pubs. Singers were actually on the lowest rate – that's why so many of them started putting in a few jokes to work under the title 'comedy vocalist', to up their money

As comics were now going out of fashion (everybody had to be an impressionist at that time) I had the chance to get myself on the musical bandwagon if only I could overcome my reservations of my ability to sing. My husband John has always been very open about what he thinks of my singing. He says I sing as good, as Les Dawson played the piano!

Joy was, as usual, encouraging: "Everyone, absolutely everyone, can sing about six songs. You just have to find out which ones," she told me. I must admit that having listened to a lot of acts I could see what she meant. So I went over to Joy's house in Long Eaton and we went through as many songs as we possibly could. She kindly gave me a load of backing tracks to practise with and, guess what, yet another club act doing the good old 60s and 70s numbers.

It was also through Joy's influence that I went on another TV talent show of its time *Sky Star Search* in 1989. Mike drove us down to Hammersmith for the auditions. I passed the audition so it was off to London Weekend television's studios for the show proper a few weeks later. Keith Chegwin was the host of the show and he would be joined on the show by two celebrity judges each week. Some acts were undoubtedly very good, others not so good as is the case in all talent shows though it wasn't too flattering when later on in an out-takes show *TV Nightmares* he said: "Anybody who wanted to be on it, was on it."

My two 'celeb' judges were Dana, the Irish singer a previous winner of the *Eurovision Song Contest* in the days when people voted for the best song, not the country, and Derek Nimmo, the very popular comedy actor who never seemed to be off the TV in those days.

My act consisted mostly of my own material and this went down particularly well with Dana. I actually came second on the show. I was beaten by a male vocalist who got one mark more than I did. I did however get a consolation prize. Keith Chegwin used to present his Frog Award to the best newcomer at the end of each show and this went to me, along with £50 for being the runner up.

My Dad had been so very proud of me appearing on this show that he'd told everyone who cared to listen – and probably quite a few who didn't – when on duty at the Town Hall the weekend of the filming but on the following Monday he suffered a massive stroke and within a month had died, ironically on the day that the show was televised.

I did many shows with Joy, Mike and her daughter Rachel. Joy and Mike later moved to Spain to work as entertainers in a holiday complex. Tragically, Joy died in her early 50s.

155

One place that will always have a big place in my memory is The King's Cabaret at Birmingham, now sadly demolished. A good many of the acts there were semi-professional singers. I appeared on my first heat of the talent show with a good dozen of them, all of which would have probably taken the singers on *Pop Idol* and *The X Factor* to the cleaners. Some were working almost every night of the week, as, at that time, there were so many clubs in Birmingham you could work at a different one every night of the year and they were all crying out for entertainers.

However like me there were also some people appearing who were outright amateurs. I remember one girl 'would-be-vocalist' turning up with a single piece of music only to be told she had got to sing three songs or she wouldn't be allowed to go on. She went on stage and sang the same song three times, much to the bewilderment of the audience! All music had to be live at that time. We had professional musicians backing us. These were the very same musicians who played for the top stars that appeared at the Kings Cabaret, including Shirley Bassey, and they were brilliant. When I first appeared there, I hadn't a clue what the musicians were talking about when they asked me for my 'dots'. It had to be explained to me that this meant my sheet music! There are a lot of showbiz terms you have to get to grips with along the way.

The resident host for Kings Cabaret was Nick Berry and he was compering the talent show. Nick was a really nice man whom I got on with so well but who sadly died in his early 50s. Kings Cabaret was a beautiful looking cabaret club set in the middle of a housing estate. The stage was huge, I felt like I was working in a West End theatre. They had women on the door, which was very unusual then. They were smartly dressed in red jackets and long floral skirts. This was a really good idea by the owner of the club. He said he had had no trouble at all since employing them. It certainly worked very well at Kings Cabaret Club.

King's was a cabaret base for all the top variety stars of the time such as Ronnie Corbett, Max Bygraves, Stan Boardman, Des O'Connor, Bernard Manning, Joe Longthorne, Bob Monkhouse and two Leicester groups Showaddywaddy and the Dallas Boys.

With a dozen singers in my heat it meant I got on stage really late. It was close to midnight when I made my entrance, supported by an enthusiastic and loyal following from the dancing school and work. After what seemed to be the longest walk of my life from backstage to the microphone, I was honestly beginning to wish I hadn't entered. I said my opening line and heard the very welcome sound of laughter. It was Nick, the compere. If I could get such a professional comic as him to laugh, I thought, I couldn't be that bad after all! This was, after all, a more reliable judgement of my ability as a comic than the kind of local shows I was more used to performing in where most people knew me. This gave me the incentive to really go for it and I had a very good evening. Altogether I must have appeared at King's a good half-a-dozen times.

I got through to the semi finals of the talent show. But more important than the result was the interest that Nick took in me. He put together six acts from the show and took us round the Birmingham clubs for more invaluable experience. I remember going to Smethwick WMC, Chelmsley Wood Cons Club, Handsworth Horticultural Club, Cradley Heath Ex-Servicemen's Club, Allen's Cross WMC, Sheldon Royal British Legion and the Avenue Social Club at Whoeley (pronounced 'wheeley') Castle.

I vividly remember at one of these clubs coming off stage and going to the bar where a big fat drunk man was eyeing me up. "Were you the comic up there just then?" he slobbered, I said 'yes' and he then said "Well you looked better on the stage". I replied; "In that case it's a pity you can't go and stand up there then!" As I walked away I was very tempted to tread on his toes with the heel of my stiletto shoe, à la Elizabeth Taylor in *Butterfield 8* for which she won an Oscar by the way, but I resisted!

Mark Reynolds, a comedy impressionist, was the winner of the King's Talent show. He was fabulous and everybody raved about him. I remember Mark saying to me in the dressing room he wanted to be a star for the lifestyle, the fast cars, houses, money and all the other 'perks' of being famous. That had never even occurred to me. I just wanted to stand on a stage and perform. Nothing else mattered! I was delighted after my appearance in *Emmerdale* to receive a card from Mark after all these years.

I appeared in one talent show in Scarborough where I won my heat. A girl who was 14-years of age had won a previous heat and she came to watch with a friend. I seem to remember her having short curly dark hair. I was told she was fabulous at impressions and that her name was Debra Stephenson. She later went on to star in *Bad Girls* and then as 'Frankie' in *Coronation Street*.

Leicester City Council ran a heat for a National talent show in a community centre in Mantle Road, Leicester. I appeared with Andrew Chettleburgh, a young boy magician, from Coalville in Leicestershire. He did go on to become a professional artist and we are still in touch today.

A talent show at Leamington Spa had important consequences for me. The organisers offered to provide us with a video of our performances for £15 but, at first, I didn't think I would bother, as I might not do a good spot. But there were agents in attendance and, as I enjoyed a very good turn, I asked afterwards whether I could buy a copy of the video. A few weeks later one of the agents from that talent show night rang to say that he'd had a phone call from Granada TV after I'd been spotted in the *Showcall* book. Apparently producers of a new comedy programme were looking for someone to join Pauline Daniels, as she was the only female on the show. They had been to see three other women comics and hadn't decided on any of them, so did I have a video? Needless to say I sent my video from Leamington Spa off to Granada TV and they were quickly in touch to say that I was on the show. I once again had to send a script off to the producers of the show beforehand as I had with *Opportunity Knocks* and that wasn't all. I then had to go up to Granada TV studios in Quay Street in Manchester and go through a face-to-face meeting with about five other comics. We each went through our respective acts, to check if there was any doubling up between us or for anything we might not be able to say on TV! Altogether I only had about four days in order to gather myself before going on the cult TV show *The Comedians*, compared to most of the other comics who'd had a good two months to prepare.

On the day there was a large audience seated waiting to laugh. Ted Robbins, before *Phoenix Nights* fame, was the warm-up comic. He did a superb job getting the audience, who'd been bussed in from here, there and everywhere, in the right mood. Therefore you can imagine how I felt when I started to walk out to hear the director shouting 'Stop!' This took me aback for a short while. Then it was explained to me that my hands and, with an open-neck jacket, part of my bosom were coming up 'too white' on the TV monitor, so I needed touching up, so to speak, in front of the audience by the make up girl and out I went again to start my 20 minute spot.  When I had finished my act and gone back to the dressing room my blouse and pink jacket were ruined by the make up but that didn't upset me as I was so thrilled to have filmed a spot for this iconic TV show that I could never imagined ever being on. I could always buy a new blouse and jacket!

The only other direct contact I had with the show itself, a very big Granada hit, was going back to Manchester for the photo shoot with all the comics who would be appearing on this new series of *The Comedians* for a supplement for a Sunday newspaper. It was there that I got talking to Ian Sludge Lees and Johnny Casson, a well-known northern comic who had appeared several times on the Des O'Connor show. He told me that he had been paid off many times in club land and had even had glass ashtrays thrown in his direction. I thought if this could happen to such a great talented comic like him then it wouldn't put me off from carrying on trying to be a comic if it happened to me. Johnny said he kept himself going in those situations by saying to himself 'think of the money'!

When the show was broadcast, as with the original version in 1971, it was edited to give short clips from each comedian and ran them one after another. This meant that my act was broken up and I actually appeared on several of the programmes but had no idea until sitting in front of my own TV exactly what was coming next.   One pleasant surprise some time later was getting a royalties cheque from the video.  I hadn't even known I was on it!   It's difficult now to think of a show like *The Comedians*, which consisted in effect of continual stand-up joke telling, being so popular these days.  Audiences now are looking for more observational comedy, rather than straight wall-to-wall joke telling and some of the material might not have delighted the politically correct lot either.  But back then it went down an absolute storm.

One place where straight jokes were definitely in demand was in 1998 at ASDA Supermarket, of all places! They launched their own competition for anyone to send in jokes as they had got to the point where they thought everyone had read and heard all the jokes inside Christmas crackers.  There were many, many entries and I got in the final six.   The TV people wanted some of the finalists to appear on early morning TV before the actual competition and I said I would go.  It was hectic stuff getting down to London so I could perform my jokes early morning.  The previous night I was appearing at the Aylestone working men's club in Leicester at a ladies night and there was no way I was going to cancel that! I walked off the stage that night at 11.30pm and was whisked straight into a car still in stage costume.  A friend and fellow panto performer, Ian Smith very kindly drove me all the way to London.

The three of us who had managed to get down to London were put up for the night in a very expensive hotel before being collected by a chauffeur the next morning to be driven to ASDA in time for a 7am TV appearance.  I got on really well with one of the two men finalists, Malcolm Wilkinson from Carlisle, and we kept in touch for many years. He even used one of my scripts for his own panto production.

When we got to ASDA we were greeted by lots of reporters and TV camera crews.  We were interviewed live on TV by Martin Frizell, a GMTV reporter, and husband of long-term presenter Fiona Phillips.  It was a strange, but enjoyable occasion. Telling jokes in front of a few ASDA staff, early morning shoppers and reporters wasn't quite what I was used to.  Among the others taking part was Jayne Tunnicliffe, Cilla's friend Yana in *Coronation Street* and who also appeared in *Phoenix Nights*. Jayne told me she was working as 'Mary Unfaithful' at the time round the northern clubs with an act playing *Oasis* numbers on her ukulele!

There was just one main trouble with all the talent shows and that is the one that the winner of the talent show at the New Kings Cabaret in Birmingham found out.  After winning, he was offered a booking but he couldn't take it as he only had enough material for the 15 minutes he had done in the heats!

*Gimme that one more chance.......................................................!*

In safari gear on *Opportunity Knocks* 1970

Joan Neal and Hughie Green

# CHAPTER 9

## LET ME ENTERTAIN YOU!

I HATE being called a 'comedienne'. I prefer the term 'comic'. Having said that, I don't like the current trend of actresses calling themselves actors and like to be known as an actress. How contrary is that!

As much as I desperately wanted to be a comic there was one thing holding me back, I was afraid I didn't have enough material. Over the years, I'd written endless scripts, learnt songs, thought up audience participation, the lot - but did I really have enough material to do it for real? It's alright filling a few minutes in front of a panto audience full of family and friends or even a three to five minute cameo for TV, as I did for *Opportunity Knocks*, but another one altogether if you are going to make it on the harsh and critical working men's club circuit.

Years ago in the heydays of the clubs there would be two or three acts in one night - a real cabaret show. That has long gone and one act now is booked to perform all night. The usual set-up today in clubs for singers is three half-hour spots, or even three 45-minute spots, sandwiched between the bingo, meat raffle and open the box! A comic, on the other hand, is usually expected to do a 60-minute one-off spot or two 30-minute spots and that, believe me, is a long time to keep people laughing, now you can see why anyone who could sing had a big advantage. My breakthrough came with the help of a timely piece of encouragement. I was at Ann Oliver's Thursday night cabaret in Leicester where I met Mervyn Jaye, a professional impersonator, who had just appeared on *New Faces* and gone down a treat. I told him that I didn't think I had enough material to work and he said: "Nobody ever thinks they do, you just have to give it a try." If he hadn't have said that, I don't think I would ever have given it a go!

My first professional appearance was at a Leicester club. The entertainment secretary at Belgrave Liberal Club in Leicester had seen me in talent shows and also at Ann Oliver's and he asked me to do a short spot. This was about 20 minutes for £25 on a Saturday night when they also had two singers appearing.

# Dee Quemby

It may not have been a full club comic's booking, but it was certainly a way of getting me going in the clubs. I had a really good spot between the singers and people were asking the entertainment secretary afterwards to give me a proper booking. I was called into a small bar at the side of the club and an elderly man - I only remember that his first name was Jack - who was a well known agent from Thurnby Lodge, said: "My wife loved you, she said give that little girl some work!" I told him that I didn't think I could do an hour spot yet, and he told me to let him know when I had sorted myself out. He kept ringing me for a year, but at the time I just didn't have the confidence to do it, so I kept putting him off. Jack died that same year and I didn't get to work in the clubs until many years later.

Talking about agents if you are thinking about doing the clubs, it is all pretty pointless being without one. Usually you do a 'shop window' that is on a Sunday after the entertainment secretaries meeting. Anyone can do this, and if the ent secs like you, they'll most likely book you for their club. Unfortunately a lot of ent secs do not stop after these meetings, so if you don't impress the few that are there, you then have to try the talent shows that advertise 'agents will be there' but very few ever are, if any! In effect this empty promise provides a cheap show for the venue that is staging it.

When you do eventually get an agent, you soon realise that there are three sorts in club land - the good, the not so good and the 'absolute shite'. I have been to bookings where I was told; "we didn't ask for comedy, the agent said you could sing." This type of agent will tell them anything (in other words 'taurus excretum'!) to get a booking for an act and so get his 15 per cent commission! Luckily, if you are not too bad when you start working on the clubs, you soon build up a reputation and better agents will contact you. In this way you now start to move up the agents' ladder.

When you are fairly well established, clubs and venues will contact you direct. I have got to the stage now where I promote my own panto tour, ladies' nights, 40s night and cabaret shows, as well as working for a fair few agents. My first booking with an agent, however, was at Gotham British Legion. I did my three half hours, plus an encore, and, you've guessed it, I hadn't even used half the material that I'd prepared. Mervyn, you were right!

A PA (sound system) for an entertainer is essential. Gone are the days when you could walk into any club and just pick up a mike (mic') and as for live backing, you're more likely to see a carpet fitter's ladder! Of course to begin with you buy the cheapest kit possible, as your career might not last long. No sense in wasting good money! Over the years you upgrade and build up a reasonable amount of good, reliable and always very heavy kit. When an agent rings with a booking the first thing you ask is where the concert room is and pray he isn't going to say it's in an upstairs room! How well I remember carrying heavy speakers up an outside fire escape with very icy steps one freezing cold dark winter's night. (I know you have to suffer to be a star, I just want to know when the suffering's going to stop!)

One of the best things for any performer is a radio mike. These are great for walking round an audience (even into the 'Gents' if needs must, and has!). However sometimes they can be a nightmare! I was performing my spot in a club in Corby unaware that there was a 24-hour taxi firm's office on top of the building. Their radio frequency was the same that my radio mike was on. My act was peppered with calls to and from the taxi drivers most of them just as a tag line was coming up. Happy days!

When you first begin to work, you do the pub circuit that usually means standing in a corner as they rarely have any form of stage. Being a mere 5'1½" meant that all people could see of me was the top of my head. Imagine my amazement and delight when I began working the pubs in Nottingham and found that most actually had a concert room, being more like the working men's clubs in Leicester.

I have worked in all sorts of social and working men's clubs and theatres, bingo halls, hotels, pubs and leisure centres. It never fails to amaze me where you will be asked to work. Years ago I was asked to do a show in a cowshed. When we got there the cows were still in it! They had to be moved outside and the camping community came in with buckets that they turned upside down and sat on ready for the show to begin. I have worked at Butlins' hotels in Llandudno and Blackpool, many places in Skegness and even a car showroom at night when they were unveiling a new car. My PA was set up next to this car and many bemused people were looking at me as I went through my routine.

My friend Karen West, a professional singer, once appeared in a fabric factory and in addition to being paid, picked up some material for her new curtains!

The more unusual venues have included Rampton Hospital, various Officers' Mess's and even HM Whitemoor Prison, home to some of the most notorious criminals in the land. When I went there some of the prisoners included serial killer Dennis Neilson and several IRA terrorists. No jokes about a captive audience please as I was there to appear in front of the staff and warders! We walked into the room and a woman came up to me immediately and gave me my money. She explained that they paid the artiste as soon as they got there as if the prisoners knew there was entertainment on they would stage an incident just to upset the night for the warders and the guards. Riot gear was packed away in a cupboard. I was told that in the event of trouble, they would put on the riot gear and I'd have to pack up my PA and get out of there as quickly as I could! Anyway, we had a great show without any trouble, though on the news the next day we heard that several of the IRA prisoners had escaped during the night. Perhaps they could hear me singing!

I went with my friend Joy, 'Joie Hearts', to appear in a hotel in Skegness at a cabaret during a 'race night'. This is where they have films of old horse races and you have to bet on the horse you think is going to win before the film is shown. We had a blind singer with us from Nottingham who had had a number one hit in the charts. During his spot, he often lost his sense of direction and ended up facing the wrong way, at one time singing romantically to the wall. Fortunately he had his girlfriend to help as she kept calling out to him "quarter to three", "ten to six" and such like so he could negotiate his way back to face the audience.

I was booked to do an RAF family club in the south and when I got there they were very apologetic. They hadn't realised that on the same night they had a big show on in the main hall with a 'star comedian' who years later would achieve even more fame in a much-loved soap on TV. They thought that because of the competition they would not get much of a turn out in the family club that night, so asked whether I would come back again a few weeks later. This I did and on going back was told that the night in question had not gone as well as expected as a lot of the squaddies had got very drunk and the heckled star had performed for ten minutes and then walked off, having been paid a few grand in advance.

On my level you don't get paid until you finish your spot. So that's enough motivation to keep you going! As you can imagine, hearing this didn't exactly fill me with too much confidence for my stint in the family club. But worse was to follow shortly after I'd started my act in what was now a well packed venue as the fire alarm went off. So we all had to stand outside and wait for the fire engine to arrive. Fortunately it was no more serious than a false alarm. This was, however, a moment when my heart well and truly sunk. You have been going great, working the audience on your side when you have to stop for an unscheduled break such as this. On many occasions trying to get them going again would have been impossible and the night would have gone flat. But, somehow, we had a great night and they recommended me to other RAF bases as a result.

All of us who have taken to the stage have experienced the audience from hell and there are different ways of dealing with it. The best way of dealing with abuse is to fight back. Any comic who has been working for at least a year will have a few well-rehearsed put downs up their sleeve to make any heckler – usually a man – look a complete prat. This will also win the heckler's friends over to your side and shut him up!

A booking for a really well known agent up north provided just such a challenge. I will save face by sparing the exact location, but I can safely say that it was one of the worst places I have ever appeared at. We got to this dismal, dirty pub surrounded by old cars, bikes and rubbish. When we walked in we were greeted with the sight of unfriendly, scruffy people. There was nowhere for me to stand, which wasn't too much of a surprise. After being introduced as "a comic all the way from Leicester", the first comment from someone in the audience was "f\*\*k off back to Leicester!" My reply to the heckler was: "I don't do requests." I was going to do an impression of a prat but you've just beaten me to it." This raised a laugh but it wasn't any guarantee that I'd last the evening. I can honestly say that they were the most ignorant lot of people I have ever come across and when you've worked the clubs as long as I have, that's saying something. But this only made me more determined to carry on regardless. So I 'upped' my microphone and did the full hour.

The agent came to pay me at the end and said: "Comedy's changed these days. You don't have to be funny any more, just 'eff and blind' all the while. I really admire you for doing your full spot tonight." This only made me more resolved to carry on with my own interpretation of comedy. Yes sometimes you do have to use the odd swear word here and there to get a point across, but to my mind if you swear every other word you are only giving the audience half an act.

These days we hear swearing everywhere. In the streets, in shops, at work, in schools and many children are growing up thinking this is perfectly normal. Years ago we were performing the touring panto at a Royal British Legion Club. Chubby Brown, at the time, had his own 'version' of *Living Next Door To Alice* in the pop-charts. There was a notice on the wall in the dressing room saying this version of the song was banned and on no account was it to be sung in the club. Not one of the very nice young girls in my show could understand why this was! Well after all, if you hear swearing all the while it loses its shock value! What do these people do if they want to swear? I always remember being told years ago about a young child coming home from school and constantly using a four-letter word. His mum said: I don't mind you saying that, but if I ever catch you saying Trent Bridge.............!" That cured him.

Coventry was a great place to work years ago. There were several Irish clubs and many social clubs a lot of which were named after the different makes of cars that were manufactured there at the time like the Standard-Triumph and

Jaguar. I went to the Jaguar Club to do a showcase. It was massive room with a very long catwalk from the large stage that went out into two thirds of the audience. At that time there was a horror group called *Nightmare* who combined horror and music and they were very big all over Europe. They were working a lot of the music cubs here and they were doing this showcase too. I had read a review of their act in *The Stage* and knew there would be buckets full of blood, realistic hangings and beheadings. At that time I was very squeamish and when I saw the gallows, blocks and axes covered in dried 'blood' filling the stage, I felt quite ill. I knew a lot of the agents and when this act was announced I stood at the back of the hall behind a pillar determined not to look. These agents and their wives were looking at me and laughing, the music started and after about 15 seconds into the act everybody was looking decidedly pale and ill. The act finished and I went backstage. The stairs up to the dressing room were covered in blood footprints, I opened the dressing room door and the girl in the act sat there covered in dripping blood stuffing a hamburger into her mouth! It really put it all into perspective!

Corby was a place I worked many times years ago and every club I went into was full of burly tough looking Scots with the strongest accents ever but what great nights we had, I couldn't understand them but they could me! And I was told that they particularly liked women comics!

I believe that if you are standing on a stage in front of people you should make the most of yourself. I once worked with a singer who set his PA up in ripped jeans and a dirty T-shirt and even dirtier trainers. When he walked out to perform he was wearing the same clothes! When we held the talent show at Scraptoft working men's one of the acts couldn't understand why there was a mark for 'appearance' and went on to perform in a very crumpled old jumper and dirty jeans. Needless to say he didn't get through his heat to the next round.

I have worked with Stan Boardman at Caesars Palace, Luton; this was one of the best cabaret nightspots years ago and now sadly gone, George Roper, one of the original Drifters, Emile Ford and The Platters. I was booked to appear with 'The Platters' in a Birmingham working men's club. When we arrived the whole stage was swamped with their PA. It looked more like a music shop than a stage. There was no room for mine and The Platters' roadies/technicians told me I could go through their kit. The Platters arrived later on and were hastily taken straight to a room until it was time for their 'star' spot. When they walked out to perform they looked more like teenagers than the middle-aged people the audience were expecting. Probably one of them was an original but the others certainly weren't. At the end of the night there were people queuing up for autographs holding old LP covers and looking confused at the group and then at the album cover. No one got an autograph the group were whisked straight off the stage and into a waiting car.

I've been lucky enough to meet some of the top comedy stars in my time and I've got to say that the much-missed Bob Monkhouse was at the top of the list. I first met him while I was doing the talent show at King's Cabaret at Birmingham. Bob Monkhouse was just one of the stars I met many times there. I found him both immensely encouraging, polite and genuinely interested in a 'no-name' just-getting-started comic. If you've ever considered Bob Monkhouse's public image, he was nothing at all like that. A lot of people thought of him as being smarmy and smug but how wrong they were, he was both warm and very willing to help someone obviously trying to make their way in a business in which he had reached the top.

He very kindly promised that he had some great material for a woman comic and would send it to me. I was very thrilled, as you can imagine, but wasn't expecting Bob Monkhouse jokes to drop through the letterbox. Imagine my surprise, therefore, when a few weeks later I picked up an envelope addressed to me, marked 'Park Lane Hotel, London', looking like it had been written in my own handwriting. Amazingly, he had taken the time to copy very accurately my handwriting for my name and address on the outside of the envelope. Inside I could hardly believe my eyes! There were three pages full of jokes and a two-page handwritten letter from Bob Monkhouse. Goodness knows how much that would have cost if he had been writing for me professionally! I didn't actually use any of them, although that was scarcely the point. My style of humour and Bob Monkhouse's were very different. Where he would have endless topical jokes and was a great writer of them, my act was far more likely to contain day to day events of what had happened to me at the hairdressers, the doctors, in the supermarket or with the kids! I have always been into what I would term 'observational comedy' and that's what I think audiences respond most to in my case!

I will always feel grateful and honoured that one of the all-time great comedians took the time and trouble to support and encourage me at a time when women comics were not in demand. Today there aren't that many traditional stand-up comedians. Comedy has changed more than any other form of show business.

One of our greatest actors today is Sir David Jason, known to millions for his TV roles as Del Boy in *Only Fools And Horses*, *Jack Frost*, Granville in *Porridge* and many other excellent TV dramas. It was over 20 years ago when I first got the chance to meet him in London and what he wrote to me then I've got safely locked away hoping it will actually materialise someday!

David Jason was appearing in the comedy play *Look No Hans* with Lynda Bellingham at the then *Strand Theatre*. I went to the matinée, and as I knew the stage doorkeeper I went to the stage door afterwards and stood inside. It was in the winter and I was clutching my panto script which I was trying to learn when David Jason strode across and said: "what you got there then?" and took it out of my hand. He read a few lines and laughed. What an honour, it was a script I had written myself! He then told me there was an 'actors" café nearby and how actors would go in, sit down and plonk a script on the table, even if they weren't working, just to make the other out of work actors jealous! We started talking and when he knew I was trying to be a comic he said: "What else could you be with a name like Deirdre?" In the 60s and 70s sitcoms Deirdre was a much-used name for some reason! In *Steptoe And Son* one of Harold's girl friends was a 'Deirdre'.

We went for something to eat at a nearby café in Covent Garden. We were chatting away and I couldn't help noticing that two middle aged women, whose view of us was somewhat obscured by a very large plant, kept parting the leaves to have a look at us. They didn't have any trouble identifying David Jason, but human nature being what it is they thought I must be somebody in showbiz too. They said to David Jason "Are you?" He quickly answered: "Yes I am." They looked at me and asked: "Are you Amanda Barrie?" Amanda Barrie would later play Mike Baldwin's wife Alma in *Coronation Street*, though at this time she was appearing in *Stepping Out* in nearby St Martin's Lane. I had long hair then, piled up in a bun on the top of my head and that was how Amanda Barrie wore hers too, so I suppose it was quite a logical question seeing the company I was in and I was very flattered!

166

David Jason went on to speak enthusiastically about the great Ronnie Barker and it was very obvious how much he admired him. Both actors of course appeared together in those great sitcoms *Open All Hours* and *Porridge*. He was very interested to hear that I was from Leicester and told me a little known fact and this was that he had appeared in Leicester as straight man to Bob Monkhouse many years before. He said he would come and see me perform in a talent show in London and I subsequently received loads of notes from him wishing me all the best in my career. He also wrote in one note that if I ever got my own show on the BBC, he would appear as a guest! At the time I didn't honestly see that happening at all. However I got my slightly more modest opportunity in 2004 when I hosted a three-hour phone-in programme on BBC Radio Leicester. Jennifer Norton who works behind the scenes immediately set to work to make a 20-year old promise come true.

Unfortunately it never even got off the ground, as the staff at his agents didn't entertain the idea at all. Jennifer was only going to ask if he would do a short phone interview with me for a few minutes. They didn't even return the copy of the note and photos of us together that she had sent them. Poor Jennifer it really bothered her for months. She had said to the rather snotty woman on the other end of the line: "We're not a Mickey Mouse organisation, we are the BBC!" Not to worry...........I have plenty of copies. You can bet your life on that! 'This time next year, Rodders.........!'

It's usually the case that the people around a star think themselves more important than anyone else, even the star! I really believe; that, if the now Sir David Jason had been made aware of this by the admin staff in his agent's office, he would have done it. On one of his notes he wrote 'As long as you love it keep doing it' and I've read those words many times over the years!

I had another special time with the stars when I was asked to appear in a charity show for the Roy Castle Cancer Appeal at the London Palladium. I was given the second star dressing room that belonged to Paul McGann, who was appearing in *Oliver* at the time. As I stood on that stage, I was overwhelmed by the stars that would have stood over the exact same spot over the years, like Frank Sinatra, Max Miller, Danny Kaye, Tommy Cooper, Judy Garland, Morecambe and Wise, Dean Martin, Marlene Dietrich, Les Dawson, Jimmy Tarbuck and The Crazy Gang to name but a few!

We were asked to sit in the audience and a man with a very strong Cockney accent informed us that in the case of an emergency we shouldn't panic each other and the audience by using words such as 'fire' or 'bomb'. Instead our code was 'Albert' in case of a fire or 'Arthur' for a bomb, or something very similar. This continued until I really was beginning to panic, not in case we had an emergency, but because I couldn't remember what any of these 'names' really meant! Garry Bushell, the popular and very witty TV showbiz critic came to watch the show. We still keep in touch to this day, especially on St George's Day!

Dave Vickers, who often appeared in my panto as my son or sidekick, came with me to Trafalgar Square in London to be part of an advertisement for a certain brand of ice cream. We had to take a panto cow skin with us, which proved very heavy so he brought his son's pushchair on which we wheeled 'Buttercup' on her journey around London. We got changed at the London Coliseum in St Martin's Lane, the home of the English National Opera, along with the other 'skin performers'. We all then trotted down in costume to Trafalgar Square. We found out that this coincided with the farmers' demonstration against the BSE crisis so we had to be carefully diverted away from one another, as the protesters

167

were getting a bit angry.  You can only imagine what hilarity this caused in the following day's press.

I was asked to appear on alternative comedy programme being filmed at the Camden Head at Islington.  This was at the time when alternative comedy was at its height.  I changed into my dress, that was bright yellow with big black spots on, yellow high heels and a pair of large dangly earrings.  This was the era when women decided to be make up free, wear black leggings and boots, baggy black T-shirts and shave their hair off.  My always very pessimistic husband said: "You're really going to die on your a**e with this lot!  I'm stopping down here in the bar" and it was looking like for once he would be right!  People were coming up to me, saying "Wow, don't you look different!"  The show was filmed in an upstairs room and I appeared with the Rapping Rabbi, whom I'd seen on a Friday night show on Channel 4.  For some reason he lay flat out on the floor of the Gents all night before his appearance!

Once again you can never quite tell how a show is going to go and we had a great laugh.  My heart sank when the producer said to me: "You're not an act", but he followed up with the kind words "you're a whole show!" which I took as a compliment.  Several people then came up to me and asked me to go down to London to work, saying: "All you do is walk in a pub, do 10 minutes, then move on to the next one.  "Ten minutes," I said; "That's not working, I'm used to doing an hour and a half!"

For someone, who is a self-professed non-singer, I've had to sing a fair deal over the last few years.  I started off doing a vocal/comedy act in Nottingham and Derby at a time when comics were not in demand anymore.  This was a time when TV was full of impressionist shows.  As I said previously, my friend Joy sorted out various backing tracks for me with the philosophy that everybody can sing a few songs, it's just a matter of finding out which ones suit you.  So I learnt some traditional 'easy' songs such as *Sailing, Let's Dance* and *Da Doo Ron Ron* – all specially chosen, as they are so familiar that audiences tend to sing along to them without paying too much attention to the vocalist.  This was very much in my favour!

One cold dark wintry Sunday night I had a booking at a club in Top Valley, a notorious estate in Nottingham.  We arrived early about 7pm and the club, which looked like a bungalow overlooking the estate, was in darkness with no sign of life at all.  John went to the club door and came back saying: "I can see a poster in the entrance hall it says 'Des Quemby guitar vocalist'!  A while later a man came to open up the club, so my husband went to see him and said: "I think there has been a mistake, my wife is a comic called Dee Quemby."  He replied: "Nothing to do with me, you'll have to see our president when he comes."  At least he let us in and we carried the PA into the concert room.  The stage was about 6" off the floor, about 2'0" wide and ran the length of the room.  There was a shower curtain at the end of the stage containing a chair and I was assured this was the dressing room!  I was also very concerned that there was a billiard table right in front of the stage.

A few men started to arrive and they began to play billiards on the table.  The president eventually made his grand entrance and was very put out when John gave him the news that his guitar vocalist for the night was nothing of the sort.  "We always have a male guitar vocalist on a Sunday.  It's too late to get anyone else now, she'll have to go on," he said in a huff.  The club was getting full by now and the local football team came in.  I peered out of the shower curtain and the billiard table - thank God – had disappeared.

The place was packed and it was time for me to appear. The president walked out onto the stage, picked up the microphone and tapped it three times, why do they all do this? He then made an introduction I don't think I'll ever forget if I live to be normal! "Ladies and gentlemen, we always have a guitar vocalist on a Sunday night, but tonight we have a young lady doing comedy and I sincerely hope this is not going to spoil anybody's night, ladies and gentlemen, Miss Dee Quemby" and out I walked! However, the audience was great. I went over time and finished up doing nearly two hours and had a wonderful night. The football crowd were out for a laugh and two old ladies, who had sat near my husband, put the 'icing on the cake' when they said at the end: "We've had a real good night, we get fed up with all them guitar vocalists every Sunday." Good on 'em!

I did another club in Nottingham - one of those 'cowboy clubs' where they have fastest draw contests. The audience was small, in fact it totalled six and they all sat at one of the tables playing cards! We set up the PA and, by now, were waiting to start. Then another six people walked in! I asked the ent sec when he wanted me to go on for my first spot. He said: "I'd go on now, we don't get more than this in on a Sunday" without even looking up from his cards.

So out I went and, what a surprise, they were a great! I could see my husband sat with a couple, then he moved and sat with another. During my first spot alone, he had gone through the entire audience. Then we got to bingo time and John won a game and out of embarrassment went round each member of the audience again to apologise. Clubs usually like winnings to go to their own members only, but these nice people were fine about it. At the end of the night everyone was up dancing to the six songs I could manage! The ent sec came into the dressing room and said: "Great night, the couple at the front table don't normally stop because they're deaf and dumb. But they can lip read, they've stopped all night and had a real laugh."

Like all club acts I've seen some very strange places over the years. Most places don't have dressing rooms or, if they do, they are only big enough to accommodate one very small person. I've changed in men's toilets where there is never anywhere to hang anything, a fridge in a pub on the Old Kent Road, London, in the showers at a rugby club (minus the rugby players, I hasten to add!), and in one pub I changed in the kitchen where my feet kept sliding beneath me on the grease covered floor.

I was booked to do a ladies night at a very dirty run down WMC in Leicester, now long gone. I got there early and the few people in the small bar were reminiscent of the actors in the bar scene from *Star Wars,* not really a good omen for the rest of the night! The massive concert room had rows of school canteen tables and hard chairs. The dressing room was full of broken chairs, why do clubs always keep broken chairs? A badly cracked mirror was covered in graffiti by artistes who had previously worked there mostly confirming what I now knew which was, what a 's**t-hole'! On the three-legged table, covered in beer stains and cigarette burns in front of the mirror, was an obviously worn, screwed up, pair of men's black knickers. However the night was a great success and I was booked for another show eight months later. On my return booking those knickers were still there in the exact same place; there was also a lot more graffiti on the mirror!

Nowadays one of the few live events that are put on regularly in the clubs and other venues is the ladies night. The very first one I promoted and appeared in was at Scraptoft Valley WMC in Leicester. The concert room was huge and beautifully furnished with a big circular stage and a black backcloth with twinkling lights. The night was a sell out as there must have been more than 400 women there. At the end Mark the ent sec, came up to me thrilled that they had taken more money over the bar than on New Year's Eve and that was saying something. I suggested to Mark that we organise a talent show, as I knew a lot of young people trying to get into the entertainment business. I asked agents, other acts and the well-known radio presenter Steve Merrick to be the judges.

The *Spice Girls* were all the rage at the time and we had five young girls aged 11 to 13, from the dancing school who were also appearing in my touring pantos - Erica Makin, Anisa Burton, Lara Dalby, Louise Jones and Laura Harris, who were all totally obsessed with them. They had made up a tribute band purely for fun. They got the backing tracks, and outfits and genuinely did look and sound like them and they appeared in a lot of charity shows. They called themselves *Girl Essence* and did a few numbers to get the evening started.

Erica is probably the most wonderful young singer I have ever heard and she has gone on to take leading roles in local amateur productions. She has the most amazing range from musicals to hard rock, as well as being a great natural dancer and actress and has done her stint of hard graft in the holiday camps. It's a pity we don't get talent scouts round and about any more like they used to be. There are so many young naturally talented people going unnoticed professionally who would knock spots off the ones in the charts and on the telly!

We were lucky enough to have some great amateur acts on the talent shows. One, in particular, called *Mosaic* featured four girls who danced and sang and had many quick changes. They were a big hit on the night and were immediately offered work in the clubs. One of the mothers told us that she had tried many times to get them a booking in the clubs and no one would give them a chance. But after this triumphant night they were inundated with offers. They became very popular on the Leicester club circuit and went on to work in other areas and do summer seasons before eventually disbanding.

You can never be prepared for what might happen in an audience and at one club, four men suddenly got up whilst I was doing my act on stage. They did no more than pick up an elderly woman and carry her out aloft, one shouted to me: "You carry on love she's only having a fit!"

There are numerous stories of amusing incidents in club land that you hear about on the circuit and one of my favourites concerns Neville King, a very well known ventriloquist who was very successful in the 60s and 70s. He was doing his vent act on stage in a working men's club when he became aware of the small cloth-capped ent sec creeping across the back of the stage. The ent sec came up behind him and whispered in his ear "they can't hear at the back, can you hold dummy nearer the 'mike'?"

At another venue a comic, who was not going down very well, said to the ent sec; "I think it went above their heads." The ent sec replied: "Well we did move speakers higher up wall last week."

Colin Fingers Henry is a pianist and many years back there would be a piano in a club for him to play but he always took a battered old red 'joanna' around with him to play honky-tonk numbers on. He was wheeling this piano into Belgrave

Liberal Club in Leicester where he was booked to play. The doorman looked at him and the piano and asked him; "are you a member?"

Club doormen are legendary, years ago nobody would get by them without a membership card. At one club the act on stage having had a bad time from the doorman said: "If we ever get invaded I'm coming here, no army will get in past that doorman."

I had a friend Margaret whom I had met at the Kings Talent show many years earlier and she was singing in Leicester and we went to see her perform. But her poor husband who had driven her there from Birmingham was made to sit in his car all night; the doorman wouldn't let him in without a membership card!

Club doormen can be very droll, late one-night after finishing a show I was standing in the foyer when an irate woman came barging back into the club loudly jangling her car keys. "I've got one stuck up me front and one stuck up me rear" she announced before charging into the concert room. "She's lucky at bingo as well" said the little old doorman without even looking up!

We went to see Peter Kay at a try out prior to a tour a few years ago at Ann Oliver's in Leicester. A few comics do 'try outs', Victoria Wood is one. They appear at a small venue with little publicity and then 'try out' their new material to see what to include, or what not to include, when they tour. I met Peter Kay afterwards and said that he must have grown up in working men's clubs as he had a real understanding and affection for them especially with his brilliant series *Phoenix Nights*. He said how much he loved being taken to the clubs as a child especially at Christmas. He told me how all the kids would look at Santa's shoes trying to remember which Committee men had been wearing them earlier to work out who 'Santa' was that particular year. They always did work it out. Instead of saying "hello Santa" they would say "hello Bert" or whatever his name was! I asked if he would autograph my ticket and was just about to spell Deirdre when he said: "I can spell that, it's the same as my mother's." He's the only person who has ever spelt it right first off!

Club acts are very generous and always ready to donate their services to a charity show. When the Gulf War was on and many politically correct theatres and council owned buildings were refusing to let people stage a benefit night for the Gulf War, I got very annoyed at this wimpy attitude and decided to stage one. I booked Loughborough Town Hall and asked several club acts and pupils from the dancing school to appear. We had the British Legion coming with their banners, one bearer being an ex-dancer from my men's troupe at the Neal Academy, Keith Hassall. We also had the vicar from Quorn coming to lead us in a prayer for peace at the end of the show. The tickets were not selling well and then a week before the show the war ended. I worked out it would be more expensive to pay the full cancellation cost than go ahead by putting my own money to meet the cost of the show; so this I did. But on the night what a welcome surprise: where did all those wonderful people come from? The Town Hall was packed and we were able to send a really good donation to help the families of the soldiers who had lost their lives.

An agent booked me to do a comedy spot in a 40s show and it was great to see the room decorated with flags and all ages of people dressed in uniforms and 1940s style outfits. It was a really great fun night and I decided to promote my own 40s shows that I have done now for several years. Some of the older girls from the dancing school became the 'Doodlebug' dancers. I got myself an ENSA uniform and we always have a guest singer on with us. I also appear as

## Dee Quemby

Shirley Temple, Mrs Mopp, Carmen Miranda and Marlene Dietrich. These shows have proved very popular even to younger people and this led to my Music Hall show coming into being.

Over the years the Doodlebug Dancers (Les Girls in the Music Hall shows) have changed and the guest singers have come and gone. I hope I have remembered them all.

| Doodlebug Dancers (aka Les Girls) | Guest Artistes |
| --- | --- |
| Jane Harker | Karen West |
| Lucy Brown | Neil Ashley |
| Lucy Rose | Peter Graham |
| Tracey Smith | Reg Ryan |
| Felicity George | Ted and John |
| Cassie Booth | Jay the Entertainer |
| Rachel Sullivan | Erica Makin |
| Nicola Neilson | Jonny Fines |
| Susan Thompson | |
| Stacie Hogg | |
| Semeena Ditta | |
| Anisa Burton | |
| Rebecca Newitt | |
| Samantha Foister | |
| Charlotte Barrows | |
| Natalie Drew | |
| Erica Makin | |

### 40s Spiv
Eric Makin (Erica's Dad)

### Circus Skills
Amy Burge

### Sound 'man'
John Hayward (I'm the only act in this business with a deaf soundman!)
Roger Willows - stand in soundman (not deaf!)

Thanks one and all for the great shows!

Dee X

Don't put your daughter on the stage............!

First time my name was up in a club! (Belgrave Liberal Club in Leicester)

Joy and Mike

That spotted dress!

Karen West

Evacuees in a 40s night

On stage at *The Royal Centre*, Nottingham in ENSA uniform

John as the air raid warden

The original line up of Les Girls

Mountsorrel's tribute to the *Spice Girls* (*Girl Essence*)

Les Girls today

Backstage at the *London Palladium* with Fiona Castle

With David Jason outside *The Strand Theatre* (now
the *Novello Theatre*) in London 1985

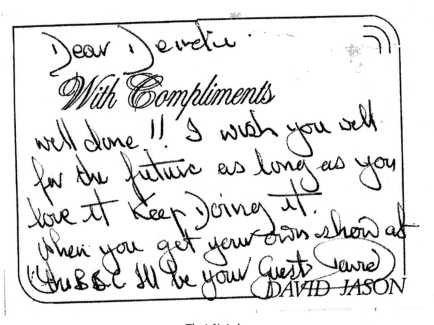

That Note!

# INTERMISSION

Bingo books and meat raffle tickets are now on sale in the bar

Confectionary, ice creams and soft drinks are available
from................. your local supermarket

## ARTISTE'S LAMENT (ANON) *found in a very old 'CLUB NEWS'*

You stumble wear from your bed
Thunder crashing in your head
Within the hour you're washed and bright
Somehow you've got to star tonight

Outside it's bright and snowing fast
Just how long can this winter last
With gear in car you set off slow
There's times you just don't want to go

Through snow, fog, ice you're on your way
To the land where little club folk play
Near journeys end and there's still some stress
The agent's given you wrong address!

You see a local club land chap
With big beer belly and flat cap
Never heard of that round here
Says he reeking of last nights beer

Eventually through dark nights gloom
A dim lit club land sign does loom
With speakers, amps and mikes on back
You stagger in like a loaded yak

The concert room with hard wood chairs
Is always up three flights of stairs
Committee man's the first you see
Thou frightened us to death did thee

We thought you'd gone and let us down
And tonight we've really gone to town
We've got bread cakes, hot peas and Sid
Club land's best backing, cost four quid!

Fast as you can you set up gear
You think "What am I dong here"?
Switch dressing closet light switch on
Only to find the bulb has gone

But "luxury", it's got a hook
To hang your bits and pieces up
No mirror, basin, fire or loo
It's just like prison there for you

## Dee Quemby

We want three-spots, hope thou's reet?
The comic got paid off last neet
He made our bingo run quite late
And that our members really hate

"I sing as well"; you quickly plead
Does th'organist and drummer read?
Read owt our Sid, best in the land
He used to play in our church band

Your heart sinks low there's no way out
A voice within you wants to shout
You think about your agent smug
He's sitting home, all warm and snug

You try to phone him, busy line
It's "off the hook" till half past nine
He don't want trouble, no not he
Fifteen percent plus V.A.T.

But further bad news lies in wait
No pick up here didn't he tell you, mate
Four letter words you keep in check
You think; "I'll break that agent's neck"

You're starting now to feel quite low
Spirits dwindle down
Your ever-smiling cheery face
Gets wrinkled with a frown

The audience don't want to know
As if you wasn't there
They sit all stony faced depressed
And in their beer do stare

Everyone is smoking
The fag smoke hurts your eyes
Then someone shouts; "you're rubbish mate"
You feel you want to die

The organist with fag and pint
Murders everything in sight
The drummer plays on clapped out drums
Broken sticks and beats not right

All night you sing, tell gags and die
But magic words "it's time" they cry!
More, more, more, just one more mate
Sing 'em "*Amarillo* cock, they really love that one a lot

Then as the crowd all clap and cheer
He drops the mike into his beer
So ever willing on you go
Your raise a smile "On with the show"!

Then end of night pack kit away
Drunk wants signed 'pic' for Auntie May
Car loaded set off down the road
To seek the refuge of your abode

You're thinking what a ruddy life
Full of stress and strain and strife
But you wouldn't change it not one bit
So next day by the phone you sit

It rings and you hear "agents here
You went a bomb last night I hear"
And then his words fill you with doom
"They want you back again there soon"

You take it manly on the chin
"A charity?" "Yes count me in"
The mirror shows your face of strain
'Cause you know you've been had again!

*But showbiz in your heart does burn that's why you'll always be a turn!*

On the back cover of a Chubby Brown video he writes............ I take my hat off to all the professional entertainers and to all the fans who keep them there because there isn't any better magic than show business!

## DRUM ROLL (IMAGINARY!)

Please take your seats for part 2 of 'I'm ready for my close up......anybody!'

# ACT II

*Keep on running...........................................................................!*

# CHAPTER 10

## HAVE PANTO, WILL TRAVEL
## - OH YES WE WILL!

HOW on earth did I ever let myself get talked into doing a touring panto, was I stark raving mad?  Had I taken leave of my senses?

It all started when I was trying out as a comic at Ann Oliver's Thursday night cabaret show nights.  Quite a lot started from there when I think about it!  Ann and her husband Eddie, who was head of drama at her studio, asked John and I to audition for a touring panto in 1986.  They were going to take their version of *Cinderella*, which had three ugly sisters for some reason (those threes again!) around the many local working men's clubs.  My husband John and his friend Robin, who were both taking parts in our dancing school pantos, went along to audition for the Ugly Sister roles even though they hadn't played 'dame' parts before.

I went along for anything Ann and Eddie thought I could do.  There was a lot of whispering going on while we auditioned, then Eddie uttered these life-changing words: "There's something not right, let the girls audition for the Ugly Sisters!"  So I auditioned for one of the Ugly Sisters and got the part.  John and Robin were given the male bailiff parts and they suited them far better.

I loved playing an Ugly Sister.  It was so much fun and the costumes were fabulous.  It was great being bitchy to poor Cinders for a change instead of being hopelessly in love with her when playing Buttons.  I loved Ann Oliver she had such a wonderful sense of dry humour.  She was tall and slim and always beautifully dressed with her hair pulled back in a tight blond bun.  She stood and walked like a ballerina and everyone had to call her 'Miss Anne'.  She had been a professional dancer, yet she was so down to earth.  During one panto performance I heard her shout at one of the actors on the stage: "They can't hear you, get yer gob round the mike!"

The following year Ann and Eddie decided against doing another panto tour for the clubs as they had been asked to provide and choreograph the dancers for the professional panto at the De Montfort Hall in Leicester. To be honest, audiences were beginning to dwindle in the working men's clubs and they didn't think there was much of a future for a touring panto. Well, as the saying goes ............Oh yes, there was!

John and I were members of Belgrave Liberal Club in Leicester and two of the committee members Roy and Alan said that it was such a shame that there wouldn't be a panto for the clubs at Christmas. As they knew I belonged to a dancing school, they asked me whether I was interested in doing one and promised me not only a booking at Belgrave Liberal Club but also a helping hand towards getting others too. If it had been left to me, I would have said a definite 'no'! But my friend Eunice was with me and she said: "Of course, she'll do it!" And that was that! I then spent weeks and weeks worrying about it. To begin with, to spin a *Jack And The Beanstalk* phrase, I didn't have a bean!

So I now had to sort out buying a van, designing and painting transportable scenery, sound equipment, props, extra microphones and Uncle Tom Cobley and all! And that was before I actually got any bookings. Friends and girls from the dancing school asked to be in the panto and I somehow managed to get several bookings. I then got started on writing the script and that's how DQ Productions came into being in 1987. Our very first panto performance was at Holwell Sports and Social Club at Asfordby with *Aladdin And His Magic Lamp* and it must have gone down well as we've returned there every year since.

Panto is very hard work but always great fun and there are always plenty of stories to tell afterwards. All together now...................... Oh yes there is!

Children love panto and there's one thing I have found out from my years as a children's entertainer - you can't fool kids. If you are doing a magic trick it's a far different thing when children are in the audience. Adults will sit and watch with a slightly embarrassed look on their face if they can see how you are doing it. Not so with children, they have no embarrassment and will speak up very loudly: "You're pulling a string!" or "It's in your other hand!" Answering back may not get full marks everywhere, but it's much needed in the panto world. Children will never let you down or will they?

On one of our first panto tours nearly 20 years ago, we arrived at a club that will remain nameless. We were met by the sight of some of the most unruly children ever brought together on a single carpet. They ranged from five to 15 years and were shouting, screaming and fighting. When we started the show, the principal boy and girl walked out to be greeted by the kids shouting: "Lesbians!" The 'baddie' received so much grief during his appearance on stage that he had a 'wee' dilemma during the interval. Desperate to go to the toilet that was at the side of the concert room, and terrified of the kids, he resorted to using the sink in the dressing room making the rest of the cast stand outside while he did! At the end of the night he wouldn't leave the dressing room until he was assured that all the kids had gone home.

The traditional chase around the audience is something the kids always love but, on this occasion, two 14-year-old boys decided to get up and rugby tackle me. The two 'Chinese' policemen, also involved in the chase came to the rescue and promptly set about them with their plastic truncheons. For some reason, the boys seemed to think this was great! At the end of the night the ent sec came up to me and said: "The kids loved it, we want you back next year." I replied:

"Don't threaten me!" Yet the show must go on and we have been back every year since.

Also in that first show was Robert Bramley Buhler who now plays dame for the dancing school shows, and is also one of the leading lights on the amateur stage in Loughborough. He was playing Wishee Washee and at the end had to throw sweets out to the audience. He came to me at the end of one show looking quite worried. He asked if he could miss throwing out the sweets in future? He said a large and abusive mother had threatened him, as her child had not been able to catch one! I'm glad to say that the children have always been much better behaved than that first time, and we never saw that particular mum again!

The first time we performed at Newfoundpool WMC there were literally hundreds of screaming kids sitting on the floor. The stage was in the corner and about six inches off the floor (another one!) and our dressing room was so tiny we had to erect our own at the side of the concert room using metal tubular rods that lock together over which we hang a curtain. As the show went on, the children were getting nearer and nearer to the stage and attempting to join in the panto by becoming part of the cast! This is the time you discover, that most working men's club committee men are generally not the bravest of people and, where kids are concerned, very thin on the ground, so we were left to build our own barricade. At the interval we had to dismantle our makeshift dressing room and erect a metal barrier in front of the stage. Walking out in the second half I felt like I was performing in *Les Miserables!*

I love the way children take things so literally and, as you can imagine, the number of laughs and highly touching moments we've had on the road over the years have far outnumbered any of the problems. The Latimer Ward Conservative Club in Leicester is one of the biggest clubs in the city and they like to do an hour's bingo during the interval. That's too long for the cast to sit around in the dressing rooms, so we always go to the bar in our costumes. Sometimes we sit at a table at the side out of the way and play bingo ourselves. One year I was sitting there waiting for the bingo to start dressed in my poor clothes as *Mother Goose*. I became aware that someone was watching me and turned round to see a little angelic-looking girl watching me with great pity. She was about six years old and had long white blond hair and big blue eyes which just added to the pathos when she said ever so sympathetically: "I hope you win the bingo 'cause you're so poor." Then she turned away and walked off her eyes filled with tears and mine were too.

A similar incident occurred at Market Harborough Conservative Club only the other year. I was playing Sarah the cook in *Dick Whittington*. When I said I had no money, a kind little boy put his hand in his pocket and said: "You can have my 10p, it's all I've got, but you can have it."

Many years back one Christmas, we were setting up in a club in Wigston for an afternoon performance of our panto and we also had another one to do that night at the Belgrave Liberal Club in Leicester. We were just about to start when one of the girls collapsed on the dressing room floor in agony. I had noticed a doctor's surgery opposite the club so I ran out of the club and into the surgery where four women were sitting at a table behind the reception desk drinking tea. I explained what had happened. They said the doctor was not at the surgery and as it was an emergency to ring for an ambulance immediately. This was before we had mobile phones and I was told I couldn't use the phone there. Talk about no room at the Inn! I ran back to the club and found their pay phone and rang for an ambulance. The paramedics came almost immediately and said that Jane, still writhing on the floor in agony, had to be taken to hospital. She wanted someone to go with her and there was no way we could get in touch with any of her family. My friend Alison whose husband Dennis, and young son Hugo were appearing in the panto said she would go with her. Fine and dandy but Alison had her new baby boy with her in a carrycot! Alison said she would leave the baby's bottles and anything else it might need and would be back as soon as she could. The paramedics then carried Jane out aloft through the middle of the packed audience with Alison following behind.

The baby lay under the small dressing room table and slept through the whole show. We hadn't heard from Alison and had no choice but to pack up and load the van and take the baby with us. We got to the next club and set up and once again the baby went under the dressing room table. Apart from waking up for the odd feed he was the perfect showbiz baby, 'born in a trunk' as Judy Garland sang. We kept ringing the hospitals from the club's pay phone but Jane hadn't been admitted at any of them. We did the finalé of the panto and the audience left the concert room. I went into the dingy small dressing room to pack up my costumes. The baby lay there fast asleep in very poor and shabby, dimly lit surroundings. All was so quiet and peaceful that it was just like a Nativity scene. I was very moved and felt it really was Christmas. I quite expected three men with long beards dressed in flowing caftans to come in bearing gifts and to see a bright shining star lighting up the beer crates and broken chairs in the club's yard outside. We packed up and Dennis took Hugo and the new baby home. We found out the next day that all the hospitals had been full and it had taken a long while to find a bed for Jane who by that time had been diagnosed with a kidney stone. Alison finally arrived home at 3am the next morning.

On one panto tour we had just finished the finalé of an evening performance of *Mother Goose* when we heard the strangest juddering noise. Everybody in the dressing room checked their mobiles and we noticed a box on one of the walls shaking and then the fire alarm went off! I was half out of my ball gown and most of the rest of the cast were in their underwear. The dressing room door was flung open by a committee man telling us we had to leave the club. I zipped my ball gown up and put my wig back on as the audience charged through the small dressing room of half naked people and out through the fire escape doors onto the car park. Another man barged into the dressing room telling us there could be a fire through half clenched teeth as he had a lit cigarette in his mouth! I walked out onto the dark freezing cold car park resplendent in my finalé outfit, tiara and diamanté jewellery and got the crowd singing the audience participation song *Tiddly Winky* again! Fortunately it was a false alarm. Apparently at the end of the show some children had left the concert room, crept upstairs and set the alarm off. Little sods! I wanted to get home so I could watch the 'soaps' I had taped.

Children love shouting "There's something behind you" but at Leicester Forest East Rugby Club halfway through the performance one frustrated boy's patience with us, was wearing thin. The ghost behind us had been perfectly visible to everyone apart from us, of course, for some time, so he folded his arms with great indignation and said loudly: "I'm not shouting anymore. I keep telling you there's something behind you - but you don't take any notice of me!"

Children are very practical and to the point as was the case in a previous production of *Mother Goose*. This panto tells the tale of a poor family finding a goose, Priscilla, and off she goes to live with them as one of the family, later to bring them great wealth by laying golden eggs. When I said to the audience of over 200 children "What are we going to do, we have no jobs, no money and no food?" all the kids shouted back "Eat the goose!"

Kids can also be very cruel as was the case when a young girl playing one of the 'babes' in *Babes in the Wood* came off stage in tears. It was the scene where the two robbers take the children deep into the woods to kill them before turning soft and letting them go. John was playing one of the robbers and when he asked the audience "should we kill them or let them go, kids?" the boys shouted back in unison "let the boy go, kill the girl!"

In the same panto the nurse has a big dog she is trying to housetrain. Every time the dog cocked his leg up the children had to shout 'Nursey, Nursey", but not at one show in Leicester. The first time the dog did this, a little boy shouted: "He's having a s**t." We were on stage trying our best not to laugh ('corpsing' in showbiz term - a big professional sin!) when he shouted again: "Look, he's having another s**t" as all the other children nodded in agreement.

In our recent *Dick Whittington*, Sarah the Cook is on a diet and every time she holds up a sweet and says: "I'll just have one of my sweets", the children were supposed to shout: "you'll get fat you silly cat." Needless to say at a lot of the shows the children made their own ending up!

Many years back we appeared at Cottesmore RAF Camp with *Dick Whittington*. All our individual details, along with car and van registrations, had to be sent beforehand and we were met at the gate by armed guards. During the desert island scene the dancing girls wore black tights, leotards, gloves and had balaclava-type masks with woolly hair on. At all previous shows this sight had been greeted by kids shouting: "It's the natives" but, on this occasion, the RAF kids shouted: "It's the IRA!" Towards the end of the first half the emergency alarm went off for a drill practice. Everything wound down and we were in total darkness much to the high-ranking officer's annoyance as he had organised the panto and he had informed the base there was a show on. He shot off and a few seconds later everything started up again. Some poor squaddies had had a right ear bashing!

We have toured with *Aladdin* many times with various different versions. One *Aladdin* was the same year the very popular film *The Full Monty* was on release. You have to keep the panto topical so in the second half Abanazar sang *You Sexy Thing* to me and the rest of the men in the panto walked across the back in black trousers, white shirts and black bus conductor caps to mimic the actors in the film. We were performing at one club and as soon as the audience of children heard the opening bars of the song, all the little boys stood up and started stripping.

Sometimes a panto calls for the Dame to do a comic strip that can be quite exhausting. I have to put on 12 pairs of knickers, corsets, petticoats and bras and have a ten-foot long sock pushed up my leg out of sight beneath my costume. If I'm feeling fit I also have a very long washing line with various comical pieces of underwear fixed to it wound tightly round my middle and someone has to 'unwind' me. I now have to stop halfway through this, as I get dizzy much quicker now! The side effect of all these many colourful garments is that I can hardly breathe or walk and it really is very tiring putting them on and taking them off again. I try to arrange the pantos so one year I do the comic strip and not the next. At one club a very serious looking boy about nine years old came up to me and asked: "Are you stripping this year?" I said: "'Fraid not love." He muttered: "Wasn't worth coming then" and walked off. Oh heck just realised,

191

there's a comic 'strip' in this year's *Mother Goose* tour. I'd better start getting fit and in shape!

In 1998 we had a 16-year-old girl Laura Harris, playing Princess Balroobador in *Aladdin*. The thing about Laura was that you really couldn't fail to notice her assets that I think measured 32F! A reporter got to hear of her ambitions to be a page three girl and an article appeared in a national newspaper with the heading 'Hey Chesto'! There was even a cartoon in the *News of the World* showing a Princess with big boobs leaning over a balcony, completely overshadowing Aladdin, with the words: "Aladdin, Aladdin, wherefore art thou Aladdin?"

This also led to a TV appearance in Germany, apparently the Germans love stories of eccentric British people and their TV researchers scour our papers for unusual stories. I had a phone call from Pro Sieben (Channel 7) in Germany. They wanted to come and film Laura at home holding up her outsize bras, then interview and film the panto crew in the dressing rooms as well as filming part of the show. It was our dress rehearsal and we had friends and family to make up the audience. A reporter flew over from Germany and picked up a film crew in this country before coming to the Mountsorrel Memorial Hall. They interviewed us in the dressing rooms and also filmed the audience clapping and cheering. I was sent a tape of the programme. Although the very serious woman reporter was speaking in German, the antics going on behind her, by other members of the cast, were hilarious and quite rude at times as you can imagine! I really should have taken the plastic truncheons off the two 'policemen' before filming began! A friend has recently watched this tape of Laura and the rest of the cast in *Aladdin* for the first time. She had tears running down her face and was in hysterics for the entirety of the video that is about ten minutes in total. As for Laura, she didn't ever full-fill that particular ambition, but she certainly kept the German TV audience happy. Laura has recently become a mum and also has a very happy baby! However, this would not be the last I heard from Pro Sieben as a year later they would come to film me for another story, and yes as we say, that's another story!

Thomas Bates is my friend Shirley Willow's great nephew and he absolutely loves the touring panto. He will quote most of the lines from the panto for the rest of the year until he comes to see the next one. For his eighth birthday in January 2006 he said he wished that a birthday present could be for him to be in one of the performances. I borrowed outfits from some of the dancing school mums who had children the same size and he made his debut in our panto for Severn-Trent. Apparently he had been up very early waiting for the panto crew to come and pick him up for the afternoon performance, driving his mum mad asking every other minute what the time was, it was a good job we hadn't been late in picking him up! He was so good in the panto that we let him do another local performance. He has booked his birthday 'present' for next year already. He was heard telling another little boy "If you're over five and you're talented Deirdre will let you do the panto." Oh will I now! Thomas really is a fantastic little actor and it comes to him so naturally. His elder sister Amy is also another naturally talented untrained stage performer and auditioned successfully for *The Haymarket*, production of *The Wizard of Oz* (*The Haymarket* in Leicester that is!) Thomas has three sisters and he told me that his mum, Michelle, 'has a disease of girls'!

One of my favourite panto stories from many years back 'starred' Cilla Black. She was appearing as principal boy with those wonderful long legs of hers. At the end when the baddy had been captured she said to the kids "what shall we do to punish him?" and a little boy shouted: "sing him a song, Cilla!"

Oh how I love those old fashioned mangles they say it all about a bygone age! I used to watch my Nan roll up her sleeves and set to with the biggest mound of heavy wet clothes and watch in awe at her great strength working this contraption! When I was taken on my birthdays to the Leicester pantos I used to love the washing scene in *Aladdin*, actors racing in and out of the doors and then through the mangle. When we first did *Aladdin* I was determined I was going to have a mangle and the father of Beverley Pike, a girl I worked with, drew up a design for a huge thing with foam rollers which we had made up and then used in the dancing school panto first. We took it with us on our first panto tour that of course was my favourite *Aladdin*. The mangle was in several parts and we used to piece it together on the floor at the side of the stage. At the first show we had over 200 kids in the audience. In the laundry scene I put Wishee Washee through the mangle and then asked for three 'little' willing volunteers from the audience. Every child in that room got up off their seats and ran down to the front, what do you do! Well of course we put every child through. Robert Bramley-Buhler was playing Wishee Washee and he picked them up and pushed them through and I caught each and every one the other side and a lot of the kids were not that little! This must had added at least half an hour on to the whole show. Robert and I collapsed with exhaustion on getting home! I'm sure some of the little beggars queued up more than once!

I hate to see children disappointed! I absolutely hate it when at the end of pantos they get kids up on stage and give all of them but one a bag full of goodies and then make out there is nothing left. How awful must that child feel? It must be like the end of the world to them and it really is so unnecessary, even though we all know they will get more than the other children did. For a brief moment his or her world must have collapsed. Shame on you!

During a previous tour of *Dick Whittington* we had a stuffed rat that appeared at the top of the scenery in the shop scene. But there was also a 'stand-in' rat, as lots of things, when you're packing up quick, can go missing on tour. The young son of the evil King Rat was dancing in the show and was also put in charge of looking after the rat's appearance. At one club, mainly full of adults, the audience was hysterical at this point of the show. I turned round and there were two 'stuffed' rats bonking away on the top of the scenery. After the finalé, I confronted the boy backstage and asked him: "What would your dad say if he knew you were doing that?" "He told me to do it!" came his indignant and difficult to argue with reply.

We have done the panto for Eddie, one of the most pleasant ent secs going, at the tiny RAOB club in Coventry for many years now. We were there one year performing *Jack And The Beanstalk* with our own version of the 'Giant'. This was a very large head made out of papier-mâché that we held over the top of the scenery. Unfortunately the RAOB ceiling is very low and there is only a 5" gap between the top of the scenery and the ceiling. So what were we going to do about the 'Giant'? As the performance went on we were no nearer to coming to a solution. We had now come to the part in the panto where the Giant's booming voice would be heard and was. Next minute all the kids were screaming. Craig Salmon, a young boy appearing in the show and he of the 'bonking rats' fame, was running round the car park with the head. It was looming up at the kids through the three windows at the side of the clubroom and was certainly more scary than popping up at the top of the scenery.

Children always want your autographs, but never have anything with them to for you to sign. In working men's clubs I have signed the back of bingo tickets and soggy beer mats and, if a child or even an adult asks for a photo, I always get their name and address and make sure one is sent to them.  During the touring panto season, we have been wearily packing up costumes at the end of a long night when there has been a knock at the dressing room door and someone shouting, "there's children out here wanting your autograph."  However late it is and however tired we are, we stop, unpack the costumes and dress back in the character we have appeared as.  These children absolutely believe you are the fairy queen, the baddie, the beautiful princess and the dame with no money.  You cannot disappoint them by letting them see you as yourself.

There's a saying that the show must go on, and it has to, come what may.  It's not the audience's fault if something goes wrong.  We were touring with *Jack And The Beanstalk* and performing at Scraptoft Valley WMC to a packed audience.  We were well into the first scene and the 'halves' of Buttercup the cow, two young girls Anisa and Louise (in showbiz terms 'skin-performers' - this term can also mean a stripper but I have never heard strippers call themselves this!) were frantically looking for the cow skin.  After a thorough search, we realised that poor old 'Buttercup' in a black bin-bag was probably still on top of the dustbin in my garage.  John was quite wound up by now and snapped: "just get on with it, we'll have to do it without the cow skin."  I said: "John how can we do *Jack And The Beanstalk* without a cow; what's Jack going to sell at the market?  One of the kids!"  One of the harassed mums said: "You can sell mine!"  Jackie, the wife of Ian Smith who was playing King Crumble (King Crumble has a daughter Princess Apricot in this panto, yes that's right, Apricot Crumble!) shot off in her car with my house keys and we had to improvise for a full 45 minutes.  Don't ask me how we did it because I really don't know.  It must have added up to the longest ever school scene in the history of pantomime!  Incredibly not one person in the audience realised that there had been a problem.  Oh no they didn't!

I usually take off my grotesque dame make up before going home but one night we were very late finishing and I went to go home with one of the mums, Jan Dalby.  She had her two children Lara and Amanda in the car, along with another girl Danielle Lemon.  As we were so late, I had not had time to wash my face, so decided it would be better to keep my wig on as well.  We were nearly home when a police car suddenly appeared with its flashing lights and pulled in front of us at The Green, Mountsorrel.  Jan was hysterical and she kept saying: "I've only had one Babycham!"  The policeman almost had a fit when he shone his torch on my 'dame' face topped with a bright carrot red wig, complete with huge dangling 'Pat Butcher' earrings!  Apparently we had been stopped because a car similar to Jan's had been stolen.  The children were in fits of laughter all the way home.  Jan was traumatised for days!

Another time near Christmas we had two shows on the same day, so I kept my make up and wig on and my first 'dame' costume as we had very little time to get to the next venue.  As it would be a late finish, I was in desperation to get my flask filled with hot water – I can't go all night without my cup of tea!  We were passing Clarendon Park Road in Leicester where a friend called Trish lived.  We stopped the van and I ran down the entry in full Dame gear clutching my flask.  I knocked on the door and went in and there were Trish and a number of startled dinner guests who couldn't believe their eyes.

We were booked to appear at a working men's club in an area of Birmingham.  Our hearts sank when we got there to be greeted with the sight of shops and houses boarded up and rubbish littering the streets.  We went inside the club that was quite run down.  But, the people themselves were great.  They made us cups of tea and really looked after us.  The children were well behaved and were given two pieces of fruit and a bag of sweets, and they generously gave them to our 'panto' children as well at the end of the show.  Every child, without any prompting said 'thank you'. You really can't judge a place by its appearance and I never have done so again.

A few years later we got very excited when an agent booked us for Lakeside Club. The mother of one of the girls immediately piped up: "That's where the darts tournament on the TV comes from."  We were all very thrilled that we would be appearing in such a big posh venue.  The panto van was playing up that night and one of the dads, Mick Lemon, whose daughter Danielle had been spared by the robbers in the wood scene even though the boys in the audience wanted her dead, said he would take us in his van which was much higher than ours.  We drove to Birmingham in the dark with gale force winds.  It was very scary driving along the motorway in such a high van.  We swayed from side to side with five cars of cast and dancers following us.  When we got to an island, John, who was navigating, couldn't decide which exit to take (no surprise there then).  So we went round the island at least seven times as John tried to decide where to turn off.  However another car had managed to get in between our convoy, the poor driver had no other choice but to keep going round with us.  The look on his face was priceless.

We got to the Lakeside Club only to discover that it wasn't the TV venue for the darts tournament at all.  As one of the dads indignantly informed us that particular Lakeside Club was a little further south in Surrey!  The club sloped down from where we had to park and was alongside a big lake with no lighting.  The ground was also very muddy.  The scenery consists of eight heavy boards each about eight-foot high that can be joined together and it takes two of us girls to carry a board though the men can manage one each.  We had to stand at the side of the van with someone else on the other side who was letting us know when the wind had dropped a bit for us to run with the scenery safely into the club.  To make things more difficult, it was a long way down to the club in the dark on a slippery slope.  We started off ok, but then the wind got up again and we found ourselves being blown sideways towards the lake.  Two of the men on their return journey back to the van had to grab us to prevent us ending up in the lake.  This happened several times as we unloaded the van.  It was really frightening at the time, but we could laugh about it later on.

One of our 'regulars' is that very same RAOB Club in Coventry. The clubroom is tiny, probably as big as my lounge and annexe.  The stage is a few inches off the floor, about three foot wide and five foot long; and there are no dressing rooms!  We carry scaffolding and curtains in case we have to build a dressing room at the side of the stage as we have done in the bingo halls we have worked in at the Leicester, Nottingham and Derby Gala Clubs and Walkers Bingo Clubs at Mansfield and Stoke-on-Trent to name but a few.  Unfortunately we can't do this at the RAOB as the floor is taken up with the audience that has a capacity of just 30.  Once again the show must go on, however, and we set the panto scenery in front of the stage.  As there are usually 15 of us in the cast, this means only a few can change in the stage area.  There is a door at the back of the stage with a small passage leading to the club's small private car park.

What we have to do is back the van as close as we can to the door and the men change in the van before making their entry to the stage via the small passage to the door.  When we do this club its usually freezing cold winter weather.  Next to the club is a huge temple and the year we were touring with *Aladdin*, John was standing at the side of the van in his black policeman's outfit wearing a plastic helmet and holding a kid's plastic truncheon waiting for his cue.  Several cars drove on to this private car park with people who were going to the temple and had nowhere else to park. On seeing my husband, they all said: "Sorry officer" and promptly drove off again.

We have been part of the Grantham Marriott Hotel's Christmas and New Year entertainment programme for a few years now and often meet the same families from all over the country who stay there over the holiday period. We perform the panto in the lovely ballroom. One year we had finished our performance of *Dick Whittington* and had packed the van ready for the off. John got in the van and said: "Oh heck!" We all looked and he was holding the gear lever up, it had come off in his hand. We phoned the AA and all the cast waited for them to come with a trailer. All the children appearing in the show were quite upset that they had to go home in their parents' cars. They thought it was great that two of the men had to sit in the van on the trailer all the way back to Mountsorrel.

We performed the panto for many years at Rolls Royce, Hucknall. One year going to a matinée performance the van broke down on the motorway. All the cast and audience sat waiting patiently for the van to arrive and, as this was in the days before mobile phones were invented, we were unaware of the problem. We eventually received a call to tell us about the breakdown and that the AA had been informed. We got the children up and played games with them to keep them from getting bored and the Rolls Royce employee who was to play Santa that year decided to get dressed in his costume and appear early instead of at the end of the show and went outside to change. By now it was dark when all of a sudden we heard a siren and saw flashing lights on the car park. The van had arrived on a trailer, so we, and the kids, went outside and there sat with John and Brett in the front of the van was Santa Claus. They made an impressive appearance with all the flashing lights and the kids were thrilled how Santa had arrived. We literally threw the scenery together and eventually performed the pantomime. One of the dads said "my son was heartbroken when he thought he wasn't going to see the show." Thank goodness it turned out all right in the end.

Our first booking at Whitwick Social Club always makes us smile. We arrived to find a long narrow concert room with a row of full size billiard tables at the bottom. I asked Phil, the manager, where we were to perform and he said: "on top of the billiard tables." I didn't think they would take the weight of the scenery let alone the cast, but Phil assured me he had had many rock groups performing on top of the same tables. He and two men covered the tables with wooden boxes to make a floor and protect the tables and we set the scenery up. Some of us were changing one end behind the scenery and the others in a small space at the other side on the floor. As always happens one person had another's hat, jacket, sword, script and other vital 'props' but there was no way of getting to each other. We had two children aged six years who thought it was great to be dropped down at the back, crawl across the floor under the tables to the others and back with whatever was needed, it was like a escape tunnelling scene from a war film.

We worked on the tables and the boxes moved when walking on them and even more so during the tap routine. The heels on our shoes kept dropping down the side of the boxes, but we managed to do the show without any accidents. We still perform on top of these tables to their wonderful audiences but the covering is now more secure.

Our first booking at Aylestone and District was also a minor miracle. They had a steep sloping stage and the scenery was on casters. The cast not on during a scene had to hang on to the scenery whilst the others performed and vice versa! We have also worked in bingo halls where they have a fixed bingo machine in the middle of the stage and have been told: "It can't be moved, we're linked", and somehow we have always been able to work round it.

We had performed the panto at Scraptoft the previous year and when we arrived for our next annual performance, which was also going to incorporate a presentation of a cheque for various charities to the Lord Mayor of Leicester, there was a rock band taking all the stage and a girl singer bringing a PA in. I went to see Mark, the ent sec, and he said that, as the panto only lasted an hour and the club would be full, he had hired the band and the singer. Where he got the idea from we were performing for an hour I don't know, especially as the year before the panto had been close to three. We reached an agreement and the band moved their equipment to the back of the stage that was still in our way. The girl singer's PA was put to the side and she would go on at the interval of the panto, we would then do the second half and the band would take over. We finished at approximately 11.30pm and were dismantling scenery round the band as they were playing and the audience was leaving the club.

Another unusual distinction is that we must be one of the first and quite probably the only panto company to appear in a gay club. I had appeared in cabaret a few times at the Dover Castle and George, the landlord, asked me if I would do the panto as he thought it would be something different for his regulars! We put on *Aladdin* and had a great time. The barman collapsed in fits of laughter when my husband asked for a drink in a straight glass! At one time the 'flash' for the geni's entrance didn't work. My husband without thinking remarked: "We need a little puff" and we were met by the biggest show of hands in an audience ever! Much more hilarity ensued when Abanazar said he had a magic ring! Followed by me innocently asking what his magic ring did. He replied: "Stand back for when I rub it, something wonderful happens!" Oh dear! The audiences in gay clubs are always up for a laugh. We had one of the best nights ever there. Gay audiences really do have a great sense of humour.

Our last performance of the tour is always for the local charity Heartlink that my friend Gill Smart and her husband started many years ago. All the cast and crew donate their services to help this wonderful charity that has raised money to buy the necessary and life saving equipment for Glenfield hospital. Gill and her husband ran our local paper shop for many years and held many fund raising days in the shop. My father would put on his commissionaire's uniform and stand on the shop door for them. We offered to do the panto and for many years performed at the Groby Road Hospital. A lot of the children would be brought in wearing their pyjamas and night dresses, many attached to a drip, along with their parents, family, friends, doctors, nurses and heart surgeons. The surgeons would have their pagers on and often we would see one get up during the performance and rush off, another poor little soul was being brought in to the hospital in need of urgent attention. When Groby Hospital closed, New Parks Social Club kindly offered their premises for Gill to use and we perform there annually in February to past and current patients and families.

My friend Kay, mother of my godson, Craig, shouts louder than the kids and really gets carried away at the panto performaces. She was working in admin at the old Loughborough General Hospital in Baxter Gate and I had an appointment. I went in the full reception room, walked up to the counter and said: "It's Mrs Hayward" only for the girls from the office to jump up and shout "oh no, it isn't!" Kay had seen my name on the appointments list for the day and had been rehearsing them for my appearance at the counter. I sat there with all the other patients, who were wearing puzzled as well as worried looks by this time. A few minutes later Kay appeared at the reception desk and said in a very serious and loud voice: "Listen everybody, I am going to put this marker pen at the side of the counter. If you see anyone go near it, I want you to shout; haemorrhoids!" and with that off she walked back into the office!

We were asked many years ago to perform our panto for a local factory, 3M at Wharncliffe Road, Loughborough. We set everything up and all the very serious children were frog marched in. No matter how hard we tried we couldn't get them to join in. They sat silent and motionless and some looked frightened to death. At the interval I expressed concern to a very stern looking lady that the children didn't seem to be enjoying the panto and she told me that all the children had been warned repeatedly that they had to be quiet and sit still! All the cast went round the children and explained it was a panto and that they were supposed to shout and join in. Needless to say the audience and the cast enjoyed the second half much more.

We were touring with *Dick Whittington* in 2005/6 and at the last show at New Parks Club for Heartlink and as in most shows the children were so into the story that they left their seats and came to the front of the stage. We were well into the docks scene when I looked down at the footlights and there was a boy about seven-years old looking very much like the 'Milky Bar Kid' holding all the leads and wires in his hands and attempting to bite through them!

We did *Puss in Boots* in a club years ago that was in a very poor area of Leicestershire. We had to perform on the floor and the children sat on the floor right up to the mikes. It was very obvious to us that they had never seen such a show before and they were absolutely mesmerised. I play Queen Gertie III when we perform this panto and in the ballroom scene when I was dressed in my very sparkly ball gown I looked down and there was a little girl about six years old lovingly stroking my dress totally unaware of anything else. It was a very humbling moment.

We were yet again at Leicester Forest East Rugby Club with another panto where we have to perform on the floor. The children sit in seats right up to the mikes. Halfway through one scene a very serious little girl stood up wanting to go to the loo. She looked either side of her and decided she couldn't get by. She did no more than walk straight through the cast, then round the back of the stage to the loo. She made the return journey back to her seat the same way. When you've gotta go, you've gotta go!

I'll always remember the first time we appeared at the same club. We had arrived there early to set up the panto. A game, in its last stages, was being played on the rugby field. My friend Sue, that stalwart of the ladies nights, watched the end of the game through one of the windows in the clubhouse. "Oh look at them big hunky beefy rugby players," she said excitedly. Only to find out later, when they came into the clubhouse to shower and change, that it was actually a ladies team playing!

People often ask me about panto and why this most traditional form of live entertainment is still so popular when theatres and clubs generally seem to be struggling. The answer is simple people love it and it crosses all ages and boundaries and we take it for what it is, pure entertainment. Unfortunately over the years a few stuff shirted 'modernists' have tried to bring panto up to today's world and to put across a social message!

I went to see a professional production of *Jack And The Beanstalk* in Leicester where they had tried to do this, unbeknown to most people who were expecting to see a proper traditional panto. Jack complete with back to front baseball cap, ripped jeans and trainers lived in a council house. The Princess turned up on a bus wearing a tiara and trainers and, that would probably have been a better name for the panto, 'Tiara and Trainers', though just the initials would sum the show up, TAT! The beanstalk looked like a rubbish heap in the middle of the stage and Jack used his computer to destroy it! There was little scenery, no dancers, no comedy, no sparkly costumes and effects and in all a cast of about five people! The moans and groans from people sitting around me in the audience said it all! The message was loud and clear 'Don't mess with our pantos'!

I can't stand snobbery about panto. If an actor has not been seen, or heard of, for a while, other people in the profession will sneeringly say: "Oh, he's probably doing panto now" with a long look down their nose. Panto is very hard work! You have to be able to put across all the emotions just like any other actor, as well as keeping in complete control of a very mixed age, and often very noisy, audience.

Just look at the audiences pantos get around the country and you can see how popular it is as entertainment for all ages. Surely that's what theatre is all about – being entertaining. A lot of other types of productions would like to be so well attended! And don't forget the Queen, when Princess Elizabeth, and Princess Margaret used to stage their own lavish pantos for the rest of the Royal Family, playing principal boy and girl. If it's good enough for them...........................!

I love Sir Ian McKellen. Not so long ago, 'proper' actors would have turned their noses up at appearing in 'soaps' and 'panto', it would have been beneath them. Because of him, they're now queueing up to appear in both! Well done, Sir!

Recently we have seen more of our great actors appear in panto such as Simon Callow and Nigel Havers and top actresses Frances Barber, Maureen Lipman, Susan Hampshire, Stephanie Beacham and Patsy Kensit. Big American stars are now even crossing the 'pond' to appear in our pantos, Patrick Duffy from *Dallas* and Henry Winkler (The Fonz himself from *Happy Days*). It looks like panto is becoming 'legit' theatre again and quite right too. It is one of our greatest and very original traditions of theatre and, most importantly, is often a child's first introduction to theatre.

Panto used to be what every actor aspired to in the 1800s and the shows in London, especially at Drury Lane's *Theatre Royal*, could last for hours and include as many as 36 scenes with a cast of hundreds. There could also be many horses and other animals, real fires and waterfalls and royalty and gentry alike used to attend them. These over the top colossal shows gave birth to the saying 'it's a right pantomime'.

The theatre-going public at that time were horrified when 'common' acts from the music halls such as Marie Lloyd started to appear in panto. In those days there were hundreds of titles for pantos, many based on all the nursery rhyme characters. Today we have about six of these titles left for pantos.

During the 'swinging sixties' all the star variety acts topped the bill in pantos up and down the country and the script virtually went out of the window. The panto was very much built around a 'star' name. There was a very popular Australian entertainer, Shirley Abicair, who often appeared on TV playing her

199

zither. In one panto in which she was starring she uttered these immortal words: "While I wait in the woods for them hither, I'll just play a tune on my zither." And did just that!

Mind you a similarly dreadful pun had been done many years before during the classic music hall days. Gertie Gitana, who made the song *There's An Old Mill By the Stream, Nellie Dean* famous (another one sung to me by my Gramp in the pub) also played the saxophone and she was playing the title role in *Cinderella*. Everyone had gone to the ball. She was sitting by the fire all forlorn and said: "Here I am all alone, I think I'll play my saxophone." She then put her hand up the chimney and pulled out a saxophone and blasted out a tune on it! Leicester's own Engelbert Humperdinck playing the title role in *Robinson Crusoe* at the London Palladium was very conveniently locked in a cage in one scene so he could sing his number one hit record *Please Release Me*!

Many years back panto was popular in America for a short while. However disasters hit a few theatres where pantos were being staged. A fire burnt one theatre completely to the ground and at another a murder took place. And so to Americans pantomime became associated with bad luck and was considered a jinx and theatres stopped staging them. Well in today's world, it's one thing we can say is still British. Have you ever tried to explain to a foreigner what pantomime is about!

Pantomime originally developed from the religious plays in mediaeval times that were performed all over England in villages by touring players. That is why in pantomime the baddy always loses. Traditionally, there is a good side and an evil side of the stage and that is why the fairy will appear from the 'good' side and the evil character from the other every time they make an appearance. In panto I like to stick to tradition apart from the fact that I play Dame. However, if we kept to the strictest traditions of the stage no women would appear at all. They were banned from doing so until Charles II was on the throne. He then had to give in to a certain actress by the name of Nell Gwynne and changed the law.

I quite like to see a man play the principal boy in professional pantos and, to be honest, a lot of kids can't understand why a girl plays a boy anyway these days. Often when my principal boys puts in his/her first appearance backstage you can hear the kids muttering to each other in disbelief saying: "It's a girl!" But they soon forget the 'sex-change' and get wrapped up in all of the magic and madness. Nevertheless, a girl playing principal boy and slapping her fishnet-clad thighs still goes down very well with the dads in the audience! Sir Norman Wisdom played the part of Aladdin as far back as 1956 and was a tremendous draw. Other popular male principal boys have included Frankie Vaughan, Engelbert Humperdinck, Tommy Steele, Cliff Richard and Jimmy Tarbuck.

A lot of professional pantos these days have cut down on some of the traditional parts. You rarely see the Brokers men in *Cinderella* any more, which is a great shame. These were wonderful parts for the big comic duos such as Cannon and Ball and Little and Large, but we haven't got these sorts of acts any longer - and, sad to say, we don't have many men who can play Dame.

Famous dames like Terry Scott, Arthur Askey, Billy Dainty and Les Dawson have all long 'hung up their boobs' and gone to the panto finalè in the sky. Christopher Biggins is one great dame still strutting his stuff in the best traditional way and he now also directs the pantos. There doesn't appear among the present-day younger comics anyone who can, or even who wants to try, to fill their boots or should that be 'boobs'? It is very sad that the dame parts are being cut as a result.   I saw a 'pro' panto recently where a top-notch comic of yesteryear who must be nudging 76-years-of age played Wishee Washee and a young man played his mother.  It seemed so odd and the poor dame only made about four appearances, had very few lines and just a couple of costumes!  Perhaps it's time for some' girl power'.   Just imagine what great panto dames the likes of Fern Britton, Barbara Windsor, Wendy Richard, Victoria Wood, Pam St Clement and Julie Walters would make.

It never fails to amaze me how naturally talented some young people can be.     On our last tour of *Mother Goose* one of my dancing pupils joined the show for the first time.  Fairy Liquid (we call her in this panto 'cause she goes that little bit further) had to miss a night and this young girl learnt the part and carried it off without a rehearsal.  She also quickly learnt the part of Chardonnay Beaujolis Blossom-Hill (don't ask!) but didn't get to do it as the girl playing this part recovered from a chest infection.  Another night one of the Bailiff's men had an emergency and had to drop out at the last minute.  This young girl walked into the dressing room and I said to her: "you're doing the bailiff's man part tonight with John." "OK" she replied even though she was shaking a bit.  One of the girls had a black trouser suit and we dressed her up.  Out she went with a quick run through with John before each appearance (and it's a big part) and she was word perfect.  On stage she probably looked about 17 or 18 but was incredibly only 12 years old.  Well done, Emma Smith!

We tour with our panto for three months.  We see each other at our best and our worst, at our most defensive and our most vulnerable like a family and so became a 'panto family' and after 20 years that's a lot of relatives!  When we see someone who appeared with us many years ago it really is like meeting a long lost relative. There is a real sense of belonging and camaraderie.   So I'd like to give a mention to those who have worked so hard over the years.   We have had many talented people taking part in the touring pantos.  The casts, dancers and helpers change yearly due to other commitments.  I would like to thank all those that have worked so hard with us for the first 20 years, not only appearing but carrying boxes, scenery and costumes into venues, looking for John's knickers (his spare pair!) and my many props, helping set up a panto stage, erecting dressing rooms, lights and PA systems, zipping costumes up and fetching cups of tea.

I hope I have remembered you all.  If I have missed anyone out I do apologise and I do assure you that you, too, are very much appreciated.

## Principal Boys
Anisa Burton
Jeanette Davis
Rachel Sullivan
Helen Farrer
Amanda Jones
Erica Makin
Claire Woolley
Karen Martin
Sarah Howarth
Natalie Drew

*Dee Quemby*

## Sons and Sidekicks
John Lovett
Paul Schofield
Robert Bramley Buhler
Anthony Riddle
Dave Vickers
Jim Robertson

## Principal Girls
Rachel Tilford
Danielle Lemon
Lucy Rose
Laura Harris
Sarah-Jane Heffer
Samantha Foister
Linda Pawlyn

## Fairy Queens
Charlotte Barrows
Ruth Salmon
Louise Jones
Jenny Billson
Susan Thompson
Holly Baddeley
Emma Smith

## Bailiff's men/robbers/Kings and Emperors
John Hayward
Craig Salmon
Wayne Riches
Ian Smith
John Tilford
Dennis Newell
Robin Davies
Stuart Court
Rod Billson
Brett Katchick
and Emma Smith!

## Stage managers/technicians/dressers/'gofers'
Mick Green
Steve Newitt
Carol Tilford
Eunice Salmon
Sue Newitt
Paul James
Craig Valentine
Debbie Burge

Simon Court
Chris Ditta
Shraz Ditta
Eric Makin
Aaron Davis

## Evil Baddie
Pete Salmon

## Dame
Dee Quemby

## Dancers, Chorus, villagers, 'stand ins' etc
Megan Baddeley
Amy Burge
Emma Smith
Emma Newitt
Rebecca Newitt
Nicola Sykes
Stephanie Bond
Hayley Limmage
Natalie Drew
Sophie Bunce
Trish Watts
Cara Bond
Kelsie Sibbald
Valerie Pearson
Nikki Crane
Meghan Court
Jane Harker
Felicity George
Claire Buhler
Katie Hawksworth
Cheryl Billson
Nicola Neilson
Sarah Matthews
Claire Hamilton
Lea-Anne Bailey
Tracey Pawlyn
Hugo Newell
Jake Smith
Carl Salmon
Lara Dalby
Amanda Dalby
Semeena Ditta
Samantha Schofield
Tracey Smith
Cassie Booth
Lucy Brown
Helen Higgins

## Dee Quemby

Kerry Williams
Lorna Hughes
Amy Hartwell
Melanie Hall
Karen Moss
Jessica Ditchfield
Danielle Willows
Thomas Bates
Katrina James
Ashley Pryor
Zoe Katchick
Kelly Frew
Laura Kidger
Danielle Burkinshaw
Catherine Pittwood
Thomas Harris
Pauline Davies
Alison Wallis
Karen Stock
James Court
Joanne Swann
Alexis Slater
Katie D'Arcy

## Scenery/props

John Hayward
Steve Newitt

## The voices of Janet and Lol Holmes in *Mother Goose!*

A big thank you all from Dee, oh yes it is!

There is nothing like a Dame...................................!

As ugly sister (kneeling) for Ann Oliver

The first touring panto production *Aladdin and his Magic Lamp!*

*Puss in Boots* (Queen Gertie III goes for a ride)

Got the bird again! (as *Mother Goose*)

With Buttercup the missing cow!

Those natives in *Dick Whittington*!

Another touring version of *Aladdin*

The '*Full Monty*' lads!

On board the Saucy Sue in *Dick Whittington* (courtesy of Clive Rasin)

A happy touring panto cast in Leicester

Queen Gertie has a turn! (courtesy of Clive Rasin)

Queen Gertie does the 'royal wave'

*Babes in the Wood* in Leicester

That Leicester City frock!

(See 'Barnardo's'
Chapter 14)

211

*Mother Goose* on tour

Alone on a deserted island (courtesy of Clive Rasin)

A get together of panto dames in a London Hotel for 'breakfast' TV (me seated on far banister wearing a crown – Christopher Biggins at foot of stairs on right)

Touring with *Mother Goose*

News of the World Cartoon 'Big Boobs at the Panto'!

# CHAPTER 11

## DRAG QUEENS AND
## GENTLEMEN ARTISTES

IF EASILY offended or of a nervous disposition, you're probably best giving this section a miss and moving onto the next chapter.   **Don't say you haven't been warned!**

~~~~~~~~~~~~~~~~~~~~~~~~~~~~~~~

I ONLY went to two ladies nights before I started working as a comic and I felt very uncomfortable, as did most of the other women.   I hated them both!   Both were compered by a male 'blue' comic who obviously would have preferred to work to an all male audience and both shows had two, not very good looking, ridiculously costumed strippers doing very silly things. They would have looked better in their costumes than without!   Would you believe one came out dressed as ET; he even had a light on the end of his finger, well I think it was his finger?   What a stupid costume for a male stripper anyway!   I even heard of a stripper in a Peter Pan costume of all things!   Also on one of these shows was a 'drag queen' and she seemed to be still working out 'her' act.

It was 18 years ago when I was first asked by an agent to compere and do two comedy spots at a ladies night in Peterborough at a restaurant with a male stripper from London.   After the two shows I had seen, I was not at all happy about doing it. John persuaded me to give it a go and I reluctantly told the agent I would.   What a night it was and a real eye opener!   It was a top class restaurant and the women were all dressed up to the nines.   I had a great first spot and the handsome male stripper walked out looking like a top male model in a designer suit.   The second spot was just as good and I realised I could do more topics that the women associated with than I could with a mixed audience.   I now saw that this sort of show could be real good entertainment and kept more 'high class' than the two I had been unfortunate enough to see.

My next ladies night was in the Midlands at a bus depot. The bus company's fleet of double-decker buses had picked the women up to bring them to their massive canteen. They had all enjoyed a good meal and were ready for entertaining.   This is where I met one of my dearest friends, Russell. He had originally come from Leicester, but was now living in Birmingham and working as Miss Sandy Laine.   We had such a laugh on stage and in the dressing room. At the end of the night he and his friend had helped me scrape all the uneaten ham off the plates for me to take home for my many 'rescued' cats, and our lifelong friendship had begun.

Russell also worked in a drag trio called High and Mighty with two other drag queens; Mighty Megan and Folly B and they gave me a lot of work in their shows in Birmingham.  Russell often worked in London at a very top class hotel.  The owner, Mark, had become his partner and Russell lived with him.  I had been asked by Garry Bushell to appear on his TV programme *Bushell's On The Box* and needed to be at Garry's home in Eltham early in the morning.  Russell rang the night before I was going down to London and persuaded me to go and stay with him.  I got to St Pancras railway station and was met not only by Russell, but also a Bentley and a chauffeur!  We went to a luxury block of flats 'Shad Thames' to leave my case.  Russell told me Joan Collins and Jimmy Nail had apartments in the same block though he had not yet seen either of them.  We were then chauffeur driven round London for the day.  Getting out of the Bentley at Selfridges, I must admit it was great to be asked:  "What time do you want the Bentley here to pick you up madam?"  I could get used to that!

I met Mark later and what with the flat and the Bentley, I have never been so looked after in my life. I woke up the next morning looking out of the massive window to see Tower Bridge, the tower and many boats sailing past.   What luxury and kindness and what an experience!

Other great drag queen friends were The Showgirls, Kevin and Leon, I was working with them a week after my mother died and they were so kind and caring.  Sadly Kevin died of a massive heart attack at the age of 45.  Two weeks before he had been zipping me up in my stage dresses at the Latimer Ward Cons Club in Leicester.

We went to Kevin's funeral in Birmingham with Shirley and Roger and what a send off it was.  There must have been over 200 people at the crematorium.  All the drag queens were there and how handsome and smart they all looked in their designer suits getting many admiring glances from the women.  Also there were most of the strippers and four of them carried the coffin into the crematorium, Rebel Red, Double Impact, Wild Warrior and Scorpion, three dressed in their white *Officer and Gentleman* uniforms.

The Wake was at The Wellington, a fabulous gay pub in Birmingham where I had been part of the cabaret a couple of years before for Kevin's birthday. The food was out of this world and generously provided by the pub, then we had a cabaret.  A fabulous male Shirley Bassey impersonator, Champagne Shirley, who actually sang live, and another drag queen singer with a tremendous voice, Vanilla Rimmer, brought the house down.  We left at teatime, but I was later told the cabaret went well on into the next morning. That's the way to do it!

My friend Sue and I had a really good costume tip from one drag queen 'Alfie'.  Sue was desperately trying to make the 'Wicked Queen' costume from *Snow White* for one of the dancing school shows.  Whatever she tried to stiffen the collar with wouldn't work.  The collar just kept flopping down and Sue was at her wits end! Working one night with Alfie, he walked out on stage in a fabulous costume with a high collar. In the dressing room Sue asked him what he had used and he said: "The collar the vet put on our dog to stop it scratching!" There's always a way!

To work with drag queens is an eye opener. Their humour is razor sharp and outrageous and they are great fun. It opened me up to a broader sense of comedy. Who would have thought a few years ago that men would have come with their wives and partners to the many cabaret nights we do with just me, and a drag queen? They have truly become the last bastions of the great British traditional sense of humour and just love cabaret. When did you last see anyone dressed up like Shirley Bassey on a stage? Everything is so plain and dowdy these days. Surely we need glamour on a stage, not an act looking like they've come to mend the boiler.

We were booked to do a ladies night at the White House, Scraptoft and I, the stripper and Russell, aka Miss Sandy Laine, had to change in the men's toilets. The women were all seated in a room waiting for their meal when the lights fused and we were all plunged into darkness. "How come we can see?" asked the stripper and Russell replied: "It's the emergency lighting, you know all about emergency lighting when you're gay!" One of the staff found their way to us and told us they were going to have to move everybody out into the main restaurant where they had lighting and wanted to start as soon as possible. This meant we would have to walk through the pub that was by now packed. The problem was Russell now had his 'slap' on and was dressed in a white basque, stockings with suspenders and high heels. You can imagine he's quite a sight as he is well over six feet tall even without the four-inch high heels and wig! However the show must go on. So he put his wig on, picked up his case, held his head up high, and walked magnificently through the many startled people having a quiet drink!

I picked up my stuff and walked through the dark room. I was intrigued to see the chef in his whites picking up bowls and cutlery to take into the restaurant with the aid of two small blue lights on the table so he could see. I asked him where he had got these from and he said matter of fact: "I borrowed two light up vibrators off the Ann Summers girl!" Eat your heart out Gordon Ramsay!

As most people know, I am particularly fond of leopard-skin and have worn it for years, long before it came back into fashion. The drag queens tell me all my clothes are very camp and I have often been performing on stage and gone back in the dressing room to find the 'girls' trying on all my clothes.

Over the years I have worked with some great drag duos, some of which have unfortunately split up; I had great nights with the High and Mighty, Gone Wrong Sisters, Fatz and Small, Just Friends, The Showgirls, Hollywood Hookers, Bossom Buddies and Kopy Catz. Not only were they superb acts; they were also very kind and caring people who became my very good friends.

I was now doing so many ladies nights that I was being asked to promote my own nearer home. We went to Scraptoft Valley and were met by the sight of over 400 women. We had the Gone Wrong Sisters, Double Impact and another stripper on the bill. This club was overwhelmed at the amount of women and struggled to cope at the bar and the show began to overrun. The first stripper was doing his second spot when a grumpy and rude committee man came up to my husband, who was working the PA. He shouted at John that he was shutting the club. So John handed the microphone to him and said: "Here you are you can tell all these women you're closing and Double Impact won't be appearing, cause I'm not!" The committee man paused for a moment, looked at the seething audience of excited woman and muttered through clenched teeth: "Carry on" and walked off.

Mark, the ent sec, was over the moon at the end saying they had taken more money over the bar than at New Year's Eve. We packed the PA up and went out to the car to see many miserable looking men who had been standing outside in the wet and the cold for ages waiting to pick up wives and girlfriends. How many times did we hear women being snapped at: "Just shut up and get in the car!"

At one ladies night a lady of 85 years was so taken by the naked stripper that she ran up the front of the stage and wouldn't let go of him. The now terrified stripper was desperately trying to fend her off! I was sat at a table of women and one of them said: "Good God I know her, I'm her care worker. I replied: "Well if she's dead in the morning at least she'll have gone happy."

I always like the house lights up when on stage, that way I can see the opposition! Joking apart, I like to sometimes talk to individual women in the audience and have a chat. At another ladies night at Scraptoft Valley there was a girl in the audience who had a leopard-skin polo-neck top on and I made a comment about it every time I appeared. She stood up and said: "Do you want to buy it off me for a fiver?" I got £5 off John, handed it to her and she promptly took it off and gave it to me, putting a jacket on over her bra. Goodness knows how she explained that when she got home!

Some comments you get from the audience mean so much. At the Brush Club in Loughborough a young girl came up to me and said: "I've never met you in my life, but I feel like you're a mate chatting to me up there on the stage ". She'll never know how good she made me feel saying that.

We did many ladies nights in Leicester for a lady named Jill who was trying to raise money for a young football team in New Parks. At one of these nights there was a middle-aged woman in the audience a bit the worse for wear. She was slowly, and very carefully, sliding herself down the wall towards the stage when the stripper was on for his second spot. The second spot is always the 'Full Monty'. A stripper never 'flashes' in his first spot, unless of course he's only doing one spot! I always go out in the audience when the lads are on in case any of the women get a bit too friendly and I have to have a quiet word with them. I was keeping my eye on this one, she got to the fire door that promptly flew open and she disappeared. In a second she was flung back in wide eyed as if nothing had happened, it reminded me of Del Boy in *Only Fools and Horses* in the famous bar scene. She picked up a chair and carefully carried it down to front of the hall, put it down and did no more than sit down on the wrong side and ended up the floor where she stayed for the remainder of the night.

Drink can cause a lot of trouble and can spoil a good night, fortunately it doesn't happen that often and we always nip it in the bud. Two occasions however have stayed with me vividly over the last 18 years.

Women are usually very good with each other but at one ladies night with an audience of over 400 some of the women got up and started to dance while the stripper was on. This is a total 'no no'. The drag queens and strippers want people to watch them not dance in front of the audience and once again I usually have to have a word. John was working the PA that was set up on the floor and two women were pulling each other's hair. John thought they were dancing! And so did the stripper. An almighty row broke out ending with one woman on the floor out to the world. We stopped the show and went down to help and after about five minutes a very large woman stood up at the back of the hall and shouted "stop f*****g about with her, carry on with the show or I want my money back!" All the other women agreed with her! We decided this woman was more drunk than hurt and she was moved to the side and left there to recover – so much for compassion that night!

At one ladies night, we had been finished for over half an hour, and most of the women had gone home. We were busy packing up the equipment when we heard the sound of bottles and glasses being smashed. We rushed out of the dressing rooms and saw two women really going for it. The drag queen rushed up to them and tried to calm things down, but failed. Friends of the two women pulled them apart as they shouted abuse at each other ending with one woman screaming: "I don't care if you are my f*****g mother, I'm going to kill you!"

As we drove home we saw these women literally being carried home by their friends. The next time we performed at that club I asked their friends what had happened after they had got them home and they told me the girl and her mother couldn't remember anything about it the next morning and wouldn't believe they had even fallen out!

I was now getting so many bookings and this is where I came across a really good agent, Ann of Telstar Entertainments and her friend Dot who works in the office. I book all of the strippers through Anne because she doesn't use any of the cheap ones. Her acts are good and reliable and always give a good performance whether it is in a big club or a tiny dirty bowling alley and most importantly they always turn up! I have done many a ladies night where they have booked the stripper direct. Not only hasn't he turned up; they also couldn't contact him on any of the numbers they had got for him!

If there is any illness or other problem where they can't make it, Ann will move heaven and earth to find a good replacement even if it means losing out on the commission. How many other agents will do that? As for me, I must be the only person in Britain with a stripping agency on my BT list of family and friends!

Many of Ann's lads have over the years won the prestigious title of UK number one male stripper and she had all the finalists in a major male stripper competition that was actually shown on late night TV with the appropriate title: *A Thong For Europe*!

To be a drag queen means one thing and one thing only and that is glamour. I have been watching many a drag queen going through 'her' act when male members of staff of wherever we are performing have said: "I wish these drag queens would give women some tips on how to dress and make up." Yes the men still like the old fashioned glamour. Mind you, the women are always very envious of the drag queens' legs that are usually very long and slim. It is an interesting and little known fact that many of the fabulous 'legs' pictured on the old packets of stockings were actually men's!

Sparkle, sparkle, sparkle, the Queens love it! I have been ready to walk out on stage dressed in my long sequin frock, feathers and diamanté jewellery when I have heard the drag queens rummaging around in their jewellery boxes. I am just about to walk out and they grab me and ram more diamanté bracelets on my wrists, another diamanté necklace round my neck, more rings on my fingers.

## Dee Quemby

"I've got enough on, " I protest, and I always get back a very indignantly said: "Dee, it's impossible to have too much sparkle!"

A friend Graham, aka Spangles Galore, worked in a drag duo, The Gone Wrong Sisters. They had a booking in the North and it was in a very bad area where the club was very run down. The concert room was packed with stocky heavily tattooed women who looked as tough as old boots. There was no compere so the 'girls' opened the show and soon became aware of a rift between the women. On one side were the family and friends of a girl who had been murdered and the other side were the family and friends of a man who had at one time been a suspect. The women started shouting obscene abuse at each other and a fight broke out. The men from the committee came into the room but they gave it up as a bad job before the law arrived. The police were forced out of the room by the women and one woman jumped up on the stage ripped her clothes off and shouted obscenities that would have made a sailor blush, and did! Graham said: "I wouldn't have minded Dee but while all this was happening I was stood on the stage dressed as a f*****g brownie!" This from an ex-sailor who had been decorated with a medal as a Vietnam veteran!

For people who have never been to a ladies night they will imagine a room full of young women. Not so we get all ages. At a lot of venues women come up and tell me that they are there with their mother, grandmother and daughters – a real family show! There were a couple of older ladies who used to come regularly to the Brush Club ladies nights in Loughborough. I had taught one of the women's daughters dancing many years ago. She said her husband didn't mind her coming when she told him it was 'one of Deirdre's shows'...........little did he know!

A lot of women have told me that they only go out when it is one of my shows as they fell safe which I feel is very sad. There are a lot of places women will not go these days because of fights, drugs and abuse. A lot of men have asked me if it is possible for them to come as they have heard what a good laugh it is – sorry lads, the only men allowed in the shows are artistes, roadies and staff.

Often I am told by a lot of girls that they have been to other ladies nights where the stripper was ugly and had dirty costumes as well as not much of an act. Male ent secs will book a stripper as to them a stripper is a stripper end of story and it is the same with male agents. Come on lads, the women want to see a good looking young man up there, preferably in a uniform, who is unobtainable and who does a dignified and well rehearsed act.

Most of the 'lads' are really nice men. I often have to change with them and they always turn their backs as I put on my stage-dresses, though it doesn't bother me. At my age I'm grateful if anybody looks! And yes, they may show all they've got on stage but in the dressing room they are very polite and modest. If I walk in they immediately grab a towel and say: "Sorry Dee." If we are in with the drag queens as well, I often end up with my stuff under a chair or a table. Believe me, when you're in with a drag queen you have no chance of getting anywhere near the mirror all night!

When I have had new strippers who are doing things I think are unnecessary I have told them. If they are that good looking they don't have to resort to cheap tricks. I want all the women at my shows to go home having had a good laugh and not feeling embarrassed. We have a good reputation and in the audience we have had doctors, councillors, policewomen and even JPs.

How women love the male stripper that goes out into the crowd and involves everybody regardless of age or looks! There is always a big affectionate 'ahhhhh' from the women when the stripper selects an older woman to rub the baby oil on him. Our record at the moment is 94 years of age, the woman not the stripper that is! Many years back in Northampton we had a special needs young woman in a wheelchair sat at the front with her friend. The stripper was walking round and she eagerly held out her hands. He poured some of the baby oil into them and positioned himself so she could rub it on his rear end. Unfortunately the poor girl's co-ordination was all to pieces and no matter how he moved, and her friend moved the wheelchair, she couldn't make contact. The stripper in the end turned round, took hold of her, and gave her a big kiss instead. She had the biggest smile on her face for the rest of the night.

Working early on with strippers when all music was on tape, I always took pencils with me to the shows. We'd be in the dressing room and the show would have started and the stripper would hold up a tape saying he had forgotten to get it wound back. I would sit with the tape and a pencil patiently winding it back to the start. Thank goodness for the invention of mini discs and CDs!

How many times have I had men say to me that women only like gay men because they're safe with them! Well that just proves how much they know about women! At the end of the shows the drag queens, out of drag, are always surrounded by many admiring women. I have heard women pleading with them to go home with them for the night convinced that they can turn them straight. One very tired drag queen wanting to go home and fed up with persistent ever-hopeful women came back with a very witty retort, which is far too rude to print here!

A lot of the drag queens had long since said I should do the gay clubs. But, although I knew the 'girls' laughed at my act backstage at the ladies' nights, I still felt unsure about what this sort of audience would go for. An agent rang me and asked if he could book me for Lily's Lounge at The Cross Keys in Peterborough, a gay pub more commonly known as 'the crossed legs'. The date was several months later and, when it arrived, I had gone down with laryngitis. I rang the agent who in turn rang the pub. The agent got back to me and said: "They want you to go still. They've had it in the press that you've been in *Emmerdale,* there's people coming down especially!"

So off I went apprehensively with John and my friend Sue. This was a mixed gay club and I had to change in the toilets and Sue came in with me. There I was standing in my long sequin frock, feather boa and diamanté jewellery when in walked two lesbians. They looked me up and down and said seductively: "Are you stripping for us?" I said: "At my age, if you want to see my boobs, I'll just lift the hem of my frock up!" and we all laughed.

Out I went to Lily's Lounge and got a great reception. I could just about talk, but not sing, and got a lot of the audience involved in participation. I knew there had been a lot of photos taken during my act and I was sent a copy of Peterborough's gay magazine *Out and About* with me on the front cover. The words 'serving the gay and lesbian community in Peterborough' were at the bottom across my feet and I hoped nobody would take this literally! Inside was a full-page article, in which it said that I'd become a gay icon overnight, well at least in Peterborough!

I now realised from this that I could do the same act for these audiences and went on to do more gay clubs. I was even asked to go to Dot Cottons Club in Cambridge, a large factory that had been converted into a club. Apparently the real soap star, from *EastEnders*, had been there herself only a few weeks previously. I was to appear in the clubroom that was upstairs, far away from the head banging music, the hundreds of whistle blowers and sparkly stick wavers. I expected this to be something special, yet it was a very small room with a tiny bar. "Where's the stage?" I asked, only to be shown something that can only be described as the trolley your luggage is put on to go to the plane at the airport. I had to stand on this, which was on casters, and face the audience over the large handlebar at the front.

I then extended my circuit of the gay clubs and again Russell, who was by now running The Jesters gay bar and a pub The Queen's Arms, in Birmingham, gave me many bookings. Every time I appeared at one or the other Russell loved to heckle me from the bar all through my act! Another great friend and oh so funny is Dec, aka Phyliss Stein, he always looks after me when I'm appearing with him and we always have a great time with his wonderful sense of humour and that wicked Irish accent. I'll never forget the night Dec was in the audience at The Jesters. He and Russell came alongside me on stage, picked me up and held me upside down as I continued singing! Russell had a wig and whatever he was doing with it brought howls of laughter from the audience! I wonder if this ever happened to Shirley Bassey?

Two of my favourite gay clubs are The Wellington in Birmingham and The Dover Castle in Leicester. The Wellington's concert room at the back of the pub is almost Victorian with paintings adorning the ceiling. I could readily imagine all the great stars of the Victorian Music Hall days appearing there. At the Dover Castle I appeared in cabaret and had a wow of a time. I was even asked to appear for Gay Pride at their tea party. All the mums were there and we had 'dainties' on the now never seen three-tier cake plates that every house would have had in the 1950s, along with tea in floral patterned china tea pots and cups and saucers – and loose tea, no tea bags of course it had to be done 'proper', and quite rightly so!

A lot of the drag queens tell me that I am really a drag queen, which I take as a great compliment. Perhaps it's appropriate that my initials are DQ!

I have actually stood in for a drag queen at Loughborough. Russell rang me in a flap saying he was appearing in Loughborough at the East Midlands Hotel, the site of the first house I lived in at Loughborough funnily enough. He had been booked through an agent as a duo but for some reason the other drag queen couldn't make it, so would I go? He said: "You've got a red sequin frock, so have I; you've also got a turquoise one, so bring them; you've seen the act that many times you know it." John was away and Russell came and picked me up. We did the show and not one person asked me if I was a man or a woman.

I was appearing at another show with two strippers and at the interval a girl on her mobile phone was saying: "It's a fab show, we've got a great drag queen" she looked at me and said: "Are you a drag queen or are you a woman?" What a compliment!

'Drag queens' are so generous. Russell rang me one night when I was panicking. I was appearing somewhere in Wales many miles away that night and John had hurt his leg and couldn't drive. With no hesitation Russell said that he'd come and take me. He drove quite a distance with his new partner. They packed my PA in their car, drove me to the venue, worked my PA for me and also for the drag queens Hollywood Hookers and the stripper Stallion, brought me home and unpacked my PA. Russell wouldn't even take any money for the petrol! That was the first time I had worked with Stallion or as I call him 'my little pony'! When John saw him for the first time, I said: "Just wait they'll all scream when he take his hat off." John replied: "Don't be daft" but when he did and that long hair fell down John was deafened.

One of the funniest nights I ever did was a ladies night at King Richard's Road WMC, Leicester, a small down-at-heel club. We were asked if a group of women from a deaf centre could come and bring a signer with them. They did and they sat in a packed to capacity audience. Every woman in the audience watched me when I spoke and then they all suddenly turned their heads to watch the signer it was like being a solo player on centre court at Wimbledon. Of course when the drag queens got on the stage they went out of their way to say the most outrageous things they could think of and we all watched the poor signer getting redder and redder as she struggled to sign some things she obviously never had call to use before or would again. She took in all in good fun though the hand gestures seemed to be getting bigger and bigger. We all learnt how to sign some of the rudest words ever that night!

One winter's night I arrived at Syston Brookside Club. A massive poster with a photo of the male stripper was in the front window advertising the ladies night I was there to compere. Right next to this was a very old yellowy poster with big black bold letters saying: 'No ball games allowed on these premises'!

We have done many shows of all types at Syston Brookside Club and numerous ladies nights. Tony, one of the committee men, usually stands guard outside the door on the ladies nights. One night after a fabulous full to capacity show he called me over and said very seriously: "Dee, can you get better strippers next time some that the women will like. All I can hear when the strippers come on is the women shouting ' off, off." It was very late, I was very tired and, for a moment, I thought he meant it. Then he winked at me!

At another show at Syston Brookside, a woman in her 40s came up to me and said: "When the girls said we've got you a ticket for a ladies night, I thought I was coming to a talk on the menopause, but this has done me much more good!" Well, it must have done because not only did she come to the next one; she also brought her mother with her!

Anyone who has been to see me perform knows that no matter how glamorously I am dressed if my high heels start to make my feet ache I have a pair of old battered slippers I will fetch and put on and carry on with my act. Even though I was brought up in a pub I do not drink alcohol or even soft drinks, I just don't like them, I much prefer a cup of tea and my flask goes on every booking with me. This always caused much amusement to the drag queens I worked with. Getting to a venue I would be greeted with "I bet you've got your flask and slippers with you Dee?" by the 'girls'. So when I started working the gay clubs I decided to call my show *The Flask And Slippers Tour – The Menopausal Years!*

Working with strippers and drag queens you have to be very down to earth and prepared for anything, embarrassment goes out the window! I was standing on stage in a top notch place in Birmingham going through my routine dressed glamorously in sequins, feathers, diamanté jewellery with a really nice expensively dressed posh group of women when from the wings the drag queen whispered: "Can you do another ten minutes the stripper's not got a hard on yet!" My face never moved a muscle!

223

## Dee Quemby

I have only ever done one stag do. I was approached by an agent to compere a stag night at Peterborough FC, my husband, a big football fan, encouraged me to take the booking because the agent had said some of the top footballers would be there. Someone from the club had seen me in a showcase and they wanted an all-woman show, so I reluctantly agreed to do it. I was treated like royalty by the staff at the club and the two female strippers were top class. I had a great night and a lot of the men came up and spoke to me. One actually said: "Thank you for not 'effing' and blinding at us all night because we're men", another said: "It was so great not to hear all the old stag jokes again tonight." However I have never done another one, as I was not comfortable with it. Women go to ladies nights for a good laugh and a bit of fun. It's a very different atmosphere with an all-male audience.

Over the years a lot of the women in the audiences have become old friends such as Elaine at 'The Stute', 'Wilco' Karen at Syston, Jo, 'Sticky' Vicky and Rachel (anywhere Double Impact is on!). They say hello and have a chat with me in Leicester and Loughborough when out shopping or at the Gala or Mecca Bingo Halls. I get many Christmas cards from them and I was very touched to receive cards from Margaret and friends from Birstall when my Mother died even though they didn't have my address. It amazes me how many letters I get just addressed to Dee Quemby, Mountsorrel!

I really believe that you should give it all you've got and make the most of your appearance on stage especially on ladies nights. For these women it is not a cheap night even though the tickets might be. They will have had their hair done, bought a new dress or top, paid for a babysitter and also a taxi and, let's face it, women do not drink cheap drinks so they deserve the best show you can give them.

Whatever your opinion of these nights they do make a lot of much needed money for many charities and women can be more than generous. As well as any money made on the tickets, the people organising the night and the clubs usually do a raffle and bucket/tray collection for a particular charity and I have seen women putting in £10 notes, who else would do that!

Oh the curse of mobile phones! How can people forget to switch them off when they are in an audience, but they do and we now have to have put downs not just for hecklers but for mobile phone addicts as well! When the stripper makes his appearance you see a room full of women holding up their mobiles to take pictures or video them, it's like being at a Barry Manilow concert without the candles. The best I ever saw was in Northampton a girl was rubbing baby oil on a stripper and talking on her mobile at the same time. It takes all sorts!

The film *The Full Monty* was a massive hit and ladies nights appeared everywhere. Instead of them being seen as seedy they were now very acceptable, and top hotels and theatres started to put them on. This in some way killed the ladies nights it made them 'respectable'. You could go to one every week if you wanted to it was no longer a bit daring and special. A lot of men thought there was nothing to becoming a stripper and some very poor acts started to appear especially locally that led to the downfall of ladies nights at a lot of venues. It takes a lot of hard work to be a good stripper, most of them spend every day in the gym to keep looking their best and there is definitely an art to it. Let's face it we all laugh at men we know messing about having a bit of fun pretending to be a stripper but just try it in front of a 300 or more capacity audience of strangers, who have seen all the top strippers go through their routines and keep their interest! That's a completely different ballgame, oops!

224

These days we see and hear it all on the television in our own homes so people are not so affronted by it now and this is leading to a loss of audiences at these events. Anyone on the circuit will now tell you that the stag nights have almost had it. When we have had a really good packed to capacity ladies night at a club the men always demand a stag night but when the club puts one on very few of the men will actually buy a ticket. At a big club where we had packed 400 women in, they put on a stag night and had about six men in. The acts had to perform in a corner of the club rather than on the massive stage. Most variety acts, including the big stars, have at some time worked with strippers. It's part of show business and everything you do adds a bit more to your own character and understanding of people. From these nights, I have made some fabulous friends both backstage and in the audience.

Shirley my friend started to promote ladies nights and we have worked together on some great nights in Leicester always with capacity audiences.

Traditionally drag queens' names should be their first dog's name and their mother's maiden name combined. However today a name is more likely to be based on humour such as Miss Understood, Hedda Lettuce, Miss Dot Com, Emma Roids, Sister's with Blisters, Amber Dextrous, Vida Las Vegas, Nora Carrot, Fonda Boyz, Betty Swallocks, Ann Droid, Anty Biotics, Mary Hinge, Miss Demeanour, Kitty Litter and, who will ever forget, Kenny Everett's 'Cupid Stunt'.

I have listed all the drag queens and strippers below that I have, up to now, appeared with. If I have omitted anyone I do apologise, but as you can see there have been so many.

## DRAG QUEENS

## GENTLEMEN ARTISTES
### (Strippers aka willy-wavers!)

| DRAG QUEENS | GENTLEMEN ARTISTES | |
|---|---|---|
| Miss Sandy Laine | Double Impact | Andy King |
| Mighty Megan | Stallion | Gemini |
| Phyliss Stein | Sebastian | Johnny XL |
| Folly B | Cock Robin | Pegasus |
| Spangles Galore | Lethal Weapon | G-Force |
| Tilly | Wild Child | Jackhammer |
| High & Mighty | J J O'Neil | Jet |
| Alfie | Rebel Red | Bullet |
| Showgirls | Romeo | Axle |
| Just Friends | Private 69 | Angel |
| Miss Andre | Paul Grant | Wild Thing |
| Bossom Buddies | Brewster | Buddy Brown |
| Gone Wrong Sisters | Stevie Dynamite | Black Desire |
| Miss Marcia | Scorpion | Tyrone |
| White Wine & Soda | Kat | Raw Deal |
| Rag & Ritches | Ectasy | Marco |

## Dee Quemby

| | | |
|---|---|---|
| Sisters' Slim | Stryker | Highlander |
| Fatz and Small | Armani | Solid Gold |
| Mrs Mills | Knight Ryder | Eclipse |
| Kopy-Catz | Reno | Onyx |
| Kruger Sisters | Blue Steel | Young Blood |
| The Harlettes | Rogue | Juice |
| Hollywood Hookers | Wild Warrior | Hustler |
| Mitzi Munroe | Nico | Nicky Storm |
| Candy Martell | Adrenalin | Smooth Operator |
| Pretty in Pink | Inferno | |
| Moma Trish | | |
| Pam | | |
| Terry DuCane | | |

A very special mention to 'Betty' and our medical adviser 'Dr Pete'!

*Love from Dee, Shirley and Sue!*
*XXX*

*Oh yes it's ladies night ...........................................!*

High and Mighty! (Russell and Paul)

The Showgirls (Kevin and Leon)

Miss Phyliss Stein (Dec)

Fatz & Small (and they are!)

Miss André

Gone Wrong Sisters

Miss Sandy Laine (Russell)

Stallion (or as I call him 'my little pony'!)

Double Impact

Romeo

Rebel Red

Armani

# CHAPTER 12

## LIGHTS, CAMERA, ACTION!

IN the 1990s many television programmes were being filmed at the now long gone Carlton Studios in Lenton Lane, Nottingham and they needed a lot of extras and nearly all of them they used had a variety background. My friend Joy was already working as an extra and she asked me to go along with her. I appeared in the then popular TV shows *Boon, Harry's Mad, Woof, Signs And Wonders* and *The Back Up* and many other dramas. I have spent many hours sitting in rooms, catering buses and out in the open talking to jugglers, magicians, children's entertainers, singers and comics waiting to be called for filming.

At that time the majority of TV and film extras were in the actor's union Equity. I was with Barbara Plant whose agency had an office in Birmingham in the Central TV offices. She would ring me up and say they want you for so and so, the director has asked for you. Alas gone are the days when, if the director liked you, you graduated to speaking parts and very often stardom! Barbara told me the directors usually asked for me and said: "she gets the others organised and motivated." I was often asked to provide other extras and one time they wanted rock 'n' rollers for *Harry's Mad*. My husband and I had been members of the Loughborough Rock 'n' Roll Society so that was no problem. Tony 'the Tiger' and his wife came, as did a future Mayor of Charnwood, Councillor Mike Jones and his wife Marjorie. I had worked at Herbert Morris Ltd with Mike before his political career! Another time they needed cowboys who could lasso. One of my dancing pupil's dads, Ron Emmett and his wife were members of a cowboy society that spent weekends away re-enacting famous gun fights and battles and so we all turned up in cowboy costumes for yet another episode of *Harry's Mad*. Ron and friends were a bit put out when they found out they had to lasso pot garden gnomes in front of a hotel.

One actor filming this episode told us, during one of the breaks, that he had just appeared in a film with Kevin Costner and that was *Robin Hood – Prince Of Thieves* a big box office hit. We hadn't recognised him at all as he was now costumed as General Custer. He'd had a very big acting part in the film as Robin

Hood's father's faithful servant who had been blinded by the Sheriff's men and was in many of the scenes with Kevin Costner!

Extra work is hard going, you usually have to be at the studios by 7am or earlier some extras even having a three hour's drive to get there. They would then put you on a bus and they would ship you out to whichever location they were using. You would have been told by the agent what you were meant to be and you had to provide your own clothes; you would then parade pass the open door in the costume trailer for the wardrobe people to make sure you looked right for the part and if not they would dive into rails of costumes and re-dress you. It was always great for your own clothes to be used, as you would be paid more! You would then sit around for hours waiting to be called. In one episode of *Boon* I had to wait until 5pm for my call and then had to walk past the back of a car in which Michael Elphick who played *Boon* and another actor were talking. It was a 'one take' and that was the day finished for me!

On my first day as an extra, I couldn't understand why the 'seasoned' extras kept looking at their watches. I soon found out that if we went over a certain time we would be paid more! If the director came into the room and asked who would be prepared to say a couple of words, everybody would jump up, as this would mean more money too! I hate sitting around and if that was the sort of filming day I had, I often went home tired out and with a headache – not such a glamorous life as people imagine it to be!

Michael Elphick always gave me a smile when he saw me turn up, but he never spoke to anyone. He and the actor who played Harry always stayed in their trailers when not filming and had meals taken to them. Queuing up with other extras at the catering van I turned round to find Neil Morrissey, who played Rocky and Gemma Craven who was guest starring in that particular episode, in the queue behind me. They were talking and laughing with everyone – no big egos there.

One time I was asked to provide a family of children for another episode of *Boon*, that Dora Bryan was guest starring in, I was asked to go as chaperone. I went through all my dancing school pupils to find four children who looked like they were related. I had a girl, Claire Cullen, who was 11 but looked a lot younger; another girl Laura Hughes who was 12 years old; a boy, Julian Robbins, aged eight years who is now a doctor; and Nikki Walker who was a mere four years old.

I had an urgent call from Barbara the day before filming and she said: "the producer wants you to bring a dog as well!" Oh he does, does he? I was teaching dancing that evening and asked some of the mothers and pupils if they had a very friendly dog. One of the mothers had a brother who worked at the butchers in the High Street with such an animal. The next morning a man appeared in the Market Place, where we were waiting to set off early morning, with a dog and handed him over to me. The dog was wonderful, and he took to us immediately. The dog was such a big hit with the producer and crew that he got to do extra scenes on his own! Getting back into Loughborough, I said to the children: "We have to go to the butchers to take the dog back." A very worried young boy asked: "Deirdre, who's going to eat the dog?"

When filming you have to be very, very quiet. Time is money and one scene can take several takes to get right. We were filming in a very expensive hotel, cameras were rolling and the two actors playing the parents of the children drove up in a car, got out and walked up to the hotel reception, so far so good, the 'mother' placed four year old Nikki on the counter who immediately, unscripted shouted "I want my dinner." Even the producer laughed which is unusual. This was the last episode of *Boon* to be filmed and for some reason this episode was not televised until a few years later much to one of the older girls' embarrassment.

In later years adverts would appear in local papers where filming was taking place for anyone to audition to be an extra, the successful ones would be paid less and food did not have to be provided for non Equity members. Equity tried to stop this practice with little success at that time. However some of these 'extras' could be very unprofessional continually talking during filming, wandering off and missing their calls. There were even cases of these 'extras' being costumed in an expensive suit, or given an expensive camera if playing photographers and then completely disappearing off the face of the earth as the suits and the cameras could be sold for more than they were getting paid for the day! They were probably never found as, if not in Equity, you could always give a false name when registering at the start of the day's filming!

I appeared as a social worker in a BBC police drama *The Back Up* and was asked to take a young boy with me to appear as a battered child. Hugo Newell, another dancing pupil, who was five years old was made up to look battered and in filming I had to snatch him from his 'weeping mother'. I really enjoyed that! At the end of the day's filming on a very derelict and vandalised council estate in Birmingham I went to the mobile toilets parked in the street, the steps were very wobbly and steep. On the way out I had to put my hand at the side to climb down, the producer of the episode walked up and pushed the door back, crushing my thumb in the door. I had paper towels wrapped round my bleeding thumb and was driven to Selly Oak Hospital with Hugo in a BBC car and left there. We sat in the waiting room, me still bleeding. Hugo, being a typical boy, refused to wipe his make up off his face, as he liked looking all bloody and battered! We had many concerned looks from staff and public alike. My nail on this thumb has never grown back properly, it is split down the middle and I have to keep it really short, and so that was the day I was maimed by the BBC!

I was asked to provide a young girl, Danielle Lemon, for the children's TV programme *Chucklevision* starring the Chuckle brothers. I can honestly say they were two of the nicest men I have ever met, so down to earth and friendly – no big egos.

Much later I eventually did get a speaking part and my agent at the time told me; "no more extra work, you just become known as a reliable extra."

I now needed an agent for TV work in my own right, not as an extra. TV/film agents have very little work nowadays for the actors they already have and everyone in the business will tell you, you have to have a London agent. Most things are cast in London, even the locally filmed vamped up flop *Crossroads* that was filmed in Nottingham was. No London agent is going to take you on with little or no experience, so I had to try nearer home.

The local Equity newsletter often printed names and addresses of agents willing to take on new actors and I contacted a very nice lady in Melton Mowbray. She had been a business consultant and had opened an acting agency but unfortunately she failed to get going so after a year I was now looking for another agent.

*The Stage* newspaper had an advert for an agent, Lena Davies. I went to see her at her farmhouse in Cogenhoe in Northampton. It was a luxury farmhouse and she had her own theatre building next door. There were stables with ponies, dogs, cats, chickens and a stable with big white rabbits in. I was interviewed by Lena, and her associates and she signed me up there and then.

Lena was very well known in her own right. Years before she had written a song that had become a number one hit in the charts for her then partner, Polly Perkins, who had starred in the TV soap *Eldorado*. Lena dressed all in black and had long dark hair and I loved her London accent. Lena was a big friend of Tracey Ullman who was now starring in her own TV series in America. Lena told me Tracey Ullman had been offered the lead opposite Michael Douglas in the big hit film *Fatal Attraction* but had turned it down because of the scene as the 'bunny boiler' as she didn't want to upset Lena! I later met Tracey Ullman at one of Lena's do's. Unfortunately for me, Lena decided to move away from TV and film work to do charity fund raising and so I was now left looking for another agent though we do still keep in touch.

I was approached by an agency in Leicester and went to see their super offices and was very impressed by the Ferraris outside on the car park. Unfortunately after a few months they were arrested for running a scam – another case of anybody can be in films and TV just send us so much to register to be on our books. Equity will tell you if an agency asks for money forget them! A good agency will make money from the work they get you. I know so many people who have parted with hundreds of pounds not to hear anything and when writing to see why they had heard nothing, having their envelopes sent back to them marked with 'not known at this address'.

I was so lucky to get an audition for *Emmerdale*, the very popular TV soap. I had had no luck with agents for TV/film and so I decided to promote myself and I sent a load of CVs and photos round to casting directors. About six weeks later I had a phone call from the Yorkshire TV office asking me to go for an audition for *Emmerdale*. I said I no longer did extra work and then I was told it was for an actual part for a character called 'Tallulah Dingle'. This is the moment you have been waiting for all of your life and you suddenly became an incoherent mumbling idiot with shock!

I was working at Charnwood Borough Council at the time and had never watched an episode of *Emmerdale* in my life as it was on at a time I was taking dance classes. Michelle, one of the girls in the office who was a big fan, said: "You'll get it, you'll fit in with the Dingles." On finding out this family was a set of thieving but likeable rogues I thanked her very much! Being at the council the news of my audition flew round like the Red Arrows and I was inundated with phone calls from other members of staff wanting to know all about it. The director of our section, Geoff Henshall, was from Yorkshire and he loved *Emmerdale* and I was sent for and asked "any chance of Kim Tate's autograph?"

I went to Yorkshire TV in Leeds for the audition. I walked into the massive reception area and saw a very welcome sight. Hung on a wall was a very large photo of our own smiling Bill Maynard, who was starring in *Heartbeat*. I said: "Give me some good luck Bill." I only saw one of the other actresses who was auditioning and on her way out and my way in she wished me good luck and that worried me as we all know you should say 'break a leg'!

Michelle the girl at work was pregnant and had been told she was having a boy. Her partner was a big fan of Bill Maynard in *Heartbeat* and she was desperately trying to talk him out of naming their baby boy Greengrass! Fortunately for the baby she did!

At the audition, I was asked if I had ever appeared in a drama before (the TV powers that be do not call them 'soaps') and I replied I had not. I read my part and on the way out asked when they would let the person who had got the part know. I was told "in a few days time" and set off back to Loughborough.

Soaps incidentally are called that because when they started on American television they were sponsored by washing powder companies and, during the breaks, the commercials would be for that particular soap/washing powder and hence the nickname. Thank goodness they weren't originally sponsored by haemorrhoid cream!

On the way back home we had to call in at the vets down Meadow Lane in Loughborough to pick up some special biscuits for one of my cats. We got home and the answer phone was flashing away, I listened quickly to a message that seemed to say I had left something in the TV studios so I didn't bother to ring back straightaway. About an hour later I listened to the message on the answer phone again. This turned out to be two messages; the first was that we had left the biscuits in the vet's waiting room and the second to ring Yorkshire TV urgently! I rang the number given and was asked: "What news would you like to hear?" and I immediately turned back into an incoherent mumbling idiot again. I was told I had got the part and would be filming the following week. The script would be in the post and on no account was I to let anyone know my part or story line. Needless to say by now with the 'bush telegraph' nearly all of the council staff and many people in Loughborough, Shepshed and Mountsorrel knew what part I had gone for anyway.

In those days there weren't the countless TV soap magazines there are now and the very detailed story lines in the TV Times and Radio Times of what is coming up for that week. Story lines were kept secret and I was told at the end of filming my script would have to be shredded as one actor had put his in the dustbin and, of course, the plot had been leaked to the press.

The script came and it was for the whole episode. My husband, at that time an ardent soap fan, explained who everyone was but I wouldn't let him see the script and sat and learnt my part in a couple of days.

I was asked to go back to the TV studios to see the costume people and to take any outfits I thought the character might wear. I took a leopard-skin swagger jacket and a leopard-skin straight skirt, low red top, hoop earrings, white ankle strap stilettos and black lace tights which the wardrobe people thought were great and so I ended up wearing my own clothes as 'Tallulah' otherwise 'Aunty Lulu'. I was sent a list of hotels and bed and breakfast hotels to find somewhere to stay and this proved a real headache. It was July and graduation time at the Universities and of course everywhere was full. John rang the last B & B on the list and the owner said he was full but he kindly nipped next door to another B & B and they had one room left which he booked for me. We got to the B & B the day before my first day's filming and I had the attic room that opened up on to Headingley Cricket Ground much to my husband's delight. Early the next morning I reported to the TV studios to a very nice lady in the reception. She had a fantastic voice very slow, husky and oh so well spoken. When she made announcements over the tannoy-system everybody would stop just to listen to her.

The first day of filming arrived and a taxi picked me up and took me to the Dingles' house. Time is money and as the soaps are on so often, they have to shoot quickly. Usually each episode is six weeks in advance. We stood in a circle to do the 'dickies' ('dicky birds' i.e. words) and then went for a take. Screen acting is so very different to acting on a stage. Everything has to be slower so the camera can follow you and 'less is more'. You cannot use the facial expressions and gestures that you would on a stage as if your whole face filled a TV screen, you could frighten viewers to death. This took a lot of getting used to and the director, John Michael Phillips, was very kind and helpful to me as were a lot of the cast, especially Steve Halliwell, the actor who plays Zak Dingle, and Jane Cox, who plays his other half Lisa Dingle. Jane very kindly used to take me back to my hotel in her chauffeur driven car.

It was so strange to sit in the canteen and see Kim Tate in a beautiful designer suit head and shoulders over the rest of the cast queuing for a cup of tea. Lisa Riley, as Mandy Dingle, was very popular then but unfortunately she was not in my episode as she was on holiday. I would have loved to work alongside her. All the 'Dingles' were great to work with and as there have been so many of them over the years, it's not surprising some of the regular cast members get confused! On the third day of filming Marlon played by Mark Charnock said: "Remind me, what relation are you to me?" 'Seth' on a break during filming asked me where I was from and told me he had played nearly all the working men's clubs in Leicester as a pianist. Bobby Knutt, also a comic, was playing Zak Dingle's brother Albert, father of Marlon, and he and I swopped 'horror' stories of the different venues we had appeared in as comics.

Other days we filmed in a church and in *Emmerdale's* pub The Woolpack and it actually has real beer in the pumps. My friend, Dave Vickers, when appearing as an extra in The Woolpack said they had all been told to sip the drinks slowly as there had been cases of slightly tipsy extras in the past! My few days of filming were over and I was asked to go back for another day. I had used holidays from the council to do the filming and the day I was asked to go back the girl I worked with, Trudy, had booked this particular day off, but she very kindly changed her day so I could go. I filmed my last day and John Michael Phillips told me, as this was my first big TV part, I could keep my script that I still have. Back home waiting for the episode to be shown I was pestered and pestered for details of my part but I couldn't tell anybody anything about it. The episode was shown in September and I sat there ages after it had finished waiting for my Mother to ring. Eventually after half an hour I rang her worried she might be ill but she told me she was still sat there just thinking about it! My friend Russell aka Miss Sandy Laine, rang to say he knew I had said I had got lines but not actual 'close ups'. He was over the moon for me.

I went into my local health store 'Elf' in Loughborough the day after the episode was televised and there were a lot of people at the counter queuing up to pay. Ian who runs the shop shouted: "You can get out, we don't serve Dingles in here!" These customers were obviously not 'soap' fans by the way they looked at me before they realised Ian was joking! *Emmerdale* is such a popular soap and shown in many countries. You receive royalties when your episode is shown and yes you really do get cheques for amounts like £1.68 for being televised in New Zealand or Sweden or some other country! I was walking home one night and there were three little girls walking towards me whispering to each other. They stopped and the eldest one asked shyly: Were you in *Emmerdale?*" I said "yes" and the tiniest girl about six years old looked at me wide eyed and said: "Are you rich?" I should have shown her the cheque for £1.68!

Being in *Emmerdale* was a fantastic experience and I know I was very lucky. It really was a case of being in the right place at the right time.

I love *EastEnders* and was thrilled to be called in for an audition for a very small part as a stripper. John was driving me to the Borehamwood studios to audition and as usual we seemed to have missed our turn. Why is it men drivers will never stop and ask for directions?   We stopped in a quiet county lane and I was getting a bit 'het up' as it is the ultimate sin to be late for an audition.  A motorbike rider rode by on the other side of the road followed by a huge black car, I recognized the couple sat in the back and waved at them. John was looking at his map very irritated when I said: "The Queen and Prince Phillip have just gone by in a car." "Don't be stupid"; he snapped back, so I decided not to press the point.

We got to the studios and I read my part. If you're going to do something, I believe you give it 100 per cent and so, I had taken a 'basque' costume, a feather boa and cassette tape of Shirley Bassey's *Big Spender* for my audition.  I was told there was no need to actually strip but as I had taken the trouble would I do it anyway. The director of the particular episode and Matthew Hickling, the casting director who had auditioned me for BBC Talent in Leicester, were in hysterics at my attempts as an 'exotic artiste' which they filmed!  Well you can't be good at everything!   I hope they destroyed the film afterwards!  After all this I was told that I didn't look old enough to be one of the two strippers.  What?  I was in my 50s!  How old did they want them?   Well if anything crops up in the future that I am suitable for, at this rate it will have to be for somebody's 'granny'!

We got home I put the News on and there were the Queen and Prince Phillip being shown round the *EastEnders* set that very day by Barbara Windsor!   Well you can't argue with that.

What have Margaret Thatcher, Joan Collins and Judy Garland got in common?..........ME!   I cannot do impressions and accents and I really admire people who can.    The only impression I have ever come close to is Margaret Thatcher who first put in an appearance in my Punch and Judy shows, and then in cabaret shows.

When she was Prime Minister a lot of people got a lot of good work out of impersonating her.    As my vocal impression went down well in Punch and Judy I took it a step further.  I bought a dark blue suit, silk blouse, a black handbag, pearl earrings, a string of pearls and a strawberry blond wig and wrote a monologue. This act I did for several years but once the person you are impersonating is no longer in the public eye you might as well forget it and I did.

'Joan Collins' didn't come about through me.  I went to audition for a TV/film agent and whilst I was going through my paces, he was looking at me very quizzically.   When I had finished he asked me if I had ever thought about being a Joan Collins look-alike. Well frankly no I hadn't!  He said that I had the bone structure and, with wigs and make up, he thought it could work.  I forgot about this for several months and then the agency rang me up to go for an audition for a fresh fruit commercial for Swiss TV.  I was to be a woman in a designer tracksuit with a lot of 'bling' and a lot of hair.  The girl in the agency told me to go as 'Joan Collins'.  I found an old black satin tracksuit in the attic trimmed with sequins that had huge shoulder pads and bought a cheap black wig.   The cheap bling jewellery I already had! I walked into the audition room holding the wig and when I put it on the casting director screamed "oh my God", I thought what have I done and began to panic. The next minute she said: "It's Joan Collins!"  Everyone in the room was nodding in agreement and when I got back into the dressing room and looked in the mirror it shocked me too.  But I now had the confidence to go for it and when I got back home I arranged to have photos done and was taken on by a top London look-alike agency. I must say Joan Collins is a lady I admire greatly and I was dead chuffed that I could do a passable look-alike. I watched her in every episode of *Dynasty* and those fantastic Cinzano ads with Leonard Rossiter. I saw her brilliant one woman show at the *De Montfort Hall* in Leicester. She really is an amazing woman!

Six days after my mother died the agency I was with at the time rang to say I had an audition for a part in a TV drama/documentary *Death By Excess – Hollywood Goddesses* as Judy Garland. I was already due to go to London that day as we had got tickets a long while before for an interview and a questions and answer session at the Theatre Museum in Covent Garden with my former dancing pupil and now top choreographer Stephen Mear. We were going with two friends John and Yasmeen and they thought that I wouldn't be going now but I couldn't see any point in stopping at home it wouldn't change anything.

My Mum always thought I would get that 'break' one day and had always said to me: "Don't ever let me stop you from doing anything, somebody will always look after me" which was usually John or her good friends Christine, Jackie, Brian and Clive. My Mum had loved Judy Garland and I thought if I didn't try for it I would be letting her down so I told the agency I could get to the audition in the morning. I auditioned at the film studio's offices and the agency rang me a few days later to say I had got the part.

I filmed my part in London and it made a real change not to do comedy, I had to cut my throat, have convulsions, wreck a dressing room, take drugs and do other nasty things and it was great. At the start of filming the director came in gingerly holding a sugar bottle and said: "These are very fragile and expensive and we have only got four to last us so be very careful" and then promptly dropped it! Sugar bottles are horrible things and they get sticky from the heat of your hand. I filmed smashing two in various scenes and then he carefully handed me the last bottle. The director motioned how he wanted me to swing it back and then throw it at the mirror. I said: "You want me to swing it back and………." As I copied his action I heard the bottle smash behind me on the wall and I just froze. The camera crew were helpless with laughter and so was the director, thank God! We managed the scene with me throwing the half bottle quickly so it would look like a full one. Oh well even Humphrey Bogart dropped the Maltese Falcon and badly damaged it early on in filming!

It was several months before *Death By Excess - Hollywood Goddesses* was televised. But when it was shown, for once my very critical husband couldn't find anything to pull me up on!

At the moment I am sat at home waiting for the phone to hopefully ring. I really am ready for my close up......................anybody!

*Hooray for Hollywood* .................................................!

As 'Joan Collins' (Julie Oswin photography)

Maggie Thatcher responds to a member of the public!

Tallulah (Aunty Lulu) Dingle takes a break from filming *Emmerdale*

# CHAPTER 13

## IT'S ALL IN THE STARS!

CAPRICORN                December 22 to January 19

| | |
|---|---|
| Symbol | A goat climbing upwards |
| Lucky birth stone | Garnet |
| Ruling Planet | Saturn |
| Element | Earth |

### Character Traits

Conscientious, Ambitious, Conservative,
Lonely, Melancholic, Controlled emotionally
Practical, Law Abiding, Careful, Organised,
Hardworking, Thrifty, Purposeful, Down to
Earth, Traditional, Humorous, Reserved,
Trustworthy, Old in youth - young in age

# SHOWBIZ and other famous CAPRICORNS

| | | | |
|---|---|---|---|
| Ava Gardner | Cary Grant | Danny Kaye | Bebe Daniels |
| Oliver Hardy | Kevin Costner | Jane Horrocks | Jose Ferrer |
| Elvis Presley | Shirley Bassey | Humphrey Bogart | Irene Handl |
| Marlene Dietrich | Sir Anthony Hopkins | William Bendix | Oscar Levant |
| Jane Wyman | Steve Allen | Lloyd Bridges | Tony Martin |
| Ethel Merman | Ray Milland | Sheree North | Margaret O'Brien |
| Zasu Pitts | Moira Shearer | Robert Stack | Sylvia Syms |
| Russ Tamblyn | Loretta Young | Faye Dunaway | Jackie 'Mr TV' Pallo |
| Jim Carrey | Nicholas Cage | Denzel Washington | Mel Gibson |
| Gerard Depardieu | John Thaw | Jon Voigt | Jude Law |
| Annie Lennox | Joe Orton | John Singleton | Joey Adams |
| Sir Ben Kingsley | Kate Moss | Marilyn Manson | Mary J Blige |
| Mary Tyler Moore | Paul Merton | Quentin Crisp | Robert Duvall |
| Melanie Chisholm | Emma Bunton | Rod Stewart | Rowan Atkinson |
| Ted Danson | Howard Hughes | Tia Carrere | Val Kilmer |
| Victor Borge | Janis Joplin | Diane Lane | Orlando Bloom |
| Ricky Martin | David Bailey | Al Capone | Conrad Hilton |
| Gracie Fields | Marion Davies | Des O'Connor | Patricia Neal |
| Richard Widmark | Anna May Wong | Gwen Verdon | Gypsy Rose Lee |
| Helena Rubenstein | Elizabeth Arden | Muhammad Ali | Eartha Kitt |
| Philip Lynott | Lucy Davis | Carol Smiley | Carol Vorderman |
| Joely Richardson | Jason Connery | Mack Sennett | Maggie Smith |

*************************************************

Poor old Capricorn, the stubborn goat
Plodding on even though thought remote
Courteous, respectful and knows his place
A worthy star-sign for the human race

But be not taken in by this solemn pose
Inside this goat great thoughts have rose
Ambition burns bright and hopes are set high
To be the brightest star in the dark night's sky

He will bide his time and wait for his turn
While hopes and expectations in his heart burn
He takes all disappointments in his stride
And ventures on when others hide

So be ever watchful for there comes the day
When the Capricorn goat leads the way!

~~~~~~~~~~~~~~~~~~~~~~~~~~~~~~~~~~~

ALL showbiz folk seem to be very superstitious and some star signs are definitely better than others to be born under if pursuing a career on the stage.

The general traits of Capricorns are quite depressing, solitary, traditional, melancholic, lonely, hard working, serious as a child though supposedly we do have a dry witty sense of humour, are creative, trustworthy, good at organising and, like the goat, we go over much bumpy ground before eventually reaching the top albeit may take a very long time - well that bit's coming true anyway! Ava Gardener was a Capricorn and said it was the worst sign to be born under! We are also supposed to get better looking with age in which case, I should be quite a cracker at 90!

I hate garnets. I had a garnet ring, years ago, and whenever I wore it something 'unlucky' seemed to happen even though this stone is supposedly my 'birthstone'! Why couldn't it have been either a diamond or a pearl for Capricorns – my two favourites!

How many times have I said to myself I am not reading my horoscope in a newspaper or magazine any more, if it's good it never comes true and if it is slightly upsetting it worries me all day! I never read my daily horoscope if I have a show or audition on that day, that is definitely a NO NO!

Horoscopes in newspapers came about by Princess Margaret's birth. One newspaper printed on the day that she was born that any child born that same day would have certain qualities. This was so popular that it prompted many people to write in and ask for it to become a regular feature, and it did, worldwide.

I am a very superstitious person probably due to my Romany and spiritualist background and my Nan! Opals are only supposed to be worn if your birthday falls in October, my Nan's was on 15 October. Nan was given a bag of opals by Great Uncle Harold, brother-in-law to Gramp's elder sister Ethel. He had been mining in Australia in the early 1900s. Even being born in the right month did not console my superstitious grandmother and she flushed the lot down the toilet! I was always told by my Mum and Nan never to take part in the very popular Ouija board sessions of the 1960s, as with my background and ancestors you never know what could appear!

My Mum and my Nan bought everything in threes, shampoos, pairs of stockings and especially underwear which most people did, it was known as 'wash, wear and spare'. The majority of superstitions can be traced back to religion and this was thought to come from the Holy Trinity and is more associated with good luck than bad.

My personal superstitions are touching wood; ancient Britons used the bark of the wood as medicine. The bark contains salicylate acid which is natural aspirin but to them, as it cured some illnesses, it meant a god lived in the tree and to touch a tree would bring them good luck. My Nan said never to stir the tea in the teapot with a spoon as this stirred up trouble. I always place a shiny coin outside on New Year's Eve and when I've seen the New Year in I go and turn it over in the moonlight.

There's also not going in one door and out the other unless I have sat down on a chair. I often go in Boots front door, sit down on a pharmacy waiting chair count to five and then go out the back door, I will not put new shoes on a table, nor cross another person on the stairs, I will not put red and white flowers together as it means death although some people do say it means blood and bandages, I never leave the teapot lid off, I will not walk under a ladder, nor open an umbrella indoors and I always throw salt over my shoulder at mealtimes even if I have not spilt any. I have never done any washing on New Year's Day or Good Friday as my Nan always said if you did you would wash someone out of the family and I never cut my nails on a Friday or on a Sunday. I don't like signing anything in black ink, my friend Lilla Patel said that was an Asian superstition too, probably a throw back to my Romany ancestors!

If out and I see a solitary magpie I have to 'salute it' to ward off bad luck. If I accidentally put any of my clothes on back to front, they have to stay on until bedtime and I go hysterical if I see crossed knives. My Nan said that if you gave someone a purse as a present you had to put a coin inside and if I ever move house again it won't be on a Friday!

My elephant ornaments always face the front door to signify there is a welcome in the house, the other way round means bad luck. The great American showman, Florenz 'Flo' Ziegfeld, producer of the famous *Ziegfeld Follies* loved pot elephants and was given one for good luck for every one of his show's opening nights. A pot elephant sent to him in the post was smashed to pieces and he died shortly afterwards.

Variety performers usually have a personal lucky routine they carry out before going on stage. They will never tell you what it is but I have seen some very strange sights in dressing rooms. Yes I have one too and I do it three times and no I'm not telling you what it is either!

Theatre superstitions are many fold, you cannot say the name of a certain Shakespeare play. You have to refer to it as 'The Scottish Play' and if someone actually says the name backstage they have to go to the stage manager, apologise and say to him: "Angels and ministers of grace defend us" or if said in the dressing room go outside turn round three times and then knock the door. It is bad luck to say the last line of a play at rehearsals, this we never do in the panto - we always wait for the first performance. It is also bad luck to say good luck to anyone opening in a show; you have to say break a leg.

It is considered unlucky to carry live flowers during a performance and to wear green on stage. The great actor Peter Sellars refused to wear anything green when filming or on stage. It is unlucky to peep through the curtains at an audience before the show starts and whistling backstage is absolutely forbidden, I have one member of the panto cast who never remembers this and he gets shouted at every year!

Not whistling backstage made good sense in the early days of theatre in London and this is where this particular superstition must come from. Out of work sailors would be employed to lift and lower the backcloths that had heavy weights attached to them. At sea sailors would lower and raise sails and other objects by a series of whistles so if anyone whistled backstage a cloth or heavy weight could be dropped on them by instinct and I believe an unfortunate actor was actually killed by doing this.

Many top hotels will not serve 13 people at one sitting.  This is considered unlucky, another religious superstition due to the Last Supper, but there are always ways round everything.  The Savoy in London used to keep a large toy teddy bear and, if 13 people were dining together they would set a place at the table for the teddy and sit him there for the entirety of the meal.

James Stewart, the great American film actor, had been a pilot during the Second World War and had flown on many dangerous bombing missions.  Even after the war had ended he would not fly as a passenger unless his lucky tie was packed in his case.  When Noel Coward was asked if he was superstitious he replied that he never slept more than 13 in a bed!  Jean Harlow always wore a lucky ankle chain that is often visible on screen.  She also had a lucky mirror and would not leave the room without looking in this mirror first.

I have only ever had my palm read once.  The palmist didn't come from round here and would have no idea what I did.  She kept looking at my hand very puzzled and asked me: "Why do I see a lot of women?"  This quite impressed me, she'd obviously tuned into a ladies night audience.  I once was asked to do a show for a Spiritualist Church, I sorted out children to take who would dance and one of the dads said to me "you won't be able to do any jokes, they'll all know what the endings are!"

Johnny Casson does a superb gag about a fortune teller: "I went to see a fortune teller and she said I'd be broke and miserable up to the time I was 40 and I said what happens after 40?  And she said it won't matter, you'll be used to it by then!"

Did you know I've been on page 3 of *The Sun*?

The reporter who had done the story on Laura Harris in the travelling panto always used to ring me and ask if I had any news, we mentioned superstitions and my doing things in three's and this led to a feature in *The Sun* newspaper.  A photographer was sent to my home and took photos of me holding things up in threes, among them cans of beans and bras.  I was called the following day and asked; "Guess what page it's going on in *The Sun* newspaper?"  Yes it was the infamous and very popular page 3!

I was doing a ladies night that week and two of the strippers, Double Impact and Stallion (Dean and Dave) said they were coming home late from a booking, called in a garage bought an early copy of *The Sun* newspaper and nearly crashed the car when they saw me on page 3.  This article also resulted in a TV appearance on *Trisha* that was filmed in Norfolk.  Trisha had just taken over from Vanessa Feltz due to the bad publicity regarding fabricated stories.  Another appearance was on a programme for Sky filmed at Granada Studios, Manchester and yet another appearance on a Sky TV show *The Guilty*.  And yes the German population had found yet another eccentric Britisher and a reporter and camera crew came from the German TV channel Pro-Sieben to Mountsorrel once again!

I also have a numbers and characters routine I do in 3's that is far too complicated to explain here so I won't!

The same reporter also had a feature on my allergies in a women's magazine.  I suddenly became extremely allergic to anything I ate and drank at the age of 38 years.  My husband had gone out on a Sunday evening and my face was beginning to swell up like a football one side and it was getting worse by the minute.  My Mother rang me late at night and I could hardly talk, she came straight round, had a fit when she saw me and rang the doctor who came out immediately. I was flat out on the settee with the doctor sticking all sorts of needles into me when John came home. "Who's the prat who's parked halfway across our drive, I've just run into his car?" said John and then saw the doctor glaring at him!

I had many years of living on rice, lamb, pineapple, pears and hot water and went down to six stone. This meant I couldn't go on holidays for 20 years. If I did go out, I had to take a flask of hot water with me, and whatever I could eat. At work the first time someone saw me they were on the verge of ringing the police thinking I was a victim of abuse at home which was a great worry to John! It was also a time when people didn't think allergies were that serious and there wasn't the food that you can buy now for people who have food sensitivities. We would spend hours in supermarkets reading labels and packaging and it would be a long while before rice cakes and other things that are quite common in shops today would be on sale.

The morning of the first performance of my touring panto I woke up with a badly swollen face over which I slapped my make up. The show must go on!

The buffet bar staff on the trains to London always refused to give me hot water on days out as they said it was too dangerous to give to the public. Didn't they realise what a mess hot coffee would have made anyway let alone hot water! Haven't they seen Lee Marvin throw a cup of hot coffee in Gloria Grahame's face in *The Big Heat*! I can eat and drink fairly normally these days and they now ironically give you the tea and coffee separately and a cup of steaming hot water to make your own!

My face would often swell up looking like I'd gone ten rounds in the boxing ring and it would take a good week to go fully down, thankfully I seem to be a lot better now, but in the end I got quite philosophical about it. When you've eaten and you're not hungry any more you could have eaten anything you wanted to imagine. Most of us as we get older have something wrong with us and at least it wasn't as dreadful as some of the things people unfortunately do get.

John and I had bought a terraced house at 15 Hawcliffe Road, Mountsorrel in 1976 that needed modernising. The house had the old quarry tile floors that we had arranged with a builder to do that winter. The builder came with his apprentice dug all the downstairs floors up and said; "I'm just off I'll be back in a bit to finish", by the time his van had got to the end of the road severe winter conditions set in and in a short while we were up to our neck in snow. For almost a week we had to walk on soil, John put down some planks and used copies of *The Sun* to put over them. My mother used to walk down from St Peter's morning service on a Sunday to see us. She went in to look at the living room floor and we could hear this rustling noise that went on for some time.

When she left to go home I went into the living room. She had turned every one of the 'page 3s' over that displayed Samantha Fox's two main talents. My Mum would have thought these were 'not nice' and it was on a Sunday too..........!

*Wishing on a star*.............................................................!

# CHAPTER 14

## THERE'S NO BUSINESS LIKE SHOW BUSINESS AND A FEW OTHER THINGS I WANT TO MENTION!

THIS chapter is like *Coronation Street's* Betty Turpin's immortal hot pot, a lot of things thrown in together that hopefully will come out all right and be digestible! The main ingredients are nostalgia and showbiz and bring to mind a line from a famous film:

As Vivien Leigh as Blanche DuBois said in the 1951 film *A Streetcar Named Desire*: "I don't want realism, I want magic!" (**And so do I!)**

### SYDNEY GREENSTREET

Whenever I think that's it, I might as well pack it in I say to myself; "remember Sydney Greenstreet!" (Yet another Capricorn!)

Kent born tea-planter Sydney Greenstreet gave up the tea business and returned to England to manage a brewery and found time to take acting lessons. At the age of 61, portly and bald, his big break came in Hollywood when he appeared in his first film as the 'distinguished' villain Kasper Guttman alongside Humphrey Bogart who was playing the popular shamus Sam Spade in *The Maltese Falcon*. George Raft being the first choice for 'Sam Spade', but he turned the part down as he didn't want to risk his reputation with a new director by the name of John Huston! Well we all make mistakes!

Although Sydney Greenstreet had been a stage actor for many years, he was that nervous on his first day of filming that he asked the female lead in the film, Mary Astor, a film veteran with over twenty years of filming behind her, to hold his hand as he was worried he would make an ass of himself! Two statuettes of the Maltese falcon were used during filming due to Humphrey Bogart dropping the original one and damaging it early on during shooting.    The damaged falcon can be seen to this day in the Warner Bros museum in Hollywood.

The next year Sydney Greenstreet was again cast with Humphrey Bogart along with Peter Lorre and Ingrid Bergman in one of the best films of all time, *Casablanca*.  This film was based on an unproduced play *Everybody Comes To Rick's*.  The extras singing the *Marseillaise* to the Nazis in 'Rick's Café Americain' had real tears in their eyes as most were displaced Jewish Europeans who had fled to America during the Second World War.  German Jewish actors, who had also fled Nazi persecution, were ironically playing Nazis. The German actor Conrad Veidt, the film's Nazi Major Strasser, had an SS death squad sent after him in America.

Claude Rains, another British actor, also starred in *Casablanca* and many other American movies in the 1940s.  As a youngster growing up in London, he had worked as a callboy at the then *His Majesty's Theatre.*  Claude Rains was the first actor to be paid one million dollars to appear in a film.    This was the 1945 film *Caesar and Cleopatra* in which he and British actress Vivien Leigh took the title roles.    Claude Rains failed his first screen test but went on to receive, though never won, four Academy Award nominations for an actor in a supporting role.

Due to being filmed during World War II, *Casablanca's* airport scene could not be shot at an actual airport for security reasons.  A sound stage was used and a cardboard cut out of an aeroplane was in the background.  Dwarfs were employed as 'technicians' to make the plane look full size.

Ingrid Bergman was taller than Humphrey Bogart and he had to stand on a box or sit on a cushion during close ups with her, he also wore platform shoes during filming.  Alan Ladd, a very short but very good actor (size isn't everything unless it's a ladies night!) had to have a trench dug for his leading ladies to walk in when being filmed alongside him.

*Casablanca* won three Oscars in 1943 for Best Film, Best Direction (by Michael Curtiz) and Best Screenplay.

*Casablanca* was recently voted third best film of all time and has some memorable lines:

  ◦ Here's looking at you kid
  ◦ Play it Sam, play *As Time Goes By* ('Sam' played by Dooley Wilson was actually a drummer and couldn't play the piano which had to be dubbed by a pianist behind a curtain so Dooley could see him and copy his hand movements)
  ◦ Of all the gin joints in the town, in all the world, she walks into mine
  ◦ We'll always have Paris!
  ◦ Round up the usual suspects!

Ronald Reagan and Ann Sheridan were Warner Bros first choice for the leads in *Casablanca,* also considered were Dennis Morgan, George Raft and Hedy Lamarr.  Somehow I don't think this film would have been the worldwide success it was without Ingrid Bergman and Humphrey Bogart!

Sydney Greenstreet went on to star in a lot of films, mainly as a villain and usually with the small, very odd looking bulging eyed Hungarian actor, Peter Lorre.  Peter Lorre had a small part in *Casablanca*, being killed off very early in the film.

My most favourite Peter Lorre film is where he is Raymond Massey's sidekick, struck off plastic surgeon Doctor Einstein, in the fabulous Frank Capra 1944 film *Arsenic And Old Lace*. The stars of this film are Cary Grant and Priscilla Lane who appear along with character actors Jack Carson, Edward Everett Horton and Jackie Gleason. Elderly actresses Jean Adair and Josephine Hull have a ball as the 'dotty' murdering aunts. It is one of the most hilarious witty films I have ever seen and no one, absolutely no one, could do it as perfectly today!

## DIANA DORS

I think Diana Dors was one of the most beautiful and talented British stars we have ever had and a great dramatic actress as shown in her performance in the 1956 film *Yield To The Night* and as Mrs Wickens, the evil guardian of two children in the 1972 film *The Amazing Mr Blunden*. Her real name was Mavis Fluck. Whilst her father didn't mind her changing her first name, he was opposed to her changing her surname until she pointed out to him that if her name ever appeared in lights and the seventh bulb had blown, it wouldn't look very nice!

Many years ago she came to Loughborough Town Hall to open a Business Exhibition. She was no longer a top name and had put on a lot of weight but she was still very beautiful. She arrived in a Rolls Royce, wearing a mink coat and walked into the hall every inch a star. There was not a huge crowd waiting but she made a wonderful speech and walked round each stand and spoke to everybody there before leaving, a very beautiful, gracious and much missed lady.

## ALAN BATES

What a nice man the actor Alan Bates was. Years ago one of my dancing pupils' mums, Val Gilbert, loved London and the theatre and seemed to go every week on her own. I started to go with her and Val always went round to the stage door at the end of every show even if we were pushing it to catch the last train home. This is how we got to know the Derbyshire born actor, Alan Bates. He loved it that we came from the Midlands and he would always come down to see us at the stage door. We went to see him in a play at Hammersmith and we were waiting for him in a room. He came into the room and some bigwig producer went to speak to him and he said: "Not yet I have to see my two ladies from Leicester first" and walked over to us! When he was at the National he had passes left for us at the stage door so we could go backstage before the performance to see him.

The *National Theatre* has very long corridors that look the same and had three stages, all with productions on that night. I spotted the famous director, Peter Hall, who was directing the play Alan Bates was in so we followed him and eventually made it to the right part of the *National Theatre* to see Alan Bates before the performance. The corridors are hung with many pictures of famous actors and Alan Bates told us he could only negotiate his way round these endless corridors to get to the stage and back to his dressing room by remembering which actors' portrait were where!

Apparently the late much loved comic/actress Beryl Reid also had the same problem. Many years ago when Albert Finney was appearing in *Othello* on one of the National's stages, Beryl Reid was appearing on one of the others. She had been out to do some shopping and coming back into the National she got lost and walked out, complete with shopping bags, onto the stage where Albert Finney was giving his all in front of a packed auditorium. "I'm terribly sorry Albert, I've come in the wrong place" said Beryl and walked off the stage as if nothing had happened!

## GRACIE FIELDS AND GEORGE FORMBY

Oh how I loved watching the old black and white films in which these two stars appeared when they were shown on television as a child and if ever one appears on afternoon TV I still do and I still laugh as much as ever.    These films contained a cavalcade of the great British variety talent of the time and very witty lines and routines.  My Nan used to sing *The Biggest Aspidistra In The World* and *Turn Father's Face To The Wall Mother* to me as a child and she had many of Gracie's old 78rpm recordings in the pub that I would play over and over again.

I love the film in which Gracie Fields is mistaken for a dancer and is thrown around the room by a man to very dramatic music.  This was known as an apaché dance, apaché being the French word for hooligan!   These dances were very dramatic and involved the woman dressed in fishnet tights, split skirt, tight top and beret (in other words looking like a 'tart'!).  She would be thrown about and slapped by a man dressed in tight black trousers, striped top, and beret.  She then gets stabbed to death at the end (no encore then)!   A lot of variety shows in the 30s and 40s would include this sort of 'turn' as it was so popular.  This style of dance was featured in the 2001 Baz Luhrmann film *Moulin Rouge*.

Gracie Fields was born in Rochdale and she was the 'pop idol' of her day.  She was asked to appear in a West End Play and the other actors were a bit off with having to appear with what they thought of as a 'variety turn from up North'.  One day she got to the theatre, hitched her skirt up and did cartwheels all round the stage, she stood up and said; "How many of your buggers can do that?"   This of course was a great leveller and everything went much better after that.

I love Gracie Fields because she was so normal and down-to-earth and didn't put on airs and graces.  Well after all she was a Capricorn!   When, as a big star, travelling on the *Queen Mary*, the captain asked if she would give a performance to the first class passengers.  She said she would but she would do it in the boiler room for the lads who were running the ship.  She did just that and the first class passengers came down to her!

Unfortunately Gracie Fields had an unhappy and turbulent personal life and she spent her last years living on the Isle of Capri where she would quite happily chat to British holidaymakers and pose for photos with them.  She was made a Dame of the British Empire in 1979 and she died the same year.

If anyone asks me if I can play a musical instrument I say; "yes, the radio!" I did try to learn the accordion at George Hames' music shop in Loughborough and I would have to carry it to and from lessons on the bus.  I went for a couple of years but playing this instrument can become very uncomfy for a growing girl! If ever I could have learnt to play one instrument it would have been the banjo. George Formby was the highest paid star of his day and his numbers are still remembered.  My juvenile dance classes love to dance along to *Chinese Laundry Blues* and one dad had to find a CD with it on for his five-year-old daughter who never stopped singing it at home.

We had a wonderful 'turn' on our early 40s nights, Peter Graham, who was the master of the banjo and often met up with ex-'Beatle' George Harrison to play guitars and banjos together.  Wherever he appeared with us and no matter how old or young the audience was; they were fascinated by his wizardry of this instrument.

## ANTHONY HOPKINS

I became a member of the Actors' Centre many years ago and I received an invitation to the opening of the new premises in Tower Street, London on 17 September 1994 at 2pm by Anthony Hopkins, but unfortunately it was a Saturday afternoon when we had a matinée of the dancing school's *September Show*. The very generous mothers of my pupils said: "You never miss any lessons and you're not missing this, we'll look after the children." So, thanks to them I set off in the morning got to the actors centre and to my great disappointment, it had already been opened several hours before! I bumped into Richard Wilson who was starring on TV in that wonderful series *One Foot In The Grave*. He told me they had invited all the VIPs in the morning and he thought Anthony Hopkins would be long gone by now

The centre was packed and I suddenly saw Anthony Hopkins sporting a white 'bob' and dressed casually but immaculately in a room being interviewed. I stood and waited and out he came. People stepped aside and smiled and I thought to myself I've come all this way I'm going to speak to him and I stepped forward and said: "Excuse me Mr Hopkins but I've come all the way from Leicester where you had your first professional booking at the *Phoenix Theatre*." He paused for a moment and said: "Yes you're right" and gave me a heart melting smile with his mesmerising turquoise eyes. He gripped my arm and started speaking to me and autographed my invitation card. When he eventually walked on I could see everybody staring at me very enviously. Well they had their chance and didn't take it! I rushed back to Loughborough on the train ready for the evening performance of the dancing school show and proudly showed everybody my autographed invitation card.

## MARIE LLOYD

I love Marie Lloyd. Born in Hoxton in the East End of London on the 12 February 1870, her real name was Matilda Alice Victoria Wood. But her family called her 'Tilly'. At the age of 10 she told her parents she was going on the stage and rounded up her younger sisters and friends to form the *Fairy Bell Minstrels* and they appeared in the many Mission Halls in London.

Marie (pronounced Mah-rey) Lloyd was a hugely popular vibrant, dark haired, petite, well endowed Victorian music hall star known as 'Queen of the Music Halls' and, more affectionately, 'Our Marie'.

She picked the exotic stage name Bella Delmore for her first professional appearance in 1885 at the Grecian Assembly Rooms then part of the Eagle Tavern in London's City Road. Her father worked there as a part-time waiter in the evenings. He also had a full time day-job making artificial flowers for women's hats, for an Italian merchant. Marie's mother was a dressmaker. A very wise manager advised her to change her name to something simple that the public would remember. She had always liked the name Marie, and Lloyd came about on her seeing a billposter advertising a newspaper, *Lloyds Weekly News*.

She became famous for singing songs with titles such as *She'd Never Had Her Ticket Punched Before* and *Every Little Movement Has A Meaning Of Its Own*. She told innuendos and with her cheeky personality accompanied by a nod and a wink, the public fell madly in love with her. She would walk out on stage with a folded up umbrella, hold it aloft and say to the packed audience "Do you know I haven't had it up all week!" After appearing and not going down well in Sheffield she told them 'they could stuff their knives and forks (and anything else they made out of steel) up their jacksies'. What a girl! A star at the age of 16 she was earning £100 a week and, at the height of her career, was earning the incredible sum of £600 a week. In those days of the music hall each act would have a number on a board and when Marie's number appeared at the side of the stage the crowd would go wild.

Some of her many famous songs were *My Old Man, Come Into The Garden Maud, One Of The Ruins That Cromwell Knocked About A Bit, Don't Dilly Dally On The Way* and *Oh Mr Porter* everyone of them sung to me by my Grandad. A complaint was made about a line in one of her songs 'she sits amongst the cabbages and peas' which Marie obligingly and wittily changed to 'she sits amongst the lettuces and leeks'. With her cheeky personality she could even make a simple song like *Come Into The Garden Maud* very suggestive!

Listening to recordings of Marie singing these songs it is hard to believe that she was considered 'blue' but this was a time when a woman could not show her ankles. Even table legs had to be covered in long chenille cloths! Of course as soon as the dresses came into fashion with a split in the middle so you could show a leg, Marie was one of the first to wear these. She always held a long black cane in front of her. This black cane would be placed on her funeral car many years later.

Like many variety acts, Marie was very generous and would always help out with fund raising shows for charities even going so far as to buy over a hundred pairs of boots herself for poor people. She appeared in many shows in support of the First World War. Even though she was a top star she took the side of the poorer paid and very often badly treated music hall artists and became a picket outside the halls in the music hall strike of 1906/7. When another not so famous 'turn' on the halls ex-opera singer, Belle Elmore, tried to cross a picket line and Marie was on picket duty, Marie, obviously not a fan of Belle's, shouted: "Let her go in, let her play, she'll do more to help break the strike by playing than by stopping out!" Belle Elmore did achieve fame however in 1910 after she was murdered by her husband, the infamous Dr Crippen!

Marie's songs are still sung all round the country today in music hall shows. My grandparents would sing all these songs and other music hall medleys to me whilst cleaning the pub. I would be sat on the bar singing along, swinging my ringlets, and holding aloft a glass of Vimto.

Marie Lloyd was the eldest of 11 children, two dying in infancy. Her sisters, Daisy, Alice, Grace and Rose also performed 'on the halls' and all but Daisy adopted the surname 'Lloyd'. But Marie was undoubtedly the star of the family. Marie's daughter also trod the boards as Marie Lloyd Jnr, but never achieved the same fame as her mother.

Marie used to make her own extravagant dresses but, as the work came piling in, her mother and her aunt took on the task and then later on a professional dressmaker, Jefferson Arthur Leake, made all her beautiful dresses up to the end. At Marie's funeral he sent an empty dress box covered in flowers with the words 'my last design, the dress box but no dress'.

Making your own costumes was something acts did at that time. Panto dames would make their own outfits, the more outrageous and extravagant the better. A 'dame' would be booked for a panto not on his acting ability but on how good, and how many outfits he had. John Inman from *Are You Being Served?* is reputed to have made all his own panto Dame outfits.

Marie Lloyd was refused entry into the USA in 1913 as she had shared a cabin with her new 'beau' and they were not married which was a shocking situation in those days! Bernard Dillon was the new paramour he was 18-years her junior and a Derby winning Irish jockey. Marie, at that time, was still married to her second husband. They were arrested and charged with 'moral turpitude' and detained at Ellis Island alongside murderers. Marie Lloyd had a very well known dramatic life and a turbulent marriage with Dillon, who eventually became her third husband. When she sang *One Of The Ruins That Cromwell Knocked About A Bit,* thanks to him she didn't need any make up!

She was not included in the very first *Royal Command Performance* at the Palace Theatre in 1912 that was actually commanded by King George V, due to the suggestiveness of her material in her act and her very well known personal life. Marie retaliated by staging her own show at the London Pavilion calling it *The Popular Command Performance, Commanded By The People* and she played to sell out audiences. The first *Royal Command Show* was in front of a very stiff and stodgy audience but Marie's audience at the other end of Shaftesbury Avenue were the complete opposite, cheering, clapping and shouting for more all night. After this show a slip was pasted over the bills outside the theatre proclaiming her 'The Queen of Comediennes" and 'The Queen of Comedy' and proudly stating 'Every performance given by Marie Lloyd is a Command Performance by order of the British public'! So there missus!

Vesta Tilley, another famous music hall act, who sang dressed in male attire usually a uniform, appeared in that first *Royal Command Performance*. Queen Mary, our present Queen's grandmother, refused to look at Vesta Tilley on stage as she was dressed in 'trousers that a man would wear' and she instructed the rest of the ladies in the royal party to do the same!

As she got older Marie began to drink heavily affecting her voice and her act. In Edmonton in 1922 whilst singing one of her famous songs *A Little Of What You Fancy Does You Good* she staggered around the stage, the crowd loved it thinking she was acting 'drunk'. She walked off the stage and collapsed in the wings. She died three days later at the age of 52. At her funeral the streets of London were filled with over 100,000 mourners and 12 cars were piled high with wreaths. Shops were closed along the route of her funeral car. Significantly, one wreath was of a huge birdcage in memory of one of her songs. The cage door was open, the cock-linnet gone for good.

I love old theatres and music halls and the Old Bedford Music Hall in Camden High Street, sadly now gone, was one of the most famous. Marie Lloyd appeared there from the age of 15. Her famous song *The Boy I Love Is Up In The Gallery* was 'pinched' from another music hall act, Nelly Power, who died in poverty in 1887. Marie first sang this song at the Old Bedford Music Hall and cunningly placed her young brother in the gallery with instructions that he should wave his handkerchief when Marie sang this particular song. This caught on and in no time at all the whole audience would wave their hankies every time Marie Lloyd rendered *The Boy I Love Is Up In The Gallery*. There really is nothing new under the sun, just think of the Barry Manilow concerts where women hold up candles!

Marie celebrated her 50th birthday on stage in pantomime at the Old Bedford and also appeared in panto at Drury Lane for three years as principal girl with Dan Leno, the greatest panto dame of all, from 1891 to 1893. Marie and her sisters all played principal boys throughout their careers.

I was asked to go and give a talk to a senior citizens' group in Syston, Leicestershire and I spoke about the only thing I know showbiz! I mentioned Marie Lloyd and, at the end of the evening going around talking to some of the people there, an old lady called me over and whispered to me in a London accent; "Marie Lloyd was my great aunt!" She said she remembered Marie Lloyd giving her a doll and I was amazed when she said she hadn't told anyone else, as she didn't think anybody would remember Marie Lloyd. Bless her heart!

## BOB MONKHOUSE

Bob Monkhouse seemed to be on the TV screen all the while in the 1950s and 60s and not for nothing was he known as King of the Quiz Shows! In 1957 he was the comperé of *Val Parnell's Sunday Night At The London Palladium* and hosted a very popular cover version of the controversial American quiz show the *$64,000 Question* on TV that began in 1956. Whilst in America a contestant could win this amount, in Britain the top prize was £6,400. This was because the Independent Television Commission would only allow prize money on TV shows to go up to £5,000 and special permission was given for this to be £6,400.

Bob Monkhouse's most remembered TV shows must be *Candid Camera* that began in 1960 and *The Golden Shot* that ran from 1967 to 1975 and along the way he took time to also host *Family Fortunes* and *Celebrity Squares*. Bob Monkhouse was also a very fine actor; I saw him in a couple of televisions dramas, *Carry On Dentist* and also in a *Jonathan Creek* TV episode but his great love was writing comedy material and drawing cartoons and he sold his first gag to a comic at the age of 15. He also wrote material for the showbiz greats like Frank Sinatra, Dean Martin, Jerry Lewis and Bob Hope. He was also an avid silent movie collector of the great stars like Buster Keaton, Charlie Chaplin and the Keystone Cops. Bob also said *Opportunity Knocks* from 1987 to 1989 but this show really didn't produce the stars that the original Hughie Green series had and then Les Dawson became the host. I met him several times when starting out and he always took the time to talk to me and give me advice that I really appreciated. Bob Monkhouse was respected and acknowledged by all comics old and new as 'the master'. He was awarded an OBE in 1993 and died In 2003.

## ROY CASTLE

I loved Roy Castle because he was such a brilliant tap dancer. Years ago when he was a big star on TV he came to Loughborough Town Hall but unfortunately not a lot of tickets had been sold. He walked out looked round and asked: "Did you all come in the same taxi?" This immediately broke our embarrassment at the poor turn out; he then asked us all to move down to the front seats. He did a brilliant show and even jumped off the stage and tap danced round us. I met him in his dressing room after the show and said how sorry I was about the lack of audience expecting some caustic answer. But he was so easy going about it and gave me a big tip. He had children's toe taps fixed on to the heels of his tap shoes because they gave a better sound and so did I after that.

Variety people are full of advice and tips and I remember years ago being told that an old vaudeville and variety tap dancer's trick was to place a sixpenny piece (6d) on the underneath of the toe of the shoe before the tap plate was screwed on, so it rattled when you danced and made more sounds!

I remember taking a child with me to his dressing room. Recently talking to Stephen Mear's Uncle Stuart, he said that he and his wife Joyce and Stephen's cousin Fay went with me to that show. Fay would have been around eight years of age at the time and she said she wished that she could meet Roy Castle. I took her to the dressing room entrance whereupon a man abruptly told us we weren't allowed in. I apparently pulled myself up to my full 5'1½" inches and said very authoritatively: "We're something to do with it!" and he let us straight in. Fay never forgot this and when Stuart, Joyce and Fay were ever going anywhere they would laughingly say "we're something to do with it." Isn't it funny what other people remember about you!

Roy Castle was thrilled I had passed the audition for *Opportunity Knocks* and offered to be my sponsor on the show. When the time came and I was called to appear, he had to go off to Sweden to film a TV show and wrote to say how sorry he was. I still have his letter today. Years later I appeared at the London Palladium and Fiona Castle, Roy's widow, came and we presented her with a cheque towards the Roy Castle Cancer Fund Appeal.

## GLORIA GRAHAME

For making such an impression on me in the 1950s in the film noir *The Big Heat*, that at the age of seven years I decided I was going to be a film star and change my name to Deirdre Grahame!

## JUDY CAMPBELL

I had been several times to see Omar Shariff in *The Sleeping Prince* at the *Haymarket Theatre* in London in the 1980s. This was the stage play of the Laurence Olivier and Marilyn Monroe movie *The Prince and the Showgirl*. This is where I met the wonderful actress Judy Campbell, mother of Jane Birkin the actress, film star and she of the notorious number one hit *Je t'aime* fame. Judy Campbell was also starring in the play. I wrote to her and she invited me to go and see her in her dressing room and I went to see her a few times during the run. She said to me: "I love that name, Deirdre Quemby" and kept saying it in that fabulous husky regal voice of hers. This made me think that perhaps Deirdre Grahame was not such a good choice for a name as an actress and I may have to reconsider. Judy Campbell must have been in her late 60s and she told me stories about the theatre ghost and how it was supposed to appear in the mirror in her dressing room but so far she hadn't seen it. She had a lovely wry sense of humour. I could have listened to that fabulous voice all night.

I mentioned that I had met Omar Shariff at the stage door many times and how serious and quiet he was. She said that as this was a very old theatre, dressing rooms were all over the place and on different levels and Omar Shariff had been moved after complaining that he was not on the same level as the stage. She told me she had said to him: "Darling, Ralph Richardson had the dressing room you were in when he was very elderly and he managed those stairs several times during every performance!" So there!

## GINGER ROGERS

Oh how I idolised Ginger Rogers and Fred Astaire. Today there are very few couples or even dancers that can spell bound an audience like these did. Fred Astaire learnt to dance with his sister, Adele, and they became a double act in American variety and also came to London to dance. Adele met and married an English Lord in 1932 and became Lady Charles Cavendish. She left show business and Fred Astaire auditioned at a film studio in Hollywood and he had this comment written down about him 'can't act, can't sing, slightly bald, can dance a little'! However he was given a chance to dance in film and teamed up with a certain Ginger Rogers in 1933.

Fred Astaire danced with other leading ladies such as Judy Garland, who will ever forget *We're A Couple Of Swells*, Joan Crawford, Eleanor Powell and Rita Hayworth to name but a few. But it is 'Fred and Ginger' that we all remember best.

Fred was a perfectionist and insisted on gruelling rehearsals that led to lots of rows with Ginger. But it never showed on screen, they were the ultimate professionals. One big row came about a dress Ginger had picked for a certain dramatic dance number in the 1935 film *Top Hat*. It was covered in ostrich feathers and as they danced the feathers would literally get up Fred's nose and this led to another big row. However at the end of filming, the dance number being a huge success, he gave her a silver 'feather' charm. As Katherine Hepburn said of them: "He gives her class and she gives him sex!"

Fred Astaire was brilliant, but don't forget Ginger did it all backwards and in three-inch heels! Ginger's name was actually Virginia but a young niece had difficulty in pronouncing it and so it stuck as 'Ginger'. The actor Liam *Star Wars* Neeson's first name is actually William. He also had a young relative who had difficulty in pronouncing his name, and that's how his stage name came about as well!

When Ginger Rogers was much older she came to London to star in *Mame* at the *Theatre Royal* Drury Lane. I booked my ticket months in advance to see my idol. I got to the theatre and there was a huge notice in the foyer. Apparently Ginger had gone off on a two-weeks cruise for a rest and Juliet (*GI Blues*) Prowse was covering the title role! It was unkindly said the next day in the press and on London TV that Juliet Prowse was much better in the part being younger. Well she was good but I wanted to see Ginger even if she had to have been helped on to the stage and then just sat in a chair for the whole performance!

## WILL HAY

This man to me was a genius on stage and in his old black and white films most of which I have on video and regularly watch, he can make me cry with laughing and also makes me realise what a lot of really great talent we had in those days. 1933/4 saw him star in a stage play *The Magistrate* that was remade as the film *Those Were The Days* in which a very young John Mills played his son. The plot sees them end up in a Victorian Music Hall that showcased many top draw music hall acts of the time.

# MAX MILLER AND THE LITTLE GOLD BOOK!

Before television comics only needed one act. There were so many places to work you could travel the country with that one act. Nowadays with millions watching on TV you need so much more material as people rarely laugh twice at the same gag or routine. I found I was being asked to go back again and again to the same clubs so my 'little gold book' came into being. I note down the topics I have talked about and when I am due to return I carefully note down what they were and make sure I don't use the same material. They may not remember jokes to tell their friends that they have laughed at but when you are standing there going through the same routine they come flooding back to them and they never ever laugh twice at the same material.

The great Max Miller had a 'blue' book in which he supposedly kept his risqué jokes. He would always ask the audience whether they wanted the white book or the blue book and they would always shout back "the blue book!" He is said to have asked this at a Royal Command show winking at the Royal Box only to hear King George VI (our present Queen's father) allegedly shout back 'the blue book'! Max Miller's blue book gave birth to the term 'blue joke'.

Max Miller wore outrageous floral patterned jackets, matching plus-four trousers, a gaudy kipper tie and a pair of white and brown golfing shoes, topped with a jaunty trilby. He would walk on stage in a long bold patterned coat trimmed with fur which he would take off and hang on a hook that was fixed on the back cloth to gasps at his gaudy finery and say invitingly to the audience: "I wear some nice clothes, don't I ducks?"

Jean Kent, an actress of the 1940s/50s, appeared in variety shows with Max Miller and said he was very different off stage. He would tell the chorus girls off backstage if he heard them swearing or being rude. Max Miller would never go on last as top of the bill even though he was the 'star turn'. He always timed the end of his performance to the exact minute so he could leave the theatre and catch the last train back to Brighton where he lived. One night he was a few minutes late and they actually held the train up for him.........now that is a star!

I am a member of the Max Miller Appreciation Society, Roy Hudd is the President, and, in a small way, contributed to his statue in Brighton. Max Miller would say: "There'll never be another" and he was right!

# MY FAVOURITE ACTRESSES AND ACTORS OF YESTER YEAR OF THE SILVER SCREEN

| James Cagney | Jean Harlow | Robert Mitchum | Cary Grant | Carol Lombard |
| --- | --- | --- | --- | --- |
| Errol Flynn | Judy Garland | Lana Turner | Jean Arthur | Myrna Loy |
| Hedy Lamarr | William Powell | Margaret Rutherford | Peggy Mount | Marjorie Main ('Ma Kettle') |
| George Murphy | Joan Crawford | Humphrey Bogart | Bette Davis | Ginger Rogers |

## Dee Quemby

## CHICAGO – the musical

Anybody who is interested in musical theatre has known about this wonderful musical for years.  When it was mentioned that this would be made into a film all the critics predicted it would be a flop as, according to them, nobody was interested in film musicals any more.  Well the money paying public proved them wrong!  *Chicago* picked up quite a few awards at the Academy Awards with our own beautiful and elegant and then very pregnant Catherine Zeta-Jones winning an Oscar as 'Velma'!  Catherine Zeta-Jones was at one time British Tap Dancing Champion, another reason why I love her!  She was also the winner of a talent show at a Butlins holiday camp!  Another coincidence here, Stephen Mear danced in *42nd Street* at Drury Lane *Theatre Royal* alongside Catherine Zeta-Jones.  I'd love to meet her; I bet she's a right laugh!

I was thrilled that when Catherine Zeta-Jones won this award, her husband, Michael Douglas was bursting with pride.  Dead chuffed he was!  I can't understand why not one of these award shows, like the Olivier's, isn't shown on TV any more, it's so annoying.  I used to book the day after the Academy Awards off work, set two videos up the night before just in case one didn't tape, get out my long frock and 'diamanté' jewellery and sit there on the settee the next day dressed to the nines watching the whole ceremony.

Did you know the Academy Awards have 'seat stand-ins'?  Apparently anyone can put in to be one.  The Academy picks so many from all over America and they stand out of sight at the awards.  When anyone in the audience has to nip to the loo during the many hours of the awards, the seat stand-in sits in their seat.  This is done so when the camera makes a sweep of the audience during the televising there are no empty seats to be seen.  If I were a seat stand-in I'd have to have my own seat stand-in as well, as this ceremony lasts for many hours and often overruns!

The plot of *Chicago* is based on a true story of a murderess and Ginger Rogers played the title role in the 1942 film *Roxie Hart* along with George Montgomery, the wonderful character actor Adolphe Menjou, Phil Silvers in an early role long before his famous *Sergeant Bilko* and I believe the rather stocky old looking newspaper boy at the end with one line is William Bendix though he is not listed in the credits.  For Ginger this was a non-dancing role though she did manage a bit of the Charleston in the prison and few tap steps on the stairs, Ginger was actually a prize winning Charleston dancer.  She won an Oscar for her performance as Roxie Hart.

I was thrilled to see my friend from Loughborough, Nikki Hughes, play Velma in *Chicago* in London, I sat on the front row and at the end when Roxie and Velma were presented with bouquets, Nikki leaned forward and gave me a red rose.

## ELTON JOHN

I love Elton John.  To me he is the supreme showman!  The talent, the campness, the showmanship, the humour and the sheer love of entertaining are all there in his performances.  Those wonderful over the top shows of his!  He is exactly the same age as my brother David would have been.  I'll let you into a little secret; I used to imagine to myself that he was my brother!  What shows we put on!

## 20ᵀᴴ CENTURY FOX AND (LEO) THE MGM LION

For me, as a child, the two most awe inspiring things in the cinema were the opening fanfare for the 20ᵗʰ Century Fox films, and the roaring lion for the start of the MGM films! Pure magic!

I was in Las Vegas in October 2004 with friends Shirley and Roger and every morning I would walk across the bridge from the Tropicana Casino into the MGM Grand Casino to see the lions, lionesses and occasionally the two cubs 'Chilli' and 'Pepper' as they were not brought in every day. A lot of the lions and lionesses are descended from the original MGM lion whose name was Leo.

A massive bronze lion stands guard proudly outside the MGM casino. The statue is actually 45 feet tall and 50 feet long and weighs 50 tons. I would look up and say hello to him every morning. My Mum would have loved the MGM Casino. It's bright green!

As I went in the MGM Casino every day the trainers would talk more to me and I was told that the original Leo was bought from a zoo in Ireland by the Goldwyn Picture Corporation and Leo's first roar was heard, via a phonograph record, at the start of a silent movie *White Shadows Of The South Sea* on 31 July 1928. Goldwyn pictures merged with Metro and Louis B Mayer and became MGM. In keeping with their showbiz background some of the lions' and lionesses' names are Metro, Goldie and Louie B. Get the picture!

Polish-born film mogul Samuel Goldwyn's original name was Samuel Goldfish. Somehow I can't see a roaring goldfish being so impressive at the start of a film! He did not have a really good grasp of English and is noted for his 'howlers' and amusing quotes that are legendary amongst actors and are known as 'Goldwynisms'.

Gentlemen, include me out
A verbal contract isn't worth the paper it's written on
Anyone who goes to a psychiatrist should have his head examined
On someone admiring his wife's hands: Yes I'm going to have a bust made of them
If Roosevelt were alive he'd turn in his grave
I can answer you in two words, Im possible
A hospital is no place to be sick
I don't think anybody should write their autobiography until after they're dead
If I could drop dead now I'd be the happiest man alive
Spare no expense to save money on this one
I never put on a pair of shoes until I've worn them at least five years
Let's have some new clichés
Give me a couple of years and I'll make that actress an overnight success
Colour television, I won't believe it until I see it in black and white
If people don't want to go to the pictures nobody can stop them
I'll give you a definite maybe
Our comedies are not to be laughed at
I am willing to admit that I may not always be right, but I am never wrong
This scene is dull; tell him to put more life into his dying
Modern dancing is old fashioned
A wide screen just makes a bad film twice as bad

I don't want any yes men around me. I want everybody to tell me the truth even if it costs them their jobs!

And: The reason so many people showed up at his (Louis B Mayer) funeral was because they wanted to make sure he was dead!

The 'Lion of Hollywood' was Russian-born, Louis B Mayer, known as LB, an ex-ragman, fur trader and ex-scrap iron dealer. He was also the founder of the Academy of Motion Picture Arts and Sciences that in turn gave birth to the Academy Awards. In 1927 he organised a dinner at the Ambassador Hotel in Los Angeles to unite the film companies against their fight of mobster control and so the Academy came into being. At that time many film companies were paying enormous sums of protection money to the mob, if not cinemas their films were being shown in would be hit by many disasters. Films would be run backwards or without sound and key scenes cut out by blackouts. This even happened to the famous 'no under shirt' Clark Gable scene in *It Happened One Night* that many women had been waiting all through the picture to see. Can you imagine their reaction!

Even the Kennedy family were part of these set-ups. John and Jack and their other many siblings' father, Joe Kennedy was a bootlegger during the Prohibition Days from where he made his fortune. He then went to Hollywood during the 1920s where he took control of many of the cinemas apart from one chain. The elderly Greek owner, Alex Pantages, refused point blank to sell to Joe Kennedy.

A little while later, Alex Pantages was accused of rape by a young girl. Alex Pantages had little command of English and this gave a bad impression to the jury and the public and he was convicted and sent to jail. However for his retrial case he had the good luck to hire an unknown lawyer, who through his brilliant handling of this new case, would become known as 'Lawyer of the Stars' to future studio stars in trouble, his name was Jerry Giesler. The girl who had previously turned up in court demurely dressed, in flat shoes and her hair in pigtails was proved by Jerry to have quite a track record that shocked the new jury and he also showed that the mop cupboard she had alleged the incident took place was so small it could only accommodate one person apart from her and an elderly portly man. Pantages was now declared not guilty with lots of stars and studio bosses noting down Jerry Giesler's phone number just in case! Years later the woman on her deathbed admitted it was Joe Kennedy who had instigated the frame up so he would be able to buy up Alex Pantages' cinema chain while he was in prison! Joe Kennedy also found time while all this wheeling and dealing was going on to have an affair with Gloria Swanson.

MGM studio motto was 'Art for Art's Sake' and for their musicals 'Do it big, do it right and give it class'. MGM had a famous photo taken of all their stars together in the 1940s that was published in *Life Magazine* with the studio's proud boast 'we have more stars than there are in Heaven'. Among them being Elizabeth Taylor, Gene Kelly, James Stewart, Joan Crawford, Bette Davis, Buster Keaton. Greta Garbo, Lana Turner, Clark Gable, Laurel and Hardy, Frank Sinatra, Judy Garland, Mickey Rooney, Fred Astaire and Ginger Rogers. Two MGM stars, Spencer Tracey and Katharine Hepburn hold the records for the most Academy Award nominations and actual wins by an actor and actress, though Katharine Hepburn never turned up to receive any of her Oscars. If she'd have asked me I'd have picked them up for her, I've got my Oscar outfit ready and waiting!

MGM also produced the highest money making film ever *Gone With The Wind* and the ever popular *Wizard of Oz*. I have seen this Judy Garland film so many times I now expect to see my name come up in the end credits!

A lot of incidents involving studio stars would be hushed up and kept from the very moral public's knowledge. Clark Gable, while drunk and driving a car, had hit and killed a woman and a minor studio employee had been very well paid to take the blame and the prison sentence and on release a guaranteed lifetime job at the studio. Clark Gable's brush with homosexuality, as was Errol Flynn's, to advance his film career was also kept quiet.

At this time the casting couch was the main and probably the only way of getting on in the movie business and most stars had countless bi-sexual affairs and liaisons with each other as well as with the heads of the studios and other executives. This was all accepted as perfectly normal in 'Tinsel Town' though they had to appear to the public as extremely moral people, happily married with a family. Loretta Young's adopted daughter was actually her own child by Clark Gable. She went away on the pretext of being ill and was not seen by the public for a while. The newborn baby girl was then placed in an orphanage for many months so Loretta could be seen to visit the orphanage and 'clap her eyes' for the first time on the toddler she wanted to adopt! The child's telltale ears were kept covered and operated on as soon as possible to pin them back.

Later on Rock Hudson would be made to marry his agent's secretary by the studio he was signed to, to conceal the fact that he was gay from all the many millions of female fans madly in love with him, Van Johnson also had a studio arranged marriage for the same reason, and cross dressing grey haired 'all American action man' man Jeff Chandler's wife often came home to find him in her dress or negligé. Her blue negligé was apparently his favourite, which of course was kept, like Jeff, under wraps by the studio.

These studios were all powerful and there was no question of not doing what they said. Busby Berkeley, the creator of those wonderful dance sequences in the 1920s and 30s, whilst driving drunk had hit and killed three people and he himself had sustained serious head and leg injuries. Charged with second degree murder he would be wheeled into the court room on a stretcher every morning and guess who the lawyer defending him was......yes the now not unknown, but famous or rather infamous Jerry Giesler hired by the studio. He would also be called on later to defend celebrity clients like mobster Bugsy Siegal, Zsa Zsa Gabor, Charlie Chaplin (paternity case), Errol Flynn (statutory rape), Robert Mitchum (possession of drugs), Marilyn Monroe (divorce from Joe Di Maggio). 'The sweater girl' Lana Turner (murder of her mobster boyfriend by her 14 year old daughter Cheryl, or was it actually Lana who gave her finest acting performance ever in the witness box?) and many more notorious cases involving 'stars'. In fact at the hint of any trouble the studios and stars would cry: "Get me Giesler!"

Warner Bros film studio had Busby Berkeley contracted for three pictures at the time of his trial and these films were their main concern not the trial nor the murder charge or even his serious injuries! They re-arranged filming schedules to take place during the night where Busby would be wheeled from the court room straight on to the set to direct the elaborate dance sequences until the early hours of the morning before making his next court appearance. The first two trials ended in hung juries and it was the third trial that Jerry Giesler's brilliant defence brought about the now totally exhausted Busby's acquittal. This man's many dance sequences were so masterly and original, especially his 'wedding cake' shots and never before done close ups of the chorus girls' legs, that even today to do a 'Busby Berkeley' means to stage a huge dance sequence.

Some film studios even had their own police department and they would be called in first even if it involved murder. A lot of crucial evidence would be removed and never seen again. Jerry Giesler was called to the Lana Turner mobster boyfriend's murder scene at her house long before the police were informed.

The film studios were so powerful in those days and very strict with their stars and even controlled their private lives. Paramount studios in the 1920s had a 'Potato' contract that their female stars had to sign. This stipulated they had to maintain their weight at the time of being taken on by the studio. If they put on more than 5-lbs they would be instantly sacked and this resulted in many of them resorting to diet pills and health wrecking crash diets. Actors would be supplied by the studios with all sorts of pills to keep them performing at their peak to make money for the studios.

Actresses of the 40s would be completely taken over by the studio and they would then be totally made over into glamorous stars. One of the best films to see this process in is the 1954 *A Star Is Born* where Judy Garland as 'Esther Blodgett' of all names is remodelled to stardom as 'Vicki Lester'. This film was a musical remake of the 1937 film of the same title that had starred a very popular American movie actress, Janet Gaynor. Janet Gaynor was the first ever winner of an Academy Award for best actress. She won the award for not one film but three (those threes again!) and these were *Seventh Heaven, Sunrise* and *Street Angel* (how weird all three begin with 's'). This was because the Oscar was awarded to her for her work in film over the previous year. Sweet girly Janet Gaynor is said in a recent book, allegedly, to have had a lesbian affair with Larry Hagman's mother the American musical theatre star Mary Martin. Not another one! Perhaps this is where I'm going wrong in the business?

Real names would be changed to more exotic ones, hair would be styled and coloured and make up artists would give them their own special look. Movie magazines would show their female readers amongst other things how they could copy a Joan Crawford 'mouth' or Carol Lombard 'eyebrows'. Joan Crawford had several of her back teeth removed to give her the fashionable hollowed cheek look and even then plastic surgeons would be poised at the ready. The top film costume designers would create a special fashion look for each star. So powerful were these designers and make up artists that their names were as well known as the stars.

The women stars were idolised, with their glamorous designer clothes, make up and hairstyles being copied worldwide by their female fans. Joan Crawford was the first woman to have shoulder pads sewn in to her clothes to accentuate her shoulders, a fashion fad that has never gone away and was taken to ridiculous heights in the over the top but oh so glamorous and much missed American soap operas *Dynasty* and *Dallas*. This 'new' fashion was copied by women everywhere and resulted in them all looking like American footballers for a decade! Linda Gray who played Sue Ellen in *Dallas* was originally a model and interestingly it is Linda Gray's pair of legs on the famous poster for the 1967 Dustin Hoffman film *The Graduate* not Anne Bancroft's, as most people believe.

Not only clothes and make up influenced the movie going public. In the Bette Davis 1942 film *Now, Voyager* her co-star, Paul Henried, put two cigarettes in his mouth, lit them at the same time and then handed Bette one.  This scene became screen history and was copied by men all over the world.

Actresses could never appear in public without being dressed and made up to perfection.  Joan Crawford was told by L B Mayer at MGM to always remember she was a star and to dress like one and never to be seen without make up even if only taking rubbish out to the dustbin.  The film moguls of those days must be turning in their graves at how so many female stars appear in public today.

This was a time when glamour was everything and actors and actresses would be signed for their looks very few of them had ever taken acting lessons. Nowadays actresses are expected to down glamorise, no make up, hair scraped back, no bold hair colours, plain clothes, what a turn around.

At that time contracted female stars had to ask the head of the studio for permission to marry and if they were told 'No' that was the end of that otherwise they would be dismissed never to work again.   Affairs between stars at the studio would be ended if the studio didn't like who was involved with whom.  The film bosses would always know every detail of their actors' and actresses' private lives.  More often than not the stars' dressers, assistants and secretaries would be 'spies' for the studios, reporting back every little detail!  A married female star would be told when she could or could not have children and her husband would be told as well.  If she had pictures to film for the studio and did become pregnant secret abortions, which were illegal at the time, would be arranged.  Most of the famous female stars of the 40s and 50s had plenty of these.

All movie stars had to appear to the public as having perfect lives and to be seen as proper and decent, even saintly, role models.  Their private lives were just the opposite and could never be made known like today to the movie going public who revered their stars and put them on pedestals and this is probably why there is such fascination with these stars today.   Any star whose behaviour was cause for concern by the studio, whose real 'concern' would be that the public might found out something that had been going on for years, would be warned and if they didn't toe the line they would be sacked and their career ended.

It took a two year search to cast an actress to play Scarlett O'Hara in the 1939 film *Gone With The Wind* with all the top female actresses competing for the role and they were all screen tested in the famous 'lacing up' scene in costume. Paulette Goddard was the hot favourite, but it was becoming public knowledge that she was living with Charlie Chaplin and they were not married and this cost her the role.  Remember this was a time in films that a married couple would be seen on screen in twin beds and if a shot called for an actress to be in a bed and a man sat on the bed he had to be fully clothed and keep one foot on the floor throughout the scene!

Filming started before Scarlett was cast.  Vivien Leigh, an unknown British actress, was eventually given the part.  Amazingly the studio had no inclination that she was living in secret with Laurence Olivier otherwise she would have been struck off the list too.  They were both actually married, but not to each other! Vivien Leigh walked off with the best actress Oscar as did Hattie McDaniel, the first black actress to be awarded an Academy Award, as best supporting actress for their roles in this film.   Hattie McDaniel's private life involving two other actresses, Tallulah Bankhead and Ethel Merman, was also another very well kept Hollywood secret!

Films had strict codes to abide by and swear words could not be used. Clark Gable as Rhett Butler in *Gone With The Wind* had the immortal line: "Frankly my dear I don't give a damn." 'Damn' was then a not-to-be-uttered-in-public swearword! The film company was told by the Hays Office, the film regulation body, that censored the content of films, that it had to be changed to 'Frankly my dear I don't give a darn'. However many negotiations later and after two scenes had been shot using both lines, the original line was allowed to be used in the film.

MGM even ran their own extremely well kept secret brothel in Hollywood for their business associates and male stars. In the 1930s the 'ladies' at the establishment were look-alikes of the top female film stars of the day such as Clara Bow and Greta Garbo. In his biography Mickey Rooney mentions, in his day as MGM's biggest money earner, the T & M Studio that was a Hollywood brothel with celebrity look-alikes. This was the theme of the big hit Russell Crowe, Kevin Spacey 1997 film *L.A. Confidential* that was set in the 1950s with the then, happily married to Alec Baldwin, Kim Basinger winning an Oscar for her performance as the hair over one eye 'Veronica Lake' look-alike call-girl.

Veronica Lake was a very popular American husky voiced glamorous film star during the Second World War. Women here and in America copied her then very distinctive and novel hairstyle where her hair flopped over one side of the face completely obscuring one eye and this hairstyle was known as the 'Peek-a-boo Bang'. This created problems with the women in this country working in munitions factories for the war effort as their hair frequently got caught in the machinery and it became compulsory for them to wear their hair back and in a snood whilst working in the factories. They probably bumped into a lot of things as well!

It is hard to imagine these days how controlling these studios were of their 'stars' when we see how many film and TV stars are allowed to behave now. I watched Olivia de Havilland, one of the stars of *Gone With The Wind,* on a chat show years ago. She said that the big studio bosses in the 1930s and 40s even had their female stars 'monthly' charts on a wall so they could see the days when not to do any close ups as they would be too puffy!

Any likely scandals in your background before you hit the big time would be hushed up, as was Joan Crawford's early porn films and life as a prostitute and also Jeanette MacDonald's early escort days. Most 'stars' had 100 per cent fabricated previous lives made up for them.

Merle Oberon, one of the most beautiful actresses even today with her oriental exquisite looks, had an elderly Indian maid for many years and on Merle Oberon's death it came to light that this maid had actually been her mother which accounted for her dark beauty. In those days to be born of mixed parentage was unacceptable and you would be called a half-caste. Marriage between black and white people was illegal in America and even carried a prison sentence in some of the states. Merle Oberon would never have worked with any studio if they had known. It has only recently become known that the great British beauty Vivien Leigh came from a mixed race marriage. Ava Gardner played the half-caste Julie Laverne in the 1951 musical *Showboat* with Howard Keel and again in the 1956 film *Bhowani Junction* with Stewart Granger as did Yvonne de Carlo with Clark Gable in the 1957 film *Band of Angels* though neither actresses were of mixed race parentage.

If any star scandals were found out and hit the newspapers the studios would be horrified and immediately suspend whoever it was tarnishing their saintly studio, even though they had probably known what they were up to months before. Many journalists continually tried to sniff out any wrong doings, the most powerful being two women, Louella Parsons and Hedda Hopper. Studios bosses and stars lived in fear of this pair who could make or break a career by the written word. Both women became as famous as the movie stars and hated each other as much as Joan Crawford and Bette Davis did.

James Cagney however was not in awe of the studio system and had many rows with Warner Bros over parts and money. In 1936 he was the highest earner in film and the number one box office star, but he was unhappy that he could not share in any profits of his successful films, that he had no say in what he thought were mediocre scripts and poor leading ladies and he resented always being cast as a gangster. He took Warner Bros to court and won and was released from his contract. He unfortunately signed with a company that was a network of minor studios and he was cast in two unsuccessful films. It was alleged that Warner Bros saw to it that they were unsuccessful! He eventually returned to Warner Bros who took their greatest star back at a much higher salary. He was now able to have a 'happiness clause' inserted in his new contract that said Cagney could end his contract at the end of any year or after any motion picture if he thought that his relationship with the studio was obnoxious or unsatisfactory to him. This contract was the envy of many movie stars!

Bette Davis was the first actress to challenge the studio system in 1936. She was not happy with the parts she was getting and informed Warner Bros, of which there were four, that she wanted parts worthy of her talent. Instead of just meekly bowing down under pressure, she upped and left and came to England to work, but the studio blocked her contract and wouldn't let her work with anyone else. She sued Warner Bros. saying her contract was a form of slavery and lost. On her return they gave in to her demands so all things considered she did win in the end and with the bonus of a huge increase in salary. She went on to star in some wonderful films though losing out to Vivien Leigh for her Oscar winning part of Scarlet O'Hara in *Gone With The Wind,* Bette Davis was compensated by the studio by being given the lead part in *Jezebel* for which she won her second and last Oscar. So powerful did Bette Davis become after this that she was known as the fifth Warner brother!

The MGM casino's theme is Hollywood's Golden Age with black and white stills of bygone film stars hung everywhere. I have a wall in my house full of these black and white stills that I get from 'Back to the Wall' in London's Covent Garden, a permanent market stall that backs on to a wall! It is next to my friends Pam and Keith's costume jewellery stall and both are well worth a visit on the Monday market.

Meanwhile back at the MGM Las Vegas Lion Habitat............the animals are only in the habitat for a few hours each day and are on a rota basis. They are obviously well looked after and pampered. The habitat is wonderful and the lions and cubs cannot see or hear anything other than the waterfall and the trainers who sit with them and have been accepted as part of the pride. They have the best of care and can expect to live at least eight years longer than a lion in the wild. The MGM Casino and Keith Evans, the owner of the lion ranch in Las Vegas and master trainer, also donate money to many other wildlife preservation organisations. Some of the lions and lionesses love the habitat so much that they don't want to leave when it is time to go back to the ranch affectionately known as 'The Cat House'!

267

*Dee Quemby*

Shirley and Roger renewed their marriage vows in the garden of the Tropicana Casino where we were staying and I was the maid of honour. Who else could they have to perform the ceremony in Vegas but one of the many Elvis impersonators? How I stopped myself from cracking up when he asked Shirley to vow: "never to step on Roger's blue suede shoes" I'll never know! It was an experience not to be missed.

## RITA HAYWORTH

Rita Hayworth was the most beautiful classy woman ever; tall and svelte with long red hair. She was also a wonderful dancer. I could watch her over and over again performing *Put The Blame On Mame* in the 1946 film *Gilda*, in which she played the title role. Her singing voice however had to be dubbed by Anita Ellis. During this number she did a mock striptease peeling off her long black gloves and through this became Hollywood's number one sex goddess and millions of pin-ups pictures of her were sent to American servicemen overseas.

During a day's filming on a film set under the strong lights she would have to have her long thick hair set at least four or five times and later in life she said that she had spent more time under a hairdryer than actually working. She was born in Brooklyn, New York. Her father was a Spanish dancer, and her mother was from an English and Irish background. She danced professionally from the age of 12 years. She danced with her father, under the name of Rita Cansino, in cabaret where she was spotted by a film scout. At the age of 15, she was put under contract to Fox's film studio.

The studio set about remodelling her. They raised her hairline by electrolysis, changed her original black hair to red and changed her surname to Hayworth. She also danced with Gene Kelly in *Cover Girl* and Fred Astaire in *You'll Never Get Rich* and *You Were Never Lovelier*. Rita Hayworth was cousin to Ginger Rogers by marriage.

Of all the films she appeared in she was always remembered for *Put The Blame On Mame* and she had a very dramatic personal live. After many marriages and divorces and becoming an alcoholic she said: "Every man I knew had fallen in love with Gilda and wakened with me." A true legend!

## GENE KELLY

For a long while all the men in musical films were slim, dignified and a bit 'twee'. Then along came Gene Kelly who looked like he'd walked straight off a building site! Rugged and very masculine and a trained gymnast he brought sex appeal to the films and was the first person to dance with a cartoon character. He danced with many famous names of the time though later on said: "As for my leading ladies at MGM, the hardest thing was finding dancers who could also act and sing. Most of them couldn't even say hello!"

Gene Kelly did not have much praise for most of his leading ladies apart from one, Judy Garland. His first film appearance at the age of 30 was opposite her in MGM's *For Me And My Gal* in 1942. Judy Garland was a big star at the time but she took the time, and the trouble, to help him, an unknown newcomer, and gave him tips and advice on filming. He always had the highest respect for her. This film also starred one of my favourite 'song and dance men' George Murphy and was directed and choreographed by Busby Berkeley.

Gene Kelly appeared with Frank Sinatra and those two wonderful dancers Ann Miller and Vera Ellen in the film *On the Town*. Another coincidence here, Stephen Mear choreographed *On The Town* at the *Royal Opera House*, London in 2005.

## SINATRA AT THE LONDON PALLADIUM

For my birthday in 2006 Stephen Mear gave me two tickets to see *Sinatra At The London Palladium*; which Stephen had choreographed. We were blown away by it, it was absolutely incredible and of course the dancing was fabulous. It was a night performance and after the show I nipped to the loo and when I came out most of the packed audience had gone. A woman grabbed my arm and asked me what I thought of it and then I saw a camera. It was for London Weekend TV and I said how brilliant it was, the dancing was superb and how great it was to see all the audience singing along and being thoroughly entertained. A few months later someone jokingly asked me if I was receiving any royalties for the promotion of this show. London taxis and buses are now fitted with TV screens and apparently I was on the ad for this show! Of all the performances and all the thousands of people going to see this wonderful show, this is another one of life's little coincidences.

It is impossible to describe the sheer brilliance of this show. Frank Sinatra appeared on many moving screens and was backed by a full live band and he even talked about his life to you! It was almost as if you were in the presence of 'Ol' Blue Eyes/The Voice' himself. This show cost £5m to put on and the beautiful classy 50s dresses of the female dancers in the first half cost £2,000 each. This show was first produced in New York in association with the Sinatra family. Apparently, the American backers were so impressed by how this show was staged here that there is even talk of it opening in Las Vegas.

After one of the first shows, outside the stage door, stood a man clutching an autograph book. After some time he asked the stage door keeper: "Is he coming out?" When asked:"Who?" He replied indignantly: "Sinatra of course!" Well I did tell you it was a good show!

To see a live show especially in London is very expensive, there are no reductions for children and senior citizens. For more years than I care to remember I have taken parties of dancing pupils to London. We get half price tickets from the ticket booth at Leicester Square on the day and over the years have seen some wonderful shows at prices they can afford and you really have to see a show in London to see what it is all about. There is something so special about a West End show. Over the years many of the girls from the dancing school have met Stephen at the stage door of whatever show he was appearing in at the time as they have another Loughborough born successful West End performer, Nicola Hughes.

Many years ago when I first started taking some of the dancing pupils to London the half price tube fare was 50p and the girls were always told to take plenty of 50ps. We were walking through Soho where all the 'Peep' shows had 50p entrance notices. One of the younger girls casually remarked to another girl; "I can see why you need a lot of 50ps in London!"

269

## MARTI CAINE, VICTORIA WOOD AND PAM AYRES

Growing up I can only recall two funny ladies and these were Joyce Grenfell and Beryl Reid. They didn't tell jokes but performed monologues. With *New Faces* the world opened up to me with Marti Caine. Here was a woman actually standing on stage and telling jokes like the male comics did and I wanted to do the same!

Marti Caine's stage name came about because she was so slim and someone by chance remarked she looked just like a tomato cane!

I was never lucky enough to meet her but I did take a party of girls from the dancing school to see her as the wicked Queen in *Snow White* in London. I wrote to ask her if she could mention them and put down all their names in the letter. We watched the show and as with *Snow White* there is no sing along at the end this didn't happen. Three weeks later a letter came to the dancing school and it was a handwritten letter from Marti Caine in which she said she was sorry she couldn't give us a mention but it wasn't that sort of show. She had enclosed an autographed photo for each child and had taken the time, and trouble, to write their individual name on each one, what a nice lady. When I went to Granada TV studios in Manchester to film *The Comedians* the production team there told me how much they liked working with her and that she really was a nice woman in real life. This is something you don't always hear about a lot of 'stars'.

Victoria Wood also appeared on *New Faces* and here was something new, a woman who just talked about situations in life and made them hilarious. She also wrote her own material and that was unique at the time. These two women paved the way for women comics and I am very grateful to them both.

Pam Ayres was brought to the public's attention via the TV talent shows. She wrote and recited wonderful witty poetry and came from the same area as my Grandad. My Grandad always maintained she was in someway related to us.

## FAITH BROWN

I got to meet Faith Brown by being a member of the British Comedy Society and when she came to the Birmingham Hippodrome to star as Norma Desmond in *Sunset Boulevard* my friend, Sue, and I were invited to see her backstage.

I wasn't sure if I would like a musical version of this great film but it was tremendous. *Sunset Boulevard* is one of Andrew Lloyd Webber's best musicals. Faith Brown was magnificent, and it was said that she was by far the best 'Norma Desmond' to appear in the musical version. Another 'turn' from the working men's clubs who made good, and such a nice lady.

## THE CRAZY GANG

I absolutely loved the Crazy Gang as a child. The 'Gang' was made up of three comedy double acts, Flanagan and Allen, Nervo and Teddy Knox, Charlie Naughton and Jimmy Gold and one solo comic, 'Monsewer' Eddie Gray. It is impossible to convey to youngsters of today how popular and incredibly funny they were. They appeared in countless films and Royal Command Performances and were in so many shows at the *Victoria Palace Theatre* that it became known as the home of the Crazy Gang.

On a Jack the Ripper walk around London, I was thrilled to see a blue plaque on a wall of a house in Hanbury Street in Spitalfields saying that this was the birthplace of Bud Flanagan.

## THE BILLY COTTON BAND SHOW - Wakey Wakey!

The whole family used to listen to the *Billy Cotton Band Show* on the radio, with his catch phrase 'Wakey Wakey', when I was a child, as did countless families up and down Britain.

I met Sir Bill Cotton Jnr, an ex-head of the BBC, at the unveiling of the plaque to Larry Grayson at the ceremony at the Empire Theatre, Shepherd's Bush. He laughed like a drain when I told him that I was still using one his father's old band tracks in the clubs *Nobody Loves A Fairy When She's Forty!*

## POUND SHOPS

Oh how I love my pound shops, my eyes light up whenever I find one! I even managed to find a dollar shop in Las Vegas out in the desert!

## SHIRLEY WILLOWS AND FAMILY

At all of my first ladies nights in Leicester there would be a woman in a wheelchair at the front, she had hearing aids on both ears and she always wore a hat. I later found out she had lost her hair due to treatment for leukaemia. Her husband would wheel her to the front and leave her there. Sometimes she came with two girls who were her daughters, Suzanne and Maria.

We got talking one night and have been best friends ever since. Shirley had two other young daughters, Jo and Danielle, at home whom I later met. Shirley had in fact in total had six daughters but two had died very young.

Shirley battled on with various treatments and is now able to work and can be seen smiling and helping customers in Shoe Zone in Beaumont Leys in Leicester. Her youngest daughter Danielle had an amazing voice and became a singer on the clubs as Danni-Jane, but has now finished.

Shirley and Roger Willows, her husband, were a great help to me with my Mum and one occasion I remember particularly well. My Mum wanted to go on the London Eye and when we got to the booking office to pick up our tickets there were two flights of steps outside. Roger is the strongest man I have ever come across. He just picked up the wheelchair with my Mum in it, with no effort at all, and carried her and the chair up the steps. The many tourists taking photos of the London Eye now were taking photos of him! Roger often 'roadies' for me if John can't go to any of my bookings.

As my Mum needed help we didn't have holidays and Shirley and Roger and family invited John to go abroad on holiday with them, which he has done for several years. All Shirley's girls and many grandchildren call him Grandad John.

When my Mum was spending her last days in hospital, my friend Carol took me and often stayed with me. Shirley, Roger and family came many times as I was sleeping in a chair at the side of the bed after several mishaps, ill treatment and run-ins with the staff of the ward she was unfortunately on. I wouldn't leave,

271

## Dee Quemby

as I wanted to make sure my Mum got the treatment and respect she deserved. I really can't believe how bad things have become in hospitals today. You get more compassion at the vets! Though I must thank one specialist and two 'older' nurses who helped me even though my Mum wasn't under their care! Shirley, Roger and Jo came just as I was told it wouldn't be much longer. They were with me when my Mum died and helped me do her beautiful long white hair up in a bun whilst we waited for the Roman Catholic Priest to come.

If I hadn't have decided to promote my own ladies nights I would never have met Shirley and Roger, their daughters Suzanne, Maria, Jo and Danielle, grandchildren Hannah, Lily, Lucy and Olivia and extended family of Anita, Taz, Yasmeen, Riaz, Kath and Julie, Michelle and Daz and their children Amy, Charley, Libby and Thomas, along with Russell, Mark, Ashley and Dave. I have called Shirley and Roger friends but we are 'family.'

## PAT WARD AND SHEILA LUCAS

These are two remarkable ladies I have met through dancing. One day at South Street when it was warm I had the door open and an elderly lady was looking through the door at the children. I asked her if she wanted to come in and sit down and watch and that was the start of a wonderful friendship, Pat had danced in the 1920s and had some wonderful photos to show me. She lived on her own and joined my adult tap dancing class in which she carried on in up to the age of 85 years. She still comes to watch all my classes and shows and at the age of 94 still takes the dancing school show posters round to shops. She used to swim every day but now does it every other day, as she wants to take it a bit easier now!

Sheila Lucas is an ex-pupil's grandmother and had been in show business as a dancer. Her mother had 'theatricals' lodging at their house. One of the acts asked her mother if she could tour with them. Off Sheila went to London and at the age of 13 years she was appearing at the *Windmill Theatre* dressed only in a hat and a string of pearls! She looked much older than she was and she had told Mrs Henderson, the owner of the theatre and Mr Van Damm that she was 16 years old. She had auditioned in the morning and went straight into the show that same night. Years of summer shows and revues all over Britain followed working with the then big names like Danny La Rue. Sheila had a book of poems published a few years ago and I am very proud that I was included in one of them. I often see Sheila when I go to Loughborough and she's always demanding to know why I'm not on the television or working at a big theatre and telling me to write to all sorts of people she knew. Unfortunately it's not so easy these days to get work, as it was when Sheila was starting out!

I often pass the *Windmill Theatre* in Great Windmill Street in London. It is built on the site of an actual windmill that stood there in the reign of Charles II. The theatre was closed for a long while which is ironic as it never did during the Second World War apart from 12 days at the start of the War when it was made to close down by the Government who were worried about the capacity audiences it was getting during the bombing raids. Its motto was 'We never closed' often changed to 'We never clothed'! Doris Barry, the sister of prima ballerina Dame Alicia Markova, who was on my audition panel for *Opportunity Knocks* in the 1960s, was a dancer and soubrette at the Windmill Theatre during the war years.

In the 1960s it re-opened as a cinema/casino and is now home to a lap-dancing club. The film *Mrs Henderson Presents* with Dame Judi Dench, Bob

272

Hoskins and Will Young was wonderful and had a really witty script and as well as its sad moments. During the Second World War this theatre carried on mainly because like a few of the old London theatres the auditorium and stage are under ground and lights would not have been visible during the blackouts. They would do six shows a day and there would be a long queue of men waiting to buy a ticket to see the nude and scantily clad girls and the fan dance number which no other theatre had put on before due to the censorship laws at the time. Laura Henderson and Vivian Van Damm found a loophole in the censorship laws and that was if the nudes didn't move it would be considered as art! They didn't however call it a nude review; it had the more respectable title of *Revudeville!*

In between the girls' routines and nude tableaux, a comic or some other type of variety act would perform often to the same disinterested audience impatiently waiting for the girls to come back on. Among them being Jimmy Edwards, Tony Hancock, Arthur Haynes, Barry Cryer, Terry Scott, Harry Secombe, Eric Barker, Bruce Forsyth, Peter Sellers and Alfred Marks. Kenneth Moore that wonderful actor and his brother Joe, worked at the Windmill as stagehands. Sheila Lucas let me into a little known fact and that was that Kenneth Moore's father loaned Vivian Van Damm the money to put up for his share of the *Windmill Theatre*.

Once in, the men and many servicemen of all nationalities could stop and watch all the six shows that were performed throughout the afternoon and night and many of the men in the audience, especially those in long raincoats, did just that! Des O'Connor got his first break at the *Windmill Theatre*. He was on his fifth show of the day when he completely dried. A man, who'd obviously been in the audience for every previous show shouted at him: "You do the one about the parrot next!"

The men in the back stalls would wait for the men in the first six rows, which were the best seats to get a good view, to get up and leave. When they did the men at the back would rapidly climb over the seats to get to the front. This became known as the 'Windmill Steeplechase'.

## UNCLE ERNIE LEADER & CAROL LEADER

Uncle Ernie, Nan's youngest brother, joined the Salvation Army and went to London to work. He met Kathleen, who was a Captain in the Salvation Army and they had to get the Salvation Army's permission for them to get married, as he was a lower rank. Aunty Kathleen appeared in the famous film *Major Barbara* about the Salvation Army, starring Wendy Hillier, the Salvation Army was asked to provide the 'extras.' Aunty Kathleen in later life became the Mayoress of Ely.

My father had the deepest respect for the Salvation Army, as did most soldiers. He said that no matter where you were in the Second World War, they were always there with a blanket and a cup of hot cocoa! When I was young the Salvation Army went round the pubs selling the *War Cry* and most people would buy a copy. If they are collecting in the town centre or selling the *War Cry* I always make a donation in gratitude on behalf of my Dad and the other soldiers.

Uncle Ernie and Aunty Kathleen had two daughters, Pauline and Carol, who were slightly younger than me. Pauline is a Quaker and does a lot of work for the Quakers in London. Carol became a successful actress. She was the receptionist in the first series of *Casualty*, the second lead in the hugely popular TV drama *Flambards*, appeared in a sitcom *The Sally Ann* and hosted *Play School,* the

*Dee Quemby*

BBC children's TV series. Carol no longer works as an actress. She is actually mentioned in Leicester authoress Sue Townsend's number one, and very funny, best selling book *The Secret Diary Of Adrian Mole Aged 13¾*.

## RED HAIR

It has only just struck me going through my early memories how much people with red hair have influenced me! Marti Caine, Moira Shearer, Rita Hayworth, Ginger Rogers, Joan Neal and James Cagney. Yes he had red hair but with the cream men used on their hair in the 1920s and 30s and appearing in black and white films people assumed he had dark hair. He was also a brilliant dancer and many impressionists copied his style of walking up on his toes that was very distinctive. As a young man dancing on Broadway he often had to dress as a woman and wear high-heels and he said that this had resulted in him walking this way.

## LEZ COPE-NEWMAN

Lez is one of Loughborough's characters and as I put pen to paper attempting to become Charnwood's Mayor! Lez has come across a stipulation in the Borough's laws that if he can come up with a certain amount of signatures he can stand as Mayor and he is very near to getting there. If Lez succeeds in his ambition, his partner, Derek, will get a hat allowance!

Over the years I have performed with him and watched him in many shows and like me he is a great theatre fan. I went to see Andrew Lloyd Webber's musical *The Woman In White* whilst I was filming *Death By Excess – Hollywood Goddesses*. It was far too dramatic for me and I didn't find any of the music unforgettable but I was overwhelmed with the staging of it which was really just projected on to the stage pretty much like an actor working in front of a blue screen and I did love the live mice and large rat that made their appearances in the second half. Lez went to see the show and hated it. He said he had walked out into the foyer at the interval and thrown his ticket in a bin. A very camp usher told him he would have to have his ticket to get back into the theatre and when Lez said he didn't like it and wasn't going back in, the young man said: "I know what you mean sir, we call it The Woman In Shite!"

I went to see *The Witches Of Eastwick* at Drury Lane *Theatre Royal* in which Stephen was assistant choreographer. At the very last minute in came Lord Andrew Lloyd Webber with his wife and another man and sat two seats away from me. This show was a preview and was running very late, it got to ten to eleven and I was catching the 11.15pm train at St Pancras. I had no choice but to get up and go and said: "Excuse me your Lordship but I've got to catch the last train back to Leicester " and had to squeeze by them and unfortunately stepped on his lordship's toes. That's my career in the West End over before it's even started then!

I have actually appeared on stage many times in the West End...................... the West End WMC in Leicester that is!

# THE BRITISH COMEDY SOCIETY

I joined the British Comedy Society several years ago and its aim is to preserve the great names and traditions of British comedy. They have several charity fund raising events and lunches and have unveiled many plaques to great stars of the past and present. At Elstree Studios they have a Wall of Fame. They also hold many tribute lunches at Pinewood Film Studios where they have a Hall of Fame. Occasionally they have 'Evenings With.........' at top London Hotels that so far have included Victoria Wood, Jim Dale, Bruce Forsyth and Dame Thora Hird.

At some of the lunches I have met and sat with Jean Ferguson, Sir Norman Wisdom, Jenny Hanley, Faith Brown, Tom O'Connor, Burt Kwok, Spike Milligan, Shirley Eaton, Dora Bryan, Pearl Carr and Teddy Johnson, Angela Rippon, Jeffrey Archer, the families of Morecambe and Wise and many more 'stars.' At Pinewood for the unveiling of a plaque to Morecambe and Wise, Ernest Maxim the producer of the Morecambe and Wise Shows, whilst talking about them had tears in his eyes and said: "I do miss them so much," as we all do!

Dora Bryan OBE seems to be ageless. In 1986, I went to see her in the revival of *Charlie Girl* in London starring an icon of the 40s and 50s Hollywood musicals ex-ballerina, Cyd Charisse. I had originally seen this musical in 1968 at the Adelphi in London with Dame Anna Neagle and Derek Nimmo. Dora Bryan would not be that young then. We watched her do a little dance routine and then all gasped and broke out into applause as she jumped straight down into the splits. She now of course is in that wonderful and long running TV programme, *Last Of The Summer Wine*. She lives in Brighton very close to where Stephen's flat is and recently was trapped for some time in a lift in a store in Brighton. Ever the trouper she started to sing to the rest of people in the lift until they were rescued. I hope she passed her hat round at the end! I will never ever forget seeing her in *A Taste Of Honey* in 1961. We all thought of her as a comedienne and were knocked out by her dramatic performance in this film, a performance that she quite deservedly won awards for.

Talking of Dora Bryan OBE brings back a story going round Herbert Morris when I was working there at 17. At that time we knew all the directors and they all knew us by name. Their offices were located near ours and we would see them in the offices and corridors several times during the working day. How unlike today when company directors are just names and usually based somewhere up in London, or even overseas! However a very important client had rung up to say that he hadn't realised there was a director on the board with an OBE and he was very impressed. He had received a letter with a director's signature followed by the letters OBE. Well frankly there wasn't any director at Herbert Morris holding this honour. Investigations followed and a young boy office worker was found to be the culprit. He was the last to leave the offices and had seen this important letter on the director's desk and had noticed that it was marked urgent. He knew this contract had to be out that night and so he had signed the director's name and posted it. All well and good he was told, but why had he put the letters OBE? He replied: "Because I was the only bugger 'ere!"

The British Comedy Society invited me to the Larry Grayson plaque unveiling by Sir Terry Wogan at the *Empire Theatre* Shepherd's Bush. This theatre was where the *Generation Game* was filmed when Larry Grayson was the host. Of course with my early association with Billy Breen, I was very honoured to go. All of the showbiz celebrities at these events are so friendly and take a great interest in you. It's well worth being a member if you are interested in show biz.

Larry Grayson spent 30 years doing the rounds of working men's clubs, variety halls and summer seasons before getting his break on TV. I've been at it 20 years now, so only another 10 to go! At the unveiling I met the late Queen Mum's butler, William Tallon, who was affectionately known as 'Backstairs Billy'. We were told at lunch that the Queen Mum loved Larry Grayson and she had sent William Tallon to Larry Grayson's funeral to report back all the details in great depth to her.

The Queen Mum was renowned for having a great sense of humour and for being an avid theatregoer. Tommy Steele appearing in a *Royal Variety Show* in her presence many years ago in front of a very reserved audience asked them to clap along to a song. They were not used to being asked to do this and it wasn't until the Queen Mum leaned forward in her box so the audience could see her and started to clap that they joined in!

This brought back to me a story about our much loved and missed Queen Mum. Apparently many years ago when King George VI was King, and she was Queen, she was woken up by the noise of two male members of staff having a very loud and heated argument below stairs. She went downstairs and said to them: "There's only one Queen in this palace and it's me!" You tell 'em!

A recent British Comedy Society 'do' hosted by Christopher Biggins, a truly hilariously funny man, was held at *Pinewood Film Studios* to celebrate the 250th episode and 35th year of production, and BBC producer/director Alan J W Bell's 25th year at the helm of that wonderful now longest-running TV programme in the world (yes it's overtaken *I Love Lucy!*) and that is *Last Of The Summer Wine*. I sat next to a man in his 80s, Royston Coe, whom I had met previously at the Larry Grayson ceremony, along with his daughter Jan and her two friends Sheila and Jane. Royston has a lovely London accent and has never ever been in show business.

Just when I thought I couldn't find anything else to put in this book, Royston told me another story! In the 1960s he was a chauffeur in London and he used to drive a model, Bernadine, to her modelling sessions. He and Bernadine started 'stepping out' as they used to say. However Bernadine met a young ex-electrician turned actor who had just signed up with her agent. She parted company with Royston and started going out with this young actor. Her agent confidently said about her new beau: "He's going to be a top star one day." The young actor's name was David White, which he would change to David Jason. I wonder if he made it!

## THE BOOK COMPANY

The Book Company in Loughborough is a tiny quaint shop that specializes in unusual and second hand books and is run by Jacqui and John Gallon. I had a book about Marie Lloyd on order that no matter how hard they tried they couldn't get. One day, months later I was walking past the shop and John called me in and gave me a tiny old book with brown pages entitled *Marie Lloyd Queen Of The Music Halls*. The picture on the front and back of the book is the Old Bedford Music Hall in Camden, there is no date in the book but it is very old and it is written with great love about Marie Lloyd. There is even a chapter that describes some of her wonderful dresses in great detail. I was over the moon, Jacqui and John wouldn't let me pay for it they said it was a gift!

I get all my showbiz books from there and they now know me so well that when I go in to order a new publication that has been advertised as just coming out they tell me that it is already on order as they knew I would want a copy!

## THE BRITISH MUSIC HALL SOCIETY

I have been a member of the British Music Hall Society for many years and the great Roy Hudd is President. They send members a magazine *The Call Boy* that has many articles of the old musical hall stars and the great stars of variety through to the 60s and is another society trying to preserve our very British theatre traditions and well worth joining.

## COVENT GARDEN

Covent Garden is famous for many things; one being that it is where the first Punch and Judy show was performed and watched by Samuel Pepys in May 1662. This was commemorated in 1962 by a plaque being put on the front wall of St Paul's Church by the Punch and Judy Society. This church is immortalised in the film *My Fair Lady* as where Eliza selling her flowers first meets Professor Higgins. St Paul's Church in Covent Garden is the actors' church and inside there are many plaques to famous actors, actresses, dancers and musicians. Well worth a look inside.

The Punch and Judy Society's patron is that everlasting and over running comic Ken Dodd! One Sunday a year in May the Punch and Judy Society hold a May Fayre in Covent Garden and in 2006 it was the 31st May Fayre to celebrate Mr Punch's 344th birthday with most of the society's members getting together with their 'bottlers' and performing their individual shows. A 'bottler' is the person who stands at the side of the booth and then goes round at the end of the show for donations. They are called 'bottlers' as in olden days they would collect the money in a glass bottle. A service is also held inside the church for the society's members. When a Punch and Judy Professor dies a wreath, with a photo of the late Professor, is hung near the plaque. That's the way to do it!

## DRESS CIRCLE AND THE SEVEN DIALS

Dress Circle is the showbiz shop of the world in Monmouth Street, London near to the Seven Dials. This is so called because there is a large sundial on a plinth in the centre and seven roads exit from it. Dress Circle has CDs, DVDs, mementoes, etc from all over the world and even sells programmes and other memorabilia from past and present West End and Broadway shows. The Seven Dials is actually mentioned in one of Marie Lloyd's songs.

My friend from Loughborough, Nikki Hughes, who has starred in *Chicago*, *Tommy* and *Fosse* to name but a few and appeared in countless West End shows and even made a recent appearance in *EastEnders*, brought out a CD that I could not get locally or anywhere else come to that. I got it from Dress Circle!

## THE QUEEN'S 80TH BIRTHDAY PARTY AT BUCKINGHAM PALACE, and A 40s NIGHT!

I was thrilled that the two musical numbers in this televised show for children from Buckingham Palace were Stephen's from *Mary Poppins*. On a very much smaller scale I was asked to provide a show for Mountsorrel's residents who were over 80 at the working men's club in honour of Her Majesty's 80<sup>th</sup> birthday after having had their own tea party. We did our 40s show with old friends Monty Katchick (ex-club singer Monty Martell) and Trevor Ison providing songs. The dancing school pupils from three years up dressed as evacuees, oh how small children love the songs from the 40s especially Flanagan and Allen's *Run Rabbit Run!*

*Run Rabbit Run* was often the participation song at the end of the pantos when I was a child. These days they seem to write such complicated lyrics to an unrecognisable piece of music for panto participation songs that even the adults can't follow it. Keep it simple!

I really have to mention one 40s night I was booked to put on. Two young women had approached me at a ladies night. They had their mother with them, and unbeknown to her they asked me if later in the year I would be able to do a surprise 40s night for their mum's 60<sup>th</sup> birthday. I gave them my telephone number and thought no more of it. How many times do we working men's club 'turns' get asked for cards and phone numbers never to hear from these people ever again!

In the summer Tessa, one of the girls, rang me and booked the 40s night for a Saturday in November at the Three Horseshoes pub in Willoughby in Leicestershire. I assembled the dancers and a wonderful singer, Neil Ashleigh, and we set off in the dark through the countryside. As we approached the village we could hear Chamberlain's speech and 40s music blaring out and as we drove into the pub car park a wonderful sight met us. It was just like being on a film set; well it was more than that it was really like actually having gone back to the 40s! They had built a bunker on to the opening of the pub that was covered in camouflage nets. They had hired rifles, a machine gun, ammunition boxes and shells that were placed inside the bunker. The whole pub had been taken over and both rooms were decorated with wartime posters and flags and all the staff were dressed in 40s outfits.

My friend Sue who had got there earlier with her daughter who was one of the dancers told me I had to go immediately and look in the annexe. This was a small room with an old fireplace and on the mantelpiece there were sepia photos of the 60<sup>th</sup> birthday lady as a child in old frames. A small table covered in an old lace tablecloth had on it an old black 40s phone, an identity card and many other 40s items and to top it all, the mother of the lady whose 60<sup>th</sup> birthday it was and who was well into her 80s, sat on an old fashioned armchair next to the fire wearing a crossover pinny and 40s hair-snood. When the guests arrived this was also a wonderful sight, the men so handsome in their uniforms and the women so glamorous in the 40s dresses, make up, hats, shoes, stockings and fur stoles. They didn't half all scrub up well. Not a cap with a peak the wrong way round, or a pair of thongs, or trainers in sight!

Wayne, one of my panto stalwarts and brother of one of the dancers, arrived late. He was driving and they had got lost. His sister couldn't believe that he stopped the car in the village, wound down the window and said to a man walking down the road dressed in a Nazi uniform: "Are you going to a 40s night?"

The woman, whose birthday it was, was completely overwhelmed and it was one of those magic nights that you never ever forget.

## AUDIENCES

You can never prejudge an audience. I hate it when someone says to me: "These look like a good audience" or: "You'll go down a bomb with these." Those happy friendly people can become the audience from hell and the rough and ready noisy lot can be the best you have ever played to. Comics 'test the water'. If a certain topic isn't going too well you switch to another to hopefully make them laugh. Laughter is a comic's applause!

However sometimes a singer can get it wrong. A female vocalist appearing at a Royal British Legion Club during the conflict in the Falklands wondered why she was met with stony silence after singing *Don't Cry For Me Argentina* in a big white frock! I'll always remember a magician being totally floored, and lost for words, when asking a woman in the audience to pick a card and she shouted back: "Christmas!"

Jimmy Tarbuck many years ago was appearing at the Talk of the Town, a famous nightspot in London. He was at that time Britain's number one comic. On doing his spot, he appeared in front of an almost silent audience. Later on backstage someone told him that the audience was full of Portuguese businessmen who couldn't speak English!

I should point out that showbiz terms do not always cross the 'pond. If someone says to you in America you went like a bomb it means you were a flop!

## LEICESTER (pronounced 'Lesta' see Addendum!)

It was said during the hey-days of variety that for an entertainer the worst three-weeks in show business were Holy week (Easter), Christmas week and a week in Leicester! I'm saying nothing!

We did a few years back have a film première in Leicester; which if memory serves me correctly was *Batman Forever* in 1995 starring Val Kilmer as the caped crusader. We were all amazed a film would première in Leicester. However someone did say to me that rumour had it that this was due to a typing error, Square had been missed off after Leicester! By the time all the invitations and press releases had been sent out it was too late to change it.

Did you know film director Stephen Frears was born in Leicester? (Thought I'd just throw that in!) Everybody thinks the Attenboroughs (Lord Richard ('Dickie') and David) were born in Leicester but actually it was Cambridge, they moved here as children.

On a recent short visit to Leicester, one member of the *G4* group (they came second on the *X Factor* 2005) said to a local newspaper reporter: "It's a place you usually drive past, Leicester, isn't it!"

As an entertainer who has worked in a lot of places all over the country, I can honestly put my hand on my heart and say Leicester is one of the cleanest brightest friendliest cities going. Though not many people seem to know much about Leicester. On being asked where I have come from and answering the Midlands, they always presume I mean Birmingham!

## Dee Quemby

Leicester has been responsible for two very important and major effects worldwide. The first ever package holiday tour started here with Thomas Cook and Leicester is where DNA testing was developed. Where would we be without either of these two?

Leicester town centre has many really nice shops and stores all very central and a variety of top-notch restaurants and cafés. There is also a central very large undercover market all week long. The nightlife is good too. As well as the many bars and clubs, there are many professional and amateur shows being performed all over the city. We also have a wonderful space centre. The only other one I have ever seen is the Griffiths Observatory in California! If you smile at anyone in Leicester they'll immediately start up a conversation with you as though they've known you for years. They'll even affectionately call you 'me duck'. Though how long will it be before we're not allowed to say that anymore is anyone's guess these PC days? If you go in a shop more than once they always remember you and greet you with a smile.

Leicester is also a very multicultural city. We have some wonderful Asian run shops in the centre. At Christmas they are stocked with all sorts of Christmas novelties, cards and gifts that they sell to people of all nationalities and religions. These shops are all trimmed up and play Christmas music and all the staff say ' Merry Christmas' to everyone. What is this Winter Festival some places are forcing on the public instead of Christmas? In Leicester we have Diwali, Eid and Christmas lights all together. Why can't these PC 'bullies' just let ordinary people get on with their lives alongside one another? They do in Leicester. Haven't we got anyone left in this country with any common sense?

Independence for Leicester I say with Paul O'Grady as President, Elton John as First Lady, Ricky Gervais as Deputy President, Johnny Depp (foreign affairs!) and Peter Kay as whatever he wants to be because he'd be a right laugh!

AND next time instead of driving past, give Leicester a go!

## THE ROYAL OAK AND THE BOWLTURNERS IN LEICESTER AND QUORN CONS CLUB

When not working as 'a turn' on a Saturday night I go with John and friends to these three places and have had some of the best nights and biggest laughs ever. The Quorn Cons Club bingo session 'bingo calls' are so witty and funny that first timers have tears running down their faces, political correctness goes out of the window, which is probably why! When number 89 comes up, we all have to sing a full rousing chorus of *We're Almost There*.

## EMPTY THEATRES

When working in a theatre I love to get there early before everybody else and walk out on to the stage in the semi dark and look at the rows of empty seats and just take it all in. It is a wonderful feeling, almost spiritual, and nothing else comes anywhere near it.

## FLOORS

I love floors. If I walk into a building where they have a nice shiny wooden floor I immediately want to start tap dancing, and often do!

## UNFULFILLED AMBITION

To be asked to play the 'mother' of Catherine Zeta-Jones and Johnny Depp. I'll work cheap and I'll even provide my own clothes!

## AUNTY ETHEL

Aunty Ethel was actually my Great Aunt. She was Gramp's sister and, as he was the youngest of a large family, she more or less brought him up. She married Fred Simms and their fabulous wedding photo is one of my all time favourites, and that is why I have included it in this book. It is so perfect that they look like actors on a film set. She lived in Aylesbury in Buckinghamshire and as a child I often stayed with her.

Aunty Ethel lived to a week off 102. She would never reveal her age to anyone. When the local press came to take a picture of her on her 100th birthday she put her hanky over her face and refused to remove it. She told my Mum, that when she died that she didn't want anyone putting her age on her gravestone. She didn't want anyone to know how old she was!

## CHRISTINE, JACKIE, CLIVE, 'THE RIDDLES' AND GILL 'OVER THE ROAD'

Friends we have known for years who were there day and night for my Mum.

## MY HUSBAND, JOHN

Yes, he can be a moaning old bugger and he's always right but his heart is in the right place. He was wonderful to my Mum and there was nothing he wouldn't do for her. He is as soft as grease with the cats and helped me for the many years I had severe food allergies which was very upsetting for me and he had to miss 15 years of holidays as I couldn't go anywhere because of them.

Many years ago there was a wonderful comic/raconteur, Mike Harding, on British TV and John looked like his twin brother and they both wore red plastic framed glasses. We would always be asked if John was Mike Harding wherever we went. We went to Morocco for a holiday and the hotel we were staying at held on the first night a get together for the newly arrived holiday makers from all the other hotels. So many people came up to me to ask if John was Mike Harding and no one would believe me when I said he wasn't. As the night progressed, John got slightly 'merry' and ended up in his underpants perched on several Moroccan stools on top of each other. He wouldn't believe me in the morning until he saw a photo someone had taken pinned on the visitor's board of which the hotel sold a record number of copies!. John got asked for his autograph so many times it became embarrassing. In the end we had to say he was Mike Harding incognito as he needed a rest and could they please keep it to themselves so we could get on with our holiday!

Many years back I was told by a friend, about a taxi driver in Loughborough who had seen John in Mountsorrel and was convinced that he was 'Mike Harding'. This taxi driver used to drive round the village in his spare time with Mike Harding LPs in his car boot hoping to get them autographed!

*Dee Quemby*

A thought has just occurred to me concerning holidays and a friend, who shall remain nameless! She had booked a holiday in Spain and kept asking everyone where a place called Aoa was? She had looked at maps and asked countless people and nobody had ever heard of it. It suddenly dawned on me when she said she was lucky to get a last minute bargain holiday that it wasn't a place at all, AOA was the abbreviation for 'allocated on arrival'!

## JOYCE HARRIS

I had just got two poor little abandoned kittens, Sheba and Indy, from a rescue centre and we were touring with our panto *Puss In Boots* and we had raised some money from putting on the panto in a night club for the Kegworth Air disaster. I also wanted to give a little of the money to an animal charity. Pat Ward told me of a wonderful couple who took in cats and kittens and I went to see them. This resulted in me nipping up every Friday lunchtime from work and taking endless poor cats home that gave me that look that says 'please look after me and love me' much to my husband's growing concern when we had ten cats in the house. He did say once after a particular argument: "If you bring any more cats home I'm leaving!" I resisted the temptation all week to go and fetch another one! I often did my Punch and Judy show for Joyce on some of her open days to raise money to help keep the cat sanctuary going.

Joyce is that dedicated to helping these poor creatures that she does not have central heating in her house, but the cats' pens in the garden do!

## GREEN SHIELD STAMPS

We all collect points at various shops and supermarkets these days. But this has all been done before. When I was a teenager, Green Shield stamps would be given to you in different shops when buying anything. You would go in people's houses and they all would have lots of sheets of these stamps inside vases and jugs on the sideboard and we did too. The whole house seemed full of them. You had to paste them in little books and all the family would sit down at the dining table one night and do just that in one go. You would then take the full books to the Green Shield Shop and come back home with various items such as electric kettles and hairdryers. I believe you could even exchange them for money? We seemed to have a house full of them though my mother probably collected them just because they were green!

## THE EMRICKS

When Mum, Dad and I, at 11 years of age, left to live in Mountsorrel my grandparents stayed in the pub for a couple more years before coming to live near us. Every day during the school summer holidays I would go on two buses to the pub to see my grandparents and then travel back to Mountsorrel. A teacher lived in the house opposite the pub and he had exchanged his job with an American teacher who lived in Ventura, near Los Angeles, California in the USA for one year.

One day I was on the pub car park and got talking to the two young American children, Pearl and Steve. Their parents John and Cora came into the pub for drinks and we all became friends. I used to go across to the house and watch Cora struggling with the washer and ringer and she would tell me about the fabulous equipment they had in the States that did a lot of these jobs for you and she couldn't believe how hard British housewives had to work. She couldn't believe women here would spend time making cakes from individual ingredients hadn't we heard of cake mixes? She and her husband John told me about something called a microwave that they had used on one of their trips to a National Park in the States that cooked meat in minutes but a lot of people in the States were not happy with these new machines as they thought they gave off radar waves and they weren't proving very popular.

John recently recalled how, on their first visit to Shepshed in 1957, they were amazed that we didn't have coffee makers, toasters, washing machines, clothes dryers and central heating. However, they thought it was an excellent idea that shops were not open on Sundays and wished it were the same in California! Cora wore trousers and British women didn't. To Cora as an American, trousers were 'pants'. She was so embarrassed to find out that in England 'pants' meant knickers, especially after saying: "I'm wearing my new pants today" and receiving very odd looks! Both John and Cora loved the fact that British women at meetings in the afternoon or for tea in someone's house would wear a hat.

They wanted to know why all our electrical equipment came without a plug already attached? How many times in those days did British children lucky enough to get an electrical present from 'Santa' have to wait for the shops to open days later so their dad could buy a plug for them to be able to play with it! It was also the same with toys that needed batteries. The Emricks also couldn't understand why we had to buy boxes of matches in England. In America, shops and supermarkets would give customers books of matches at their checkouts for free.

But the most amazing thing to them about life here in the 1950s was that nearly everybody used a bicycle for transport. Very few had cars and those lucky ones with the luxury of this modern form of transport would not tax their cars during the winter, as they wouldn't drive them then!

Life after the war was very basic here then, especially in a village - not at all like living in California in the 1950s. John particularly recalls Cora taking a young Stevie to the butchers in Shepshed. While Cora was looking at the meat, Stevie wandered into a room at the back and saw a lamb's head and asked if he could have it to take home. The butcher put it in a brown paper bag and gave it to him. John and Cora were horrified when Stevie pulled it out of the bag at home! Incidentally, the name Shepshed is supposed to be derived from 'sheep's head'.

There were however other benefits. They were amazed that a doctor would visit you in your own house if you were ill; this was unheard of in America! They were startled to find a pint of milk on their doorstep in the morning. In America you would have to drive to a store to buy milk. They wanted to know what a 'milkman' and a 'milkfloat' were.

We British are not at all embarrassed to say that we are going to the toilet and why. In fact a lot of people will even loudly announce it! The Emricks, like most Americans, however couldn't bring themselves to do this. They always asked if they could go the 'bathroom' or 'powder-room'; and it was always to 'wash their hands'. But we all knew why they were really going!

When eating a meal with the Emricks, we became very aware that our every move was being watched. They were fascinated by our use of a knife and fork. Americans stab food with a fork and then proceed to saw a piece a food off with the knife, then they put the knife down and eat with just the fork. The Emricks tried to use a knife and fork the British way but after a year of living in Shepshed and being unable to do so, gave up. I had the same problem with chopsticks in Hong Kong! Even now if on a visit or holiday to America, using a knife and fork as we British do is always of great intrigue to Americans and always guarantees an audience.

The one thing Stevie and Pearl really missed here was something called 'peanut butter' – how did they make butter from those little peanuts we all wondered! However there were great British treats for the whole Emrick family. They couldn't believe how good our chocolate was and John loved Birds custard for which they have no equivalent in the States. He used to wait until all the children had finished their pudding and left the school dining room. He would then scrape all the left over custard on to his plate! Needless to say on our visits to the Emricks in California, we had to take chocolate and packets of Birds custard powder.

Whilst staying with John and Cora, I asked if I could have some vinegar to put on my salad and they had to search for it in their cleaning cupboard! And I will never forget sitting in a diner with them for breakfast and feeling violently sick as I watched other diners pouring syrup over their ham and eggs (bacon and eggs) first thing in the morning. But I did love how you paid for a cup of coffee and the waitress kept coming over and filling the cup up at no extra cost.

John and Cora used to take me for days out in their car with Pearl and Steve. I was introduced to root bear, potato salad and watched in horror as Pearl put cottage cheese in her bowl of fresh fruit. We found it very strange that Pearl and Stevie were sent to bed every afternoon for a 'nap' even if they weren't at all tired. Apparently in 1950s America all young children would have an afternoon nap every day.

John Emrick taught 'English'. He was fortunate enough to receive his American wage while he lived here. The poor British teacher however had to struggle on his British wages in California and almost lived in poverty for a year!

The Emricks often came to our house in Mountsorrel and we all had lovely trips together. When they returned to the States they often came back to England to see us. In 1978 John and I went to stay with the Emricks in Ventura. Well yes it is the same language but oh so many different meanings! I said we were on our holiday fortnight and they had no idea that a fortnight meant two weeks and of course they don't have holidays they have vacations. I asked for a 'beaker' to put a drink in and was met by blank faces. When I said we had a new shopping precinct back home they all laughed as a precinct in America is a police station, and on seeing a strapless top in a shop and saying: "I like that boob tube, I think it would fit me" they thought I was talking about a television set! Did you know in America a bum bag is a 'fanny pack'? I hope they don't ask for one here!

I recently came across this language 'difference' on my trip to Las Vegas in 2004. BBC Radio Leicester wanted to interview me live from Las Vegas after doing a comedy try-out. I worked to a few Americans and had to explain that an attic was a 'loft', and of course they had never heard of a milkman! It's the same language, or is it? My Mum used to tell me about a Leicestershire vicar and his wife staying in a hotel in America. Mrs 'vicar' had asked at the reception if she could be 'knocked up in the morning'. Here we all know this can also mean 'an early morning call', but in America it only means to be pregnant! Whoops! There was probably a long queue outside their hotel door that next morning!

Whilst on holiday, we met the wonderful 1940/50s husky voiced movie star, June Allyson. Her husband was a prominent dentist to the stars in Ventura and she did an autograph signing in his very large office building. She was busy writing autographs one after another. When she heard my accent she got up and put her arms around me and said: I've just come back from London, I love England". We spent a long while talking to her about her movies, especially the wonderful 1953 film *The Glenn Miller Story* with James Stewart.

We were taken to a cinema to see a new movie called *Grease* that we loved and thought might become quite a big hit! No one went out at night and everywhere was locked and bolted at 9pm and security patrols drove around the housing area. John went down to the ballpark which closed really early every night and got talking to some of the teenagers. They said they all wanted to come and live in England as they had heard you could walk about at night, places were open until late, go to a dance, even a pub and didn't have to wait to be 21 to drink alcohol, none of which they could do in the States. I couldn't help thinking how we as teenagers had thought life in the States would be fantastic!

John Emrick and John used to go jogging on the many school's various sports tracks early in the mornings. John told me in amazement how every school had an Olympic size swimming pool.

We couldn't get used to how many TV channels there were. We were told don't worry if you miss the end of a movie it would be bound to be repeated on another channel the next day. They had an Education Channel and a lot of British programmes would be shown but not the whole series. They had had one episode of *Poldark* and one episode of *Fawlty Towers* that they thought was hysterical and wanted to know all about John Cleese.

As a child I used to get some fabulous presents from them, they often sent me the latest Elvis 45 rpm disc before it was released here and then I would have to go to Eugene Cooper's to buy the plastic inserts so it would play on my turn table. One Christmas I had a pretty powder bowl with jewels on the top containing dusting powder by a certain cosmetics company called Avon that we had never heard of but was apparently very big in the States. Cora and Pearl sadly died some years ago, but we are still in touch with John and his second wife Gerry to this day.

## BARNARDOS

I have had a long association with Barnardos. Out of desperation for panto garments I started looking in charity shops. Where else could you buy a pair of corsets, shawls, a cross over pinny, and flowery hats? Though in the early days of the charity shops the elderly lady assistants would all be wearing flowery hats and cross over pinnies! All the film, TV and stage costume people search these shops for clothing for actors and sometimes outfits you are given to wear in filming can be very old and very smelly, but what the heck you're in show business!

In Barnardos and other charity shops they always seem to have a lot of curtains for sale, usually new, and these make wonderful costumes for panto, especially the heavy brocade ones. Many of my panto Kings, baddies and captains have had wonderful frock coats made from these. I bought some brand new thick cotton curtains with fruit all over them. They made a great, though very heavy, outfit for Sarah the Cook in *Dick Whittington.* One year I bought another pair

285

of curtains decorated with the Leicester City Football Club logo. What a cheer I got coming out on stage in this outfit from the kids and adults in the Leicester audiences!

I found on looking through the clothing that a lot of it was very good and unusual. This set off a passion for these shops that I still have. Karen West, my friend in Birstall, the very well known local professional singer, and I often go for a day out to a different town to see what their charity shops hold.

I got to know Liz, the manageress at the first Barnardos' shop in Market Street, very well and on certain promotions provided her with children from the dancing school. Many times we had 'fairies' and 'bunnies' sat in the window. This probably wouldn't be allowed today as a Health and Safety issue! The children loved being in the windows and watching startled passers-by shriek when they realised they were actually live children! We also had children dressed as 'vegetables' and soldiers out and about with collecting tins, accompanied by an adult of course. One year I asked all the children to donate toys they didn't want which we put in bin liners. At the finale of the panto we invited Liz on stage and gave her all these many full to capacity bags. I was invited to open the newly furbished shop, which I did with great pride wearing a donated leopard-skin coat I had bought in the shop of course!

The shop moved to bigger premises in High Street and now had a new manageress, Linda, and an assistant manageress Angie. Once again I was very honoured to be asked to open this new shop. Linda organised many charity fashion shows in the shop and I was asked to compere and provide the models from the dancing school. We had children, girls, women and men from the dancing school on the catwalk. At the end of the fashion show the men, including my husband, dressed as 'ladies' and strutted their stuff down the catwalk to hysterical laughter.

We did a really good fashion show one year in the Victoria Room at the Town Hall. The theme was Cinderella going to the ball. I wrote a script and stood at a lectern as the narrator. We had dancers as maids and soldiers, the juveniles were fairies, a girl Louise, whom I worked with, was Cinderella and my friend Janet Holmes was the fairy godmother. Another friend Monty Katchick, Mountsorrel's 'fishman' and ex-club singer Monty Martell, was Prince Charming and sang a song he had written himself. A lot of friends from work were also catwalk models. Somebody said: "It's dangerous knowing you, you never know what we might be asked to do!" When Cinderella said: "I have nothing to wear to go to the ball", the fairy godmother produced two tickets and told her she was taking her to Barnardo's fashion show. They left the stage and re-entered the hall at the back of the audience and had two seats reserved at the front for the fashion show. Of course the finale was Cinderella's wedding with lots of bridesmaids!

Princess Diana was Barnardo's patron and in 1990 Linda excitedly let me know that the Loughborough shop would be having a royal visit. I was asked if I could act as a customer in a short sketch showing the life of a bag of items donated to Barnardos in front of the Princess (my first royal command show and probably the last)! I was asked to select children and adults from the fashion show to meet the Princess. The security was unbelievable and we had a visit from a Lady in Waiting to Princess Diana to look over the shop and us beforehand. When the day came Princess Diana just seemed so normal and it was so easy to talk to her. On looking at the photos of the fashion show she spotted a photo of the 'ladies' doing their bit at the end of one of the previous fashion shows. Princess Diana laughed and said: "I like the men."

Barnardos kindly allows photo displays for the dancing shows to be put in their windows and also allows the dancing school to use the shop as a booking office twice a year and the dancing school makes many donations to Barnardos from these shows.

## DEM BONES, DEM BONES, DEM DRY BONES!

My Nan had to take Mum when she was three years old in the 1920s to Leicester Hospital. There was an unusual case of a young boy who was losing the use of his arm through having too many bones. The doctors had asked his mother if she had a relation with a young girl they could examine and take X-rays of. My Nan was contacted and off they went. My Mum remembers at this age refusing to take her vest off, always the lady! Apparently they found many of these tiny bones in my Mum as well. These bones would float round and get stuck and before she got rheumatoid arthritis she would often have to massage her hands when they arrived there. I used to wake up with pains in my feet when this happened to me. Fortunately those little bones seem to have moved on.

My little fingers are very crooked but they do match and when going for an audition for commercials you have to hold up your hands for this very reason. If you have any problem with your hands they will make sure they are out of shot when filming or use a hand model.

My Nan was told that anybody else with these extra bones would be related in some way. My Mum's cousin, Nora, the GI bride, living in New Orleans, wrote to say how her daughter had the same problem.

Years later I went to the hospital and the doctor lifted my leg up and dropped it quickly. He asked me if I knew I had a large bone in the thigh that shouldn't be there. I told him not only did I know but I had a matching one in the other leg too and many more in other places!

Now I realise this may not be of interest to most people reading this book but I have included it as I am now an orphan and running out of relatives fast. So if you have extra bones like mine, please get in touch, as we must be related!

## TECHNOLOGY

How did we live without all of today's technology? Much more happily actually! I worked with a man in his 50s who had never fathomed out how to work his video timer. He lived not far from the council offices and would look through his newspaper to see if there was anything on the television in the day that he wanted to tape. If there was, he would nip out 10 minutes before the programme started, go home, press the record button and come straight back to work! There's always a way!

## ESCALATORS

I was terrified of escalators as a child and my Mum would always take me up the stairs in shops instead. In 1952 Princess Elizabeth became Queen and my Mum had read in a magazine of a woman in the East End making statuettes of the Queen on horseback in her home and they had to be fetched, I would have been six years old at the time.  Off we went to London with Nan and we all went to this lady's home in the East End and picked up the statuette.  We had to use the tube to get back to the train station and of course when I saw the escalator I just froze with terror.  A very kindly man with a very strong Cockney accent picked me up, put me on his shoulders and comforted me all the way up.  I think this is where my love of London and the Cockneys really began.

I did a cabaret spot at a Cockney wedding some years back and they really are fabulous people and know how to enjoy themselves and are not at all as miserable as they come across in *EastEnders*!  The buffet was in the ballroom and in the hall there was a trestle table piled high with whelks, eels and other things I couldn't bear to look at and they didn't half give it some welly!

I have always enjoyed playing to audiences in the south, the first time I appeared at Caesar's Palace, Luton (sadly now gone) there were bus loads of Cockneys shipped in and although I didn't go on until nearly midnight they were a great crowd.

To us in the Midlands, Oxford is the south and I really have to mention Rosehill Community Centre.  I was booked to do a cabaret on a Bank Holiday Saturday night and wasn't expecting many people in. Well it was a sell out and there was a great singer, Jimmy Love, from Blackpool, who appeared with two tremendous girl dancers.  Not only were they a great audience for me, they also listened to Jimmy and clapped every number.   There were quite a few young people in and amazingly we didn't see or hear a mobile phone all night!

I often go to see vocalist friends working and can't believe how noisy people are and then at the end of the night, not having listened to one song, they all shout for more when the poor singer has had enough, done the spots he has been paid to do and just wants to pack up his PA and drive home!  But these people at Rosehill were great, just how club audiences used to be.

## EARLY DAYS AT THE COUNCIL

When I first started working at Charnwood Borough Council it was in the general office as an audio typist.  We had all the letters of complaints to answer and we also had to do legal typing.  I loved typing the conveyances on the thick parchment paper (no computers or electric typewriters then) and sewing them up with green tape and using the sealing wax.

People, especially older folk, are so funny without even realising it and that's why I love to listen to conversations in the doctors, on buses and in the supermarkets.  I have created many a comedy sketch from doing just that.  In the general office we had many letters to reply to that made us laugh so much the tears would be running down our faces.  One woman wrote that she was having trouble with her back passage and it was making it very difficult for the milkman!  Then there was the elderly man who demanded that the Council come round immediately and remove his bollards!

When I went to work in the Improvement Grants Section of the Council a woman wrote to ask if the Improvement Grants Officer could go round and look at her damp patch and we had a letter from another woman to say that she had a large bush around her opening and was it something the Council could deal with!

Bless them all for making us laugh and for providing me with more comedy material.

I loved working with the public and was very sad when this contact was taken away from me but it's how everything is going these days as we are all going to be electronic apparently and soon there will be no need at all for human contact. We worked in a small office and our boss would even e-mail us rather than talk to us a few feet away!

Everything is so impersonal now and I hate the term 'service user' and 'client'. If I asked what the service user's name was there would be a lot of rustling of paper as they tried to find out. What's wrong with using someone's name in the first place? There won't be any point soon in having one. We'll all be given a number! I still can't believe that when I was working at the Council I was actually snapped at for being 'far too helpful with the public'.

## HALLOWEEN

My Mum, being very religious didn't hold at all with Halloween and thought it should be banned. I have no feelings either way about it and through teaching dancing for so many years, countless children, accompanied by a parent in the background, seem to find their way to my door on this night.

On All Hallows Eve, I decorate my window with a witch on a broomstick, cobwebs, spiders, old candelabras, parchments, goblets and hang a notice on the front door saying 'Only knock if you have your death certificate with you'!

I put a long black dress and wig on, my large spider diamanté brooch, blood red lipstick and nail varnish looking just like Lily Munster. I also play a horror effects CD and dim the lights and sit and wait with my cats. It's great fun and we take a lot of photos of the children, some in fantastic outfits, with me.

One Halloween a couple of years back, two older girls knocked the door and came into the kitchen followed by a young boy about eight years old. He was dressed in an immaculate tail suit, high white collar shirt, diamond stud pin and cape lined in red satin with his hair parted in the middle and plastered flat to his head, his fangs looking more than realistic! I gave the boy some sweets and then the girls. I said to the girls: "Who's the little boy with you, he looks fantastic?" The girls said they didn't know, he had just followed them in. We all turned round and he had vanished and I couldn't see him anywhere in the street. Creepy or what?

John Brindley first came to see me to discuss the idea of me doing a book (yes its his fault!) on All Hallows Eve. I really should have told him beforehand that I dress up. The look on his face when I opened the door!

## IF ONLY!

It's amazing whom the big film moguls originally wanted to star in many of their films. We all identify Harrison Ford as Indiana Jones and really couldn't imagine anyone else in the part. Tom Selleck of *Magnum* TV fame was first choice for this whip cracking all action hero but he couldn't get out of his TV contract and had to turn 'Indy' down.

# Dee Quemby

Deanna Durbin had the most amazing singing voice and was very pretty. Turned down by Disney at an audition to be the voice of *Snow White*, she was told that she didn't sound like a child. She was recommended to MGM and appeared in a 'short' with another young girl by the name of Frances Gumm. Louis B Mayer watched the screening. He phoned a studio executive and said: "Sign the flat one." (Apparently, on odd occasions, Deanna Durbin could sound a bit flat). The studio executive misheard and thought that he had said: "Sign the fat one!" Deanna Durbin was sent home and Frances Gumm signed up. Frances Gumm's name was changed to Judy Garland. Over the years Judy's amazing talent made millions for MGM. Louis B Mayer affectionately called Judy 'my little hunchback'. Deanna Durbin, one of my Mum's favourites, was eventually signed by Universal and made many films that showcased her fabulous voice and her sparkling personality and also made millions of dollars for Universal.

Shirley Temple was to be Dorothy in *The Wizard of Oz* but the Fox studio would not loan her out to MGM. A 17-year-old Judy Garland, with her boobs strapped down, stepped into the 'red slippers' and won everyone's hearts in a part she would forever be associated with. For her roles in *The Wizard of Oz* and *Babes In Arms* both made in 1939, she was awarded a special Oscar for 'her outstanding performance as a screen juvenile'.

Humphrey Bogart was second best to George Raft in film classics *High Sierra, The Maltese Falcon* and *Casablanca.* Bad judgement, George! Everybody remembers 'Bogie'! Though I'll never forget George Raft as the ex tea salon gigolo performing the bolero with Carole Lombard in the 1934 film *Bolero.* In a 1970s documentary *That's Hollywood*, it was revealed that the more difficult movements in the long shots during this dance sequence were actually performed by professional dancers. Talking of luck, 12-year-old Carole Lombard was spotted playing baseball in the street and was immediately offered a film contract! Tragically, later on, when married to Clark Gable, she died in a plane crash. Incredibly, Bette Davis failed a Goldwyn screen test, though Universal had the good judgement to sign her up!

Can you imagine anyone else other than handsome swashbuckling Errol Flynn as Robin Hood in the 1938 top box office film *The Adventures of Robin Hood*? Well Warner Bros could, as their first choice for the title role was James Cagney. But, due to his contractual dispute with the studio, Cagney walked out of Warner Bros leaving them high and dry.

Following Errol Flynn's worldwide success in the all action film *Captain Blood* he was then offered the role of Robin Hood. Errol Flynn however was not the first choice for *Captain Blood.* Robert Donat had to drop out from playing the heroic English sea Captain due to ill health and this gave, the then bit player, Errol Flynn his chance of movie stardom.

Nan and Gramp gave me the book of *The Adventures of Robin Hood* film when I was 6, as a present for dancing in the Poole Academy's 1952 Christmas panto *The Pied Piper*. This book is still intact to this day and as well as containing dialogue it also has 16 fabulous full-page colour plates from the film and many black and white stills. As hard as I try, I just cannot see James Cagney, my all time favourite movie star, in this role though no doubt if he had played Robin Hood we wouldn't have been able to imagine anyone else in the role!

James Cagney was a brilliant natural actor as shown in the 1935 Warner Bros beautifully filmed version of *A Midsummer Night's Dream* in which he played Nick Bottom the weaver, to great acclaim. He also proved this over and over again in the many 'gangster' movies especially as the psycho Cody Jarrett in the 1949 Warner Bros film noir classic *White Heat* ("Made it ma, top of the world!"), *Angels with Dirty Faces, The Roaring Twenties* and *The Public Enemy.* In the 1931 film *The Public Enemy* he made screen history by pushing half a grapefruit in Mae Clarke's face and then going out and picking up the blonde bombshell herself, Jean Harlow! This sort of behaviour had never been seen towards a woman on screen before. This film was so popular on release that it ran for 24 hours in Times Square. Mae Clarke's real life ex-husband had the scene timed to perfection. He would often buy a cinema ticket just a few minutes before so he could go in and watch his ex-wife get smacked in the face with the grapefruit and then promptly leave. It must have been a bitter divorce!

James Cagney was swept to international stardom and put on the Hollywood 'A' list for his performance as 'gangster' Tom Powers in the Warner Bros 1931 film *The Public Enemy* based on the novel *Beer and Blood.* This came about because of a last minute casting change! Up to that time all leading men in film, even 'gangsters', were expected to be tall, dark and handsome (threes again!) and to have a good clear speaking voice due to the early days of film sound equipment. Debonair actor Edward Woods had been signed to play Tom Powers. The film was in its third day of shooting (more threes!) when Darryl F Zanuck 'spotted' James Cagney in a supporting role. He liked the young short and stocky, brash and cocky, fast-talking unknown actor and, taking a big risk, changed him to the star role. And so a screen legend was born! Edward Woods however was not so lucky. The studio did not renew his contract when it expired and he retired from acting. I'm with Darryl here, I just can't see Edward Woods staggering about riddled with bullets, hitching his trousers and saying "I aint so tough" and then being delivered home looking like an Egyptian mummy to fall flat on his face! However the two young actors playing the gangsters as children had already filmed their scenes. Even though they looked very much like the older actors, their roles were not reversed and these scenes were left in the film.

James Cagney's performance in the 1938 film *Angels with Dirty Faces* earned him an Oscar nomination and also won him the New York Film Critics' Best Actor Award. After the 1939 film *The Roaring Twenties*, as bootlegger Eddie Bartlett, alongside Humphrey Bogart (I can see Gladys George now as 'Panama Smith' at the end of the film kneeling at the side of his body saying "He used to be a big shot!" after a very stylised and probably the longest lasting Cagney 'gangster' death!), James Cagney did not play another gangster role until Cody Jarrett in the 1949 cult film *White Heat.*

James Cagney's individual (and often lengthy) style of 'dying' in his gangster movies (he didn't survive in most of them!) would be copied by variety acts and impressionists for years to come, as would the line: "You dirty rat." However he never said this. His line from the 1932 film *Taxi* was actually: "Come out and take it, you dirty, yellow-bellied rat, or I'll give it to you through the door!" In the 1930s gangster movies, expert marksmen would be hired to fire real bullets around the actors as they filmed. No wonder he was quick on his feet!

Allegedly, for some unknown reason, the Mafia had a 'contract' out on James Cagney. A studio light was to be dropped on him whilst filming! His friend the actor, George Raft, another great dancer, with mob connections and friend of Bugsy Siegel, used his influence and got the 'hit' stopped. George Raft's New York gangster past is shown in the 1961 film *The Spin of a Coin* with Ray Danton playing George Raft. This film also starred Jayne Mansfield whose daughter Mariska Hargitay is one of the 'regulars' in the TV series *Law and Order: Special Victims Unit* created by Emmy award winning producer Dick Wolf.

As we know poor old George had the misfortune to turn down three roles that made Humphrey Bogart a mega movie star. He had turned down *High Sierra* as he didn't want to die at the end. As previously mentioned, he also turned down *The Maltese Falcon* as he didn't want to work with an inexperienced director, a certain John Huston. However these bad decisions may have also been due to the fact that he couldn't read and he just sent many scripts back that he didn't like the look of! How did he learn his lines?

James Cagney's wide range of acting parts is shown in such films as *Mister Roberts*, *13 Rue Madeleine* and as Lon Chaney in *Man of a Thousand Faces*. One of my favourite Cagney films is *Love Me or Leave Me,* the story of the life of singer Ruth Etting, with Doris Day.

*Angels with Dirty Faces* also had in the cast Humphrey Bogart and 'The Dead End Kids'. The Dead End Kids were a gang of fast talking teenage boys who had starred in a series of popular comedy films. However in this film they played juvenile delinquents who are whipped into shape by the gangster they hero worship, Rocky Sullivan, who of course is played by Cagney. The scene in the gym where he 'slaps' them about is the best 'choreographed' scene I have ever seen. Many of 'Jimmy' Cagney's gangster films had an Irish priest, always played by Pat O'Brien, an old friend from his early Broadway days. Long before Frank Sinatra's famous or infamous, depending on your point of view, 'Ratpack', Cagney was part of Hollywood's 'Irish Mafia' along with such stars as Pat O'Brien, Spencer Tracey and Ralph Bellamy. However they did nothing more sensational than meet up and go out to dinner together.

A great non-trained 'natural' dancer (you learnt your trade on your feet in those days) James Cagney was sensational tap dancing with Ruby Keeler in Warner Bros *Footlight Parade.* He also played the great patriotic American showman and composer George M Cohan in the 1942 film *Yankee Doodle Dandy* for which he won an 'Oscar' as best male actor. The Oscar was presented to James Cagney by American movie star Gary Cooper; in actual fact Gary Cooper's parents were British and he had spent his childhood in Dunstable, Bedfordshire. *Yankee Doodle Dandy* was James Cagney's all time favourite film in his long and brilliant career and he was the first actor in a song and dance role to win an Academy Award. His tap dancing routines in this film have never been bettered. I can see him now doing a buck and a wing as he comes down the stairs of the White House and can also hear those immortal words that went into screen legend "My mother thanks you, my father thanks you, my sister thanks you and I thank you!"

James Cagney played George M Cohan once more in the 1955 Paramount film *The Seven Little Foys.* This film was based on the life story of the great vaudeville star Eddie Foy, played in the film by Bob Hope. James Cagney took the part on condition he did not get paid. He played the role as a tribute to Eddie Foy. When James Cagney was a struggling actor on Broadway in the 1920s, Eddie Foy would provide meals to out of work actors, one of them being James Cagney. Eddie Foy's son, Eddie Foy Jnr, played his father in *Yankee Doodle Dandy* alongside James Cagney.

In *The Seven Little Foys,* James Cagney and Bob Hope tap dance on top of a long dining table. Both could tap dance but it is Cagney who has 'style' during this routine. Bob Hope is what we would call a 'hoofer' meaning he could 'do the steps' but not as well as a dancer could. This is what Gene Kelly affectionately called Judy Garland when working with her in the musical film *The Pirate.*

James Cagney's advice on how to become an actor was simply: "Learn the lines, plant your feet, look the other actor in the eye, say the words and *mean them!*" Well that'd save on Uni fees!

James Cagney was at one time the number one box office movie star and deservedly so. Not bad going for an ex-female impersonator as a teenager in vaudeville! He was also a fitness expert and martial arts fighter. As said before, you never know where a great actor started! If there were one person I could have chosen to meet in the whole world, it would have been James Cagney.

*West Side Story* star George Chakiris would not have been elevated to stardom if Elvis Presley had signed on the dotted line for the part of the leader of the 'Sharks' in 1961. George Chakiris, as 'Bernardo', also picked up an Oscar for best supporting actor! *West Side Story* had an incredible 11 Academy Award nominations, winning ten of them! John Travolta had the bad judgement to turn down two starring roles in *American Gigolo* and *An Officer And A Gentleman,* both films being box office hits; not that Richard Gere minded as he was propelled to international stardom in taking them on. John Travolta also turned down the role of Billy Flynn in *Chicago,* as he didn't think this stage musical would adapt to the big screen. Well he got it wrong again and Richard Gere was there once more to step into his shoes. He took on the role of the sleazy lawyer and amazed everyone with his dancing prowess. Richard Gere however, had been in a stage musical long before *Chicago.* He played the part of Danny Zuko in *Grease* at the New London Theatre near Covent Garden in the 1970s.

Kevin Spacey wouldn't have an Oscar on his mantelpiece for best actor in *American Beauty* if Tom Hanks had not turned the role down due to work commitments. Kathy Bates would not have picked up an Oscar for *Misery* if the original choice of actress, Bette Midler, had not rejected the part.

I bet they're kicking themselves now!     *IF ONLY!*

This brings to mind one of my favourite films *42nd Street,* where a demure young girl Peggy Sawyer, up from the country, arrives in New York, seeking her fame and fortune. She gets a job as a 'gypsy' (dancer) in the chorus of a stage musical. Her big break comes when the leading actress injures her foot on opening night and is unable dance. Out Peggy goes a 'nobody' and comes back a star! How could she fail with Busby Berkeley choreographed numbers!

This film was made in 1933 during the Great Depression. So successful was it, that it saved Warner Bros from bankruptcy. A certain young Ginger Rogers had a small part in the film as the worldy-wise chorus girl 'Anytime Annie'. The mind boggles! Ruby Keeler, the then wife of super-star Al Jolson, in her movie debut played Peggy Sawyer. As a nervous Peggy waits to make her first entrance, the producer 'Warner Baxter' takes her to one side and says: "You're going out a youngster; but you've got to come back a star!" And she does! Pure Hollywood!

Coincidentally in 1927, Al Jolson like his wife, Ruby Keeler, saved an almost bankrupt Warner Bros studio. The four Warner brothers, Sam, Harry, Albert and Jack took a big gamble with a new sound system 'Vitaphone' that many said wouldn't work as this was at the height of the silent movies. Well it did work and the public couldn't get enough of it.

Many popular silent movie stars lost out due to what they now sounded like when heard speaking on film. Actors and actresses in silent movies did not have to learn lines and just said whatever came to mind when filming. The words they were supposed to have said would then be shown on the screen for the audience to read. In romantic scenes silent movie heart throb John Gilbert would just say over and over "I love you" and did so in his first talkie. This had the audience in hysterics with tears running down their faces, as his voice was very high like a woman's and so his film career was over. Though it has been said that Louis B Mayer wanted a reason to sack him due to personal reasons and had the sound system tampered with!

The coming of sound and with it the ending of film careers is parodied in the wonderful Gene Kelly, Debbie Reynolds and Donald O'Connor 1952 film *Singin' In The Rain*. On a TV chat show Debbie Reynolds said that at the age of 19 she took the part of 'Kathy Selden' in this film not being able to tap dance and Gene Kelly was opposed to her getting the role. She was often in tears at the long gruelling rehearsals as Gene Kelly was a hard taskmaster and she often went home with bleeding feet. Well her dancing was just amazing in this film – some people are just born naturals!

Al Jolson was the first man to be heard speaking on film in *The Jazz Singer*, when he said: "Wait a minute, wait a minute, you aint heard nothin' yet!" However, *The Jazz Singer* was not really a 'talkie'. It was a silent movie with musical numbers added. Of course with the coming of sound, Warner Bros. made a packet only to lose it a few years later during The Great Depression! But then along came *42nd Street* and Mrs Jolson!

Al Jolson however was not the first choice for *The Jazz Singer*. George Jessel turned it down and lost the chance to go down in history as the first person to be heard speaking on screen!

So popular was Al Jolson that when he died the lights on Broadway were switched off, just as the lights in Las Vegas would be for Frank Sinatra when he died. Two of the greatest superstars ever!

## ST PATRICK'S, SOHO SQUARE

It never fails to amaze me how much we walk past in London and never notice. One dark wintry night, I was walking through Soho Square and a big wooden door was open, light was showering down on the pavement, so I peeped inside. It was a very old Roman Catholic Church, St Patrick's. I could just imagine Bing Crosby as the priest standing in front of the altar, as he appeared in that wonderful 1945 film *The Bells Of St Mary's*.

Me, and my Mum would go inside every time we went to London. We would light three candles for Nan, Gramp and my Dad. Sadly now I go in to light four. When my Mum was in hospital, prayers were said for her in this church. Opposite is a little park and on going by I always imagine Anthony Hopkins sat on a bench there in a scene from the 1987 film *84 Charing Cross Road* in which he starred with that wonderful actress Anne Bancroft. The film is based on a true story of two people with a love of books. One is an American woman, and the other a man who lives in London. They correspond through the war years but never meet.

## GREAT LADIES

Over the last 20 years I have appeared as some great 'ladies' in the touring pantos, 40s shows, music hall shows and TV. I hope I did, and will continue to do, them homage:

Tina Turner
Mae West
Margaret Thatcher
Lily Munster
Carmen Miranda
Marie Lloyd
Shirley Temple
Marlene Dietrich
Princess Diana
Joan Collins
Judy Garland
Kylie Minogue
Cruella de Ville
Barbara Woodhouse
Lady Penelope (*Thunderbirds*)
Purdy (*The Avengers*)
Mrs Mopp
Agnetha from Abba
Sheila Ferguson (Three Degrees)
Betty (as in Wilson, Kepple and Betty)

And a couple of men, Charlie Chaplin and Wilson, or was it Kepple, (as in Wilson, Kepple and Betty)?

## WHAT'S IN A NAME?

Someone in showbiz said a long time ago: "It doesn't matter what anybody writes about you so long as they spell your name right!"

When I was a child there were not the exotic names about that there are today. At school in the 1950s the popular girls' names were Margaret, Barbara, Jane, Susan, Christine, Kathleen, Jacqueline, Diana, Jane, Carol, Elizabeth, Wendy, though we did have a Pearl, Ruby and Beatrice. Boys' names were likely to be their grandfather's or father's first name like John, David, Eric, Robert, James, Charles, Peter, Leonard, Arthur, Michael and Trevor. All sound very plain today.

Today at dancing classes I have a wide range of names like Skye, Summer, Paris and Echo. You can always tell each generation of people by their names, when I was a young dancing teacher in the 60s we were inundated with Karens, Traceys and Sharons, followed a few years later with the Shelleys, Cheryls, Rachaels and Kellys and later on the Chloes, Emmas and Mollys, followed by the Courteneys and the Kylies! I am just waiting for a Chardonnay to start dancing!

I never thought of my name being unusual but as I got older people would ask me, on hearing my name for the first time: "Are you foreign?" When I was 11 and had moved to Mountsorrel, I went to a shop nearby to fetch something for my Mum. The girl in the shop asked me what my name was, I told her and she said: "If you ever become a film star you won't have to change your name." I didn't have the heart to tell her if that happened I would be Deirdre Grahame!

Quenby is a Leicestershire name and was a name of a hamlet near Hungarton, Leicestershire where there is a Quenby Hall. When I was a child in Shepshed there were two lots of families, the Quenbys and the Quembys who were adamant they were in no way related. My Father's parents were John Arthur Quemby and Mary Ann Hickling but I never knew them. When my paternal Grandmother died my Father was given her wedding certificate. The surname is spelt with the letter 'n' not 'm' as we use. This could have been a mistake by the verger of the church at the time or even my grandparents spelling it incorrectly as a lot of poor people, including vergers, could not read or write properly in those days.

The whole family went to Quenby Hall in Hungarton many years ago when it was bought by Squire de Lisle and renovated and opened to the public. I was in my early 20s and had driven my Grandad's turquoise Austin car there. The Squire was standing at the front door and said: "Who's coming in next?" My Grandmother pushed me in and he announced: "You're our 1,000 visitor and I personally am going to take you round." He nearly collapsed on the spot when my Grandmother told him my name was Quemby! Another one of life's little coincidences.

Another way of spelling Quemby is Quimby, as in Mayor Quimby in *The Simpsons*. My father loved his *Tom and Jerry* cartoons and would sit waiting for the end credits to roll looking out for his 'his mate' Fred Quimby. Fred C Quimby was ex-general manager and director of Pathé films. He moved to MGM and was in control of all their 'short' films including their cartoons that, from 1935 to 1945, incredibly won 15 Academy Awards. My father was convinced Fred was a relation.

My Mum as she got older said so many people referred to her as 'Deirdre's Mum' she was beginning to think it was her name!

Originally my Mum was going to name me Rosemary! Can you imagine that? A 'Rosemary' I am definitely not! Shortly before I was born, she went to a cinema in Loughborough. A very dramatic Irish film was playing. At the end of the film a dying man was praying to 'Our Lady Deirdre' and that was that! Apparently Deirdre means full of sorrow, very appropriate for a comic Mum! My Mum said she liked it because she didn't think it could be shortened or made into a nickname! Joan Neal always called me 'Dreary'!

Names are very important for club acts, I started off with my real name Deirdre Quemby but it was beyond the grasp of most ent secs. They would usually introduce me as: "Miss Deirdre, 'er what's your name?" A lot of people in the audience thought that was my stage name! An agent suggested I become Diane, but I said I would settle for Dee although I much prefer to be called Deirdre.

Equity is very strict on names and when you apply to join they search the registers here and abroad to check that an existing member of the union does not have the same name you are proposing to use even if it is your real name, if so you have to come up with another name for yourself. Stewart Granger, the very popular British film star of the 40s and 50s had this problem. His real name was James Stewart but because an American actor, James Stewart, was already a member, the real James Stewart became Stewart Granger.

One of the best 'stage' names I think is the name of a very old variety act, Nosmo King. Apparently this came about from 'NO SMOKING' being painted on fire doors in a theatre. On seeing the doors open with NO SMO on one door and KING on the other, he thought it made a novel name for a performer and it did!

During the 1920s in Hollywood there was an actress, who often appeared in silent movies with Douglas Fairbanks Snr. She had what I think is a wonderful name for an actress which was Jewel Carmen, I just think that is so exotic and star like! However her real name was the not so flamboyant Evelyn Quick. Her career was short lived with her association in the suicide or was it murder of another film star Thelma Todd?

'The Vamp', Theda Bara, America's first sex symbol of the silver screen in the 1920s was supposedly of an exotic Eastern background being born in the shadow of The Spinx, in fact she was plain old Theodosia Goodman from Cincinnati. Her name is an anagram of Arab death. It was devised by shortening her first name, then using part of her Swiss grandfather's middle name! The term 'vamp' comes from the word vampire as Theda Bara had very dark smouldering looks and heavy black eye make up very much like Dusty Springfield. Another one I think is wonderful is 'King Vidor', the name of a 1920s Hollywood director.

New names can be very useful. I was told of a very bad male vocalist who always got paid off. He was booked at one Leicester club three times with different names before they realised who he was!

## STAR NAME CHANGES

## REAL NAMES

| STAR NAME CHANGES | REAL NAMES |
|---|---|
| Michael Keaton (*Beetle Juice*) | Michael Douglas |
| Tom Cruise | T C Mapother IV |
| Hedy Lamarr | Hedwig Kiesler |
| Yvonne de Carlo (Mrs H Munster) | Peggy Yvonne Middleton |
| Roy 'Chubby' Brown (comedian) | Royston Vasey |
| Veronica Lake | Constance Ockelman |
| Alicia Markova (prima ballerina) | Alice Marks |
| Cliff Richard | Harry Webb |
| Judy Garland | Frances Ethel Gumm |
| Bruce Lee | Lee Jun Fan |
| Chuck Norris | Carlos Ray |
| David Bowie | David Jones |
| Rita Hayworth | Margarita Carmen Cansino |
| Gene Kelly | Eugene Curran Kelly |
| Roy Rogers (singing cowboy movie star) | Leonard Slye |
| Fred Astaire | Fred Austerlitz |
| Ginger Rogers | Virginia McMath |
| Cyd Charisse | Tula Ellice Finklea |
| Bruce Willis | Walter Willison |

| | |
|---|---|
| Cary Grant | Archibald Leach |
| Diana Dors | Mavis Fluck |
| Asta (dog 'film star' of 1930s) | Skippy |
| Benji (dog star) | Higgins |
| Eddie (dog star of *Frasier*) | Moose |
| Lauren Bacall | Betty Joan Perske |
| June Allyson | Ella Van Geisman |
| Mickey Rooney | Joe Yule Jnr |
| Woody Allen | Allen Stewart Konigsberg |
| Joan Crawford | Lucille Fay LeSueur (aka Billie Cassin) |
| Jean Arthur (film star of the 1940s) | Gladys Greene |
| Tony Curtis | Bernard Schwartz |
| Doris Day | Doris von Kappelhoff |
| *John Wayne | Marion Michael Morrison |
| Jean Harlow (film star of the 1920s/30s) | Harlean Carpenter |
| Amanda Barrie | Shirley Broadbent |
| Michael Caine | Maurice Micklewhite |
| Boris Karloff ('monster' star of the 1920s/1930s) | William Pratt |
| Elton John | Reginald Dwight |
| Audey Hepburn | Edda Hepburn van Heemstra |
| Rock Hudson | Roy Scherer |
| Dean Martin | Dino Paul Crocetti |
| David Jason | David White |
| Jayne Mansfield | Vera Jayne Palmer |
| Sean Connery | Thomas Connery |
| Brigette Bardot | Camille Javal |
| Whoopi Goldberg | Caryn Johnson |
| Cilla Black | Priscilla Marie Veronica White |
| Alice Cooper | Vincent Damon Furnier |
| Vic Reeves | Jim Moir |
| Helen Mirren | Ilyena Mironoff |
| Cher | Cherilyn LaPiere Sarkisan |
| Les Dennis | Leslie Hestletine |
| Tina Turner | Annie Mae Bullock |

And of course the one we all know thanks to Reginald Dwight, sorry Elton John!

Marilyn Monroe                                Norma Jean Baker

Norma Jean Baker was named Norma Jean Mortensen on her birth certificate but baptised as Norma Jean Baker. Her father Edward Mortensen deserted her mother, Gladys Baker (née Monroe) before she was born. Marilyn had a half-sister Bernice Miracle and a half-brother Robert Baker who died at the age of 14.

Marilyn Monroe was notorious for always being late especially when filming. When in 1956 in England to shoot *The Prince And The Showgirl* with Laurence Olivier, he at his wits end after endless days of her being late on set and sometimes not turning up at all said to her: "Why can't you get here on time for f\*\*k's sake?" She replied: "Oh do you have that word in England, too!"

Marilyn though, in all fairness, was once heard to say: "I've been on a calendar but never on time!"

Marilyn's famous wiggle, allegedly, was due to the fact that every pair of shoes she had she made sure one of the heels was one-inch shorter than the other!

Hugh Hefner head of the Playboy Empire bought the empty crypt next to Marilyn's at the Westwood Memorial Park, Los Angeles for his final resting place.

## AND ONE WHO WOULDN'T CHANGE HIS NAME!

In the early days of his career Frank Sinatra refused point blank to change his name to 'Frankie Satin'! Well that's a relief!

## OCCUPATION NAME CHANGES

Why oh why do we have to have these ridiculous occupation name changes these days. On a packed train last year an announcement was made: 'The revenue protection officer is on the train'. We all looked at each other as this sounded something really serious when this little middle-aged man came into the carriage saying:"Tickets please." We all burst out laughing, what the heck is wrong with ticket collector? I bet his wages didn't go up with his fancy job-title nobody understood. I remember a man I worked with, head buried in his hands, crying: "I don't know what my new job-title means, I don't know what I should be doing!" No, nor do we mate!

One of the men in my dance troupe was a dustbin man, and many years ago in the 70s, a reporter and photographer came from *The Echo* and asked for their names and occupations. I said; "Roy's a dustbin man." He grandly said: "No I'm not, I've been told I'm now a refuse engineer!" Well didn't he come in for some stick from the rest of the men. Even he thought it was ridiculous!

I'm just trying to imagine what fancy title they'd give 'panmen' these days! The mind boggles! I've even heard bouncers being called 'eviction technicians'………………oh pleazzzzzzzzzzzzzzzzz!

299

*Dee Quemby*

## INTERNATIONAL DRAG QUEENS' NAMES

| | | | |
|---|---|---|---|
| Annette Curtain | Rhea Listick | Della Cantessant | Dyna Might |
| Eva Destruction | Tess Tosterone | Dee Flaytable | Paige Turner |
| Tequila Markingbird | Ida Slapter | Penny Traition | Patty O'Doors |
| Micra Waive | Dyna Rod | Marcel Waive | Ella Faracket |

and the rather wonderful, and very imaginative, Lois Carmen Denominator!

## NAMES DRAG QUEENS CALL THEMSELVES

A bag in drag
A cock in a frock
Knackers in knickers
A pig in a wig
A mess in a dress

## FAMOUS FILM STAR DOG NAMES

Toto (*The Wizard of Oz*)
Asta, the dog formerly known as Skippy - star of the 1930s *Thin Man* films with William Powell and Myrna Loy as his human 'co-stars' Rin Tin Tin who was rescued from the trenches in Germany by an American pilot in World War I
Eddie in *Frasier*
Benji, who was actually female
and the many 'Lassies' all of which were male apart from the first one!

Animals in film have their own special 'Oscars' called 'Patsys' which stands for Picture Animal Top Star of the Year. Due to the death of a horse during the filming of a western *Jesse James* starring Tyrone Power in 1939, the American Humane Association initiated the award with the first winner being Francis the talking mule. Lassie, Benji and Asta from the *Thin Man* films were also Patsy winners as was Trigger, the singing cowboy Roy Rogers' horse. Arnold the pig In one of my favourite childhood TV shows *Green Acres* starring Zsa Zsa Gabor won two Patsy awards. Well done Arnold you old ham!

I am including these film star dogs as recently I had my piece of wood out in the back garden and my tap shoes on as I had an audition in London for a TV commercial and they actually want to see people over 40 (yes that's right – over 40!) who can tap dance! As I tap away to Frank Sinatra's version of *Get Happy* in the brilliant July sunshine the dog two doors down keeps barking, obviously not a showbiz lover and no there is no reason why this piece follows names for drag queens!

## SHOWBIZ QUOTES

I love quotes, anecdotes and famous lines from films. I loved watching and listening to great storytellers, like Peter Ustinov and Kenneth Williams on chat shows, sadly both no longer with us. Unfortunately these days, apart from Billy

300

Connelly, Paul O'Grady, Ricky Gervais and Peter Kay who are just as funny and witty on and off stage with wonderful stories to tell, especially on the Michael Parkinson show, we seem to be running out of these clever witty people. It seems that wit is now out-of-fashion and has been replaced by slapstick humour.

However here are a few of my many favourites. I hope they bring a smile to your face too!

Peter Ustinov late in life at the end of a function was greeted by a vision of a portly elderly lady in tight white satin pants, a quilted sequin parker, over made up and adorned in gaudy jewellery charging towards him who confided in him: "Don't tell anyone but I've been in love with you for 50 years." Peter Ustinov assured her it would remain their secret!

This brought to mind a night in a gay club in Birmingham. I had just finished my late night cabaret spot and a timid middle aged plainly dressed man with tears in his eyes came up to me and whispered "I loved you, I loved you that much that when you're here again I shall put on my dress just for you!" I was really touched this meant everything to him and he was going to do it just for me! Earlier that night during my act a drunk gay man had come up to the stage, that stood a mere 6" off the floor (yes another one!), lunged forward, looked me all over and said at the top of his voice: "Oh no it's a f*****g woman!"

Bette Davis (on making a film with Joan Crawford whom she hated and the feeling was mutual)
The best time I had with Joan Crawford was when I pushed her down the stairs in *Whatever Happened To Baby Jane?*

Bette Davis and Joan Crawford really did hate each other with a vengeance. *Whatever Happened To Baby Jane?* was a massive box office hit. Both actresses were scheduled to appear in another film *Hush Hush Sweet Charlotte*. Joan Crawford successfully feigned an acute illness to get out of working a second time with Bette Davis. British actress Olivia de Havilland, obviously made of stronger stuff, replaced her!

Bette Davis:     (on hearing of Joan Crawford's death)
I never speak ill of the dead, Joan Crawford dead?.................
Good!

Bette Davis:     I will never be below the title!

Bette Davis     With the newspaper strike on, I wouldn't consider dying

Julie Andrews to Rock Hudson on the set of *Darling Lili*: Remember, I'm the leading lady!

George Burns     At the age of 90 years on asked if his doctor knew he was smoking: No, he's dead!
Acting is all about honesty, if you can fake that you've got it made.
Too bad that all the people who know how to run the country are driving taxi-cabs and cutting hair.

301

Happiness is having a large loving, caring close knit family..........
in another city!
It's hard for me to get used to these changing times, I can
remember when the air was clean and sex was dirty!

Tony Curtis on kissing Marilyn Monroe in 1959 in *Some Like It Hot:* It was like
kissing Hitler!

(*See name changes above for this one!); During the filming of *The Alamo;*

John Wayne to Laurence Harvey:      Can't you even walk like a man?

Laurence Harvey:                    What's that Marion?

John Wayne's reply is not known!    XXXXXXXXXXX!

Humphrey Bogart to Frank Sinatra:  The only thing you owe the public is a good
performance

Judy Garland:  What do I do when I'm down?  I put on my lipstick, see my
stockings are straight and go out there and sing *Over The Rainbow.*

Noel Coward (on seeing a play with a child prodigy):  Two things in that play
should have been cut.  The second act and that child's throat!

Noel Coward on seeing the ill fated and short running musical *Gone With The
Wind* at the *Theatre Royal* Drury Lane in which appeared a child prodigy with a
shrill voice and ringlets and a live horse that, performed a natural function on
stage:  If they'd stuffed the child's head up the horse's a**e, they would have
solved two problems at once!

Noel Coward to writer Edna Ferber on seeing her wearing a trouser suit:  My God!
Edna, You look almost like a man!    Edna Ferber to Noel Coward:  So do you!

Edna Ferber:  When a desk clerk rang her hotel room to ask if there was a
gentleman in her room: Wait a minute and I'll ask him!

Several of Edna Ferber's books were made into films, two of them being the
hugely successful *Show Boat* and *Giant.*

Sir Robert Helpmann (the famous ballet dancer who was the child catcher in the
film *Chitty Chitty Bang Bang)* when touring in a ballet in America the company had
to perform in a stadium.  Sir Robert was given the umpires' changing room.  The

callboy knocked the door and opened it to see Sir Robert balancing precariously on a chair that he had put on top of a table so he could reach the light bulb. He was holding a mirror close to the dangling naked light bulb and attempting to put his make up on. "Are you alright sir?" asked the callboy. "Yes" replied Sir Robert "but goodness knows how those umpires manage!"

Sir Robert on attending the opening night of the first nude musical *Oh Calcutta:* The trouble with nude dancing is that not everything stops when the music does!

Arthur Askey speaking on the radio programme, *Hello Playmates,* when asked about television:
Television, no I never see it the only time there's anything worth watching I'm too busy doing it!

Casting is a process whereby a studio decides which of two faces the public is least tired of............ ANON

Gene Kelly: When Ginger Rogers danced with Fred Astaire, it was the only time in movies when you looked at the man, not the woman

Laurence Olivier: Acting is not a profession for adults!

Jack Benny, at an awards ceremony: I don't deserve this award, but then again I have arthritis and I don't deserve that either!

Victor Mature on having his application to join a club turned down because he was an actor:
I'm no actor and I've got 64 pictures to prove it!

Spencer Tracy when Katherine Hepburn suggested she, as a woman, should get top billing in a film they were making: This is a movie, not a lifeboat!

Irving Berlin: There's no business like show business!

Al Jolson (the first person to be heard talking on screen in *The Jazz Singer* in 1927): Wait a minute, wait a minute. You 'aint heard nothin' yet! (He was actually only supposed to sing but got carried away. I know the feeling!)

Groucho Marks: I never forget a face but I'll make an exception in your case!
Do I believe in computer dating? Only if the computers really love each other!
Either he's dead or my watch has stopped (*A Day At The Races*)

Here's to our wives and girl friends...........may they never meet!

I must say I find television very educational.  The minute somebody turns it on I go to the library and read a book

If you want to see a comic strip, you should see me in the shower

Women should be obscene and not heard!

Will you marry me?  Did he leave you any money?  Answer the second question first!

(*Duck Soup*)

When asked of his opinion of the film *Samson And Delilah* starring Victor Mature and Hedy Lamarr:
First picture I've ever seen where the male lead has bigger tits than the female!

Ginger Rogers:  There are no small parts, only small actors!

Margaret O'Brien (child film star of the 1940s):  When I cry, do you want the tears to run all the way or shall I stop halfway down?

Jean Harlow:  I like to wake up feeling a new man!

Jean Harlow was at the receiving end of a great witty put down from high society Margot Asquith, wife of Prime Minister Herbert Asquith.  Jean Harlow kept pronouncing 'Margot' with a 't' at the end.  Margot Asquith's brilliant snub was; the 't' is silent, as in Harlow!

Male half of an unsuccessful singing duo, on being thrown out of room by an 'eviction-technician' at the *X Factor* 2005 auditions:  Sing 'em a song Della! (This had Sharon Osbourne in 'stitches' and me too!)

Hughie Green:  We need people who can make us laugh.  I mean that most sincerely folks!

Carole Lombard on Clark Gable (known as the King of Hollywood):  If Clark had an inch less; he'd be Queen of Hollywood!

H M Warner, Head of Warner Bros. Studios in Hollywood in the days of the silent movies:  Who the hell wants to hear actors talk?

Walter Winchell:They shot too many pictures and not enough actors!

Playwright Jack Rosenthal to wife Maureen Lipman when watching a reality show on TV:  Do you realise we are actually watching paint dry!

Sir Peter Ustinov remarked that laughter was; the most civilised music in the world!

*Coronation Street's* 'Jack Duckworth' on reaching 70:  I now live in a world I no longer understand!
**(He's not the only one!)**

Un-named studio worker in the 1930s sent to meet Bette Davis on her arrival in Hollywood and going back to the studio without her:  No one faintly looking like an actress got off the train!

From the late 1920s there was a train that ran from Chicago to Los Angeles and it would be packed full of 'hopefuls' with stars in their eyes heading to Hollywood. The train was known as *The Chief*.  It is not known if this was the actual train Bette Davis arrived on but it could have been.

Billy Wilder to cameraman, Johnny Seitz, when setting up the attempted suicide scene for Gloria Swanson in the film *Sunset Boulevard*:  Johnny, it's the usual slashed wrist shot.

Billy Wilder to same cameraman on same film: Johnny, it's the usual dead chimpanzee set up.

Billy Wilder to same cameraman on same film:  Johnny, keep it out of focus, I want to win the foreign-picture award.

Jimmy Durante when asked to play *Hamlet*: To hell with them small towns, I'll take New York.

Humphrey Bogart's first line on a professional stage:  Tennis anyone?

Oscar Wilde: We are all in the gutter but some of us are looking at the stars.

Michael Curtiz, the Hungarian born director whose English was not that good, arranging a scene during the filming of *Casablanca*:

Curtiz:      Very nice but I vant a poodle

Prop man:    But you never asked for one, we don't have one

Curtiz:      Vell get one!

Prop man:    What colour?

Curtiz:      Dark, you idiot, ve're not shooting in colour

*Dee Quemby*

The propman leaves. A little while later Curtiz is called outside to see the propman with an ordinary looking poodle

Curtiz: Vot do I vant vith this goddam dog?

Prop man: You said you wanted a poodle Mr Curtiz

Curtiz: I vanted a poodle in the street! A Poodle! A poodle of vater!

Michael Curtiz had Errol Flynn and David Niven hysterically falling about when he instructed the animal handlers for a scene where stray horses were to run about in *The Charge Of The Light Brigade* by shouting: "Bring on the empty horses!" which is also the title of David Niven's wonderful book.

Curtiz snapped at a junior film executive: Don't talk to me vile I'm interrupting!

I was told of a girl who went to audition in London for the part of Wendy in *Peter Pan* on stage and on being asked by the director if she had ever 'flown' before replied: "I went to Majorca last year!" Don't ring us dear!

## AND THE TWO WITTIEST PEOPLE EVER!

### W C FIELDS

I don't drink water fish f**k in it!
Some weasel took the cork out of my lunch
After two days in hospital I took a turn for the nurse.
I always keep a supply of stimulant handy in case I see a snake, which I also keep handy!
I am free of all prejudice. I hate everyone equally.
Never give a sucker an even break.
A woman drove me to drink and I never even had the courtesy to thank her.
(Asked if he believed in clubs for women) Yes, if every other form of persuasion fails.
All the men in my family were bearded and most of the women
(Invited to play a game of golf by someone he didn't like) When I want to play with a prick, I'll play with my own!
When asked "How do you like children?" He replied: Fried!
I never drink water look at the way it rusts pipes!

After being told off by a neighbour for taking pot shots at the birds on the lawn of his Beverly Hills home:
I'll go on shooting the bastards until they learn to s**t green.

W C Fields was born William Claude Dukenfield in America, the son of a Cockney immigrant and a mother of British descent. His father claimed he was a descendent of Lord Dukenfield of Cheshire!

At the age of 11 years, W C Fields starting working in vaudeville as a juggler. Later on in his career he made many black and white films. He turned down the title role in *The Wizard of Oz*. A Charles Dickens fan he was delighted to be offered the role of Mr Micawber in the 1935 film *David Copperfield*. He also appeared alongside Mae West in *My Little Chickadee* in 1940. Whilst making a film with the popular American child star, Baby LeRoy, so fed up was he, with the child stealing scenes, that he laced Baby LeRoy's milk with gin. The production had to be stopped for a day for the baby to sober up! W C Fields was heard to comment: "He's no trooper!" and wanted him sacked.

W C Fields also wrote for the screen but never used his real name in the end credits. Names he used were Mahatma Kane Jeeves (My hat, my cane, Jeeves!), Otis Criblecoblis, and Charles Bogle.

W C Fields is pictured on the Beatles' album cover *Sgt Pepper's Lonely Hearts Club Band*.

He toured America and even appeared at the London Palladium with a comedy juggling act before appearing in films and everywhere he played he opened a bank account in a false name   There are said to be over 700 of these accounts still open in America.  W C Fields also appeared with Sarah Bernhardt at Buckingham Palace and at the Follies-Bergere with Charlie Chaplin and Maurice Chevalier.  In England he would often be billed as Wm. C Fields because of what the initials W C stood for here!   When touring he had three trunks, one for clothes and the other two for alcohol.

W C Fields was outrageous and non-religious and hated most things especially Christmas.  He ironically died on Christmas Day 1946 at the age of 67.  He was seen reading the Bible shortly before his death and remarked: "I'm looking for loopholes!"

As he lay on his deathbed, his long time female companion, Carlotta Monti, turned the hosepipe on.  She aimed it at the roof of the bungalow he was in, so he could hear his favourite sound one last time of rain on a roof!  Now that really is love!

## MAE WEST

Is that a gun in your pocket or are you just pleased to see me?
It's not the men in my life that count; it's the life in my men!
A hard man is good to find!
It's better to be looked over than overlooked
Peel me a grape
Why don't you come up and see me sometime, when I've got nothing on but the radio
I used to be snow white but I drifted!
It's hard to be funny when you have to be clean!
I only like two kinds of men, domestic and foreign!
You're never too old to become young
So many men, so little time!
When I'm good I'm very good, but when I'm bad I'm better
Good sex is like good Bridge..........if you don't have a good partner you'd better have a good hand!
You can say what you like about long dresses, but they cover a multitude of shins!

Goodness what beautiful diamonds: Goodness had nothing to do with it dearie!

(On being told there were ten men waiting to see her) I'm tired send one of them home!

(On being told by a tall young man that he was six feet and seven inches) Let's forget about the six feet, and talk about the seven inches!

Keep a diary and one day it'll keep you!

Mae (Mary) West was America's highest paid star in the 1930s. She attended dance classes as a child. Also in the class were ten-year-old Adele Astaire and her eight-year-old brother Fred, as well as two teenage brothers who would later on become 'Groucho' and 'Gummo', two of the incredibly talented, funny, musical and witty Marx brothers ...............oh to have been a fly on the wall!

Mae West had a life jacket named after her by the Royal Air Force during World War II and said: "I've been in *Who's Who* and I know what's what, but this is the first time I've ever been in a dictionary."

Mae West is also pictured on the Beatles' album cover *Sgt Pepper's Lonely Hearts Club Band.*

On her father's side she was descended from English immigrants from Long Crendon, Buckinghamshire near where my grandfather came from; well you never know! Humphrey Bogart turned out to be a distant relative of Princess Diana's!

## SUNSET BOULEVARD

This 1950 film is one of my most favourites. In its time it was very groundbreaking for the hero to start the picture as a dead body and then go on to narrate the film to explain how he had ended up floating face down in a swimming pool. This film was shot in black and white with lots of atmospheric shadows and is really creepy. If this had been filmed in colour it would not have had the same effect. A lot of heads of studios were annoyed that this film would show the then saintly 'Tinsel Town' in a bad light and the film was kept under wraps during filming, even being given the code name 'A Can Of Beans'.

Mae West was director Billy Wilder's first choice for the role of Norma Desmond in the film but she turned it down saying she was far too young to play a fading silent movie star, even though she was 58 years old! In fact most of the female stars at the time approached to play this role refused to do so as they didn't want to be associated with playing an ageing Norma who was trying to revive her film career. In reality it was probably a bit too close to the truth for most of them in 1950! This was a time when glamour was everything and no one in Hollywood ever aged. 4'11½" Gloria Swanson eventually bravely accepted the role that would make her an icon to millions. She was five years younger than Mae West and quite a bit shorter! Gloria Swanson always dressed to the nines and was reputed never to wear the same dress twice.

Montgomery Clift was originally cast to play the role of the struggling screenwriter Joe Gillis but he had second thoughts about appearing opposite a much older actress. After many other top male stars turned down the role William Holden was cast.

The famous director and actor Eric Von Stroheim appeared as Norma Desmond's chauffeur. In 1928 he had directed Gloria Swanson in a huge flop *Queen Kelly*. None of this film had ever been seen until *Sunset Boulevard*. When Norma gets her chauffeur to run one of her silent movies it is actually a scene from the ill-fated *Queen Kelly*. In the card playing scene at Norma's house, one of the players is the great silent movie star Buster Keaton whom Jackie Chan, Asia's number one cinema star, based his comedy action performances on. Hedda Hopper, the all powerful showbiz gossip 'maker and breaker of stars' reporter, also appears as herself in the film as do legendary film directors Cecil B De Mille and H B Warner.

Gloria Swanson as 'Norma Desmond' in *Sunset Boulevard* said two of the most immortal lines in film history:

I am big! It's the pictures that got small!

and

*Alright Mr De Mille, I'm ready for my close up!*

**(NB: She's not the only one!)**

The name Norma Desmond was made up from two names involved in a notorious murder case of which there were plenty in the early days of Hollywood. These were Mabel Normand, a very popular 1920s silent film actress, and William Desmond Taylor, a Paramount film director. Mabel Normand was the drug taking girl friend of the 1920s silent classic comedy director, Mack Sennett. The 1960s musical *Mack and Mabel* is based on their lives. The happy ending in the musical was not the case for Mabel however as she died from a drug overdose. Her actual relationship with the 20 year older William Desmond Taylor is not known, but he was often her escort on nights out.

William Desmond Taylor was found shot dead shortly after being out on the town with Mabel but she and Mack Sennett both had rock solid alibis as did another top star Jean Harlow when her husband of two months, MGM studio executive Paul Bern, was found shot dead in 1932. The Paul Bern murder was a studio cover up. Jean Harlow had found the body and rang the powers that be at the MGM studio. And she was hastily got out of the house before the police were informed and 'witnesses' came forward to say she was not staying at the house that night. An undated alleged 'suicide' note was found, though many people believed that Jean Harlow had murdered her new husband. The way William Desmond Taylor's body was found suggested that this was probably another studio cover up and his killer was never found.

## JEAN HARLOW

Jean Harlow, the original blonde bombshell, was the idol of Marilyn Monroe. She had tremendous screen presence and was a terrific comedy actress. Jean Harlow turned down the lead in *King Kong* and was the godmother of mobster Bugsy Siegel's daughter Millicent. Often thought of as a dizzy dumb blonde, she actually came from a wealthy family in Kansas. The house she grew up in had 18 rooms. She also had a French governess and she could speak fluent French

309

# Dee Quemby

at the age of five years. Called 'Baby' at home, this name stuck and she was always known by this name at the film studios.

Originally dark haired, continual bleaching by the studio hairdressers caused her hair to fall out and she then had to wear a wig. Most of the beauty treatments at the time were so harsh and unsafe that many female stars suffered as a result. Early in her career, a make up process caused Lana Turner to lose her eyebrows and she always had to pencil them in as they never grew back, though at that time all women plucked their eyebrows completely out and drew a thin arched pencil-line anyway! Jean Harlow never won an Academy Award but she did at one time have a dog named 'Oscar'.

One of her most memorable films is the 1933 *Dinner At Eight*, the plot line of which concerns a high society dinner party where wealthy working class businessman, Oscar winning actor Wallace Beery, is invited and takes along his dumb blonde tarty wife, Jean Harlow. Two members of Hollywood's 'royal acting family' John and Lionel Barrymore, from which Drew Barrymore (*ET* and *Charley's Angels*) is a descendant, and the great character actress Marie Dressler also appeared in this film.

One of the most famous pieces of film legend is where a bemused high society hostess, played by Marie Dressler, and Jean Harlow are going through into the dining room to join the other guests. Platinum blonde Jean Harlow is in a long tight revealing dress and she never wore underwear!

Jean Harlow:     I was reading a book the other day

Marie Dressler (stopping in her tracks and looking stunned)   Reading a book!

Jean Harlow:     Yes it's all about civilisation or something. Do you know that the guy said that machinery is going to take the place of every profession!

Marie Dressler (pauses and looks Jean Harlow up and down): Oh my dear that's something you need never worry about!

## PRICELESS!

Jean Harlow died at the age of 26 years. At the age of five she had meningitis, and as a teenager scarlet fever, leaving her in poor health generally. Many rumours surrounded her death. One being that while Jean Harlow was on her sick bed, her mother who lived with her, refused any medical help due to her religious beliefs. A depressed Jean Harlow had been drinking heavily for a while and suffered from kidney disease amongst other things.

Jean Harlow's death hit L B Mayer hard, as he was very fond of 'Baby'. Years later he refused to sign Norma Jean Baker who would become Marilyn Monroe to MGM, as he thought she was a poor imitation of the Blonde Bombshell.

## FAMOUS SHOWBIZ 1946 BABIES

| | | | |
|---|---|---|---|
| Liza Minnelli | Cher | Stephen Spielberg (KBE) | Sylvester Stallone |
| Joanna Lumley | Dolly Parton | Susan Sarendon | Chris Tarrant |
| Brenda Blethyn | Felicity Kendall | Linda Ronstadt | Helen Shapiro |
| Sally Field | Maureen Lipman | Tim Curry | Alison Steadman |
| Alun Armstrong | David Suchet | Diane Keaton | Candice Bergen |
| Jane Asher | David Lynch | Oliver Stone | John Woo |
| Brian Cox | Jane Birkin | Al Green | Susan St James |
| Patty Duke | Tyne Daly | Freddie Mercury | Felicity Kendal |
| Charles Dance | Alan Rickman | Hayley Mills | Marianne Faithfull |
| Marisa Berensen | Lesley Ann Warren | Victoria Principal | Charlotte Rampling |
| Timothy (007) Dalton | Tommy Lee Jones | Barry Gibb (*Bee Gees*) | Antonio Fargas |
| Producer Dick Wolf | Noddy Holder (*Slade*) | Sir Cameron Mackintosh | Sue Townsend |
| Janet Street Porter | Lesley Joseph | Donovan | Benny Andersson (Abba) |

and Bill Clinton and George W Bush!

*Stephen Spielberg could either be 1946 or 1947. It is more than likely it is 1946 as this is the date the *New York Times* gave. Unless I meet him and ask him personally (dream on!) I cannot confirm the year.

While I think he is one of the greatest directors ever I wish I had never watched his *AI* it was the most upsetting film I have seen in years, I was depressed for months. However I have been told they are making a Leicester comedy version of *AI* to be called *A Up!*

## NON-FAMOUS SHOWBIZ 1946 BABY

Me! (All together.....................Ahh!)

## SHOWBIZ STARS BORN ON 18 JANUARY

Cary Grant      Danny Kaye      Oliver Hardy      Kevin Costner      Jane Horrocks

## FILM BOX OFFICE HITS IN 1946

The price of a cinema ticket in 1946 was 5p and cinema audiences reached 30 million a week!

311

*Gilda*
*Great Expectations*
*The Best Years Of Our Lives*
*The Big Sleep*
*Brief Encounter*
*Dual In The Sun*
*Henry V*
*It's A Wonderful Life* (voted best film of all time in 2006)
*Notorious*
*The Postman Always Rings Twice*

Every one of these 1946 films is a classic and there are so many of these old wonderful films that have stood the test of time. Most 1940s black and white films when shown on television are credited with four or even the maximum five stars in the TV magazines.

It is also incredible how many young people are enjoying the old black and white films when re-run on television and the numerous prints of the 1940s movie stars appearing in shops. Well, everything comes round again and just because it's old doesn't mean it's not good! The Mona Lisa's old but it's still art, what is it with antiques? How is it non-living things are more appreciated as they get older and living things aren't!

A few years ago if you had mentioned a musical or a pirate film people in the business would have said they were 'old hat' and nobody would pay to see a film like that these days. *Chicago* and the two *Pirates Of The Caribbean* movies turned out to be wonderful pieces of film making that would do credit to any of the great 1940s/50s film directors, with lovely eccentric character parts that we don't seem to get in films any more and they really do add so much. A lot of the younger movie going public has never seen films like these and they are 'new hat' to them.

I went to see the first 'pirate' film one afternoon in the school holidays and was surrounded by very noisy kids and teenagers all with their mobile phones to hand. As soon as Johnny Depp appeared on the sinking boat at the start they were spellbound and I never heard a peep out of them apart from laughter throughout the whole of the film. Not one of them used a mobile in nearly three hours!

Johnny Depp is truly one of our great present day actors and was only going to play Captain Jack Sparrow the way he wanted to despite the powers that be at Disney continually e-mailing saying they were not happy with his performance when watching the rushes. Johnny Depp replied: "If you want me, that's what you get!" Of course when the film was released and everybody loved Jack Sparrow and raved about Johnny Depp's performance, they sent him endless e-mails of apology and it really is his performance that puts the icing on the cake.

Today at the cinema, we all watch action films with film sets being blown to pieces, bodies flying everywhere and spectacular effects knowing they were done by computer wizardry. When watching Errol Flynn, like all the action performers at that time, you would be on the edge of your seat, holding your breath knowing he was performing the stunts by himself without any technical help.

Errol Flynn brought about the welfare of animals working in films. He was angered at how the horses were treated when filming *The Charge Of The Light Brigade* with Olivia de Havilland and David Niven. This resulted in many arguments with the film's director, Michael Curtiz. Errol Flynn reported this to the American equivalent of the RSPCA and guidelines for the treatment of animals in film were brought into force that all film companies had to strictly adhere to. It is said that Michael Curtiz never spoke to Errol Flynn again.

## FILM GUIDANCE RATINGS

A long while ago, I believe it was Michael Douglas who said that the then film guidance ratings meant:

'U'     -     No one gets the girl

'12'    -     The hero gets the girl

'18'    -     Everybody gets the girl!

## 1946 ACADEMY AWARDS
## HOSTED BY JACK BENNY HELD AT THE SHRINE CIVIC AUDITORIUM, LOS ANGELES, USA

Best Actor                          -     Frederick March (*The Best Years Of Our Lives*)

Best Actress                        -     Olivia de Havilland (*To Each His Own*)

Best Picture                        -     *The Best Years of our Lives* (Samuel Goldwyn)

Best Actress in a supporting role   -     Anne Baxter (*The Razor's Edge*)

Best Actor in a supporting role     -     Harold Russell (*The Best Years Of Our Lives*)

Best Director                       -     William Wyler (*The Best Years Of Our Lives*)

*Dee Quemby*

Best short subject, cartoons     -     *The Cat Concerto* (Fred Quimby – my Dad's mate!)


## TOP BROADWAY SHOWS OF 1946

*Annie Get Your Gun* starring Ethel Merman
*Showboat* (Revival)
*Call Me Mister*


## TOP WEST END SHOWS OF 1946

*London Town* starring Sid Field, Tessie O'Shea, Sonnie Hale, Kay Kendall and Petula Clark
*Song Of Norway*


## 1946 WORLD EVENTS

20th Century Fox sign 20-year old Norma Jean Baker, and change her name to Marilyn Monroe
Oscar winners were Ray Milland and Joan Crawford for *The Lost Weekend*
Marilyn Monroe divorces first husband, Jim Dougherty
Bananas back in Britain after the war
The Flamingo Casino, managed by mobster 'Bugsy' Siegel, opens in Las Vegas
Lurex first produced
A Mars bar cost 2p
Humphrey Bogart signs new contract and earns $5,000 a week
Try squirrel pie, says Food Ministry!
Free school milk and dinners
First Cannes Film Festival
A two-door car cost £275
Australia retains the Ashes
George Orwell's *Animal Farm* published
Gina Lollabrigida appears in her first film
Hit songs of the year are *A Girl In Calico* and *Cruising Down The River*
Vespa motor scooter designed
Government nationalises the Bank of England
Espresso coffee machine invented
Derby County beat Charlton 4 – 1 in first post war Cup Final
Dr Benjamin Spock publishes *Baby And Child Care*
Independence announced for India in 1947
Bikini swimsuits appeared on beaches
TV Licence brought out
Combined Radio and TV licence costs £2
Nylon stockings on sale in Britain
Winston Churchill delivers his 'Iron Curtain' speech in America
Food Rations Cut
Chocolate, nylons and perfume dominate the Black Market
A bottle of sherry cost £1

Scrabble game board invented
Heathrow airport opens with prefabs for terminal buildings
British GI Brides sail to America
Bing Crosby, Bob Hope and Dorothy Lamour re-unite to film *Road To Utopia* after four years
Rita Hayworth and Glen Ford star in *Gilda*
Humphrey Bogart and Lauren Bacall star in *The Big Sleep*
British European Airways created
*Women's Hour* starts on the Radio
Instant mashed potato comes into shops
The Nuremburg Trails take place
Jukebox boom begins
Jitterbugging hits the dance halls
Frank Sinatra 'the most significant figure of American mass entertainment'
Arts Council established
Tupperware parties sweep the USA
London Philharmonic Orchestra formed
The Derby and the Grand National resumed after the war
BBC introduces Radio Three
Average weekly earnings for a man £6.05
Average weekly earnings for a woman £3.25
Footballers demand £7 a week!

## AND

It was the Chinese Year of the Dog that no doubt will lead to countless jokes from my drag queen friends!

## GARRY BUSHELL

For being a mate and his continuing support of us working men's club 'turns.'

## AND FINALLY, JOHN BRINDLEY

For his patience in putting up with all the alterations, rewrites and e-mails even at Midnight!

*Memories are made of this*....................................................................!

With Alan Bates at the Riverside Studios

Pat Ward on her toes in the 1920s

Pat Ward tapping on her 85th birthday

Windmill Theatre 'girl' - Sheila Lucas

Children in Barnardo's shop window

The 'ladies' admired by Princess Diana

**A STAR IN HIS OWN RIGHT
PERSONALITY PLUS TOP VOCALIST**

# MONTY MARTELL

Monty (Katchick) Martell

Being introduced to Princess Diana in Barnardos

John gets to meet Princess Diana outside Barnardos

The Emricks in 1959 in America

(Great) Aunty Ethel and Uncle Fred on their wedding day

With Shirley and Roger in Las Vegas – MGM casino is on the right

John 'three-stools' Hayward in Morocco

Walkies!   As Barbara Woodhouse (courtesy of Clive Rasin)

As Cruella DeVille (courtesy of Clive Rasin)

# CHAPTER 15

**A DAY IN THE LIFE OF DEE QUEMBY** a stand up comic, actress, panto dame, after dinner speaker, children's entertainer, clown, radio presenter, compere, tap dancer, Joan Collins look-alike, Maggie Thatcher impersonator, Punch & Judy Professor, script writer, stage dance teacher, ladies nights and 40s nights promoter and honorary drag queen!

---

WAKE up, move indignant cat off my head, go to bathroom for shower, notice costumes used for 40s show three weeks ago still on banister will put away later in attic. Suddenly remember I have said this to myself every day for last three weeks!

Shower and dress, go downstairs feed cats.

Put on 'slap' (showbiz term for make-up). Spray hair. Use air freshener instead of lacquer by mistake! Funny enough seems to hold hair better!

Go back downstairs. Make coffee and toast for me this time, not cats!

Fetch in bowls from porch that are used to feed any stray hungry cats and 'Herbie' the adopted very large hedgehog who can't get enough of the cat biscuits. Check to see if Herbie has left a 'present' in porch! Say to myself can't believe I talk to a hedgehog at 11pm every night in the porch; he just looks at me now, doesn't even curl up.

Sort out tapes and CDs and sound effects to listen to for touring panto. Check mini disc and tape deck set up.

Type up *Mother Goose* confirmation letter. Mental note must contact everyone re rehearsals.

Phone call from agent can we do panto Christmas Eve, say 'yes'.

Order Joyce Grenfell CD and book about MGM on Internet.

Sort out photos of a changed drag act for shows in October and December. Type labels for envelopes to post out to the clubs affected by change.

Look at e-mails for any auditions I can put in for, very few being over 40! Silly me haven't I realised yet; no one of any interest over 40 lives in this country, or watches TV!

E-mail British Comedy Society about *Last Of The Summer Wine* tribute invite at Pinewood Film Studios.

Remember a few more showbiz stories for book, type up. Just when you think you've done it all a bit more springs to mind!

Sort out photos, CVs and show reels to send out to any casting director I have not sent them out to before, look through *Contacts*. Realise most of them have had them a few times by now. Hopefully one will give in eventually!

3pm realise haven't eaten yet go downstairs make cup of tea try to read another chapter of new Marie Lloyd book so I can start new Mae West book.

Feed, ever hungry, cats again!

Sort out tapes for Tuesday dancing classes.

Write notes for broadcast on Wednesday on BBC Radio Leicester.

Take phone call for dancing lessons from mother of a five-year old. Another mother rings to order purple leotard for child.

Must remember to set video for soaps as out tonight, must find two hours to watch tomorrow!

Start to write down dance routine for opening number for panto

Must ring Shirley. She had new granddaughter, born with two webbed toes on each foot, will have operation later. Mark, her dad, was told at the hospital that it is very common in newborn babies in Leicestershire. It occurs to me is that why we all call each other **'me duck'**?

Start to sketch designs for costumes for dancing school juvenile and inter troupes.

E-mail Stephen before he goes off to Broadway, the one in America that is not Loughborough!

3pm still haven't eaten, make sandwich.

Read through notes for book and type up, as John Brindley coming Friday to go through new bits.

Pick up post from porch. Leaf through my husband's copy of SAGA magazine. Look for horoscopes page, there isn't one. Well I suppose I can see their reasoning for that!

Go to hoover-up cat hair floating about like tumbleweed, forgot Hoover broken. Oh well, as Quentin Crisp once observed once dust gets to an inch thick it doesn't get any thicker!

Get ready to catch bus to Loughborough for dance classes. Wait at bus stop on hottest day of the year so far, feel spots of rain, should have brought my umbrella. More spots of rain: quite annoyed with myself for forgetting umbrella. Look up see hanging flower basket with water dripping from it! What a Wus! Take one step forward.

Take classes, small room, glass roof we all end up dripping wet through with the heat.

Get home, my cats hungry again, can't have worms just wormed them. Plenty of scratches on arms and chest to prove it!

Watch soaps taped while at dance classes as I make sandwich for me, not cats. Why do they think all food is for them? Must be ready to sit down at 9pm for my favourite TV programme *CSI – Las Vegas*. Think to myself why can't we come up with anything as good as this here? I like a good crime story with a result at end, sometimes in CSI you get three in one episode; lovely jubbly! End credits rolling, got to wait another week for next episode!

I actually wrote to Alliance Atlantis the company that produces CSI, a couple of years ago. It was in the press that they were going to film an episode in London. I sent my CV and photo to them in Canada. I said I would even play a 'body' just so I could say I had appeared in CSI. I never heard a thing from them. Don't they know DNA testing was pioneered in Leicester! Oh well at least you can't say I didn't try.

Look outside for stray ginger cat to feed him. He is lying on the mat outside the porch looking at me as if to say 'where have you been'? He is starting to let me stroke him a bit and beginning to trust me. Also put out biscuits and water for 'Herbie' the hedgehog.

Get undressed, wash and go to bed. Prop up pillows and start to read a chapter of *The Golden Girls Of MGM* by Jane Ellen Wayne fascinating stuff! They don't make film stars like they used to! Why can't they be as glamorous, as well as talented, like these were today? Open book and..............................COLLAPSE!

*It's been a hard day's night.................................................!*

# CHAPTER 16

## AND IT'S (NOT) GOODBYE FROM ME!

ATTITUDES to many things have changed over the past years. I now find that I am talking about things in my act that I would never have dreamt of talking about when I first started 20 years ago. For instance we would never have mentioned sex on a working men's stage, and the word 'condom' would have been taboo. If you used one swear word you would have been immediately stopped and paid off and never booked again.

Comedy has to change otherwise if not we would still be running around in red and yellow outfits with bells on our heads, hitting everybody with a pig's bladder on a stick as in mediaeval days.

Being an entertainer is not all about wanting to do it! You do it because it's something you have to. It's a passion that never leaves you! I have seen many talented people give up because they've wanted the fame and the money and when it hasn't happened they've stopped. They just didn't have the passion to carry on no matter what. How do you know how far you can go if you give up? (Remember Sydney Greenstreet for goodness sake!) I remember seeing Morecambe and Wise on the *Michael Parkinson Show* many years ago and Ernie Wise saying that there was probably a 65-year-old tap-dancer still doing the working men's clubs convinced his break would still come, cause that's show business! You have to keep going and if you love it you do.

Everything is hard work. Today most young people seem to think it happens all at once. When I was a teenager working at Herbert Morris, I would take my tap-shoes to work and practise for the whole of every lunch-hour. I learnt my scripts going to and from work on the bus and could often be seen singing and hopping about at the bus stop waiting for the bus. If I am learning a script or working out a dance routine I'll be doing just that as I'm shopping, or on a bus or train! As a teenager I would stop in at home instead of going on a planned night out with my friends if I needed to put any extra work in on a script or routine. At home, like Stephen, I have paper and pens in every room and often wake up in the middle of a night with an idea I have got to write down there and then.

As said before growing up in a pub as an only child made me feel a bit remote and that's probably why I love people. Also being on my own a lot I came to use my imagination more and more. Sadly we now live in an age when people don't seem to matter any more but the rules, regulations and ever increasing pointless (believe me I know what I'm talking about from experience) forms do. Whatever you do these days you are given a form to fill in to put yourself in a box. Your name is hardly used any more. These days you are known as a service user, client, or even by a number. As Patrick McGoohan, as Number 6, said in the cult 1960s TV programme, *The Prisoner*: "I am not a number!" Well neither am I. I'm not filling any more forms in. Stuff it!

With comedy you can have 99 good shows and one bad one and the bad one is the one you will always remember! It doesn't matter how good you are there will always be people who don't think you are funny at all. I remember hearing someone say to a woman after a show: "What did you think of comic?" She replied: "She's alright if you like laughing!"

All the best comics of any age have had their bad nights and that is what shapes you and gives you the edge. Even the great Morecambe and Wise had certain places where they didn't go down at all! Can you imagine that! How can you deal with a heckler if you've never had one! When I first started working a seasoned professional comic said to me: "Always remember you're the one with the mike."

At one club that shall be 'shameless', I had won over a very rough and noisy audience when a little obnoxious scruffy man jumped on the stage and dropped his trousers. Oh come on, I work with Stallion, Rebel Red, Double Impact and the rest, it wasn't going to shock me! I said: "That looks like a 'willy' only smaller, if you go flashing down by the river you'll catch a trout with that!" He pulled up his trousers and got off the stage with his tail between his legs............(oops) to catcalls and howls of laughter. One of the women behind the bar said: "He always does that to the female singers when they're are on stage and a lot of them get really upset!" Why the hell didn't they ban the prat, or at least black ball him (oops)!

I hate sitting in an audience when the people round you are talking and texting on their mobiles, or continually getting up and down to go to the loo. This seems to happen all the while these days. It's what we call 'television audiences'. It's even worse if you are on the stage performing when this is happening. All comics have their own put-downs that are usually very effective. I was at the hospital with my Mum on one of our frequent very long visits trying to pass the time reading all the various leaflets and took several of them home with me. Now if I am on stage and anybody keeps getting up and down going to the loo I give them a brochure on how to cope with incontinence!

People say about singers " I don't mind them." But with comics it is either love or hate. There's no middle line and you will never hear someone shout at a singer: "Sing us one we've not heard before." The average person can remember a maximum of five jokes and will always tell jokes they have heard themselves and you have too! They don't come up with new jokes, so if you can write your own comedy material you have the edge on other comedy acts.

I can never understand why these days a lot of people want to be miserable. In the Great Depression of the 1920s, when people really had nothing, no benefits, no social help, no free medical help, they and their children really did starve, but they would pack out the burlesque and variety shows. They flocked to the cinema to see the fabulous Busby Berkeley musicals in which women would wear dresses that would cost ten-years wages to the ordinary man. They went to escape from their reality, to laugh along with the comics. It would take them outside of their lives for a short magical while. Nowadays we all watch reality television and seem to be miserable and have lost our sense of humour – what a turn around! Did you know that when you laugh you use up a lot of calories and it is also a great stress reliever! Why are there so many depressed people these days?

A lot of young comics I have worked with are so serious about what they are doing that they are almost bordering on depression. Yes, don't insult your audience by not bothering, think about and practise what you are going to do but when you're out there you have to enjoy it as well. If you're having a good time so will they. As one of the greatest comics, Les Dawson said: "Whatever you do just have a laugh, that's all it's about. Have a laugh because if it's not fun it's not worth living!"

Judi Dench is one of the greatest actresses ever and people who have been lucky enough to work with her have said that she has a wonderful sense of humour. Dame Judi said on a *Parkinson* show "That's the most important thing of all. If you have a sense of humour you can laugh at yourself and not take yourself too seriously and yet do a serious job!" How I wish a lot of other people in this business had the same philosophy!

These days comedy seems to have gone full circle. You would take your mum and grandma to see Peter Kay, Dave Spikey and Paul O'Grady and do.

As I come to the end of this book, good old Barnardos have offered me their shop to do a book signing which must be a first! No big fancy stores for me, apparently! This brings to mind a story I heard Kenneth Williams tell about a lady novelist at a book signing in London, handing a book to an old Cockney woman with the inscription 'best wishes to Emma Chiswick'. "Wot you written in here?" asked the Cockney woman indignantly. "That's your name" replied the lady novelist, "No" said the Cockney woman: "I said 'ow much is it?"

**LOVE IT!**     There's nowt so funny as folk!

*See You Later Alligator* .................................................................!

329

# ADDENDUM

FOR those readers who cannot understand the Leicester dialect and sayings, I hope the following will be helpful:

To aid pronunciation: many words in the Leicester dialect end in 'a' i.e. mutha (mother), winda (window), jumpa (jumper), Lesta (Leicester, Garry Lineka (Gary Lineker), wank ....................er forget that one!

There is a also big fascination for birds by the frequent use of the word 'duck', probably due to the fact that webbed feet are very common amongst Leicester born residents apparently!

People from Leicester are known as 'woolly backs'! This is due to the fact that in the middle ages there were a lot of sheep in Leicestershire. Wool was a huge commodity being shipped and sold all over the world. Many local merchants grew very rich from the sale of wool; some of them even lending money to the impoverished King of England at the time.

| ENGLISH | LEICESTER |
|---|---|
| Hello | A up me duck |
| Hello (shortened) | A up |
| How do-you-do? | Ow dew? |
| Goodbye | See yar (or ta ra me duck) |

| | |
|---|---|
| I'm cold | I'm a bit nesh |
| I'm hot | I'm sweating cobs! |
| Oh dear! | Oh yer razzer! |
| Can I have a look? | Giz a gleg |
| Thank you | Ta me duck |
| Can I have a ride on your (bike) crossbar? | Giz a croggy |
| It's raining | Ark at it! |
| I've got a headache | I've gorra splitter |
| Have you got your sandwiches? | A yer got yer sarnis? |
| Anyway............. | Any road up........... |
| Have you been? | A yer bin? |
| I'm ok | I'm fair to middling |
| What's on at the cinema (movies)? | What's on at the flicks? What's on at the pictures? |
| Do you want an ambulance? | Shall I gerrum to cum then? |
| Come quick | A yer gorra minit? |
| Pardon me | Sorry me duck |
| A night out on the town | Out on the raz! |
| It looks like it's going to rain | It's a bit black ovva Bill's mutha's! |

## Dee Quemby

| | |
|---|---|
| Have you got your umbrella? | Aya got yer brolly?<br>Aya got yer gamp? |
| What's the matter? | What's up me duck? |
| Hand it over | Giz it ear |
| As well | An' all |
| Excuse me can I get by you? | Mind yer sen then! |
| We're wasting time | This won't buy the baby a new bonnet! |
| Your underskirt is showing! | Charlie's dead!  (Often said at Rawlins Grammar School for girls in the 1950s!) |
| Shut up! | Shut yer cake 'ole/shut yer gob! |
| What a face! | Wara fiz og! |
| Stop messing (fussing) about! | Stop faffin about! |
| I've got a pain in my stomach | Oh me guts! |
| That was hilarious (1) | I've never laughed so much since the mother-in-law got her t**s caught in the mangle |
| That was hilarious (2) | Laugh, I nearly crashed me fags |
| I nearly passed my cigarettes round | I nearly crashed me fags |
| I couldn't stop laughing | I was creased |
| My stomach's rumbling | The big ducks are chasing the little ducks! **(more birds.........!)** |
| I'm amazed! | Well I'll go to the foot of our stairs!  Well paste my picture to the bedpost! |

| | |
|---|---|
| Are you frightened? | Ay yer frit? |
| It's a bit far fetched | It's like s**t from China! |
| He's in a mood | He's got a bag on! |
| Isn't it? | Innit?  (often said at the end of a sentence) |
| By myself | By me'sen/on me todd |
| Where's the toilet? | Where's the bog? |
| Where's the toilet roll? | Where's the bog roll? |
| I need to go to the toilet | I'm gonna wet me sen |
| I'm going for a drink | I'm gonna wet me whistle |
| Is the bus on it's way | Is it cuming then? |
| I don't like your girl friend | I don't fancy yourn! |
| Is the wife with you? | A yer gorra wee yer? |
| Are we having a cup of tea? | A yer mashing? |
| Don't repeat this! | Between you, me and the gatepost! |

## INCIDENTALS

I remember a long while ago a friend, Nisha Orton, describing a gossiping woman as 'having a mouth like a parish oven'.  Just imagine!

Older residents of Shepshed in Leicestershire in the 1940s and 50s would swop over words i.e 'nail down to knock a kneel in' and 'go street up the straight' this practise had died out, hopefully.

## Dee Quemby

When I was a child all men and women would wear a hat when going out. No self-respecting woman however would wear a red hat due to locals saying 'red hat – no drawers'. Well at least her head would be warm!

People have always said 'bless you' one way or another as they do today, especially teenagers. When I was a child people would say to you 'bless your little cotton socks' for some reason?

If anyone were acting strangely my Nan would say 'they're three sheets to the wind' (those threes again).

As a child, people would say that 'they laughed like a drain' meaning they had found something very amusing. Why 'like a drain' I have no idea?

My Grandfather always called water 'frogs' wine' and Adam's ale. As he had family in London he would use a lot of Cockney rhyming slang and on odd occasions it would be 'fisherman's' (fisherman's daughter – water).

If I didn't eat all of the food on my plate at mealtimes I would be told to think of all the starving children in China. How it would help them if I ate it I couldn't imagine and how did my Mum and, everybody else's mum come to that, know they were all starving anyway? Most mums hadn't even set foot outside of Leicestershire! You were also told if you didn't eat the crust on your bread and butter your hair wouldn't curl. Well I did and it didn't!

All 'little soldiers' (children) would climb the wooden hill at night (up the stairs to bed). It was also up the 'apples' in our pub (apples and pears - stairs). Naughty children would be frightened into behaving by being told the 'bogy man' would get them in the middle of the night if they didn't. No child actually knew who the bogy man was or what he looked like but it did the trick!

As a child getting into Gramp's car to go back to the pub after a trip out my Nan would always say: "Home James and don't spare the horses." It was a very popular saying at the time. Everybody would say it when they were going home. It was also heard in both British and American films and songs and more recently on the 2006 James Bond movie soundtrack for *Casino Royale*. James Cagney, as Tom Powers, said "Home James" in the film *The Public Enemy* when getting into a car with Jean Harlow. This set me wondering where this came from and why it was so popular? The most interesting explanation (to me that is!) is that it was an instruction by Queen Victoria to her coachman, James Darling when leaving official functions and so overheard by all and sundry. In Victorian times, only the servants' surnames would be used but Her Majesty could hardly say "Home Darling" in public!

# WORDS THAT ARE USED IN LEICESTER AND LEICESTERSHIRE

| | | |
|---|---|---|
| Jitty | - | Small lane |
| Mardy | - | Sulky, moody |
| Larey | - | Eccentric, mad, 'nuts' |
| Wappy | - | Eccentric, mad, 'nuts' |
| Gus Gog | - | Gooseberry |
| Rocks | - | Sweets (candy) |
| Cosi | - | Swimming costume |
| Sumutt | - | Something |
| Oat | - | Anything |
| Reccy | - | Park |
| Cob | - | Bread roll (in London asking for a cob they will think you want a taxi!) |
| Cardi | - | Cardigan |
| Jollop | - | Medicine |
| Guzzunder | - | Chamber pot |
| Bung | - | Cheese (any variety) |
| jollies | | holidays (vacations) |
| jim-jams | | pyjamas |

*Dee Quemby*

| | |
|---|---|
| plimmies | plimsoles |
| manky | old and tattered/moth-eaten |
| bug-rake | comb |

## (VERY) STRANGE WORDS NO LONGER USED IN LEICESTER AND LEICESTERSHIRE!

Sniggle     Motty     Reasty     Hottie

## SHEPSHED, LEICS

Did you know that Shepshed over the years has had many names, including 'Scepeshefde Regis'.

*It's only words...........................................................................!*

# ANOTHER ADDENDUM

INSIDE each copy of Miss Quemby's next publication will be a free CD for each reader of 60s hits that you will already have, probably more than once, and bonus tracks that you will never have heard before, or will ever want to hear again! (Editor's note: they make good coasters!)

Miss Quemby is currently working on a script for a pilot TV drama based on her forthcoming novel about a plumber living on a council estate in Leicester. His name is Kevin and at nights and on Bank Holidays he does a 'turn' in the working men's clubs as a, not very good though he thinks he is, 'Elvis' impersonator. Unbeknown to him, he only gets bookings in the working men's clubs when they need a toilet unblocking as it's cheaper to pay him off as a singer than for his plumbing services. An excerpt from the novel follows:

**DRAFT** (Editor's note; does she mean daft?) **SCRIPT**

Kevin parked his van outside the Refuse Engineers' and Revenue Protection Officers' Social Club, a burly eviction technician in a black Barnardo's suit bought in the happy hour, stood on the door his knuckles trailing on the ground. The eviction technician hadn't noticed Kevin's van pull up as he was contemplating handing in his notice as he had just been told that in future he had got to wear a red jacket and a long floral skirt.

The club was sandwiched in between a sex shop 'Legoverland' (or 'Knobs are Us' name not yet decided?) and the 'John Prescott Massage Parlour'. Many elderly people clutching footballs and zimmer frames were queuing to get into both shops, as it was pensioners' night with ten-per-cent off at the massage parlour and three for two in the sex shop. Rayne Wooney, a popular young footballer, was doing a ball signing in both shops and seemed especially taken with a 92-year-old woman. "What a nice lad chatting away to her" said one not so old lady. "She must remind him of his grandma."

Opposite the club was the *Bijoux Cinema* which was showing the mega box office hit and 26 Oscar winning film *The Silence Of The Woolly Backs* set in the

337

1940s in the Midlands starring multiple academy award winning actress Deirdre Grahame, who had personally sewn all the sequins on to all of her 209 costumes, and co-starring newcomer Brad Pitt's brother, Seth.

Deirdre Grahame had been nominated for yet another academy award and extra points on her BOOTS Advantage and TESCO club cards for her role in the film as the tragic heroine Della Cowell-Osbourne-Walsh (NB: surname too long should we abbreviate it to Cow? – perhaps not).

764 pigeons, two Vietnamese pot-bellied pigs and a donkey with three-legs, called Tri-pod, had also won 'Patsy' awards for their performances.

Kevin had been to Herbert's Insect Emporium Cinema two nights before to see it with his wife Flo.   The end credits were rolling and Kevin had got up to leave.  Flo sat there transfixed reading every single credit. "Come on love", said Kevin "It's over Flo!"

Flo hadn't liked Herbert's Insect Emporium as she had to climb up a wooden ladder to get to the balcony and a rude man looking like Basil Fawlty had shouted at them because they hadn't got the exact money when buying tickets.   "Kevin love" she had said, "Can we go to a REEL cinema next time?"

The film's main theme song *Baa Baa Slightly Discoloured Woolly Backs* sung by Lionel Ritchie's brother Mabalsa, was topping the charts.   Deirdre Grahame sings this number in the film (dubbed by Lesta vocalist Karen West) in front of a cardboard cut out plane as Seth says to her: "Sing 'em a song Della". As she is doing her sixth encore, Seth seductively lights two cigarettes in his mouth at once.  He hands one to her in mid-flow and she gallantly carries on during a coughing attack.  On the film soundtrack CD you can hear something being dropped and the director shouting angrily: "Bogie, you silly cat!" or something like it!

Kevin caught his breath as he recalled that poignant moment in the film when Della boards the plane that was being held upright by six dwarfs (nowadays known as 'height challenged individuals' or 'short arses') in orange boiler suits. Kevin marvelled at her grace and speed in climbing the steps, as it was a well-known fact that she had webbed feet. She stood at the top of the stairs and incredibly performed a 20-minute tap dance ending with a sparkling finale of 200 double wings and numerous hand shimmy shakes, her black patent platform wellies being fitted with tap plates that had a 10p piece between the plate and the sole.

This number had been brilliantly choreographed by the recently knighted, owner of many theatres in London and Lesta, Sir Stephen Raincoat-Mear who can be seen during the dance sequence in the background frantically signing 'get the silly cow off now'.  Several of the animals in the film had apparently strayed on to the runway during the number.

This famous scene needed a retake as Tri-pod, the three-legged donkey on hire from 'Rent-a-Moke' a subsidiary of 'Mountsorrel Mammals', had followed 'Della' up the plane steps.  She was desperately trying to push it out of the plane door backwards.  Sir Stephen Raincoat-Mear had gallantly rushed up the steps to help her waving ripped up pieces of lino to distract the donkey that subsequently received a Patsy award for its performance.

Della looked at Seth with tears welling in her eyes that ran and, trained actress that she is, stopped halfway down her face that was already covered in runny mascara that was dripping on to her leopard-skin puffed sleeve swagger coat with diamanté buttons.

Della is never going to return, she is leaving behind her twins, played by Catherine Zeta-Jones and Johnny Depp (who had to walk in a trench alongside her when filming as they were playing nine-year olds). She turns to look at him for the last time and says: "We'll always have Lesta, me duck." Seth smiles sadly and says: "Have a good journey Della, though it does look a bit black ovva Bill's mutha's, it's a good job you've got your wellies on duck!"

Kevin smiled a wry smile to himself, was it really ten years ago he had been support act to her when she was working as a comic on the clubs before her big break came that propelled her to international stardom. He remembered that night well at the Wanlip Sewerage Recreational Cub when he first met her. She had come staggering into the dressing room dressed from head to toe in leopard-skin clutching several bags, a flask and a pair of well-worn slippers to help ease the pain of those webbed feet. He smiled as he recalled that moment when she spoke to him for the first time. "What a s**t-hole!" she exclaimed. "Yes" he replied: "Well it is next door to the sewerage works."

That night had gone really well for him. He'd only had to get his plunger out once and he had actually managed to do a full first thirty-minute spot without being paid off. He was desperately trying to remember the words to other Elvis' songs for his next spot, as he had never got this far before.

He recalled the gales of loud hysterical laughter as he sat in the dressing room as she went through her comedy routine to the appreciative audience. He smiled to himself as he remembered how, at the end of her spot the audience had clambered to buy her tape made up of the six songs she could sing. He too had bought a copy of her *Melodies For Amputation ('Songs To Have If Off With')*. He often played this tape in his van, though for some reason he could only rewind it with a pencil

At the end of the night he had helped pack her PA, costumes, flask and slippers into her car. An old woman was leaving the club and Kevin heard the ent sec ask the toothless old woman: "What did you think of comic then?" "She was alright if you like laughing" the old woman hissed. She was well known in the club for having a 'bag' on, as her mother had never taken her to the dentists as a child.

He looked back and her car was disappearing into the thick fog, all he could hear was the sound of her exhaust pipe as it clattered on the ground getting fainter by the second. He smiled as he remembered their conversations in the dressing room. "I came second in a Joan Collins' look alike competition in 'Lesta' last week" she had told him. "Really" he had said impressed. "Yes me duck" she replied "A West Indian woman won!"

He had gone back into the club looking for his plunger as he had, as a favour to the ent sec, unblocked the gents' bogs for them during the bingo and helped a man from Sileby retrieve his false teeth from out of the full toilet bowl, the man had then rinsed them under the tap and put them hastily (and upside down) back in his mouth as he rushed out for the start of the fur and feather raffle and the guess the weight of the black pudding and how many mushy peas in a pint pot competitions.

339

Dee Quemby

Kevin brought himself back to reality; he had a show to do.  He slid open the door on the side of the van that proudly bore the words 'The Plumber with a KING size service - Shepshed, Loughborough, 'Lesta', Las Vegas' and that also had two rampant crossed guitars flashing on the roof of the van.  Kevin unloaded his PA onto the pavement and then carried a heavy speaker into the run down, shabby, dimly lit, wallpaper peeling, sticky floor, smoke filled (from the previous night) club full of beer stained and cigarette burnt tables, a pair of men's Y fronts were screwed up on one table.  A middle aged bleached blonde, badly dressed, over made up barmaid who reminded Kevin of a drag queen he had worked with in Scunthorpe by the name of Miss Sandy Laine looked up and said: "A up me duck."

As he placed the speaker on the stage which stood six-inches off the floor with a shower curtain at the end for a dressing room the Ent Sec, wearing a flat cap and bike clips, carrying a ferret and stuffing hot mushy peas into his mouth said: "You couldn't do us favour me old duck and have a look at the ladies bogs during the bingo?" "Yes me duck", said Kevin. "I'll go and get me plunger out of me van now to save time." As he started to walk out to the van he thought it's amazing how many of these clubs have faulty toilets, last night's Wheeltappers and Shunters Social Club bogs were blocked as well it's lucky they'd got me booked, hey oh, another of life's little coincidences.  He then said to himself: "I hope they're going to move that bloody billiard table in front of the stage before I go on."  As he walked out the door he heard the ent sec say to the barmaid: "A yer mashing?"

He got to the van and two pensioners had come out from 'Legoverland' (NB: We'll go with this name) with lots of plain brown carrier bags and two signed footballs. They stop and look at the poster for the film.  "What do your reckon to that Seth then?" one old woman asked. "Oh" replied the other;  "I saw him when he opened supermarket last year when I went to buy a cosi for me holidays." She paused for a moment and added as she stuffed a ham cob into her mouth. "He's been touched up on that poster, when I saw him he didn't suit daylight. Mind you he's got a good face for radio." The two women walked down the 'jitty' cackling. What a 'larey' pair thought Kevin.

As he walked back into the club holding his plunger aloft, he saw the ent sec lying on the floor, he was suffocating from an overdose of mushy peas, the bar maid and the ferret were kneeling on the floor beside him.  "Shall I gerrum to cum then?" the ferret er sorry the barmaid asked wiping his hot sweaty brow with the Y fronts and a soggy autographed beer mat.................................................

TO BE CONTINUED, corrected, edited and got rid of!

NB:    Miss Quemby would like it to be known that a relative of hers actually worked as an Elvis impersonator. He didn't get many bookings though as it was in 1942 and nobody had heard of him.

ANOTHER NB:

(I did actually get in the last six out of over 3,500 ideas for a sitcom in a competition run by Garry Bushell in *The Sun* a few years back based on this idea of an Elvis impersonating plumber living in Leicester which I thought would be an ideal role for Anthony Hopkins!   A bigwig TV producer went off with the six ideas and then got involved with a new show called *Pop Idol* and nothing more was ever heard from him!  On second thoughts the plumber part might suit Peter Kay better?)

*Got to use my imagination......................................................!*

*Dee Quemby*

# STOP PRESS NEWS FLASH!

MISS Quemby, direct from the National (car park that is!) is currently appearing in a cigarette advert 'somewhere in the Middle East' (so far they are not banned there). She is seen lying resplendent on a zebra-print, chaise-longue, dressed in a leopard-skin diamanté trimmed catsuit with a florescent pink net fishtail and a pair of Primark slippers (size 4). "I'm ready for my close up me duck", she says.

A Spanish 'stripper' er gentlemen artiste, Senor Willie, wearing a leopard-skin sequin trimmed loincloth (all sequins personally sewn on by Miss Quemby in the tea break as he filled her flask) seductively lights two cigarettes in his mouth and hands her one. She closes her eyes and takes a deep drag. She slowly opens her eyes, as her mascara has melted and stuck her eyelashes together. The camera moves in as she, eyes now wide open, says: "I've tried everything, but for real satisfaction there's nothing like a Camel!"

*Hi diddley 'DEE' an actor's life for me.............................!*

342

**TEMPUS FUGIT*** as the saying goes as I look at my watch. One of many bought from the TEMPO (every one a fiver!) watch kiosk in the Haymarket Centre, Leicester.

(*Perhaps my year doing Latin at Rawlins wasn't all that wasted?)

## NEW YEAR RESOLUTION

After over a year sitting hunched up over a computer, I have decided I am never going to write another book. Never again will I do this - It has completely taken over my life! I feel as happy as John Prescott on *This Is Your Life!* (Mind you I said all this after the first touring panto!)

*And now the end is near..................................................!*

(Editor's Note: Thank God - How much more of this can I take!)

# FIN

TANNOY ANNOUNCEMENT (also imaginary):  "MISS QUEMBY
HAS LEFT THE BUILDING......clean and tidy!"

Note from editor:  Lock up quick, before she has a chance to come back!

# I'M READY FOR MY CLOSE UP........ANYBODY!

(With a cast of (owing more like!) thousands
- eat your heart out D W Griffith!)

A *DQ PRODUCTION* based on a real life story

Producers ...............................Deirdre Quemby & John Brindley

Director ................................Deirdre Quemby

Script .................................Tamara Trestle-Table aka
Anisa Alka-Seltzer (for tax purposes!)

Additional Material...........................Shalimar Sahara Stir-Fry Smith, COD
ASBO

Make up overdone by............................Dee Quemby

Hair....................................Yes please!

Miss Quemby's gowns by ....................... Primark, Peacocks, Various club
books,
Barnardos, British Heart Foundation,

Help the Aged, TK-Max, Aggie at
Wish
Age Concern, RSPCA, Cancer
Research,
Sue Ryder, Sense, Scope, Mind,
Loros, Salvation Army, Lydia's
Loughborough second-hand market
stall (Saturdays only), Mountsorrel
Menopausal Modes (sale rail), Helen
& Sylvia's Loughborough market
Stall, Top Girl, Reveal and XTC
Leicester

Costume alterations........................... Karen West and Harlequin Express

Miss Quemby's jewellery........................John's (two items for £1.50)
Loughborough market stall, A to Z
Gifts Leicester, Sylvia's jewellery
stall Leicester market and Pam and
Keith's market stall Covent Garden on
a Monday (and the lady on the next
stall)

Miss Quemby's jewellery (often repaired by) .. Her husband (under duress!) and Godkin
Jewellers, Loughborough Market

Miss Quemby's plastic surgery by ............Hugh Henderson FRCS

Production Team....................................Olive and Len Quemby

Pre Production Team .............................Dolly and Horace Edwards

Catering...............................................John Hayward

Transportation......................................John (I know exactly where I am!)
Hayward

Cosmetics bought from .........................Crystals, Loughborough Precinct

Close ups .............................................With a lot of help at Pinetree Salon,
Loughborough!

Choreography ......................................Stephen Mear (well he would have if
I'd have asked him!)

Animal Handler (and cleaner up) ............Dee Quemby

Miss Quemby's stand in ........................ Joan Collins

Supporting Artists................................ Sheba, Sophie Sixpence, Billy Winker,
Sammy Wong, Tallulah Dingle, China
Tiger Moonbeam, Renault Van-
de-Bilt, Mayling Kwan-To, Herbie
Hedgehog (nights only)

Stunt Performer ................................... Scott Bradey (jumping off a six-
inch high stage and tap dancing on
a billiard-table) in between stunts
for latest Harry Potter film and
*Emmerdale*

Casting ............................................... Yes please! (Editor's note: I have
it on good authority that she'll
work cheap and provide her own
costumes!)

Showbiz (and everything else!) critic....... John Hayward

Photos. .............................................. £25 each and s.a.e if direct; or see
Rachel at Jessops in Leicester  and
Dave Kitto at Clifton Bank Studios

Props bought from............................... Pound Plus and Poundland, Leicester

*DQ* Logo ............................................. Dave Kitto – Clifton Bank Studios
Barwell, Leics

*DQ* Logo posed by ............................... Billy Winker in his younger days

Panto/cabaret/40s nights/ladies night stills.. John Hayward

Technicians......................................... John Lovett, Matthew Parker and
Matthew Tilford  - thanks lads,
chuffing computers!

Thanks to Bill Maynard, Garry Bushell and Stephen Mear for being brave
enough to write comments for the back cover of this book!   No payment
was involved (allegedly)!

A special thank you to Dave Kitto!

Thanks to Jennifer and Sarah at BBC Radio Leicester


Julian at the BBC Radio Leicester shop  (for listening!)


Miss Quemby has been reported to the R.S.P.C.A.
(The *Royal Society for the Prevention of Crap Acting* that is!)


No animals (just a few reputations and careers!) have
been harmed by the writing of this book


None of the characters portrayed in this book are fictional..........believe me!


Written on location in the Midlands


Proof read at Gala Bingo, Beaumont Leys, Leicester on Monday nights during
the breaks in bingo (that accounts for the mistakes!)


# AT THE TIME OF GOING TO PRESS THIS BOOK HAS BEEN NOMINATED FOR A RECYCLING AWARD!


LIKE JAMES BOND, DEE QUEMBY WILL BE BACK....................UNFORTUNATELY!
(Love the new bloke  -  If they ever want a female 'baddie'
with a startled looking pussy (see logo) cat!)

*Rolling rolling rolling*...................................................................!

# Bibliography

*Marie Lloyd Queen of the Music Halls*, W McQueen Pope

*The Golden Girls of MGM*, Jane Ellen Wayne

*The Westmores of Hollywood*, Frank Westmore and Muriel Davidson

Various editions of *Picturegoer, MovieGoer and Film Review*

*A History of Shepshed (Regis),* Anthony J Lacey, Stephen Smith, Derek Jowett and Christopher Smith

*The Cinema Era in Leicestershire and Rutland*, Brian Johnson

Extra, extra read all about it..................................................!

*Dee Quemby*

Bill Maynard

Dee Quemby's book is not just a wonderfully warm read but a very actual account of the most demanding and difficult life in show business, that of the COMEDIAN!

I told Dee many moons ago that she should enter the idiom that is the easiest life in show business, that of the TV drama actor.  That of course she has done to grand acclaim.

Get the book it's a great read!                    **BILL MAYNARD**

Stephen Mear (photography Clare Park)

350

Deirdre was my first dancing teacher for 13 years and I owe her a great debt.   She is a very talented performer in her own right and it would be great to dance with her again.   I still think there's something very big around the corner for her!

**STEPHEN MEAR** (Olivier winning choreographer)


Dee was brilliant as Emmerdale's Lulu Dingle. But if she'd had access to Lulu's crystal ball and been able to see how tough it would be for a mainstream comedienne to get a break in modern TV, would she have persevered?   Dee's book is moving, honest and funny.

**GARRY BUSHELL** (TV critic and personality)

Printed in the United Kingdom
by Lightning Source UK Ltd.
119805UK00001BA/184